Microtheory

Microtheory
Applications and Origins

William J. Baumol

The MIT Press
Cambridge, Massachusetts

First MIT Press edition, 1986

First published in Great Britain by Wheatsheaf Books Ltd, 1986

Printed and bound in Great Britain

Library of Congress Cataloging-in-Publication Data
Baumol, William J.
   Microtheory: applications and origins.
   Bibliography: p.
   Includes index.
   1. Economics – Addresses, essays, lectures.
2. Welfare economics – Addresses, essays, lectures.
I. Title.
HB171.B326 1986   330   85-19881
ISBN 0–262–02245–1

Contents

Preface

I was, of course, delighted when I received a letter from Wheatsheaf Books proposing to publish a volume containing a selection of my recent articles. I knew, however, that only a few years have passed since Elizabeth Bailey completed her fine work in editing an earlier selection of my writings for New York University Press, and I was concerned that not enough papers would have appeared since publication of the book to constitute a respectable second volume. However, the bad habits of a lifetime had obviously prevailed. A cousin of mine once remarked all too convincingly, 'Baumol writes too much!', and whatever the verdict of the reader on this score (and I do rely on the reader's charity), the publisher had the task of convincing me to cut the mass of papers submitted to him down to manageable proportions. The result of this process, along with the constraint requiring that the papers be ordered into some sort of coherent pattern, is the volume that follows.

The book is not made up exclusively of reprinted materials. The introductions to the four main sections of the book are new. They represent my subsequent views on the subjects covered in the reprinted articles, and in several cases report what I consider important amendments stemming from correspondence with others. The excerpts from the correspondence with Professors Areeda and Turner seems to me to shed significant new light on the antitrust issues which have become their particular providence, and the correspondence with Professor Thweatt of Vanderbilt contributes important and delightful insights on the role of James Mill in the emergence of the Say's law doctrine.

In the preparation of this volume I have incurred some debts. First and most important is my debt to Wheatsheaf Books and to Mr Edward Elgar of that organization, whose help has been unstinting and with whom I have had a consistently cordial relationship. I also thank the publishers of the reprinted pieces without whose kind permission to reproduce them the book would clearly not have been possible. Finally and most heartfelt is my gratitude to my associates, Sue Anne Batey Blackman, Mary Mateja and Karen Garner-Lipman who uncomplainingly and competently struggled with the manuscript at various stages in its evolution. Sue Anne Blackman having left me temporarily to produce her daughter Emily, and Mary Mateja having abandoned me permanently to return to her family, it was left to Karen Garner-Lipman's masterly hand to pull the pieces together.

A final word. Wherever possible, the articles reprinted here were not reset in new type by Wheatsheaf Books but were simply reproduced from the original type with the original pagination still indicated. No blame for this should fall on the publisher who did it at my request to avoid the intrusion of new errors in the typesetting process and to facilitate reference preparation by any fellow economists who care to cite these papers in their writings.

Princeton

Introduction

While there are a number of points I want to make about the articles reprinted in this book, these comments are provided in the individual introductions to the four sections of the volume. Rather than repeat any of those materials I thought it appropriate instead to say something about myself. I was encouraged in this egotistical decision by the many kindly comments elicited by an autobiographical essay recently published in the *Banco Nazionale de Lavoro Quarterly Review* as part of its series of such essays written by various economists at the Journal's invitation. The remainder of this introduction is based on that article.

For as long as I can remember — certainly by my early teens — my desire to be an economist was never in doubt. In retrospect I can see that this was no accident. Both my parents were self-educated immigrants, but educated they were, as few undergraduates are today. Literature, older or current, language, politics and economics were constantly discussed in our house in a most fascinating manner, and I was expected from childhood to participate fully in the discussions. My father with his lower class background (his parents had run a tavern in a smaller town in Poland) was driven by passionate concern for humanity, and emotion ruled his talk. My mother, by contrast, coming from a line of Jewish Lithuanian intellectuals, epitomized logic and careful reasoning in pursuit of the same objectives. Both parents, particularly my father, were avid Marxists. The combination was irresistible. I was infected by their interests and their concerns. My reading included a sampling of Marx's logical convolutions which, combined with tales of the adventure of the buccaneers of nineteenth century business — Morgan, Vanderbilt, Gould, Rockefeller and others — sealed my fascination with the subject. Well before I entered college I had begun to read economic history, the works of the classical economists and the writings of Thorstein Veblen.

Undergraduate Education (1939–1942)

I entered C.C.N.Y. (the College of the City of New York) in 1939 as the great depression was drawing to an end and the threat of war hung over us C.C.N.Y., then, was an extraordinary institution. There was no tuition charge and the students commuted from home every day by subway. The ambitious children of impecunious immigrants flocked to it as their ticket from poverty or grinding labour. Never did so many future Nobel prize winners congregate in one place. Passionate activity, discussion and debate flourished everywhere. The dining room was surrounded by alcoves each of which had been claimed by a permanent discussion group — there was the Trotskyist alcove, the Socialist alcove and one of every other variety. (There was even an alcove at which future comedians or rather, comic social commentators, some of them to become famous later, practised their craft without let up.)

A number of economists of note emerged from there, Kenneth Arrow, Julius Margolis and Jules Joskow among them. But while C.C.N.Y. at that time had many gifted teachers, the department of economics had very few. It was clear to us students that many of them were thoroughly behind the times, and could not teach us about the work of Keynes, Chamberlin and Joan Robinson which were then at the frontier. Besides, many of them just could not communicate very well. There seemed to us to be little choice, and so we organized our own classes, each specializing in a different field, devouring as much of the relevant literature as we could and then lecturing on it to the others. I was assigned the microeconomics, and suspect that I learned more economics there than ever before or since. This experience has always engendered uncertainty in my views on teaching. Can it be that, at least for some students, what is considered to be 'bad' teaching is really teaching in its most effective form, because it forces students to think and learn for themselves? I have long advocated some controlled experiments in which parallel classes are held, some taught in the conventional way by teachers of good reputation while in the others students are asked to fend for themselves, guided only by past examinations, perhaps by a reading list, and with no access to the faculty. It is my conjecture that the first group will perform better on the examination at the end of the semester, but that in an examination five or ten years later the self-taught group will far outdistance the other.

The Department of Agriculture and Military Service (1942–46)

Graduating in 1942, I spent a few months in Washington working (though it may seem odd) in the Department of Agriculture. The shadow of the receding depression led graduating students to accept with delight virtually any reasonable job offer, and I was considered very daring by the others in my class when I held out for — and received — a salary of $2,000 a year. Happily the job was not undesirable. It was a sort of think tank for the Department, and many of the group, some of whom I still see, were exceedingly bright and creative persons. The head of the Department was Frederick Waugh, a bright and fatherly figure who then and later made a number of significant contributions to the economic literature. It was under his guidance and that of my young colleagues that I first learned how microtheory can be applied to concrete issues.

Just before leaving for Washington I had been married. We were both very young, but the U.S. had just entered the war and many others were doing the same. I have had many occasions to congratulate myself on the wisdom (or luck) that guided that decision. We have ever since worked (and enjoyed life) together in many areas, most directly in our work on the economics of the performing arts. But I am getting ahead of the story.

My years in the U.S. Army are pertinent only for the correspondence course in linear algebra I took, and, while stationed in Rouen, the mathematics books I was able to buy and devour. There, incidentally, I made lifelong friends with a French family whose fabulous cellar, including samples of every great vintage of the century, introduced me to the delights of wine which I still collect. Just after the war in Europe had ended some German prisoners gave me my first lessons in wood sculpture which I now teach at Princeton University. (Before entering the army I had studied drawing and painting at the Art

Student's League in New York City and my second main field of study at C.C.N.Y. had been visual art — painting and lithography, particularly.)

After returning from the war there was another brief stint at the Department of Agriculture. But this time the task was very different: the allocation of the U.S. grain resources among the countries of a hungry world. Two prime lessons emerged from this experience — the high costs of the negotiation process and the complexities of the calculations of fairness. The first lesson flowed from the fact that all of the senior and more experienced members of the division were almost fully employed in diplomatic negotiations involving international agencies and other governments. As a result, the actual decisions were, to our astonishment, left to another young man of equal inexperience and myself!

It was not a task to make for an easy conscience. The refrain we heard from virtually every country was the same: we are hungry. If we had one shipload to go either to country A or to country B, what were we to do if the evidence showed that we had already sent enough to A this month to provide each of its inhabitants more calories than before the war, but that B, whose per capita grain receipts were higher than A's, was nevertheless well below its prewar consumption level? We did not, of course, enjoy the luxury of indecision that is available to pure research.

The London School of Economics (1946–49)

I had assumed that on my return to civilian life I would begin my postgraduate studies. My application to the London School of Economics was rejected, and I wrote again asking when it would be possible to apply for the following year. As I found out afterwards compassion was still part of the admission process, and it was decided to accept me as a student for the masters degree only. As was explained to me later, at LSE they had never heard of C.C.N.Y. and, in any event, my undergraduate record was hardly outstanding. But C.C.N.Y. soon made up for its handicap. The training in fierce debating — quarter neither asked nor given — soon got me (in my view, undeserved) attention in LSE's justly famous seminars. To my amazement, within weeks I had not only been transferred to the Ph.D. programme, but was also offered a part-time teaching post which became full time the following year. Lord Robbins afterwards told me that he went back to the records to see where they had made their mistake in rejecting me, and decided that, on the record, they had been right, after all.

LSE was an extraordinarily stimulating place to be. Besides Lionel Robbins I got to know Friedrich Hayek, Arthur Lewis, Nicholas Kaldor and, later, James Meade, among the economists, and Karl Popper and Harold Laski outside the department. Among the students there were Frank Hahn, undergraduate Ralph Turvey and an Australian, David Finch (now at the IMF) who (in 1948!) was writing a thesis on the theory of stagflation. The weekly Robbins seminar and the stimulation in the common rooms where one met for avid and fruitful conversation were experiences I have never duplicated. The erudition and broad knowledge of Robbins and Laski revealed what humanistic learning can be. Popper, who had not yet reacquired any professional logician colleagues, was prepared to report his latest derivations frequently to a new assistant lecturer who had taken a course or two in formal logic at C.C.N.Y. Hahn, Turvey and other young people were sources of a continuing flow of new and fruitful ideas. Meade and Hayek were also full of ideas which they constantly tried out on the delighted newcomers.

Because few English faculty members had anything like a Ph.D. and did not take the degree seriously, it was possible for me to write my dissertation at the same time that I held a full time faculty position. I had already planned my dissertation during my military service, and Lionel Robbins agreed to be its supervisor. He never begrudged me time or advice, which was always very helpful. The thesis, later published as *Welfare Economics and the Theory of the State,* took off from the Marshall-Pigou theory of externalities, then a neglected subject widely considered to be of minor importance. It sought to generalize the idea to as diverse a set of subjects as the behaviour of competitors, the difficulty of cartel formation and the theory of inflation (all of which we were already characterizing as a prisoners' dilemma problem in the new-fangled theory of games).[1] More than that, I hoped to derive from the logic of externalities the rationale for all government intervention in the workings of the economy — notions later echoed in works of Buchanan and Tulloch and the writings of Mancur Olsen. In the hotbed of discussion that constituted LSE the dissertation's ideas were very much a group product. We had made an effort to revive the famous Cambridge, LSE, Oxford seminar of the 1930s, and these subjects were discussed at the joint sessions, bringing in ideas from outside the LSE. Jan de v. Graaff played a leading part, he and I spending large amounts of time discussing one another's work on welfare economics.

In the course of that seminar's travels, incidentally, I also met Dennis Robertson, Joan Robinson, R. F. Kahn, J. R. Hicks, Lionel McKenzie and others whose names already were or were about to become legendary.

At LSE I gave two courses. Lionel Robbins invited me to lecture on economic dynamics, and my lecture notes for that course formed the basis for what was to be my first book, *Economic Dynamics,* which still survives. But in return for that plum I had to give a set of lectures on the American economy, a subject on which, most regrettably, I was dismally ignorant and which, I am sure, were an embarrassment to everyone, even if most educational to me. Much of the dynamics course, like so much else, followed Paul Samuelson's pathbreaking explorations which I merely translated into forms more accessible to students. People have sometimes been kind enough to suggest that my writing on the subject is rather clear. I have responded that I tried to write the book so clearly that even I could understand it — and that was, in all seriousness, the truth of the matter.

In both my lectures and the dissertation there were substantial sections on the relevant *dogmengeschichte* on which Lionel Robbins was enormously helpful. The graphic translation of the dynamics of the Ricardian model seemed to me an obvious interpretation of a system universally understood within the profession and generally agreed upon. I was amazed to find it singled out for special commendation in John Williamson's presidential address to the American Economic Association the year after publication, and to see it cited by writers on the history of thought many times thereafter. Since then it has become clearer that the substance of Ricardian economics is far from being agreed upon, as my former student Samuel Hollander has found in his debates with the neo-Keynesians of Cambridge and Italy and even with George Stigler and Paul Samuelson.

Our happy three years in London were drawing to an end. We had used the opportunity to travel about Europe a good deal. British exchange controls in that period of postwar austerity prevented us from using either my small earnings or my wife's comparable income, both in sterling, for the purpose. Fortunately, I also received support from the

U.S. Government in U.S. currency, as an army veteran, and that permitted our travels. Of course, young graduate students did not expect many comforts while travelling or in their domestic arrangements so a small income served very adequately. There were severe shortages and strict rationing still continued. In London the foreign students and their spouses shared any packages received from abroad with their English friends. Often we would all pick up our six-week ration of one egg and one slice of bacon at the same time and get together to celebrate the feast. Heating was a great problem with tightly rationed coal of poor quality burnt in an open fireplace the main source of warmth in the home. One winter our water pipes froze for three months and produced a great indoor flood when they thawed and burst in the beautiful spring of 1947.

The dissertation was completed on schedule, and I had the most delightful oral examination on record over whiskys and sodas at the Reform Club with my examiners, Marcus Flemming and Lionel Robbins who still considered my pursuit of the Ph.D. an American aberration. Professor Robbins knew we were determined to return to the United States, but he nevertheless made me a very generous offer at the LSE if I were prepared to remain. After I had refused with thanks most deeply felt, he recommended me with his characteristic kindness to Friedrich Lutz who was then visiting LSE from Princeton. Within weeks I had received and accepted an offer of an assistant professorship for the following academic year, and have remained at Princeton ever since.

Lifelong friends were acquired at the LSE — Lord and Lady Robbins and their children, Sir Arthur and Gladys Lewis to whom we had the pleasure of extending their first dinner invitation after they were married, Anne Bohm who brought sanity and order to the postgraduate program, Frank and Dorothy Hahn, and others as well. We have since made still more close friends in London where our visits (or theirs to the U.S.) have assumed the nature of reunions. In particular, Lord Robbins in his role as Chairman of the Royal Opera at Covent Garden and as Director of the National Gallery has over the years provided us with access to London's cultural activities such as few are privileged to enjoy.

Princeton University (1949–)

At Princeton we were immediately welcomed into the community and the department. Richard Lester was chairman, and he quickly made us feel at home. Lionel Robbins had also written ahead about us to Jacob and Frances Viner with whom we remained on closest terms for the rest of their lives. I did not know Viner's terrifying reputation (which was belied completely by his natural but often deliberately concealed kindness). Consequently, I was foolish enough to disagree with him avidly and energetically whenever it seemed appropriate to the astonishment of many of our colleagues. Viner, who was obviously unused to such a response, was delighted. We spent many hours each week locked in debate. From time to time I needed information on economic history or on the history of ideas and was always very pleased when in response to literally any such question he would talk without interruption for at least an hour providing an amazing stream of illuminating material from his bottomless stock of knowledge. He would also regularly, but apparently casually, make some unsupported theoretical statement which I was sure was quite incorrect and which he would then challenge me to disprove. Each time, after a considerable struggle on my part, the mathematics showed unambiguously that he was right. Years later a friend in another city recounted how Viner told him of a young friend on the faculty for whom he had set himself the task of presenting a new, paradoxical proposition in economic theory every week. What an education that was.

The following year Lester Chandler joined the Department, and from him I learned what little I understand about money and banking. Later we wrote a textbook together which, though it was unsuccessful, was an introduction to the pleasures of collaboration.

On arriving at Princeton we met two advanced graduate students, Martin Shubik and Harvey Leibenstein, with whom we have remained close friends. Within a year or two the department attracted an extraordinary group of undergraduate students including Richard Quandt, Otto Eckstein and Gary Becker with whom I wrote an article on Patinkin's dichotomy analysis and the pertinent materials in classical and neoclassical economics. We felt, and I still do, that Patinkin's discussions of the invalidity of the dichotomy between the real and monetary sectors of the economy, and of the problems caused by the assumption that supply and demand functions are homogeneous in prices alone, were brilliant pieces of work and constituted an extremely illuminating contribution. But at the same time some of the classical and neoclassical authors he accused of the resulting errors were, in my view, quite innocent of the charges. It should be added that the dispute was conducted just as such disputes should be, and that Professor Patinkin and I have become good friends and see one another both in Israel and the United States.

Consulting Activities

In about 1953 Paul Lazarsfeld, the great sociologist then at Columbia University, asked me to work with him on one of his research projects. I quickly accepted the invitation, anxious to get to know more about his path-breaking work, and, of course, because of the additional income which greatly relieved the assistant professor's traditional poverty. A key premise in much of Lazarsfeld's analysis was that while human behaviour is stochastic, the relevant probabilities of the different options in tomorrow's behaviour depend on the state of affairs today. Thus the probability that some individual will vote Democrat in the next election will depend on whether he voted as a Democrat or a Republican in the preceding election. This immediately leads to the employment of the theory of Markov chains which yields exactly that sort of relationship. It also translates itself at once into a simultaneous system of stochastic difference equations whose coefficients are the relevant probabilities. It was this translation which had attracted Lazarsfeld to my writings, and the work I did for him was subsequently used in a substantial expansion of *Economic Dynamics* in its second edition. Later I also joined Lazarsfeld in two seminars, each lasting several weeks, one held in Switzerland and the other in the beautiful mountains north of Turin. There our families got to know one another.

Just after my work on the Lazarsfeld project came to an end I spent the spring and summer as a visiting professor at Berkeley. We travelled from Princeton to Berkeley by car with our two small children, making the country seem even more enormous than it is. At Berkeley we met many delightful people, notably Aaron Gordon, Robert Dorfman (and for the second time), Harvey Leibenstein and their wives. I also met Joe S. Bain from whose work the theory of contestable markets would later derive so much, and Howard Ellis who was then approaching retirement.

Soon after our return to Princeton, where I had been promoted to full professor, I was introduced to another remarkable person, Wroe Alderson, who was then serving on an advisory committee to the Princeton economics department. Alderson was Quaker and a devoted advocate of their social goals such as the promotion of peace and elimination of poverty. He was senior partner of Alderson and Sessions, a management consulting firm in Philadelphia. After one evening together at a meeting he invited me to come to his office to see whether a consulting arrangement would suit us both. That arrangement lasted for nearly a decade. I would travel to Philadelphia about once a week and work on one or more of the many projects on which the busy company was engaged. In those years I got some sense of the way big business in the U.S. is conducted. I worked with large firms and small, among them major firms in chemicals, steel, food products and a variety of other lines. I studied their policies on pricing, advertising, product line, location and all of the other areas of interest to economic analysis. The work made use of demand theory, mathematical programming, inventory theory and many of the other tools of formal economic analysis. It was a very valuable experience, teaching me how theoretical instruments can be applied flexibly to the complex and messy problems of reality, and, above all, suggesting how firms actually behave in reality. It also led me to revise many of my theoretical ideas, and two of my books originated from my work at the consulting firm. *Economic Theory and Operations Analysis* (1961) started off as a compendium of the analytical tools that had proved useful in application to business activities, with illustrations derived from experience with firms. In its later editions the book has gradually evolved more into exposition of economic theory with particular emphasis on very recent developments. The relationship between business experience and theory was still more direct in the case of *Business Behaviour, Value and Growth* and its sales-maximization model. Several years of association with members of the managements of large firms finally forced me to recognize that there was a systematic difference between the way matters were viewed by them and by the standard economic models. Of the recommendations made to our clients, my impression was that about 60 percent were accepted and adopted. It became clear, eventually, that those which were rejected were not chosen fortuitously, but, rather, constituted a fairly predictable pattern. It ultimately dawned on me that virtually any proposal that promised to increase profits but did so by sacrificing sales volume was almost certain to be spurned. I began to modify my recommendations accordingly and, as I remember it, the acceptance rate rose substantially.

The natural reaction of a microtheorist to such experiences was a reexamination of the standard profit-maximization models which we had all been taught to employ. I found out, eventually, that other economists had, on the basis of interviews and other forms of observation, also reached the conclusion that in practice firms pursue objectives more diverse and complex than just maximization of profits. But in one important respect the consulting experience had taken me beyond that observation alone, for it had shown that other goals such as maximization of sales or growth of assets each had their own implications for business decisions and to each of these there seemed to correspond optimal values of the firm's decision variables. In other words, abandonment of the profit-maximization premise did not leave one with no choice but chaos and indecision. Rather, it called for decisions which are different but equally determinate, and which can be analyzed using all of the traditional tools and methods — marginal analysis, mathematical programming, etc.

Some months of working on the formal analysis provided the model of sales maximization (later supplemented by a model of growth maximization) which constituted the basis of the little book *Business Behavior, Value and Growth* (1959). If this model does constitute a contribution I believe it consists not in the observation that management may have objectives other than profit, but in the demonstration that other objectives are perfectly consistent with fruitful theoretical analysis, as was later demonstrated so effectively by writers such as Oliver Williamson and Robin Marris.

Let me emphasize that I never maintained and do not believe that all firms (or even all oligopoly firms) seek to maximize sales, or that they all share any other common and simple objective. I merely asserted and still believe that many firms have some objectives other than profit alone, and that for some which I encountered sales maximization is a reasonable approximation to their somewhat more complicated goals. Those goals are, in any event, rarely formulated expressly (except for purposes of public relations), they may change from time to time, and they are at most pursued only in a rough and ready manner. Moreover, I believe that in aggregative studies of industry behaviour the differences between the predictions of profit and sales maximization are apt to be minor and unimportant. But for analysis of the behaviour of individual firms I believe the distinction is vital, as the reactions of business clients to our recommendations made under the two premises suggests strongly.

Partisans of the profit-maximization approach have suggested that the behaviour patterns called for by the two models may be difficult to distinguish, and they have questioned the evidence presented in *Business Behavior, Value and Growth* which, admittedly, is all anecdotal. They have pointed out, rather cogently, that long-run profit maximization may require resistence to elimination of unprofitable sales in the short run. I certainly cannot prove the contrary. I can only suggest that the change in the nature of our recommendations constituted what amounts to a (very poorly) controlled experiment of a sort rarely possible for economists. Moreover, the resulting observations were generally supported by careful discussion with businesspersons with whom I had established rather close relationships and who had little reason to slant their answers.

After the sale of Alderson Associates when Wroe Alderson retired, my consulting work continued through the firms Mathematica, and Consultants in Industry Economics (CIE), both of which I helped to found. This work has usually proved fruitful and stimulating to me in more general research. Microeconomists are peculiarly fortunate in this respect, for while academic consultants drawn from other disciplines generally contribute by application of the learning they have acquired through research and teaching, for them benefits rarely seem to flow in the other direction.

The Performing Arts

Sheer misunderstanding led to my involvement in the economics of the performing arts. In about 1960, the Twentieth Century Fund and John D. Rockfeller III had decided that the time was auspicious for a systematic study of that subject. On inquiry they were told of an economist at Princeton who was knowledgeable about the arts as well as economics. The person who had steered them to me had, of course, confused my activities in painting and sculpture with knowledge of the finances and organization of opera, theatres, orchestras and dance companies. My father had instilled in me a great love of the performing arts but little knowledge of the economic side of these activities accompanied my wife's and my frequent attendance.

I agreed to a meeting on the subject, having first discussed the matter with a young colleague, William G. Bowen, with whom I had worked earlier (and who has since become President of Princeton University). Talking with the potential sponsors of the study I emphasized my ignorance of the subject and then, on the basis of my consulting experience, proceeded to indicate how I believed it should be analyzed dispassionately, as though one were dealing with the economics of the most banale of commodities rather than one which commands widespread expressions of adulation (if hardly universal attendance).

As it happened, Bowen and I were then both heavily committed to other projects. When it turned out that the potential sponsors had, for better or worse, decided that we were the right persons to conduct the study, we found ourselves resisting what was to prove one of the most exciting projects we had ever undertaken — so poor can foresight be!

The research turned out to be a major undertaking. It lasted somewhat more than three years, acquired and analyzed data from several hundred organizations, distributed questionnaires to about 150,000 audience members at more than a hundred performances in dozens of cities. A small army of students and other investigators was trained and sent out to collect the materials using questionnaires which had been painstakingly designed and pretested. All of this was planned meticulously by Bowen and the work was organized and supervised by my wife, with whom all my subsequent work on the economics of the arts has been carried out in full partnership.

The overall design of the study and the planning of the empirical work is all to be credited to my coauthor. His skill in dealing with messy data made it possible to determine many fundamental attributes of the activities in question. For example, he was able to show systematically that the composition of audiences in terms of education, income, age and sex varied only minusculely from one art form to another or one city to another. Audiences in London were, essentially, no different from those in Houston, Texas — all highly educated, and well-to-do relative to the population as a whole. Generally no more than two or three percent of the audience was made up of blue collar workers; opera with seven percent of the audience derived from this economic group, constituting the only exception. Many fascinating observations peripheral to our central topic also emerged from Bowen's calculations. For example, he was able to show that the proportion of women among the musicians in the orchestra at that time was almost perfectly inversely correlated with the income of the orchestra — a very tangible index of sex discrimination!

In the early 1960s collection of economic data on the performing arts in the U.S. was no routine matter. It often took my wife to back offices, basements and lofts, where figures sometimes had to be pieced together from scraps of paper that constituted the only records that some group had kept. Since that time much more such information has been collected and some of it published on a regular basis. Indeed, we were asked to design and, for several years, collect some of the figures that now appear regularly in the official U.S. government publications.

My own part in the study involved a role in the determination of the overall objectives and the general research design. I also wrote most of the final manuscript. However, my one contribution I consider to be significant is the cost disease model, which has since been used to help explain the behaviour of the cost of education, the budgetary problems of cities, etc. The basic point is that the *live* performing arts (in contradistinction to those employing the mass media such as film and television) are extraordinarily unadaptable to productivity-increasing technical change. A Boccherini string quartet written in the eighteenth century which takes half an hour to perform, required two-person hours of performance time then and requires exactly the same amount of time today. Meanwhile, in much of the remainder of the economy productivity has been increasing virtually without interruption in a manner that compounds and accumulates. If wages in the arts do not rise far more slowly than those in the remainder of the economy (and the evidence indicates that they do not) this means that cost per performance in the arts must rise steadily at a rate faster than costs in the remainder of the economy, roughly reflecting the difference in the productivity growth that characterizes the two sectors. Over the years this can add up to an enormous differential. I estimate roughly that a typical manufactured good which cost about the same as attendance at a performance in 1800 now costs only about one twentieth as much! This means also that the funds supplied to the arts by government or private philanthropy must generally increase year in, year out, at a rate exceeding the economy's rate of inflation if artistic activity is not to be forced to retrench. Constancy of *real* contributions is simply not enough for the purpose. This, then, is what has since come to be called the cost disease of the arts (I am delighted that it is also sometimes called 'Baumol's disease'). If the hypothesis is correct (and there is a good deal of evidence consistent with it)[2] it helps to explain many economic phenomena outside the arts, such as the shift of the labour forces in a number of countries out of manufacturing and toward the services, the increasing use of disposable products to avoid repair, the rising relative cost of medical care and education, etc.

It is sometimes suggested that the mass media — film, TV and recording can provide the cure for the cost disease, but recent analysis suggests that despite their sophisticated technology many of the mass media are in the long run vulnerable, essentially, to the same problem.

As a matter of fact, the data indicate that the cost of movie tickets and the cost per prime-time television hour have been rising at least as fast as the price of tickets to the commercial theatre. The explanation, apparently, lies in the technology of the mass media of which television is typical in this respect in that it has two basic components which are very different technologically. The first includes the actual performance in front of the television cameras, while the second is the actual transmission or filming.

The first component of TV is virtually identical with live performance on a theatre stage, and there is, therefore, just as little scope for technical change in the one as in the other. The second component, broadcasting transmission, is electronic and high tech in character, and constantly benefits from innovation. Television broadcasting of new material requires these two elements in relatively fixed physical proportions — one hour of programming (with some flexibility in rehearsal time) must be accompanied by one hour of transmission in each and every one hour broadcast.

Such an industry *must* be characterized by an initial period of decline in total cost (in constant dollars) followed by a period in which its costs begin to behave in a manner more and more similar to the live performing arts. The reason is that the cost of the highly technological component (transmission cost) will decline, or at least not rise as fast as the economy's inflation rate. At the same time, the cost of programming increases at a rate surpassing the rate of inflation.

If each year transmission costs decrease and programming expenses increase because of the cost disease that besets all live performance, eventually programming cost *must*, as a matter of arithmetic, begin to dominate the overall budget. Thereafter, total cost and programming cost must move closer and closer together until virtually the entire budget becomes a victim of the disease, with the stable technological costs too small a fragment of the whole to make a discernible difference.

Because such incidents are sometimes considered noteworthy it may be worth reporting that the cost disease model entered my consciousness quite suddenly and unexpectedly, though it had no doubt lurked in my subconscious for some time before. One night I awoke from a deep sleep at about 3 a.m. with the entire model clearly in my mind. I left the bedroom, went to the next room, jotted down a few notes, and immediately went back to sleep. The next morning I was able to write the idea up systematically. Later I will recount another such incident which occurred about fifteen years afterwards.

Our study of the arts was sponsored by a private foundation, the Twentieth Century Fund, which generously paid the considerable costs of this project. Moreover, the Fund was careful to avoid interference of any sort with the nature of the research or the contents of the resulting book. Indeed, it withstood pressure from a representative of some of the larger performing organizations to suppress or weaken some of the materials showing the high incomes of the members of the audience, a piece of information which, it was feared, would make it more difficult to obtain financial support from the government and other sources. Happily, these fears proved to be unjustified.

As a matter of fact, it is now widely believed that the opposite occurred — that because of the accident of timing (or, perhaps it was no accident but a matter of good judgment of its sponsors) the book is now said to have played a role in launching substantial government support in the United States. It appeared at the same time as another report sponsored by the Rockefeller Brothers Fund (*The Performing Arts: Problems and Prospects,* McGraw Hill, New York, 1965), in which Bowen and I had a peripheral part. The Rockefeller report was prepared by a committee composed to a considerable extent of businessmen whose strong statement of approval of funding for the arts contributed political respectability to the attempt to induce the United States to embark upon the sort of public sponsorship so traditional in Europe. The simultaneous appearance of our own book, which for the first time provided systematic data and some degree of analysis on the subject, apparently contributed ammunition to the campaign for public support of the arts.

The book was launched with a burst of publicity orchestrated by the Twentieth Century Fund. There were front page stories in the *New York Times* and the *Washington Post*. Newspapers throughout the world carried substantial reports. We were most amused by the story in Pravda which reported that two respectable economists from Princeton University had just published a book showing how capitalism destroys the arts!

Princeton and New York Universities

The economics department at Princeton was an extraordinarily harmonious group, indeed. I believe virtually all of my colleagues had a deep affection for one another. We were sorry when Friedrich Lutz returned to Europe a few years after we arrived. In addition to members such as Viner, Oskar Morgenstern, Richard Lester, and Lester Chandler, the Department was fortunate to acquire W. Arthur Lewis and Fritz Machlup, both of whom were to become close friends. The Lewises had their home a few doors from ours, and our children grew up together. His lovely and charming wife also proved to be my most talented sculpture student, and has had several successful exhibitions of her own. Sir Arthur's general wisdom, his analytic intuition and his meticulous historical scholarship have always constituted standards difficult for the rest of us to emulate. Fritz Machlup, whose unexpected death in 1983 left a major gap in our lives, was an incredible generator of ideas and research undertakings which he pursued with amazing determination and energy. At age seventy-seven he undertook a research programme which was projected to yield a work in ten volumes. Three years later he had completed the first three of those books, and work on the others was well on its way.

He and Oskar Morgenstern reached retirement age virtually simultaneously. On attaining their emeritus status at Princeton they were immediately offered and accepted full term appointments at New York University, where each of them continued to teach with energy and devotion for the remainder of his life.

At just about the time Machlup and Morgenstern left for N.Y.U. I had begun to think about my position. By then I had been at Princeton for nearly a quarter of a century. Our children had grown and left home. It seemed high time to make some change in our arrangements. Yet leaving Princeton altogether was virtually unthinkable. Half our lives had been spent there and it contained most of our close friends, both outside the department and within it.

The solution to our dilemma was an invitation to N.Y.U., first, to come as a visitor for a year. Aside from visiting appointments at the Stockholm School of Economics and Berkeley this was our first protracted period away from Princeton since 1949, and it was a return to the city of our childhood. The department in New York proved most hospitable and a pleasant place in which to work. The students were far more heterogeneous than those at Princeton, both in ethnic background and in quality of their earlier training. The best of them were of outstanding quality, and they constituted a fascinating and enthusiastic group.

Consequently, when the next year I was offered a permanent appointment on a halftime basis, and received the consent of Princeton to the arrangement, I agreed readily. As it turned out, it was the beginning of what, in my own view, seems my most creative period.

It actually began with the completion of an exclusively Princeton enterprise; two volumes on environmental economics written jointly with my (then) Princeton colleague, Wallace Oates.[3] One volume was almost entirely devoted to theory while the second sought to assemble the available empirical materials, adding some evidence acquired by ourselves.

Among the results provided by the theoretical volume two will be cited as illustrations. The first deals with the victims of externalities. It has, of course, been known, at least since the work of Pigou, that (with some restrictions) optimal expenditure on reduction of pollution emissions (or other detrimental externalities) requires a charge or tax upon the polluter equal to the marginal social damage of his emissions. This 'polluter pays' arrangement forces the polluter to bear the full social cost of his emissions, and therefore, to undertake any preventative measure whose (incremental) cost is less than the value of the damage thereby avoided. But what about the victims? It would seem that simple justice calls for some sort of compensation to those whose health or even whose cost of living is affected by pollution. Indeed, this intuitive judgment is readily confirmed formally with the aid of the mathematical theory of fairness provided in the work of Duncan Foley, David Schmeidler, Serge-Christophe Kolm and others. Yet it is proved in our theoretical volume that, unless it can be provided in a way whose incentive effects are zero (i.e., as a 'lump sum' payment), *any* compensation to the victims of externalities, however small, is incompatible with Pareto optimality in resource allocation in the economy. There is a simple intuitive explanation of this result. In the presence of detrimental externalities there is a Pareto optimal level of use of resources *by the victims* to protect themselves from their effects. For example, it may be appropriate to insulate or air condition homes and workplaces, or it may be desirable to move them away from the source of pollution thereby, perhaps, increasing transportation costs in the future. But if compensation is based on the amount of damage suffered by the victims, such compensation payments will induce them to spend less on self protection against that damage. In effect, such compensation payments reduce the marginal net yield of outlays on self-protection. Here we then have a clear example of a conflict (or, rather, a trade-off) between Pareto optimality and fairness.

A second illustrative result of our theoretical analysis relates to the choice between a tax upon the generator of externalities and a subsidy to induce him to reduce his emissions. Common sense suggests that at appropriate tax and subsidy rates the effects of the two will be the same — the donkey can be moved either with the carrot or the stick. But while this conclusion (which had often been repeated in the environmental literature) has an element of truth, it turns out that subsidies have a second consequence which is likely more than to offset its pollution decreasing effect. It is true that in the short run either the tax or the subsidy will induce polluting firms to emit less. However, at least in the case of perfect competition, in the long run, the tax on emissions may *not* reduce the emissions of any one pulluting *firm,* yet it will reduce the emissions of the *industry* by encouraging the exit of polluters. On the other hand, *the subsidy is likely to increase the industry's emissions* by encouraging the entry of polluters. These results are certainly true when there is a fixed proportion between output and quantity of emission. A fixed Pigouvian tax, *t,* per unit of emissions then contributes to the firm's total cost the amount *tky,* where *y* is output and *k* is the emissions-output ratio. The resulting addition to average cost is $tky/y = tk =$ constant. Therefore, the Pigouvian tax simply causes a uniform upward shift in the firm's average cost curve, and so does not affect the location of its minimum point, i.e., its profit maximizing output or emissions level. Yet we do know from a standard supply-demand diagram that with curves of the usual shape a tax must shift the supply curve upward and therefore reduce industry output and, hence, its emissions, and the opposite must be true under a subsidy.

The investigation of the empirical data also produced a number of what, to us at least, were surprises. We had thought that the explosion in the world's population and in industrial activity would show that there was fairly universal growth in the rate of environmental damage, but the results were far more mixed. In some cases such as lead in the atmosphere and the generation of solid wastes our conjecture did indeed turn out to be true or, at least, to be supported by the evidence. But postwar emissions control efforts had substantial beneficial effects on air and water quality with, for example, enormous decreases in the sulphur and particulate content of the atmosphere in major cities of the U.S. and the

United Kingdom. In other cases, for instance, the concentration of pollutants in Lake Superior in the United States and the oxygen content of the rivers surrounding Manhattan, matters had been improving long before that. In several cases such as the depletion of oxygen in the Baltic and the concentration of mercury in tuna it transpired that there was good reason to suspect that the causes were natural (e.g., a secular decline in rainfall in the sources of water for the Baltic). We were most surprised to find (after an extensive search that took us to the conservator's quarters at the Louvre, the Metropolitan Museum in New York and St. Paul's Cathedral in London) that there seems to be no conclusive evidence supporting the view that the deterioration of ancient sculpture and of stone buildings is accelerating or that it is attributable to increasing emissions of pollutants. We found many newspaper stories claiming categorically that this was so, but careful review of the scientific evidence simply forced us to accept the verdict 'not proven'.

Perhaps partly in consequence of this work I was elected to the presidency of the recently formed Association of Environmental and Resource Economists (AERE), an organization which has since grown and expanded its activities.

Visits to Sweden and Israel

Like most academics, I have visited institutions in a number of other countries. My most protracted visits were to the Stockholm School of Economics and the Hebrew University in Jerusalem. Each of these was a source of ideas, experiences and friendships which have endured over the years. In Stockholm we became very close, among others, to Bertil Ohlin, Erik Lundberg, Assar Lindbeck and their delightful views.

I must single out Bertil and Evy Ohlin because of the very special aura that characterized them. Over the years I have met many impressive people but among economists three truly towering personalities stand out in my memory — Robbins, Viner and Ohlin. Each was unforgettable even on a first acquaintance, each was extraordinarily erudite and broad in his interests, each was a remarkable and fascinating conversationalist, each was a warm and reliable friend and their wives were all marvellous and attractive personalities whom we grew to love deeply. (Both the Robbins and the Ohlins, incidentally, were close friends of the Viners.) It would seem that they just do not make their kind anymore.

I have already spoken to Lord Robbins and Jacob Viner, both of whom were middle aged when we got to know them. Ohlin was already well into retirement when I met him, but he was still strikingly handsome. Gentle, courteous, well-spoken, his conversations ranged over a wide range of issues, though they tended to focus on political economy to which his career as an economist-politician directed him. Tax policy in an inflationary period was a matter of particular concern to him. We talked about it many times and even drafted a short joint paper on the subject, which we decided, probably wisely, was better suppressed. We often visited one another's homes in Stockholm and (once) in New York. Ohlin did not enjoy the performing arts so that we had the pleasure of taking his wife to concerts and the opera. Once in Stockholm by myself I became her regular evening companion, apparently to everyone's delight.

My visits to Israel are more recent and therefore are harder to sort out from my emotional attachment to the country. I have been associated primarily with the Hebrew

University where we renewed our friendship with the Patinkins and made friends with David Levhari, Eytan Sheshinski and their wives, among others, as well as with June Flanders from the University of Tel Aviv. There is a constant air of excitement in Israel which pervades all academic discussions as well. Add to that the indescribable beauty of Jerusalem which we were in a particularly felicitous position to enjoy from our lovely apartment with its unobstructed view of the ancient city walls some 200 yards away, and one has the ingredients of an unforgettable experience.

Several of my writings were produced in Stockholm and Jerusalem, notably some of the earlier pieces on contestable markets theory and these benefited to no small degree from the excited discussion they elicited.

The Theory of Contestable Markets

Soon after the two books on the environment made their appearance, I found myself embarked almost accidentally on what I consider to be the most fruitful piece of research in which I have ever participated. The word 'participated' is used advisedly, since the results stemmed from the work of at least a half dozen persons beside myself — my coauthors, John Panzar, then of Bell Laboratories and Robert Willig of Princeton University, Elizabeth Bailey, formerly Vice Chairman of the Civil Aeronautics Board and now at Carnegie Mellon University, Dietrich Fischer, Thijs ten Raa, then at New York University, and Gerald Faulhaber at Bell Laboratories. Obviously there were three centres of activity: N.Y.U., Princeton and Bell Laboratories.

My systematic work on the subject began with a project I had undertaken under the sponsorship of the Division of Information Science and Technology of the National Science Foundation in which an incidental part of the task was to provide a nontechnical document discussing the rationale for and principles for the determination of the proper amount of government financial support for the dissemination of scientific and technical information in general and of scientific journals in particular. Assuming that a large part of the argument would rest on the sorts of market failure associated with public goods and scale economies, I set about what I expected to be the tedious task of redescribing a set of elementary and straightforward principles. The public goods portion of the discussion turned out just as expected — exactly as it is so well described in the literature. However, the theory of scale economies and the associated phenomenon of natural monopoly seemed to resist simple explanation. Each time I attempted a description of the logic of some obvious proposition it seemed to acquire complexity and turned out not to be quite correct. For example, in the case of a publisher who provided a half dozen journals rather than only one, scale economies did not seem to account for the firm's multiproduct character. Why was the enterprise a multiproduct firm, and what would society lose by breaking up the publishing firm into six separate publishers of single journals? It was considerations such as this which later led Panzar and Willig to formulate their concept of economies of scope — the savings which a firm may (or may not) enjoy from simultaneous provision of a multiplicity of products — and which had previously led me to formulate the more technical concept of trans-ray convexity,[4] a formal criterion of continuous complementarity in the production of different goods as output proportions change. At the same time it became clear that natural monopoly, which is defined to mean that production of the industry's vector of outputs is cheaper when carried out by a single firm rather than by any multiplicity of firms, is not quite the same thing as scale economies. Indeed, it was proved eventually that scale economies throughout the relevant region of output space are neither necessary nor sufficient for natural monopoly.

Meanwhile, Gerald Faulhaber, who had been sent by Bell Laboratories to carry out his graduate work at Princeton, had quite independently, starting off from some earlier work of mine, begun research on the theory of natural monopoly. He found implications which had escaped me completely at the time the original work had been prepared. When Faulhaber showed me some of his work and asked me to supervise his Ph.D. dissertation, I was astonished at the degree of overlap with my own work at N.Y.U. Indeed, using a single-product game theoretic approach, his work was at that point in many ways ahead of mine.

The developments were sufficiently seductive to attract the attention of others, notably Panzar and Willig at Bell Laboratories, Dietrich Fischer at N.Y.U., and Elizabeth Bailey who then held positions both at Bell Laboratories and N.Y.U. and who quickly took on the task of liaison, in addition to the valuable contributions she provided directly.

Faulhaber had already proved for the single-product case that the concept underlying and, indeed, appropriately defining natural monopoly is a mathematical relationship called subadditivity of total cost. Specifically (for the multiproduct case) let y^I represent the vector of outputs of the industry and let y^i be any vector of outputs assigned to a hypothetical firm, i, in any partition of the industry's outputs, so that $\Sigma y^i = y^I$. If $C(y)$ is the total cost function of a firm in the industry, then that cost function is strictly subadditive if $C(y^I) < \Sigma C(y^i)$ for each and every set of y^i summing to y^I. In other words, the cost function is subadditive at industry output vector y^I if it is cheaper for y^I to be produced by a monopoly than by *any* larger number of firms.

Faulhaber had also proved in the single product case, first, that economies of scale are sufficient to guarantee that the firm's average costs will decrease with output, second, that decreasing average costs are sufficient to guarantee subadditivity, and, third, that the converse is untrue — that subadditivity is no guarantee of decreasing average cost. In other words, in the single-product case he had shown that an industry could be a natural monopoly even if it did not exhibit scale economies and its average costs were not declining.

Soon Panzar and Willig produced several sets of necessary conditions for subadditivity in the multiproduct case, and I provided a set of conditions sufficient for multiproduct natural monopoly, conditions which have since been used rather widely in empirical studies of cost functions and their implications for the structure of an industry.

Panzar and Willig, working together, proposed a concept which Dr. Bailey and I had also put forth on the same day — the concept of sustainability of prices. A vector of prices charged by a multiproduct monopolist is said to be *sustainable against entry* if (a) it provides revenue to the monopoly at least sufficient to permit it to cover its costs, and (b) there exists no other vector of outputs which an entrant can sell at those prices and which will permit the entrant to operate without loss. In other words, sustainable prices permit the incumbent to prevent entry without recourse to retaliatory measures or strategic responses. This concept was formulated as a first step toward transformation of the natural monopoly concept from one which was normative (when is natural monopoly the most efficient industry structure?) to something that was more or less behavioural (when will natural monopoly be immune from entry?).

Faulhaber was able to prove that where both economies and diseconomies of scale are present (at different ranges of outputs), even if a firm is a natural monopoly), no sustainable prices may exist for it. He did this with the aid of a remarkable numerical counterexample: Consider three communities for which electricity generating facilities of given capacity are to be built. Suppose any one of the communities' needs can be met at a cost of $12 million, that any two of them can be served simultaneously for $19 million while all three of them can be served by a single plant for $30 million. Costs here are clearly subadditive since provision of the output by three separate plants costs 3 × $12 million = $36 million, while two-plant production costs $12 + $19 million = $31 million. Both other options are, therefore, more costly than the $30 million outlay required for single-firm production. Yet, here, a single generating firm can find no prices which are sustainable. For if it were, for example, to propose to charge each community $10 million in order just to cover its $30 million cost, an entrant could offer to supply only two of three communities at a cost of say $9.7 million each, thus more than covering the $19 million cost of the plant required for the purpose. Faulhaber's example thus showed that in some cases freedom of entry can prevent cost minimization. But the bulk of our analysis was later to argue strongly for ease of entry.

A little later I provided a complementary theorem which rested on a result first derived by Frank Ramsey in 1927. As we know, where average costs are declining (and in a variety of related multiproduct cases), a firm which prices its products at their marginal costs must suffer losses. The question to which Ramsey addressed himself is the following. If marginal cost prices are precluded financially, what deviations of prices from marginal costs are required for the second-best allocation of resources, that is, for Pareto optimality under the constraint that supplying firms just cover their total costs? Ramsey was able to derive a formula for these second-best prices which was ignored by much of the economic literature for several decades but had by the 1970s received a great deal of attention. I was then able to prove (though the result took me completely by surprise) that a monopolist who decided to adopt Pareto optimal Ramsey prices would (under a set of rather reasonable assumptions) find those prices to be sustainable. In other words, such a commendable pricing decision would reward the monopolist by granting him immunity from entry.

I had arrived at this result in rather curious circumstances. My wife and I were attending a fund raising performance at one of New York's experimental theatres, and we were waiting in line to get in surrounded by persons in bizarre dress and make-up when, according to my wife, my face took on a rather distracted look. I told her that a theorem which hardly seemed plausible to me had come to me from nowhere, along with what seemed to me to be its entire proof.

Indeed, it transpired that the rigorous proof that emerged eventually did follow the outline that came to me suddenly in that theatre lobby, but it took weeks of hard labour by (a sceptical) Willig, Bailey (and myself) before it could be put into satisfactory form.

At about this time a small group of U.S. economists was sent by the National Science Foundation to attend a conference in Leningrad, and Willig and I were among them. We sat up all night in the airplane discussing how our analysis of natural monopoly could be extended to other market forms and constitute the basis for a theory of the determination of industry structure. The vision had been mine, but Willig was to contribute the key step to its realization. First, on our return, Fischer and I produced a paper showing how one can calculate the cost minimizing structure of an industry, thereby determining whether it is or is not, say, a natural monopoly. For example, if it transpires that the industry's output vector can be produced most cheaply by say, four firms, one can say it is a 'natural oligopoly', and we showed under what circumstances this will be true. Similarly, we showed under what cost conditions the industry will be 'naturally perfectly competitive' and so on.

Then Willig formulated the concept of what we were to call a perfectly contestable market — a market in which an entrant has access to all production techniques available to incumbents, in which the entrant is not prohibited from wooing the incumbent's customers, and in which entry decisions can be reversed without cost — that is, a market from which entrants can withdraw without loss of any of their investments. An example of an approximation to such a market is an airline route. If company A opens up for business on the route from New York to Los Angeles and business proves disappointing, he can simply withdraw and move them to another more promising route.

Where exit and entry are so easy and exit so costless incumbents are completely vulnerable to the threat posed by *potential* entry. It is possible to prove that, as a consequence, in a perfectly contestable market (a) no firm can earn any monopoly profit in the long run, (b) industry structure must always be efficient, i.e., the industry will tend to be composed of exactly the number of firms that can produce its output at minimum cost and (c) if two or more firms supply a given product to a market, in the long run the price of that product must equal its marginal cost.

Markets may be perfectly contestable even if they are characterized by scale economies in production and even if they contain only a small number of firms (even only a single firm). The theory thus generalizes considerably the concept of perfect competition, showing how ease of entry and exit and the accompanying threat by potential entrants can elicit good performance even in industries with small numbers of firms.

It must be emphasized that our purpose was not apologetics. We do not believe that most industries are perfectly contestable or even nearly so. We do believe, however, that some industries with small numbers of firms *are* highly contestable, and that in those cases government interference with the market mechanism is difficult to justify. In other cases the contestability of the market can be increased by public policy and in those cases this will sometimes prove to be the most effective means to serve the public interest.

It should be added also that we are well aware of the heavy debt contestability analysis owes to earlier writing, and have tried to suggest some of its sources in our publications. But as Viner taught me long ago, one can never hope to achieve completeness in such an undertaking.

In my presidential address to the American Economic Association in December of 1981 I sought to provide a general introduction to the theory of contestable markets. This was followed several months later by the publication of our book with its lengthy analysis of multiproduct firms and industries and its examination of the market forces that determine the structure of an industry — whether it will emerge as an oligopoly, a monopoly or something else. As is to be expected, the analysis has generated controversy, raising legitimate questions many of which are still far from being settled. It has also led to a variety of research undertakings by others, both empirical and theoretical, and that has, of course, been most gratifying.

Toward Further Work

Happily, the area in which I work has experienced relatively rapid growth in the past few decades, and so my stock of teaching capital has undergone considerable obsolescence. Many of my former students and their contemporaries are now better equipped than I to teach the various courses in mathematical economics, virtually all of which I had inaugurated some thirty years earlier.

I flatter myself that this is not quite true in my research. In the two years since the appearance of the contestability book I have embarked on several other projects. I am completing a book on applications of Duncan Foley's fairness concept to analyze such issues as the equitability of different rationing procedures, of peak-off peak pricing and of Pigouvian taxes on externalities.[5] I am working together with Edward Wolff at New York University and Sue Anne Batey Blackman at Princeton on the theory of productivity growth and the feedback relationship between such growth and expenditures on research and development by private industry. I am also considering a study of the theory of nationalized industry — of the circumstances under which operation of a firm by the public sector may be superior in terms of the general welfare to operation by private enterprise, regulated or unregulated by government. Here it should be noted that analyses such as the theory of public goods are less pertinent than may at first appear to be the case since a public good can be produced by private firms if it is *financed* by government. If nationalized firms lack the incentives for efficiency provided by the market mechanism to private firms why, then, should government enterprise ever be preferred over private? I am working on a model which will, with a bit of luck, provide some answers and, perhaps, some additional insights.

In short, as yet there is no conclusion to my story — all I can offer is a status report on a continuing stream of research . . .

Notes

1. I am not certain the term 'prisoner's dilemma' had yet been invented; indeed, I seem to remember it was proposed by Professor A. Tucker at Princeton several years later. But the ideas of game theory had reached London and in discussions externalities were already being translated there into game theoretic terms.
2. The noteworthy exception seems always to have been a period of rapid inflation. Data for the period after the U.S. Civil War, after World War I and the inflation of the 1970s indicate that in such periods growth in cost per performance has not stayed ahead of the general price level. Presumably groups are not able to raise money quickly enough, and are therefore forced to retrench by reducing rehearsal time, simplifying costumes and scenery, etc. If this explanation is correct, it follows that the cost disease is not really in remission of such periods, but that its normal consequences are suppressed and emerge in a different form — that of reduction of standards and cutting of corners.
3. Baumol, William J. and Wallace Oates, *The Theory of Environmental Policy* (Englewood Cliffs, N. J.: Prentice Hall, 1975) and Baumol, Oates and S. A. Blackman, *Economics and the Quality of Life* (Englewood Cliffs, N. J.: Prentice Hall, 1979).

4. For a formal definition see Baumol, William J., John C. Panzar and Robert D. Willig, *Contestable Markets and the Theory of Industry Structure* (San Diego, Ca: Harcourt Brace Jovanovich, 1982) pp. 79–81.

5. *Toward Application of Fairness Theory* (Cambridge, Mass.: MIT Press, 1985).

Part I
Theory of Contestable Markets

The rapidity with which the ideas encompassed in the theory of contestable markets have entered both the literature of the academics and the discussions of practitioners took me by surprise, even though I had been reasonably optimistic on this score when my co-authors and I first went public. Virtually every week I receive drafts of related journal articles for comment. At hearings before regulatory agencies and in antitrust cases terms such as 'economies of scope', 'sustainable prices' and 'contestable markets' are interjected casually as though long usage had made their connotations familiar to everyone.

Perhaps this is in part attributable to the high quality of the criticism that was originally directed at our work. Nothing seems to stimulate attention as much as a reasonable amount of intellectually interesting dispute. For that reason as well as for the insights offered by their discussions I am grateful to our critics. Though their strictures left me generally unrepentant, they did suggest some reservations and qualifications that were urgently required in preceding writings by my colleagues and myself. I will return presently to the criticisms, to the helpful and constructive reviews of our book and to some of the other work that has emerged in the literature since the appearance of the volume.

Contestability and 'Libertarian' Ideology

Before proceeding to these matters let me reiterate our ideological stance, a subject on which we have encountered considerable misunderstanding. Our position is entrenched deeply in the middle ground between the extreme pro and anti regulators. We disassociate ourselves firmly, on the one side, from those who believe (or almost seem to believe) that the unrestrained market automatically solves all economic problems and that virtually all regulation and antitrust activity constitutes a pointless and costly source of economic inefficiency. *If* a market approximates perfect contestability, it is true, matters can be left to take care of themselves. There, small numbers of large firms, vertical and even horizontal mergers and other arrangements which have traditionally been objects of suspicion of monopolistic taint and worse, are rendered harmless and perhaps even beneficent by the presence of contestability. But that observation is no whitewash and establishes no presumption, one way or the other, about the desirability of public sector intervention in any particular market of reality. For before anyone can legitimately use the analysis to infer that virtue reigns in some economic sector and that interference is therefore unwarranted, that person must first provide evidence that the arena in question is, in fact, highly contestable. The economy of reality is composed of sectors which vary widely in the degree to which they approximate the attributes of contestability.[1] Thus, the conclusion that *perfectly* contestable markets require no intervention claims little more than the possibility (which remains to be proven, case by case) that *some* markets in reality may automatically perform in a very acceptable manner despite the small number of firms that inhabit them.

Thus, it is simply incorrect to associate our writings on contestability with the extreme *laissez-faire* positions on the role of regulation and antitrust. I disagree vehemently with such a view of the world. On the other hand, my coauthors and I reject with equal conviction the position of those who hold that mere large size of a firm means that it *must* serve the economy badly, that high concentration ratios are sufficient to justify governmental restrictions upon the structure or conduct of an industry or that a horizontal merger merits automatic condemnation if it increases concentration ratios substantially. For it is true that contestability , where and if it does happen to hold sway, can remove any taint from these phenomena. Thus we emphatically part company from extreme interventionists and extreme noninterventionists alike. We believe that both antitrust and regulation have a very valuable role to play, but one that is considerably more restricted than it has played in the recent past.

Criticisms of Contestability Analysis

Several more recent critics have rejected the entire contestability approach largely because, in my view, they have misunderstood its contents, its orientation or its method of analysis. For example, more than one commentator has suggested that we believe all the world to be perfectly contestable or nearly so and that on this basis we reject all or almost all government intervention to inhibit the exerise of monopoly power. As I have just indicated, this is a complete caricature of our position. I am not sanguine about the likelihood that such distortions can be prevented in the future. I therefore prefer simply to ignore such comments, only apologizing to the degree that obscure exposition on my part may have contributed to the misunderstandings that underlie them.

However, the criticism of Weitzman[2] and that of Schwartz and Reynolds[3] which initially greeted the appearance of our work on the subject are a very different matter. These authors understand our work very well; their reservations (particularly that of Schwartz and Reynolds) are very much to the point, and it would hardly do to ignore them. My coauthors and I have provided an extensive summary of their reservations and a fairly careful and, I believe, measured response.[4] Some (revised) excerpts from our comments may therefore be in order here.

Professor Weitzman takes perfect contestability to be defined to require absolutely costless and instantaneous entry and exit, and argues that this in turn implies that returns to scale must be absolutely constant so that, for all practical purposes, perfectly contestable markets must all be perfectly competitive. Thus, in his judgment, the theory is not really applicable to any other market forms.

For clarification, Weitzman's algebra can be translated into a concrete example. Imagine a machine which operates at minimum average cost when it produces 12,000 units of output per hour and which can be moved instantaneously and costlessly from market to market. Then an entrepreneur who wishes to produce only 3,000 units of output per hour in each of four markets can shift the machine four times every hour, letting the machine run fifteen minutes in each market. Thus, in market A, for example, between 1:00 and 1:15 p.m. it will produce its desired 3,000 units of output, operating at its cost-minimizing rate of 12,000 units per hour. There obviously are no diseconomies to small scale production here.

Weitzman adds a final twist to this story. Suppose customers arrive at each market in a steady stream and will not wait. Then by 1:15 p.m., our producer would have sold only 3,000/4 units of that hour's output, leaving (¾)3,000 units in inventory. Inventory-carrying costs then still impose higher costs upon the firm whose demand flow in a market is below the machine's cost-minimizing rate of production. But Weitzman also shows a way around this problem. With exit and entry costless, the machine can just as well be shifted among markets not just four, but eight times per hour, each time operating only 7½ minutes and producing 1,500 units of output in this interval. This time, the machine enters market A at 1:00 p.m., leaves it at 1:07½ p.m., reenters market A at 1:30 p.m., and leaves it again at 1:37½ p.m. By 1:07½ p.m. the producer will have already sold 3,000/8 units, so that unsold inventory will be only ¾(1,500) units, rather than ¾(3,000), as before. Our entrepreneur need not stop there. He can move among markets sixteen or thirty-two or sixty-four times per hour . . . each time cutting his average inventory in half, and, in the limit, eliminating inventory completely. Thus all financial penalties for small-scale production can be avoided and constant returns to scale guaranteed.

On what grounds do we conclude that the Weitzman story does not hold generally? First, some items, notably services, cannot be stored at all. They perish the instant they are produced, and one cannot get around this problem by taking the time they are held in inventory to be very brief, approaching zero in the limit. Second, capital is not always capable of turning out a continuously variable rate of output flow. Some processes require an irreducible amount of production *time* and yield some fixed minimum batch of output. More generally, minimal average cost may be achieved only if the production process is run at a particular intensity over a particular span of time. In these cases Weitzman's technique of 'substituting' the perfect divisibility of time to compensate for other indivisibilities breaks down.

These are not cases of minor importance, as an air transport example shows. Along any airline route, say Philadelphia to Ithaca, suppose cost per passenger is minimized by a jumbo jet if it is used to capacity, some 400 seats. Suppose no more than 100 passengers travel this route every day. Even if airplanes could be switched from one route to another without cost or delay, there is no way the Weitzman parable can be stretched to fit. Transportation services cannot be stored. There is no way any of the capacity of the departed plane can be preserved for those passengers who wish to begin their trips after it leaves.

More important, the airplane inherently provides its services over time in one 400-seat batch. Since production of the service requires some nonvanishing interval of time, say, one hour, there is no way in which an abbreviated period of operation on the Philadelphia–Ithaca route can lead to the achievement of optimal scale. One simply cannot do it by operating a 400-seat plane carrying 100 people for fifteen minutes. Of course, it can be flown only once every four days, but that supplies a different and inferior product which a smaller and less economical plane may be able to outcompete with a daily schedule. Thus, when production via the most efficient techniques occurs in minimum batches (400 seats per plane, 12,000 shoes per production run) and the size of the batches cannot be cut by abbreviating the time employed in the process, the Weitzman argument clearly fails.

Weitzman's analysis suffers from another more fundamental problem—a mischaracterization of contestability resulting from a confusion between *economic* and technological notions of sunk costs. To produce its results, even the limiting case of perfect contestability does *not* require entry and exit to be instantaneous. Rather, it is sufficient that the process be rapid enough so that the entrant does not find his investment vulnerable to a retaliatory response by the incumbent. *The length of this time period is not exclusively a technological datum, but is also the result of business practice and opportunities in the market in question.* This period can be as long as the longest period for which it is credible for buyers to commit their patronage to the entrant. In terms of a water transport scenario, 'hit and run' entry may be possible because the entrant can sell its service by contract *and before* it brings its ships or barges into the market, not because they can move in faster than the incumbent is able to cut his price.[5]

Even if such contracting is not feasible, it is still possible for regulation, costs of communicating price revisions, or other impediments to delay an incumbent's effective price response for a period of length $T>>0$. In either case, the concept of 'hit and run' entry can survive the technological imposition of a minimum production-line requirement $t^*\leq T$, while the Weitzman parable cannot.

Schwartz and Reynolds raise an issue that is very different and in our view considerably more significant. They point out, correctly, that sufficient conditions for *perfect* contestability are virtually certain to be violated in reality, at least to some degree. They ask whether small deviations from the conditions they cite are likely to affect substantially the conclusions of the analysis. They argue that there is, indeed, a sharp discontinuity, so that minor violations of the conditions they cite are likely to cause large losses in the social benefits promised by perfect contestability.

The issue they raise is important. However, their model of deviation from perfect contestability is only one of the possible pertinent constructs and that other plausible and legitimate constructs imply that behaviour and social benefits approach those of perfect contestability continuously as the contestability of markets increases.

It is quite easy to construct a systematic analysis of the effect upon a market of the introduction of a small amount of sunk costs based on the economically relevant progression from the limiting case in which entry does not subject any capital to the risk of retaliatory responses by the incumbent (complete absence of sunk costs) to one in which a small amount of an entrant's investment must be sunk irrevocably in the market. We show that under plausible assumptions the associated change in the equilibrium price must also be small. All we require for this result is that, before making his investment in the market, the potential entrant be able to enter into contracts to supply potential customers for a nontrivial interval of time, T.

The basic scenario is quite simple. At time zero the potential entrant may offer to serve customers for a period of time T at a price $p_e\leq p_i$, the price of the incumbent. Buyers would, quite naturally, inquire whether any incumbent intended to match p_e. If one did, then entry would not occur, *but the price p_e would prevail in the market for T units of time*, whereupon an entrant can again appear with an offer waiting to be matched. Thus, in the absence of exogenous change, p_e can be expected to prevail in the market at all times. How low a p_e will a potential entrant find it desirable to offer? This depends upon the magnitude of the *economically* sunk costs. Suppose that a unit of capital purchased at a price of β per unit can be sold or utilized elsewhere after T for a unit salvage value of $\alpha\leq\beta$. Thus, one can parameterize continuously the degree of sunkenness of capital from zero ($\alpha=\beta$) to absolute sunkenness ($\alpha=0$). If $\alpha=\beta$, the potential entrant can afford to offer a price just equal to the economically efficient level of average cost, because its flow of sales is guaranteed until T, and afterwards it has no 'unamortized capital' to be concerned about. However, if $\alpha < \beta$, the entrant can offer a price only as low as *its* average cost over T, and this will be somewhat higher than the true economic average cost because some of the economic value of its plant may be lost as a result of exit or of oligopolistic rivalry which takes place after the initial contracts expire at time T. Then, incumbents can charge a price above true economic average cost without inducing entry, because of the sunk economic costs required of entrants. The sustainable elevation of price, here, is larger the smaller is α. And α will be smaller the larger the proportion of cost that is technologically sunk, and the shorter is the time period, T. Thus, it is clear that the deleterious effects of sunk costs behave 'continuously' in this framework, in contrast to their behaviour in the analysis of Reynolds and Schwartz.

The essential difference between our scenario and that of Schwartz and Reynolds is that buyers' behaviour is assigned a clear role in our version of the entry process. Buyers have an incentive to enter into contracts in the way we describe, for that is the way in which they can protect themselves from monopolistic exploitation by the incumbents.

It should be emphasized that models which support the robustness of contestability analysis follow a relatively long tradition going back at least to the work of J. S. Bain. This tradition holds that increased ease of entry and exit improves the welfare performance of firms and industries. On this subject, the theory of contestability has only sought to contribute insights on the underpinnings of that judgment. Certainly it is a view widely accepted on the basis of casual observation, though systematic empirical testing still remains to be carried out.

Subsequent Contributions

Naturally, even an author with very great equanimity can derive only limited pleasure from criticisms, however high their quality. Fortunately, from our point of view, the review articles, while not avoiding some reservations, have largely been kind as well as constructive.[6] Even more heartening, however, has been the flood of contributions by others, extending the analysis, testing it with the aid of data, both statistical and experimentally generated, and applying the analysis to particular industries. Here I cannot hope to do justice to these contributions. I can only say that many of them have been highly original and illuminating, and have in my view extended our understanding of economic processes to a considerable degree. No authors can hope for more to have been stimulated by their work.

Valuable statistical work has flown from a variety of sources, perhaps earliest from Ann Friedlaender and her associates, notably J. Shaw-er Wang Chiang. They have concentrated on truck transportation and have evaluated both economies of scale and scope.[7] Wang Chiang finds no evidence of global economies of scale in trucking but concludes that there are substantial economies of scope in short and intermediate haul shipments, suggesting that trucking firms may gain efficiency from merger of short and intermediate haul firms but that huge trucking firms would not be viable in an unregulated market.

Mayo and Kaserman have carried out an econometric evaluation of the efficient structure of the electric utility industry, providing remarkable depictions of the cost surface, the iso cost loci and even the M locus.[8]

A parallel study of the process of supplying water has been carried out by H. Young Kim and Robert M. Clark on behalf of the U.S. Environmental Protection Agency.[9] They, too, calculate the behaviour of ray average costs and estimate the shape of the M locus, concluding that in the neighbourhood of currently observable output vectors returns to scale are approximately constant.

Peter A. Cassidy[10] and John Davies [11] have applied the contestability analysis to freight transportation by water. The authors conclude that because of the mobility and saleability of the bulk of the capital of the liner shipping industry contestability theory is able to explain a number of the institutions and behaviour patterns that characterize it. Thus, in Davies' words,

> The theory of contestable markets, despite being new and in some ways still in the process of formation, thus appears to provide a much more incisive tool of analysis and one of much greater explanatory power than the other models which have been applied to liner shipping (p. 99).

Contestability analysis has also been applied to banking. Glyn Davies and John Davies have examined the pertinent policy issues and the virtues and shortcomings of bank deregulation, basing their perspicacious discussion on the precepts of contestability theory[12], though, unlike the other industry studies which I have described, they provide no statistical analysis.

Thus, the range of economic activities to which our work has been applied is very broad and the extent to which some of our analytic constructs have proved amenable to quantification has been surprising, at least to me.

Besides this sort of empirical work, a number of theoretical contributions have been offered in the general field.

Evans and Heckman have provided a modified test of subaddivity of a cost function, restricting the range of output vectors to be taken into account by the criterion. They have, incidentally, applied their test statistically to the Bell system (which formerly operated most of the U.S. telecommunications network as a monopoly) and conclude that its cost function was not subadditive in the neighbourhood of the company's output vector, that is, the firm should have decentralized more than it did.[13]

Daniel F. Spulber has contributed two very substantial papers on the theory of sustainable prices. In one[14] of them he explores the relationship between size of firm and the existence of sustainable prices. In the other[15] the author introduces a concept, 'the second best core', defined as a set of prices yielding nonnegative profits for the firm and which permits no prices which make any coalition of consumers better off. This concept is designed to deal with pricing for public enterprises with increasing returns to scale. Spilbur shows these prices to be a subset of the Ramsey prices and he demonstrates that they are related closely to the concepts of sustainability and supportability.

Spilbur's work is closely connected with that of Mirman, Tauman and Zang[16] who have analyzed the use of Shapley values as a means to divide up the total costs of a multiproduct firm. They have also devised several sets of conditions sufficient for the existence of sustainable prices and have argued that the set of prices consistent with the Aumann-Shapley values, treated as the imputation of a game encompassing the cost-sharing decision, constitutes a set of sustainable prices considerably more general than the Ramsey prices that are the focus of the Baumol, Bailey, Willig weak invisible-hand theorem. The subject is still under discussion.

Some of the most novel and illuminating work that has emerged from contestability analysis is the use of laboratory experiments to test various portions of the theory. Simulation of markets in the laboratory is, of course, a widening branch of our literature and has already provided a number of very valuable results. In two papers Coursey, Isaac, Luke and Smith report a number of ingenious experiments relating to contestability.[17]

They used cleverly designed market simulations in which the experimental subjects' payments depended on the outcome of their behaviour during the experiment. The authors report the results of twenty experiments, some involving a monopoly seller and some a duopoly. The results offer some surprises. For example:

> . . . entry cost has a profound effect on market performance over time, with only five experiments [of the 12 reported in that paper] replicating the strong convergence property [toward the sort of equilibrium predicted by contestability analysis] of the [earlier experiments without sunk costs]. The remaining seven experiments, although in the end [displaying convergence to a price nearer to the competitive than to the monopoly level, on the way] exhibited [conventional oligopolistic or monopolistic] behavior. . . . We think it significant that in twelve 'trials' not a single trial supported [the hypotheses corresponding to long term breakdown of competitive forces]. Thus, the disciplining power of market contestability remains impressive even where entry cost weakens that power enough to produce a wide diversity of dynamic patterns of interaction over time' (Courtney, Isaac, Luke and Smith, p. 83).

Harrison and McKee[18] build on the work just described. They modify such features as the limitation to one or two sellers (Harrison and McKee examine three seller cases), control for strategic demand withholding by buyers, and seek to control for risk preference and aversion. They also undertake to include the attribute that 'a potential entrant evaluates the profitability of price offers *knowing* the offer of the incumbent'.

It is probably premature to draw a categorical moral from the authors' summary statement that 'In a new series of experiments we find the evidence in favor of the contestable markets hypothesis is even stronger when one modifies the experimental design adopted to correspond to the theoretical framework' ('Experimental Evaluation,' p. 1). At this stage I am prepared only to conclude that this very fine experimental work is proving extremely fruitful and illuminating and that it promises to make contributions of enormous value to the literature of our discipline in general, and to our understanding of the determination and influence of industry structure in particular.

NOTES

1. Moreover, as Schwartz and Reynolds have emphasized (see below) it is not certain how close an approximation to perfect contestability is required in an industry before the beneficent effects of market forces can be relied upon to manifest themselves to a substantial degree.
2. Weitzman, Martin L., 'Contestable Markets: An Uprising in the Theory of Industry Structure: Comment', *American Economic Review*, vol. 73, June 1983, pp. 486–7.
3. Schwartz, Marius and Robert J. Reynolds, *loc. cit.*, pp. 488–90.
4. Baumol, William J., John C. Panzar and Robert D. Willig, *loc. cit.*, pp. 491–6.
5. Sanford Grossman first noted the importance of contracting for this process.
6. Thus, *see*, for example, Spence, Michael, 'Contestable Markets and the Theory of Industry

Structure: A Review Article', *Journal of Economic Literature*, vol. 21, September 1983, pp. 981–90 and Brock, W. A., 'Contestable Markets and the Theory of Industry Structure: A Review Article', *Journal of Political Economy*, vol. 91, 1983, pp. 1055–66. The latter piece is perhaps somewhat more critical than the former but I think I do not misrepresents either author's position.

7. For references *see* Bailey, E. E. and Friedlaender, A. F., 'Market Structure and Multiproduct Industries', *Journal of Economic Literature*, vol. 20, September 1982, pp. 1024–48.

8. Mayo, J. W. and Kaserman, D. L., 'The Measurement of Vertical Economies and the Efficient Structure of the Electric Utility Industry' (unpublished), University of Tennessee, December 1983.

9. Kim, H. Young and Clark, R. M., 'Estimating Multiproduct Scale Economies: An Application to Water Supplies', U.S. Environmental Protection Agency, Municipal Environmental Research Laboratory, Cincinnati, Ohio 1983.

10. *Australian Overseas Cargo Liner Shipping*, University of Queensland, 1982.

11. *Pricing in the Liner Shipping Industry*, Canadian Transport Commission, Ottawa/Hull, 1983 (draft).

12. *See* Davies, G. and Davies, J., 'The Revolution in Monopoly Theory', *Lloyds Bank Review*, no. 153, July 1984, pp. 38–52.

13. *See* Evans, D. S. and Heckman, J. J., 'A Test of Subadditivity of the Cost Function with an Application to the Bell System', *American Economic Review*, vol. 74, September 1984, pp. 615–23.

14. 'Scale Economies and the Existence of Sustainable Monopoly Prices', *Journal of Economic Theory*, forthcoming.

15. 'Second Best Pricing and the Core', University of Southern California, March 1984.

16. 'Ramsey Prices, Average Cost Prices and Price Sustainability' (1983) and 'Issues in the Theory of Contestable Markets' (1982), Department of Economics, University of Illinois.

17. Coursey, Don, Isaac, R. Mark and Smith, Vernon L., 'Natural Monopoly and the Contestable Markets Hypothesis: Some Preliminary Results from Laboratory Experiments', *Journal of Law and Economics*, 1984 (forthcoming) and Coursey, Isaac, Margaret Luke and Smith, 'Market Contestability in the Presence of Sunk (Entry) Costs', *Rand Journal of Economics*, vol. 15, Spring 1984, pp. 69–84.

18. Harrison, G. W and McKee, Michael, 'Monopoly Behavior, Decentralized Regulation, and Contestable Markets: An Experimental Evaluation', University of Western Ontario, June 1984, and 'Experimental Evaluations of the Contestable Markets Hypothesis', 1984 (a progress report on some current experiments).

[1]

Scale Economies, Average Cost, and the Profitability of Marginal Cost Pricing

William J. Baumol

This chapter examines the behavior of costs in the presence of scale economies in a multi-product firm. It discusses the difficult problems of definition of average cost where there is more than one output and the production function is not homothetic. It also characterizes the circumstances in which prices set equal to marginal costs yield a total revenue less than total cost.

1. Economies of Scale and Efficient Expansion

The definition of scale economies can be extended as follows to a multi-product enterprise.[a]

DEFINITION 4.1. Economies of Scale. Given a firm producing $\underline{n}$ outputs whose quantities are given by the vector $y = (y_1, \ldots, y_n)$ and which uses $\underline{m}$ inputs whose quantities are $x = (x_1, \ldots, x_m)$ if all input quantities are multiplied by the same constant $\underline{k} > 1$, then all output quantities can be increased at least $\underline{k}$ times, and if in the neighborhood of $k = 1$, they are increased by at least k^r, $r > 1$.

DEFINITION 4.2. Strict Economies of scale are said to characterize a production function if a $\underline{k}$-fold increase in each input quantity permits at least a $\underline{k}$-fold increase in each output quantity with at least one output increased more than $\underline{k}$-fold,[b] and if in the neighborhood of $k = 1$, the increases in output are at least k^r-fold, $r > 1$.

I am grateful to the office of Science Information Services of the National Science Foundation under whose grant for a study on the Economics of Information this chapter was written. I am also most thankful to Elizabeth Bailey, Dietrich Fischer, John Panzar, Janusz Ordover, and Robert Willig for their very helpful suggestions.

[a]This definition is based on Panzar and Willig. The reason for the requirement that outouts increase k^r-fold in the vicinity of $k = 1$ is that otherwise scale economies may permit a zero derivative of average cost for a proportionate increase in all outputs. The definition given in an earlier draft of this chapter was deficient in this respect. I am grateful to Panzar and Willig for pointing out the consequent errors.

[b]If resources are divisible, transferable and have a positive marginal yield in the production of each of the producer's outputs then strict economies can be taken to require that

A production function may have economies of scale which are *global* (the preceding conditions hold for all input and output combinations) or local (they hold only for particular neighborhoods).

As usual, the definitions are expressed in terms of a *proportionate* increase in the usage of all inputs.

Now, as has recently been emphasized, (See C.H. Shami and E.F. Sudit (1974). See also G. Hanoch (1975).) firms do not generally expand their input usage proportionately either in practice or even in theory. It is true that if the production function is homothetic the cost minimizing way to expand all outputs proportionately is to increase inputs proportionately. But there is no reason to expect all production functions to be of this particular type, so that efficiency may, for example, call for an increasing ratio of capital to labor as outputs rise.

In such a case, obviously, a comparison of the input-output combinations along a ray may not yield the same sort of results as a comparison along the efficient expansion path. For example, while a doubling of all inputs may only permit an exact doubling of all outputs, an efficient but disproportionate increase in input quantities may permit a greater rise in outputs at the same total cost. In that case, it would seem that we might have constant returns to scale and yet declining average costs, since the cost function gives the cost of output expansion, not along a ray in input space, but with the utilization of the cost-minimizing combinations of inputs, whatever they may be.

2. Average Costs and Scale Economies in an *n*-Output Enterprise

The counterparts of economies of scale in terms of cost functions are obviously either marginal or average costs that decline when outputs rise. Declining marginal costs can be expressed simply as:

$$\partial^2 C(w^*, y^*)/\partial y_i^2 < 0, \tag{4-1}$$

where $C(\cdot)$ is the standard cost function of duality theory, with w^* and y^*, respectively, being given vectors of input prices and output quantities.

Unfortunately, there is no such straightforward definition of declining average cost except for the uninteresting case of the single-product enterprise which is almost never found outside the elementary textbooks. The problem is that we normally have no acceptable way either to aggregate outputs or to disaggregate costs, and so it is not generally possible to define the average cost

---

all outputs increase more than k times. For let commodity n be the only output which has gone up more than $k + \Delta$ fold while all other outputs have risen exactly k-fold. Then a small transfer of resources from output n to each of the other outputs of the producer will bring each of them to an amount at least slightly bigger than k times its initial level.

corresponding either to the firm's output taken as a whole or that corresponding to the output of any one of its products by itself. Clearly Σy_i is not defined since outputs are not measured in common units. We cannot use product prices for the purpose because they themselves are likely to be endogenous variables of the problem—variables whose values decline monotonically with output levels, thus introducing a systematic bias into the calculation. We just have no easy way to determine a denominator for the average cost figure.

Nor is it any easier to deal with the numerator in the average cost expression to apportion total cost among the individual outputs of the enterprise, permitting the calculation of a separate average cost, item by item. The firm's total cost includes some outlays attributable directly to particular goods in the firm's product line and some expenditres which are incurred in common for several such outputs simultaneously. Except by arbitrary convention it is therefore impossible in general to divide up the firm's total costs in a unique manner, imputing every part of this cost explicitly to one or another of the supplier's outputs.

There seem only to be available two acceptable ways of getting around these problems. First, we may deal exclusively with *proportionate* changes in the outputs of the firm. In that case we can speak of *ray* average costs and offer two slightly different definitions of the case where these are decreasing:

DEFINITION 4.3a. Ray average costs are strictly and globally declining if

$$\frac{C(w^*, vy^*)}{v} < C(w^*, y^*) \text{ for } \underline{v} > 1 \text{ and any } y^*. \tag{4-2a}$$

Or, instead, we can use

DEFINITION 4.3b. Ray average costs are strictly declining at every point if

$$\frac{\partial[C(w^*, vy^*)/v]}{\partial v} < 0 \text{ for any } y^*. \tag{4-2b}$$

We can also define[c] an average variable cost of a particular output $\underline{i}$:

DEFINITION 4.4 The supplier's average variable costs for product $\underline{i}$ are declining if

$$\partial(V^i/y_i)/\partial y_i < 0 \tag{4-3}$$

----

[c]It is easy to show that average variable costs and ray average costs need not behave similarly. For example, if all the costs of a firm are fixed then its ray average costs will decline: $C(w^*, vy^*)/v$ will be a rectangular hyperbola; but its average variable costs will all be constant and equal to zero.

where $V^i(w^*, y^*)$ is the total variable cost of output $\underline{i}$; that is, for a given output vector, y^*

$$V^i(w^*, y^*) = C(w^*, y_1^*, \ldots, y_{i-1}^*, y_i^*, y_{i+1}^*, \ldots, y_n^*)$$

$$- C(w^*, y_1^*, \ldots, y_{i-1}^*, 0, y_{i+1}^*, \ldots, y_n^*). \tag{4-4}$$

Having gotten over these definitional issues we may turn to a more substantive matter: the nature of the relationship between economies of scale and declining average costs. Intuitively it is certainly plausible that the relationship is close. For scale economies imply that the firm can obtain larger outputs "per unit" of input as it expands its operations. The difficulty, as already noted, is that the two concepts do not refer to the same expansion path and so it is not easy to jump from information about the one to conclusions about the other. We will now argue[d]

PROPOSITION 4.1. *Strict global economies of scale are sufficient but not necessary to guarantee that* ray *average costs are strictly declining as defined by (4.2.a).*

To show sufficiency let (x^*, y^*) be an initial and efficient input-output bundle, w_i^* be the price of input $\underline{i}$ and let the input bundle $kx_1, \ldots, kx_m$, where $k > 1$, be capable of yielding some output bundle[e] $vy_1^*, \ldots, vy_n^*, v > k$. Then obviously

$$\Sigma w_j^* x_j > \frac{\Sigma w_j^* kx_j}{v}.$$

However, since the proportionate increase in input use is not necessarily cost minimizing, there may exist another bundle of inputs $x_1', \ldots, x_m'$ capable of producing vy at least as cheaply as the input bundle $kx_1, \ldots, kx_m$. Then we must have $\Sigma w_j^* x_j' \leqslant \Sigma w_j^* kx_j$ so that

$$\frac{\Sigma w_j^* x_j'}{v} \leqslant \frac{\Sigma w_j^* kx_j}{v} < \Sigma w_j^* x_j. \tag{4-5}$$

---

[d]The discussion in the next few paragraphs follow an argument put forth by Shami and Sudit (1974).

[e]For a production function with strict global economies of scale, divisibility and transferability of resources it is trivial to show that the output bundle $vy_1^*, \ldots, vy_n^*$ is attainable, provided there is sufficient transferability of inputs among the producer's outputs and free disposal. For with strict economies of scale and resource transferability with a $\underline{k}$-fold increase in all inputs we can attain an output bundle $v_1 y_1^*, \ldots v_n y_n^*$ all $v_i > k$. Now set $v = \min v_i$ and by the assumption of free disposal the output bundle of the text can obviously be attained.

That is, the increasing returns condition $\underline{v} > \underline{k}$ is sufficient to guarantee (4-2a) which is the condition of declining *ray* average cost.[f]

That $v > k$ is not necessary for the result follows if the proportionate expansion path is not efficient, so that the first inequality in (4-5) becomes a strict inequality. For suppose then that a v-fold increase in output can just be produced with a v-fold proportional increase in all inputs[g] so that in that neighborhood $\underline{v} = \underline{k}$. Then (4-5) becomes

$$\frac{\Sigma w_j^* x_j'}{v} < \frac{\Sigma w_j^* v x_j}{v} = \Sigma w_j^* x_j . \tag{4-6}$$

Thus, it is still possible (as is shown by comparing the left hand and right hand terms in (4-6) alone) for overall average costs to decline even if returns to scale are locally constant[h] or declining slightly. Obviously that will never be true, if the production function is homothetic throughout, for then the efficient expansion path will always call for proportionate increases in inputs.

However, as we will see presently, this problem can arise only for sub-

---

[f]Since we have defined scale economies to involve an increase in outputs by at least the proportion k^r, $r > 0$ when all inputs increase by the same proportion k and $k \to 1$, it also follows in the limit that $d[C(w^*, vy^*)/v]/dv < 0$, i.e., that scale economies as defined also imply decreasing average costs as given by (4-2b).

[g]This assumption obviously calls for locally constant returns and does not mean that the production function must be characterized by constant returns to scale for *all* output and input changes. If the latter were true the argument would imply that an efficient path would always involve proportionate changes in all inputs.

[h]For example, consider the function $y = x_1^a + x_1^b x_2^b$, $0 < a < 1$, $0.5 < b < 1$, whose least-cost expansion path (with input prices fixed) must satisfy

$$\frac{w_1}{w_2} = \frac{ax_1^{a-1} + bx_1^{b-1} x_2^b}{bx_1^b x_2^{b-1}} = ax_1^{a-1}/bx_1{}^b x_2^{b-1} + x_2/x_1 \tag{4-i}$$

and so is not a ray.

Yet it is not difficult to show that for appropriate values of a, b, x_1 and x_2 that

$$ky = (kx_1)^a + (kx_1 kx_2)^b \tag{4-ii}$$

has a positive root of k other than $k = 1$ so that for the corresponding interval there will be constant returns along a ray which will not be an efficient path.

For example, if we set $y = 1$, $a = 0.6$, $b = 0.9$, we have, dividing (4-ii) through by k,

$$1 = k^{-0.4} x_1^{0.6} + k^{0.8} (x_1 x_2)^{0.9}.$$

Setting $x_1^{0.6} = 6/7$ and $(x_1 x_2)^{0.9} = 1/7$ and writing $\lambda = k^{0.4}$

the preceding equation becomes

$$1 = 6/(7\lambda) + (\lambda^2)/7,$$

which is easily verified to have the positive roots $\lambda = 1$ and $\lambda = 2$. Thus with these illustrative values our non-homothetic function exhibits constant returns in the large in the interval $k = 1$ and $k = (2)^{1/0.4}$.

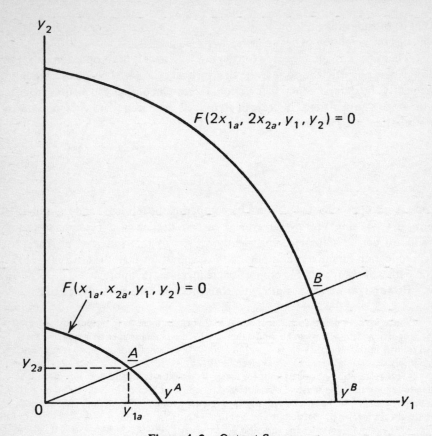

Figure 4–2. Output Space

$$C(a) = w_1 x_{1a} + w_2 x_{2a} > (kw_1 x_{1a} + kw_2 x_{2a})/v = C(b)/v \geqslant C(b')/v$$

$$(4\text{-}7)$$

which proves our result. That is, we have shown that if overall average costs fall with a proportionate increase on all inputs from $\underline{a}$ to $\underline{b}$, (which may not be the most efficient way to expand), overall average costs must certainly fall *a fortiori*, if expansion proceeds along the efficient path (from $\underline{a}$ to $\underline{b}'$) which is certainly at least as cheap as the move from $\underline{a}$ to $\underline{b}$.

Finally, we can see why with a non-homothetic production relationship we may have declining average costs overall *even without scale economies.* For suppose the move from $\underline{a}$ to $\underline{b}$ (a proportionate increase in inputs) actually increases overall average costs slightly because we have slight diseconomies of scale. Then if the move from $\underline{b}$ to the efficient expansion point saves an amount of expenditure more than sufficient to make up for the rise in costs yielded by a

MARGINAL COST PRICING   49

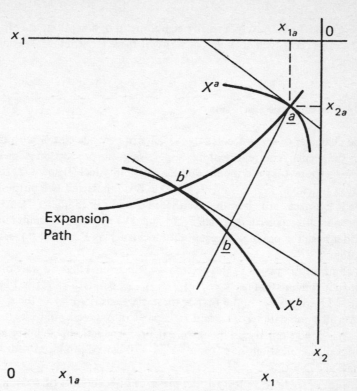

Figure 4-1. Input Space

portionate increase in input quantities from this initial point. Moreover, it requires that $\underline{OB}/\underline{OA} > \underline{Ob}/\underline{Oa}$ for *every* pair of rays in the two figures so that every point on Y^B in figure 4–2 must be more than $k = Ob/Oa$ times as far from the origin as the point on the corresponding ray on curve Y^A.

Now to show that in this case, so long as input prices are given, overall average costs must be declining we proceed in two steps: *Step i.* The coordinates of points b and B are respectively kx_{1a}, kx_{2a} and vy_{1a} and vy_{2a}. Hence, if the firm were to multiply all its input quantities by $\underline{k}$ to produce a proportionate change in outputs, its cost per unit would necessarily fall from $(w_1 x_{1a} + w_2 x_{2a})/y_{1a}$ to $(kw_1 x_{1a} + kw_2 x_{2a})/vy_{1a}$. *Step II.* Since the function is not homothetic, the firm's expansion path need not be a ray. Thus there may be a less expensive combination of inputs capable of producing output combination $\underline{B}$. In figure 4–1 this least-cost input combination is given by point $\underline{b}'$ at which the iso production curve through point $\underline{b}$ is tangent to a budget line parallel to that at the initial point $\underline{a}$. Write $C(b')$ and $C(b) = kw_1 x_{1a} + kw_2 x_{2a}$ for the total input costs at points $\underline{b}'$ and $\underline{b}$ respectively, where necessarily $C(b') \leqslant C(b)$. Hence we must have, from the preceding step,

stantial increases in output. In a small neighborhood of a point on the efficient path the average costs will decline if and only if there are strict local economies of scale.

3. A Diagrammatic Discussion

The character of the preceding discussion can be made clearer with the aid of a pair of simple diagrams representing, respectively, the production isoquants in input space (figure 4-1) and the production possibility loci (figure 4-2) for a production function $F(x_1, x_2, y_1, y_2) \leqslant 0$ in two inputs and two outputs. This function is not necessarily homthetic either in outputs or in inputs. Hence the production indifference curves (such as X^a and X^b) need not be similar in shape and neither need the production possibility loci (such as Y^A and Y^B) resemble one another.

In all of the discussion in this section we will assume that we start off with input-output combination $(x_{1a}, x_{2a}, y_{1a}, y_{2a})$, i.e., points $\underline{a}$ and $\underline{A}$ in Figures 4-1 and 4-2 respectively. In the first of these diagrams iso-product locus $\underline{X}^a$ represents all combinations of x_1 and x_2 capable of producing output *combination* y_{1a}, y_{2a}, and similarly, in the second figure, production-possibility locus Y^A represents all combinations of outputs y_1, y_2 that can be produced with input combination x_{1a}, x_{2a}.

Now let us see how we test for the presence of economies of scale in such a non-homothetic function. This is done in three steps: First we consider a hypothetical $\underline{k}$-fold increase in all input quantities (the move from point a to b in figure 4-1. That is, we consider some *proportionate* change in input quantities in order to determine the effect of a change in the scale of input usage without any change in relative input use. Second, we determine the corresponding change in the *set* of output combinations that results from the rise in input usage by the producer. This moves us from point $\underline{A}$ in figure 4-2 to any point on production possibility locus Y^B. Any output combination on that locus can now be produced by the firm. Finally, to test for economies of scale, we determine the point of intersection of Y^B with the ray through initial point $\underline{A}$. This gives us point $\underline{B}$, the largest output combination the firm can produce with its new level of input usage *if it were to choose to produce its outputs in the same output proportions as it did at A.*

We now say that there are local economies of scale if in figure 4-2 $\underline{OB}/\underline{OA} > Ob/Oa$ in figure 4-1, that is, if a given percentage increase in input quanties *permits* a greater percentage increase in all outputs, should the producer elect such proportionate changes.

Similarly, global economies of scale require the same relationships for every possible initial input-output combination $(y_1^i, y_2^i, x_1^i, x_2^i)$ and for every pro-

proportionate expansion in *inputs* it will lead, on balance, to a reduction in the overall average costs entailed in a proportionate expansion in outputs. This is why scale economies are indeed sufficient but not necessary for a curve of over-all average costs to be declining in the large.

4. Two Propositions on Scale Economies in the Small

At this point it is convenient to review two propositions, neither of which is new, though they are not widely discussed. The first reminds us that, given input prices, if we start off from an efficient input-output combination, then a small given increase in the vector of outputs can be achieved at minimum cost via *any* of a wide set of combinations of input expansions. One can achieve a small expansion in outputs at minimum cost by increasing the quantity of any one (initially non-zero) input by itself or by a suitable increase in any combination of such inputs.[i] In sum, there will be no unique expansion path in the small. The second proposition asserts that in particular, if some inputs whose quantities are positive initially also have positive marginal products, and all such marginal products are nonnegative, it will always be possible, starting from an efficient point, to achieve a small output increase at minimum cost through a *proportionate* increase of all inputs, i.e., through a small expansion to scale.

We begin by proving:

PROPOSITION 4.2. Assuming the production function to be everywhere twice differentiable with several inputs having positive marginal products, and all of them nonnegative, then starting from an initial input combination that is efficient, there will be a multiplicity of input combinations capable of achieving a given vector of small output increases $dy^* = (dy_1^*, \ldots, dy_n^*)$.

Proof: Given the production function

$$F(y_1, \ldots, y_n, x_1, \ldots, x_m) \leqslant 0 \qquad (4\text{-}8)$$

two necessary conditions for economic efficiency with a set of positive input quantities, are, first, that for any input *i*

$$w_i = aF_i \qquad (4\text{-}9)$$

---

[i]There is a simple intuitive explanation for this conclusion which may strike some as paradoxical. At any point on the efficient path all non-zero inputs will have an equal ratio of marginal product to price. Hence any such input will yield the same (small) expansion in output per dollar of expenditure upon it.

where $F_i = \partial F/\partial x_i$, w_i is the price of input i and a is a constant and, second, that the given combination of inputs satisfy (4-8) as an equality, i.e.,

$$\underline{F}(\cdot) = 0 \qquad\qquad (4\text{-}10)$$

A cost-minimizing *increase* in input quantities $dx_1^0, \ldots, dx_m^0$ must also leave (4-10) satisfied so that we must have

$$\Sigma F_j dy_j^* + \Sigma F_i dx_i^0 = 0. \qquad\qquad (4\text{-}11)$$

Next, consider any of the multiplicity of vectors $dx^* = (dx_i^*, \ldots, dx_m^*)$ satisfying

$$\Sigma F_i dx_i^* = 0. \qquad\qquad (4\text{-}12)$$

Obviously, with all $F_i \geqslant 0$ and several $F_i > 0$, there will be many combinations of dx_i^* (some positive and some negative) which are consistent with (4-12). Now define

$$dx_i = dx_i^0 + dx_i^*.$$

Then these dx_i will also satisfy (4-11) and consequently (4-10) since

$$\Sigma F_j dy_j^* + \Sigma F_i dx_i = \Sigma F_j dy_j^* + \Sigma F_i dx_i^0 + \Sigma F_i dx_i^* = 0$$

by (4-11) and (4-12). That is, these dx_i will also be capable of achieving the given increases in output, dy_j^*.

Moreover, the cost of increasing the output via the dx_i is the same as doing so via the cost minimizing input increases dx_i^0. For the cost of the former is

$$\Sigma w_i dx_i = \Sigma w_i dx_i^0 + \Sigma w_i dx_i^*$$

$$= \Sigma w_i dx_i^0 + \Sigma a F_i dx_i^* = \Sigma w_i dx_i^0 + a\Sigma F_i dx_i^* \text{ [by (4-9)]}$$

$$= \Sigma w_i dx_i^0 + 0 \text{ [by (4-12)]}$$

which is the least cost way to achieve the given increase in outputs.

Next we prove:

PROPOSITION 4.3. Under the conditions of Proposition 2 it is always possible to achieve a small increase in the vector of outputs at minimum cost if, starting from an efficient input combination, all inputs are increased to scale (i.e., proportionately).

MARGINAL COST PRICING 53

Proof: We require a set of dx_i^* which satisfy (4–12) so that by Proposition 2 they achieve the required output increase at minimum cost, and which satisfy the $m - 1$ requirements of proportionate expansion in inputs

$$\frac{dx_i^* + dx_i^0}{x_i} = \frac{dx_m^* + dx_m^0}{x_m} \qquad (i = 1, \ldots, m - 1)$$

that is

$$x_m dx_i^* - x_i dx_m^* = x_i dx_m^0 - x_n dx_i^0 \qquad (i = 1, \ldots, m - 1). \qquad (4\text{–}13)$$

Together (4–12) and (4–13) constitute a system of m linear equations in the m variables $dx_1^*, \ldots, dx_m^*$. Now, this sytem will have a non-trivial solution if the determinant of the system is non-zero. But that determinant is

$$D = \begin{vmatrix} F_1 & F_2 & \cdots & F_{m-1} & F_m \\ x_m & 0 & \cdots & 0 & -x_1 \\ 0 & x_m & \cdots & 0 & -x_2 \\ \cdot & \cdot & \cdot & \cdot & \cdot \\ 0 & 0 & & x_m & -x_{m-1} \end{vmatrix} \qquad (4\text{–}14)$$

Expanding D in terms of the elements of its first row we obtain as a typical term

$$(-1)^{i+1} F_i \begin{vmatrix} x_m & \cdots & 0 & 0 & \cdots & 0 & -x_1 \\ \cdot & & \cdot & \cdot & & \cdot & \cdot \\ 0 & \cdots & x_m & 0 & \cdots & 0 & -x_{i-1} \\ 0 & \cdots & 0 & 0 & \cdots & 0 & -x_i \\ 0 & \cdots & 0 & x_m & \cdots & 0 & -x_{i+1} \\ \cdot & & \cdot & \cdot & & \cdot & \cdot \\ 0 & \cdots & 0 & 0 & \cdots & x_m & -x_{m-1} \end{vmatrix} = -F_i x_i \begin{vmatrix} x_m & 0 & \cdots & 0 \\ 0 & x_m & \cdots & 0 \\ \cdot & \cdot & & \cdot \\ 0 & 0 & \cdots & x_m \end{vmatrix}$$

$$= -F_i x_i (x_m)^{m-2}$$

Hence D, the determinant in (4–14), must be given by

$$D = - \sum_{i=1}^{m-1} F_i x_i \, (x_m)^{m-2}$$

which cannot be zero if the F_i do not vary in sign, as assumed. Q.E.D.

5. On the Profitability of Marginal
Cost Pricing

One of the policy problems generally taken to follow from economies of scale is the unprofitability of marginal cost pricing.

For the single product firm it is, of course, easy to show that in a firm with declining average cost the sale of its product at a price equal to marginal cost must force it to lose money.

The issue then is whether a similar relationship holds for the multi-product firm. As a matter of fact, it is not difficult to show

PROPOSITION 4.4. Ray average cost declining at every point, as defined by (4–2b) is necessary and sufficient to assure the unprofitability of marginal cost pricing.[j]

Proof: Given any vector, y^*, of output levels, if (4–2b), the condition for ray average cost to decline at every point, is satisfied we must have (assuming differentiability)

$$\frac{\partial C(w^*, vy^*)/v}{\partial v} = \frac{\left(\Sigma \frac{\partial C}{\partial vy_j^*} y_j^* \right) v - C(w^*, vy^*)}{v^2} < 0 \qquad (4\text{--}15)$$

or, setting $v = 1$

$$\Sigma \frac{\partial C}{\partial y_j^*} y_j^* < C(w^*, y^*). \qquad (4\text{--}16)$$

That is, in this case the sale of each output, j, at a price, p_j, equal to marginal

---

[j]Robert Willig and John Panzar have pointed out an error in my original formulation in which I utilized condition (4–2a) instead of (4–2b) in deriving Proposition 4. But declining average costs of the former variety do not exclude points of inflexion where $dAC/dy = 0$, so that at point $\Sigma C_i y_i = C$. For a further discussion see Panzar and Willig (forthcoming).

cost $\partial C/\partial y_j$ will not bring in enough revenue to cover total cost $C(w^*, y^*)$. This shows the sufficiency of decreasing ray average costs for unprofitability of marginal cost pricing. The necessity also follows from (4–15) and (4–16). For if ray average costs are constant or increasing at some point so that the $<$ in (4–15) is replaced by a $\geq$, then in (4–16) the same replacement will be required, i.e., in such cases the revenues derived from marginal cost pricing will at least be sufficient to cover total costs.

Since strict, global economies of scale have been shown in Section 3 to be sufficient but not necessary for declining ray average costs we deduce immediately

> PROPOSITION 4.5. *Strict, global economies of scale are sufficient but not necessary to assure the unprofitability of marginal cost pricing.*

However, the profitability of marginal-cost pricing is a local rather than a global matter, involving the relationship between $C(\cdot)$ and $\Sigma F_j y_j$ at a point in $n + m$ dimensional input-output space. Now we saw in propositions 2 and 3 that, starting from an efficient point, a small output expansion can be achieved by a proportionate increase in inputs at the same cost as it can by a move along the efficient path. We can therefore prove

> PROPOSITION 4.6. *A necessary and sufficient condition for the unprofitability of marginal cost pricing is the presence of strict local scale economics. Moreover if, locally a $1 + k$-fold increase in all inputs can just achieve a $1 + v$-fold increase in outputs, then the ratio of total cost to the total revenues derived from marginal cost pricing must be exactly v/k.*

Proof: The proportionate expansion of all input quantities must satisfy

$$dx_i = kx_i$$

and the proportionate expansion in all inputs, by hypotheses, satisfies

$$dy_j = vy_j.$$

Consequently, we have as the minimum cost of the output expansion

$$dC(\cdot) = \Sigma(\partial C/\partial y_j)\, dy_j = v\, \Sigma(\partial C/\partial y_j)\, y_j. \qquad (4\text{–}17)$$

But since by Proposition 3 the proportionate increase in inputs achieves the output expansion at minimum cost, $dC(\cdot)$, we also have

$$dC(\cdot) = \Sigma(\partial C/\partial x_i)dx_i = \Sigma w_i dx_i = k\Sigma w_i x_i = kC. \qquad (4\text{–}18)$$

Equating (4–17) and (4–18) we have our result $C/\Sigma(\partial C/\partial y_j)y_j = v/k$. Finally, comparison of Propositions (4.4) and (4.6) shows at once

PROPOSITION 4.7. Strict local economies of scale are necessary and sufficient for overall average costs to be strictly declining locally.

Concluding Comment

The preceding pages have sought to characterize the relationships among scale economies, decling average costs, and the profitability or unprofitability of marginal cost pricing. We know, of course, that corresponding to any given cost function there is associated an implicit production relationship, and that the characteristics of either of these can be inferred from the other. Yet it seems useful to have laid out explicitly the cost function behavior corresponding to so important a production-function phenomenon as economies of scale. It will perhaps prove helpful in empirical work to have this relationship spelled out so that one can deal with the issue directly in terms of cost functions whose estimation may be less difficult than that of production functions.

Unfortunately, we have dealt with only one of the three policy issues that are generally associated with scale economies—the viability of marginal cost pricing. The other two issues, which are at least equally important, are closely interrelated. The first of these is the desirability, in term of efficiency of resources use, of a multiplicity of producers. Subadditivity of costs, meaning that two can be produced more cheaply than one, is not quite the same thing as economies of scale, but the precise specification of the similarities and differences remains to be spelled out. The final issue is the *sustainability* of a multiplicity of firms even where it is desirable (or the reverse—the sustainability of single-firm production where that is most efficient). It has been shown by Faulhaber (1975) that this issue is not the same as the preceding one. One can, for example, have an industry in which single-firm production is most economical but is not sustainable.

Both of these problems are global in character—they involve the entire production set and not merely its behavior in the immediate neighborhood of a point, as in the case of sustainability of marginal cost pricing. Since this chapter was written, their analysis has been explored in several subsequent papers.

References

Baumol, W.J. "On the Proper Cost Tests for Natural Monopoly in a Multi-Product Industry." (1975, forthcoming).

Baumol, W.J., E.E. Bailey, and R.D. Willig. "Weak Invisible Hand Theorems on the Sustainability of Multi-Product Monopoly." (1975, forthcoming).

MARGINAL COST PRICING 57

Baumol, W.J., D. Fischer, and J.A. Ordover. "On the Existence and Uniqueness of Pareto-Optimal Pricing Under a Budget Constraint." (1975, forthcoming).

Faulhaber, Gerald R. "Cross-Subsidization: Pricing in Public Enterprise." *American Economic Review,* Dec. 1975.

Hanoch, Giora. "The Elasticity of Scale and the Shape of Average Costs." *American Economic Review* 65 (1975): 492–497.

Panzar, J.C. and R.D. Willig. "Economies of Scale and Economies of Scope in Multi-Output Production." Bell Laboratories, (forthcoming).

Shami, C.H. and E.F. Sudit. "Generalized Concepts of Scale and Expansion Effects in Production." (Unpublished manuscript, 1974).

[2]

On the Proper Cost Tests for Natural Monopoly in a Multiproduct Industry

By William J. Baumol*

The literature is generally somewhat vague on the circumstances in which monopoly offers cost advantage over production by a multiplicity of firms. The sense of the discussion seems to be that monopoly will be "natural,"[1] that is, it can provide outputs at lower social costs, when and only when the industry has economies of scale. Perhaps the most unexpected finding of this paper is that *scale economies are neither necessary nor sufficient for monopoly to be the least costly form of productive organization.* Rather, the critical concept is (by definition) strict subadditivity of the cost function, meaning that the cost of the sum of any *m* output vectors is less than the sum of the costs of producing them separately. Since subadditivity is a mathematical concept whose properties do not seem to have been explored fully, a good part of our task will be the characterization of subadditive cost functions and their relation to more conventional concepts such as declining average costs (which, as we will see, it is inaccurate to equate to scale economies).

I

My discussion will begin with the single product firm. For these we will show that evidence of scale economies is always *sufficient* but *not necessary* to prove subadditivity. That is, it is (much) too demanding a test of natural monopoly to require evidence of scale economies or declining average costs, *even in the neighborhood of current output levels.* Nevertheless, if anything, our analysis makes it harder to prove that a particular monopoly is natural, even in the single product case. For it turns out that proof of subadditivity requires a *global* description of the shape of the *entire* cost function from the origin up to the output in question, thus calling for data that may lie well beyond the range of recorded experience.

When we turn to the multiproduct case we will find that sufficient conditions for subadditivity must include some sort of complementarity in the production of the different outputs of the industry which corresponds to a type of convexity to be specified in the next section.

Our discussion will proceed on the assumption that the menu of available techniques is fixed (no technological change), that exactly the same menu of techniques is available to the monopolist and to each of its potential competitors, *and that all input prices are fixed.*[2]

*Professor of economics, Princeton and New York universities. This paper was prepared under the sponsorship of the Division of Science Information of the National Science Foundation as part of a study of scale economies and public good elements in information transfer. The writing of this paper was very much a group undertaking with the most critical contributions made by Elizabeth Bailey and Dietrich Fischer. Important suggestions were also made by M.I. Nadiri, Janusz Ordover, Thijs ten Raa, Michael Rothschild, and Robert Willig as the analysis gradually evolved.

[1] For an interesting discussion of the origins of the concept and the term see Edward Lowry.

[2] Since we assume all input prices, *w*, to be constant, the cost function $C(y, w)$ can be written simply as $C(y)$, where *y* is the vector of outputs. Input prices are taken to be constant because an industry may be a natural monopoly at one set of input prices and not at another. For example, where capital is cheap relative to labor, single firm production may be cheapest, while the reverse may be true where low wages call for production techniques that are not capital intensive. Therefore, it seems to me that the appropriate test to determine whether an industry is *now* a natural monopoly must indicate whether it is the least costly market form at (or in the neighborhood of) current input prices. To require this to be true for all input prices would be far too restrictive.

810 THE AMERICAN ECONOMIC REVIEW DECEMBER 1977

II. Definitions[3]

A rather tedious section on definitions is unavoidable because some of the concepts have not been used widely in the literature and the extension of others to the *n*-product case is not entirely straightforward.

There seems to be some ambiguity in the term "natural monopoly" which is used to refer to one or both of two circumstances:[4]

a) An industry in which multifirm production is more costly than production by a monopoly (subadditivity of the cost function).

b) An industry to which entrants are *not* "naturally" attracted, and are incapable of survival even in the absence of "predatory" measures by the monopolist (sustainability of monopoly).

This article deals exclusively with the first of these concepts, leaving the issue of sustainability to other papers. (See Faulhaber 1975a; Baumol, Bailey, and Willig; John Panzar and Willig 1975b.)

Accordingly, we begin our formal definitions with our basic criterion of natural monopoly which is given by

DEFINITION 1: *Strict and Global Subadditivity of Costs.* A cost function $C(y)$ is strictly and globally subadditive in the set of commodities $N = 1, \ldots, n$, if for any m output vectors $y^1, \ldots, y^m$ of the goods in N we have

$$C(y^1 + \ldots + y^m) < C(y^1) + \ldots + C(y^m)$$

This is clearly the necessary and sufficient condition for natural monopoly of any output combination in the industry producing (any and all) commodities in N, for subadditivity means that it is always cheaper to have a single firm produce whatever combination of outputs is supplied to the market, and conversely.

Of course, it is possible that for some output vectors an industry will be a natural monopoly while for others it will not. In such a case we have output-specific subadditivity, meaning that the pertinent output vector y^* is produced more cheaply by one firm than by any combination of smaller firms.

We must also define precisely the other pertinent cost attributes, all of which acquire somewhat novel features in an *n*-product firm or industry. We begin with

DEFINITION 2: *Strict Economies of Scale* in the production of outputs in N are present if for any initial input-output vector $(x_1, \ldots, x_r, y_1, \ldots, y_n)$ and for any $w > 1$, there is a feasible input-output vector[5] $(wx_1, \ldots, wx_r, v_1 y_1, \ldots, v_n y_n)$ where all $v_i \geq w + \delta, \delta > 0$.

This definition in effect tests for scale economies by considering any *w*-fold expansion in all input quantities, and requiring that it permit *at least* a $w + \delta$-fold proportionate increase in each output. Note that if the production function is not homothetic *the firm may not wish to expand its input usage proportionately*, and depending on demand relationships, it certainly may not want to increase its *outputs* proportionately. Thus, our criterion of scale economies is expressed entirely in terms of hypothetical increases in input and output quantities along rays in input and output spaces, respectively.

Declining average costs, a concept usually associated with scale economies, is not so readily extended to a multiplicity of outputs. The problem, of course, is that if outputs do *not* expand proportionately we do not know how to define an index of aggregate output by which to divide total cost, nor do we have any way of apportioning

---

[3] For a fundamental article covering ground related to much of the substance of this paper see Peter Newman. For illuminating discussions of some of the definitional problems in this area and some related matters see also Giora Hanoch (1970, 1975) and also W. W. Sharkey and L. G. Telser.

[4] See, for example, Richard Posner. Gerald Faulhaber (1975a) has shown with the aid of ingenious and illuminating counterexamples that the two conditions are not equivalent; specifically that condition a) does not imply satisfaction of condition b). Baumol, Elizabeth Bailey, and Robert Willig have demonstrated the converse—that b) does imply a).

[5] I write v_i rather than v to allow for the case where *proportionate* expansion of outputs is not possible. If we assume free disposal then there is no need to do so, since if the percentage increases in some outputs were to exceed $w + \delta$ we could simply get rid of the excess.

VOL. 67 NO. 5   *BAUMOL: NATURAL MONOPOLY*   811

joint and common costs so as to calculate an average cost, item by item.[6] For our purposes, however, it will suffice to deal only with the special case in which output quantities all happen to vary proportionately *but input quantities follow the least-cost expansion path*, which in general does not involve proportionate changes in input quantities. Accordingly, we formulate

DEFINITION 3: *Ray Average Costs (RAC)* are *strictly declining* when

(1) $C(vy_1,\ldots,vy_n)/v$
$$< C(wy_1,\ldots,wy_n)/w \text{ for } v > w$$

where v and w are measures of the scale of output along the ray through

$$y = (y_1,\ldots,y_n)$$

As Definitions 2 and 3 clearly show, scale economies and declining average costs in the sense we have used it, are both ray-specific properties. We will use one other ray-specific property:

DEFINITION 4: *Ray Concavity*. A cost function $C(y)$ is strictly output-ray concave (marginal costs of output *bundles* everywhere decreasing) if

(2) $C[kv_1y + (1 - k)v_2y] > kC(v_1y)$
$$+ (1 - k)C(v_2y)$$

for any

$$v_1, v_2 \geq 0, \qquad v_1 \neq v_2, \qquad 0 < k < 1$$

This definition can be extended in an obvious way to m rather than two output vectors. The parameters v_1 and v_2 simply assure us that v_1y and v_2y are two output vectors that lie on the same ray (their outputs are proportional). The parameter k plays its usual role in the standard definition of concavity.

In the n-output case we must also have a way of characterizing the behavior of costs as output *proportions* vary. One pattern of such "transray" behavior will prove critical

6However, there is a natural extension of the concept of declining average *variable* cost of one individual product to the multioutput case. See the author (1976).

for our analysis. This concept is perhaps best described as a new formal interpretation of the phenomenon of complementarity in the production of the various goods and services supplied by the firm. We call a cost function *transray convex* at output vector $y = (y_1,\ldots,y_n)$ if along at least one hyperplane through y, $\Sigma w_i y_i = w$, a weighted average of the costs of producing separately any two output vectors on this hyperplane is no less than the cost of producing any weighted average of those two outputs *together*. That is, in geometric terms, a total cost function is transray convex at y if along some negatively sloping cross section through y in output space, costs are lower (no higher) toward the interior of the cross section than they are toward its edges (curve $C^*C^{*\prime}$ in Figure 4b), so that it is no more expensive to produce goods in combination rather than separately. More formally:

DEFINITION 5: *Transray Convexity*. A cost function $C(y)$ will be called transray convex through $y^* = (y_1^*,\ldots,y_n^*)$ if there exists any set of positive constants $w_1,\ldots,w_n$, such that for every two output vectors $y^a = (y_{1a},\ldots,y_{na})$, $y^b = (y_{1b},\ldots,y_{nb})$ lying in the same hyperplane $\Sigma w_i y_i$ through y^*, that is, for which $\sum_i w_i y_{ia} = \sum_i w_i y_{ib} = \sum_i w_i y_i^*$, we have

(3) $C[ky^a + (1 - k)y^b] \leq kC(y^a)$
$$+ (1 - k)C(y^b)$$

for any $k, \qquad 0 < k < 1$

This concept is closely related to what Panzar and Willig have named "economies of scope," in contradistinction to economies of scale.

Together, the concepts of strictly declining ray average costs and that of transray convexity turn out to be an extremely powerful combination offering us a new characterization of a cost function that is well behaved for a number of analytical purposes. We will see later (Proposition 12) that they are sufficient for subadditivity of costs. Moreover, in a closely related paper (Baumol, Bailey, and Willig), it is shown

812 THE AMERICAN ECONOMIC REVIEW DECEMBER 1977

that these go far toward giving us conditions sufficient for the existence of some monopoly prices that are sustainable against entry. It may be suspected that they will prove to have many other analytical implications.

III. Some Interrelationships Among the Cost Concepts

Having completed the tedious task of definition of our concepts, I can now summarize their relationships briefly, indicating which of them implies which. This is done in outline in Figure 1 which shows that global scale economies and decreasing ray average costs imply subadditivity along a ray, but that the former are not necessary for the latter. Moreover, they are neither sufficient nor necessary either for strict and global subadditivity, or for strict and output-specific subadditivity, the requirements for natural monopoly in an *n*-product industry.

We now proceed to prove some of the propositions underlying Figure 1. Before turning to the central issue of subadditivity we must explore briefly a few relationships among scale economies, ray concavity, and declining ray average costs. Among these cost concepts, scale economies occupies a position by itself, because all the others assume that inputs adjust optimally to output changes, that is, inputs are taken to follow along the expansion path of least costs. On the other hand, the concept of scale economies requires inputs to change proportionately, and in general, this will not minimize the cost of an expansion. (See, for example, Hanoch, 1975.) Thus, if unit cost decreases when inputs are increased *proportionately*, they must certainly decrease along the least cost expansion path. This should at least suggest the logic of a result which I have proven elsewhere (1976):

PROPOSITION 1: *Strict economies of scale are sufficient but not necessary for ray aver-*

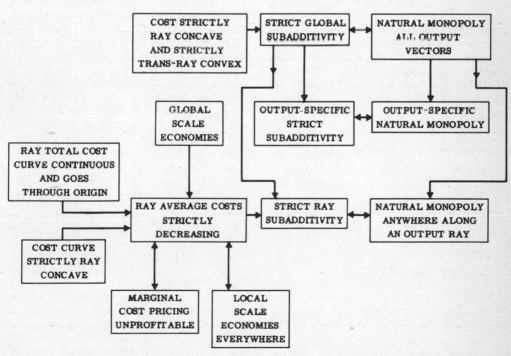

FIGURE 1

VOL. 67 NO. 5   BAUMOL: NATURAL MONOPOLY   813

age cost to be strictly declining.

We also have a relation between strict concavity and ray average costs:

PROPOSITION 2: *Strict ray concavity (declining marginal cost) of the cost function $C(y)$ and $C(0) = 0$ after subtraction of any fixed costs, are sufficient but not necessary for ray average costs to decline.*

PROOF:
By the definition of strict ray concavity we have by (2) for $v_1 = 1$, $v_2 = 0$,

(4) $C(ky) > kC(y)$ for $0 < k < 1$

which is criterion (1) of declining ray average cost.

Since it is well known that average costs can fall even when marginal costs are rising (nonconcavity in total cost), the result follows.

IV. Ray Subadditivity and its Relation to Other Cost Attributes[7]

Since subadditivity is the defining attribute of a natural monopoly, the heart of our task consists in the analysis of this property and its relation to the other cost attributes. The next few sections deal with scale behavior—subadditivity along a ray—leaving the true multiproduct case until later. First we prove

PROPOSITION 3: *Strictly declining ray average cost implies strict ray subadditivity.*

PROOF:
Consider the *n* output vectors $v_1 y, \ldots, v_n y$ along the same ray, all $v_i > 0$. By the definition of ray average costs that are strictly declining

(5) $C(\Sigma v_j y)/\Sigma v_j < C(v_i y)/v_i$

$$(i = 1, \ldots, n)$$

Consequently, $C(\Sigma v_j y)/\Sigma v_j$ is less than a

weighted average of the $C(v_i y)/v_i$, i.e.,

$$\frac{C(\Sigma v_j y)}{\Sigma v_j} < \sum \frac{v_i}{\Sigma v_j} \frac{C(v_i y)}{v_i} = \frac{\Sigma C(v_j y)}{\Sigma v_j}$$

which immediately yields our subadditivity result

$$C(\Sigma v_j y) < \Sigma C(v_j y)$$

It also follows from Propositions 2 and 3 that strict ray concavity, along with $C(0) = 0$, is sufficient for strict ray subadditivity. However, as I will show now, the converse does not hold—ray subadditivity is *not* sufficient either for ray concavity, or for declining ray average cost.

It is easy to produce the necessary counterexamples to prove this negative result—cost functions that are strictly ray subadditive and yet not ray concave throughout, and for which ray average cost does not decline throughout. An extreme case is shown in Figure 2a—the piecewise-linear cost function $OABDC$. This is clearly *not* concave, as is shown by the portion of the cost curve which lies below line segment WS. Similarly, average cost *increases* along part of the cost curve: output y_s is greater than y_r, yet the slope of ray OS is greater than the slope of OR so that ray average cost at y_s is greater than ray average cost at y_r.

To complete the argument I must now show that the cost function is strictly subadditive. A moment's consideration shows why this is so. In the case depicted, total cost for any output produced by one firm alone cannot exceed $OA + BD$. Similarly, total cost of any output produced by two or more firms in any way cannot be less than $2(OA)$, the fixed costs of two firms together. Since in our cost function $OA > BD$, we have: total cost of any output by a single firm $\leq OA + BD < 2(OA) \leq$ total cost of production by more than one firm.

We have thus proved by counterexample our desired result:

PROPOSITION 4: *Neither ray concavity nor ray average costs that decline everywhere are necessary for strict subadditivity.*

We may note also that while the extreme case shown in Figure 2a makes the proof

----

[7]A number of results in this section were first derived by Faulhaber (1975b).

_814_   THE AMERICAN ECONOMIC REVIEW   DECEMBER 1977

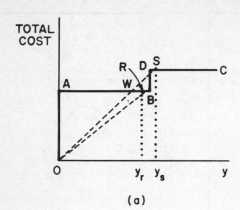

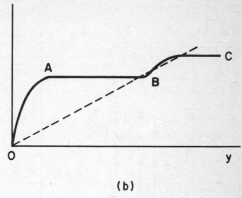

FIGURE 2

easier, less restrictive counterexamples are easy to supply. By including a series of steps in the graph of the cost function instead of the single step of Figure 2a, one can clearly produce a subadditive cost function in which average costs are rising at a number of intervals. Moreover, as Figure 2b illustrates, intervals of rising ray average costs are compatible with a completely smooth cost function that is strictly subadditive.

From Propositions 3 and 4, and since by Proposition 1 economies of scale are sufficient for decreasing ray average costs, we immediately have the following key result:

PROPOSITION 5: _Global scale economies are sufficient but not necessary for (strict) ray subadditivity, the condition for natural monopoly in the production of a single product or in any bundle of outputs produced in fixed proportions._

V. On Characterization of Ray Subadditivity

Before going further it is appropriate to say something about the characteristics of subadditive (cost) curves. We have seen that they need not be concave, nor need they exhibit declining average costs. What then do they look like in general? Three necessary conditions for subadditivity in a two-dimensional graph may offer the reader some of the pertinent flavor. First we have

PROPOSITION 6: _Strict subadditivity along_

a ray implies that for any output vector, y, in that ray, $C(y) < vC(y/v)$ for v any integer ≥ 2. That is, for any such integer v, ray average cost must on the average decrease over the interval between y/v and y.

This result follows from the definition of subadditivity which requires, for example, for $v = 3$, that $C(y) < C(y/3) + C(y/3) + C(y/3) = 3C(y/3)$ and a similar expression obviously holds for any other integer value of v. Thus, in Figure 3a the height of our cost curve at output y^* is C^*. This gives us $C^*/2$, $C^*/3$, $C^*/4$, etc., as respective _floors_ for total costs for outputs $y^*/2$, $y^*/3$, $y^*/4$, etc., as indicated by the heights of the vertical line segments. If the cost function is to be subadditive, then at output level $y^*/2$ total cost must be represented by some point such as D which is _above_ $C^*/2$, and the analogous observation applies to points B and A.

PROPOSITION 7: _If a function $C(y)$ is strictly subadditive, nonnegative and increasing in value along a ray, then either $c(0) > 0$ or the function must be strictly concave for y in the neighborhood of the origin._

For suppose $C(0) = 0$, writing $k = 1/v < 1$ in Proposition 6 we have $kC(y) < C(ky)$ in the neighborhood of $k = 0$. But $kC(y) \equiv (1 - k)C(0) + kC(y)$ and $C(ky) \equiv C[(1 - k)0 + ky]$. Consequently, in the limit as k approaches zero we must

VOL. 67 NO. 5   BAUMOL: NATURAL MONOPOLY   815

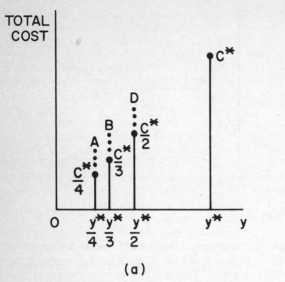

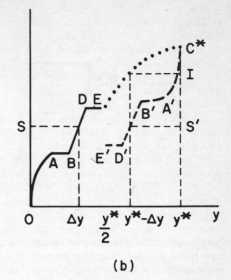

(a)   (b)

FIGURE 3

satisfy the requirement of strict concavity

$$(1 - k)C(0) + kC(y) < C[(1 - k)0 + ky]$$

A third necessary condition for subadditivity is given by

PROPOSITION 8 (Dietrich Fischer): *If $C(y)$ is strictly subadditive along a ray and y^* is any particular output vector on that ray, with $C(y^*) = C^*$, then the graph of $C(y^* - \Delta y)$ in the interval $y^*/2 \le y^* - \Delta y \le y^*$ must everywhere lie above the inverted[8] mirror image of $C(\Delta y)$ in the interval $0 \le \Delta y \le y^*/2$. That is, since by subadditivity $C(y^* - \Delta y) + C(\Delta y) > C(y^*)$, then*

(6) $C(y^* - \Delta y) > C(y^*) - C(\Delta y)$

As (6) shows, Proposition 8 follows directly from the definition of subadditivity. Condition (6) also tells us, incidentally, that with subadditivity the increment in total cost resulting from an addition Δy to an output, must be less than the cost $C(\Delta y)$ of producing that addition all by itself (its "stand-alone cost").

Figure 3b indicates more explicitly the graphic implications of Proposition 8. Let the total cost curve in the interval between

[8] The center of inversion is the point ($y^*/2, C^*/2$).

$y = 0$ and $y = y^*/2$ be *OABDE*. Now starting from C^*, the cost corresponding to y^*, draw (backwards) the curve $E'D'B'A'C^*$ which is the "upside-down" mirror image of *OABDE*. For example, with concave arc *OA* curving upward and to the right from *O*, arc C^*A' will be convex and curve downward and to the left from C^*. Now, Proposition 8 requires that the actual cost curve over the interval between $y^*/2$ and y^* (dotted curve EC^*) must everywhere lie above $E'D'B'A'C^*$.

This requirement is designed to assure us that the "incremental cost" IC^* of adding output Δy to output $y^* - \Delta y$ is less than the stand-alone cost OS of producing output Δy by itself, since, by construction, $OS = S'C^* > IC^*$.

VI. Some Implications for Evidence on Natural Monopoly

Propositions 6, 7, and 8 show that to test whether subadditivity is satisfied *just at a particular output level, y^*,* we can *not* examine only the cost curve in the vicinity of y^*. Because a claim of natural monopoly asserts that production by a single firm is cheaper than it would be in the hands of *any and every* possible combination of smaller firms, we must know the behavior of the cost curve *throughout its length in the interval between the origin and y^**. This is a rather difficult prospect for those who bear the burden of proof of the presence or absence of natural monopoly!

On the other hand, Propositions 4 and 5 imply that the tests sometimes suggested to evaluate the cost advantages or disadvantages of monopoly have in another respect been excessively demanding. In a number of regulatory hearings, much stress has been placed on the allegation that the regulated firm in question had reached a size where "economies of scale have been exhausted," implying that since output is now being produced under constant ray average and perhaps marginal costs, several firms can provide it as cheaply as one. But this is simply not true in general (on this see, for example, Seneca). Indeed, it is easy to see that single firm production will always be cheaper so long as average costs decline strictly monotonically up to any output $(y^*/2) + \Delta$ for any $\Delta > 0$ and are level thereafter, where y^* is total industry production. For if two more firms were to provide the commodity instead, at least one such firm must produce no more than half of industry output and must therefore incur average costs greater than the minimum average cost attainable. That is,

PROPOSITION 9: *A condition sufficient for strict and output-specific subadditivity along a ray is that, with y^* the given output vector of the industry, ray average cost declines strictly throughout the interval between zero and $y^*/2 + \Delta$ for some $\Delta > 0$, and that it declines or remains constant in the interval to the right of $y^*/2 + \Delta$ and through y^*.*

VII. Transray Behavior and Multiproduct Subadditivity

From the single product case, we turn finally to the conditions under which a single firm is the most efficient supplier of *all* the products provided by some industry or at least of some specified subset of those outputs.

Since scale economies refer only to the technical gains from increases in volume of output rather than those accruing from production of several goods together, it is obvious that by themselves they cannot tell us whether it is cheaper to produce two different output bundles separately or together. The issue is one relating to the behavior of the cost function from one output ray to another, rather than along any one ray. It is therefore naturally to be suspected that evidence of the presence of scale economies will be insufficient to guarantee what we may refer to as transray subadditivity.

If that were all there is to the matter, the insufficiency of scale economies for natural monopoly might seem a trivial and uninteresting observation. But there is more to the issue.

The obvious extension of the concept of scale economies to the entire cost function is concavity. Concavity is, after all, a rather strong assumption. But it is easy to show that even strict concavity is neither sufficient nor necessary for subadditivity in an *n*-product cost function. First we show:

PROPOSITION 10: *Strict concavity of a cost function is not sufficient to guarantee subadditivity.*

PROOF by counterexample:[9]

Consider the cost function in two outputs

$$C = y_1^a + y_1^k y_2^k + y_2^a \qquad \begin{matrix} 0 < a < 1 \\ 0 < k < 1/2 \end{matrix}$$

Since the sum of several concave functions is itself concave, it is clear that the cost function is strictly concave because of the values of k and a. However, we have for

[9] I am indebted for this counterexample to Dietrich Fischer. It may seem at first that a case of superadditivity such as that in the example cannot occur in reality since the firm which finds it more expensive to produce two items together will turn them out separately (in different plants). But administrative and communication costs can still make it more expensive to produce this way than in two totally independent firms. That is why, in reality, some industries are characterized by many small firms, each with their different specializations. The cost functions are such that the giant multiproduct firm just cannot compete.

VOL. 67 NO. 5

BAUMOL: NATURAL MONOPOLY

817

example, for $y_1^* = y_2^* = 1$:

$$C(y_1^*, 0) = 1 \qquad\qquad C(0, y_2^*) = 1$$
$$C(y_1^*, y_2^*) = 3 > C(y_1^*, 0) + C(0, y_2^*) = 2$$

Hence the function is not subadditive.

We also have immediately the basic result

PROPOSITION 11: *Scale economies are neither necessary nor sufficient for subadditivity.*

Nonnecessity was already proved in Proposition 5. To show insufficiency we need merely take the production function implicit in the preceding example to involve a single input (whose quantity is x) and whose price p is fixed. Then substituting $C = px$ into the cost function we see that it obviously exhibits scale economies throughout even though it is not subadditive.

It must be emphasized that this example does not represent some sort of pathological exception. Rather, as we will see next, strict concavity of a cost function involves an attribute which works in the direction opposite to that called for to yield transray subadditivity.

The main issue is what sorts of departure from concavity favor subadditivity? The answer is suggested by Figures 4a and 4b. Figure 4a depicts a cost function represented by surface OCC' which is strictly concave and exhibits scale economies throughout. Three cross sections along rays Ra, Rb, and Rc show the characteristic concave shape and, hence, the declining average costs which we have seen to suffice for subadditivity along a ray.

However, despite the concavity *and the presence of scale economies*, the cross section $CABDC'$ taken across these rays tells quite a different story. Because its lowest points are reached at the y_1 and y_2 axes, this concave transray cross section favors production of commodities in isolation. That is, it makes for increased cost of production using common facilities. This is precisely the opposite of what is wanted for transray subadditivity (or for an *interior* cost minimum along a fixed iso-revenue

curve, as is indicated by Figure 4c, the iso-cost map corresponding to Figure 4a). Rather, subadditivity is favored by a cost function which, because of complementarity in production, is shaped like that in Figure 4b whose transray cross section $C^*A^*B^*D^*C^{*'}$ reaches its lowest points in the interior of the diagram where both commodities are produced together. The corresponding iso-cost map (Figure 4d) is obviously also conducive to an interior cost minimum along an iso-revenue locus.

We come now to our key result:

PROPOSITION 12: *Ray average costs that are strictly declining and (nonstrict) transray convexity along any one hyperplane $\Sigma w_i y_i = w$, $w_i > 0$ through an output vector y are sufficient to guarantee strict output-specific subadditivity for output y.*

PROOF:

The result has already been proved in Proposition 3 for the division of y into any y^a, y^b which lie in the same ray. It therefore only remains to prove for any $y^a + y^b = y$

$$C(y^a + y^b) < C(y^a) + C(y^b) \text{ if } y^a \neq wy^b$$

By the definition of ray average costs that are strictly declining we have for any $v > 1$

$$(7) \qquad vC(y) > C(vy)$$

Let $w_1, \ldots, w_n$ be any vector of positive constants defining the cross section along which y satisfies Definition 5 of transray convexity. Now define[10] v_a, v_b by $v_a \Sigma w_i y_{ia} = \Sigma w_i y_{ia} + \Sigma w_i y_{ib} = v_b \Sigma w_i y_{ib}$ and set

$$(8) \qquad k = 1/v_a$$

so that

$$1/v_b = 1 - 1/v_a = (1 - k)$$

---

[10]As is illustrated in Figure 5, the purpose of multiplying all the elements of y^a and y^b by v_a and v_b, respectively, is to expand each of these outputs along its own ray until it is on the same hyperplane of transray convexity $\Sigma w_i y_i = w$, which contains point $y^a + y^b$. That then permits us to apply Definition 5 of strict transray convexity to the three points $v_a y^a$, $v_b y^b$, and $y^a + y^b$, to show that the cost of the latter does not exceed a weighted average of the costs of the former.

818   *THE AMERICAN ECONOMIC REVIEW*   *DECEMBER 1977*

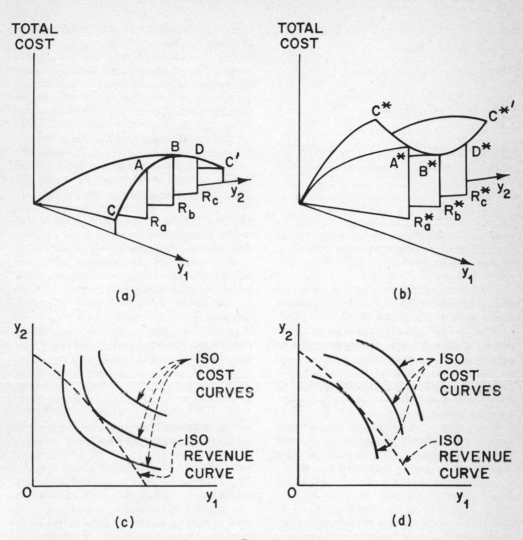

FIGURE 4

then by (7) and (3) in Definition 5

$$kv_a C(y^a) + (1 - k)v_b C(y^b) > kC(v_a y^a) +$$

$$(1 - k)C(v_b y^b) \geq C[kv_a y^a + (1 - k)v_b y^b]$$

or since $kv_a = (1 - k)v_b = 1$ by (8) we have our subadditivity result

$$C(y^a) + C(y^b) > C(y^a + y^b)$$

Note that the proof does not require *strict* transray convexity, but it does have to assume that ray average costs are *strictly*

declining over *part* of the region since the proof of Proposition 3, which is subsumed here, does require the latter. If, along the ray containing the industry output vector, average costs were not strictly declining, for example, if they increased proportionately with output, then several smaller firms might be able to produce the industry output vector at the same total cost as a monopolist. But, as Proposition 9 shows, the region in which ray average costs are *strictly* decreasing must only extend by any

VOL. 67 NO. 5   *BAUMOL: NATURAL MONOPOLY*   *819*

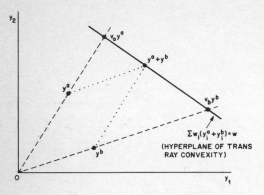

FIGURE 5

small amount beyond the *midpoint* of the ray between the origin and the outermost portion of the ray that is being tested for subadditivity.

The reason we do not need *strict* transray convexity also indicates why the conditions of Proposition 12 are not *necessary* for subadditivity. Let y be the vector sum of two output vectors y^a and y^b. Then y will be further from the origin than either y^a and y^b, and it will lie on a ray between the two. That is, it involves a larger scale than either of the component vectors *as well as* simultaneous production of the different commodities they include. Thus, even if there is no complementarity in the sense of strict transray convexity, if economies of scale are sufficiently strong, production of y by a single firm may still be the least expensive way to carry out the task.[11]

The fact that the conditions of Proposition 12 are not necessary implies that other and, perhaps, more familiar sufficient cost conditions for subadditivity may yet be

[11]Indeed, it can be shown that mild transray *concavity* can be compatible with subadditivity—the more rapid the rate of decline of ray average costs, the greater the permissible degree of concavity. The proof is a straightforward extension of the proof of Proposition 12. It can also be shown that if some outputs (or every output) in the industry product mix have their own fixed cost levels (a violation of transray convexity at the axes), then the cost function will still be subadditive if the conditions of Proposition 12 hold for the variable cost. The reason is that such fixed costs are always subadditive, and summation of two functions, one subadditive and the other strictly subadditive, always yields a strictly subadditive function.

found. It should be noted, however, that this may not be an important issue for empirical work in which data are likely to be analyzed with the aid of relatively simple mathematical forms for the cost function, whose subadditivity (or its absence) can be judged more directly.

VIII. Concluding Comment

The implications of the results of the preceding section should not be underestimated. It may seem as though ray subadditivity by itself is enough to constitute evidence for the presence of significant elements of natural monopoly in an industry and that transray subadditivity is little more than a bit of supplementary information. More specifically, it may seem that while transray subadditivity is required for natural monopoly in the production of several commodities together, ray subadditivity by itself gives us the essence of the natural monopoly, for then *each* good is still produced most cheaply by a single firm.

But that conclusion is quite misleading. To illustrate the point, suppose that the industry in question produces two commodities y_1 and y_2, and that, as in the case of Figure 6, a transray cross section has a number of minima. Then, despite strictly declining ray average costs, it can be cheapest for production to be carried out simultaneously by two or more firms. Though each firm will have a "monopoly" of production of the output *proportions* corresponding to its own ray, each will be producing the same commodities as the others. What sorts of monopolies would these really be if one were to "specialize" the production of y_1 and y_2 in a 50–50 ratio and another in a 45–55 ratio? Each firm would be producing the same two goods, only in (slightly?) different proportions, and that is surely no monopoly at all. In other words, *evidence of strict ray subadditivity is, by itself, evidence of virtually nothing of substance so far as natural monopoly is concerned*. It is consistent with the presence of a large number of firms in a cost-minimizing arrangement for the industry, and only requires slight dissimilarities in their product mix. It should

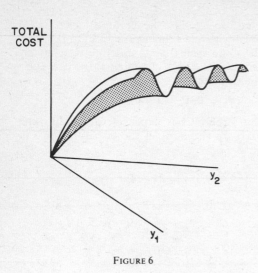

FIGURE 6

be noted that this is no extraordinary or pathological state of affairs. On the contrary, it is frequently found in multiproduct oligopoly industries in reality.[12]

We may note, finally, that though our natural monopoly criteria do not make for easy empirical testing, it is by no means unmanageable. Thus, as part of our research project on the cost of information

[12]It can be proved that if the cost function is ray concave everywhere but not subadditive, then the number of firms that minimize the cost of producing the industry output vector will never exceed n, the number of different products supplied by the industry. This by itself means that in most multiproduct industries even where costs satisfy the ray concavity requirement (which is stronger than the conventional concept of scale economies) it is perfectly possible to have dozens of firms corresponding to the dozens of products supplied by the industry. Nor need these firms specialize in the production of single products. Rather, it may be optimal for them to operate along rays in the interior of product space, depending on the transray behavior of the cost surface, as is indicated in Figure 6 where it may obviously be more economical for two firms to operate at the low points of the scalloped cross sections than above the axes. Moreover, if, on the usual (but not quite accurate) criterion of scale economies, the cost function has declining ray average costs but is not concave everywhere, then the cost-minimizing number of firms can even exceed the number of products of the industry. Examples showing this, and other proofs underlying this discussion, were provided by Thijs ten Raa and Dietrich Fischer. These materials are presented in the Appendix (Propositions 13 and 14).

supply, we have already found it possible with the aid of Proposition 12 to carry out tests of the hypothesis that there is subadditivity in the provision of a number of scientific journals by a single publisher (see the author and Braunstein).

APPENDIX

On the Cost-Minimizing Number of Firms When Ray Average Costs Decline

I conclude with two propositions which indicate how much (or how little) we know about the natural number of firms in an industry, given information only about cost behavior along each ray (economies of scale) but no information on transray cost behavior (economies of scope) (see also the author and Fischer).

PROPOSITION 13 (Thijs ten Raa): *If the cost function is strictly output-ray concave, then the optimal number of firms cannot exceed n, the number of commodities produced by the industry.*[13]

PROOF:

It is sufficient to prove that for every $(n + 1)$-tuple of output vectors $y^1, \ldots, y^{n+1}$ there exists a cheaper n-tuple of output vectors with the same total output. Because in n-dimensional space any $n + 1$ vectors are linearly dependent, $y^1, \ldots, y^{n+1}$ must be linearly dependent. Hence, one of them, say, without loss generality y^{n+1} is a linear combination of the others:

$$y^{n+1} = \sum_{i=1}^{n} C_i y^i, \quad C_i \geq 0, \quad \text{not all zero}$$

Let $\quad \lambda \epsilon \left[0, \min_{i=1,\ldots,n} \left(1 + \frac{1}{C_i} \right) \right]$

then

$$\forall i \epsilon \{1, \ldots, n\}: (1 + C_i - \lambda C_i) y^i,$$
$$\lambda y^{n+1} \epsilon \overline{\mathcal{R}}_n^+$$

[13]The proposition holds even if the concavity is *not* strict, provided there is no degeneracy in the sense used in linear programming.

VOL. 67 NO. 5   BAUMOL: NATURAL MONOPOLY   821

and the sum of these $n + 1$ vectors equals

$$\sum_{i=1}^{n} y^i + \sum_{i=1}^{n} (C_i - \lambda C_i)y^i + \lambda \sum_{i=1}^{n} C_i y^i =$$

$$\sum_{i=1}^{n} y^i + \sum_{i=1}^{n} C_i y^i = \sum_{i=1}^{n+1} y^i$$

C is output ray concave, hence

$$\forall i \epsilon \{1, \ldots, n\}: \ C\{(1 + C_i - \lambda C_i)y^i\}$$

is a concave function of λ and so is $C(\lambda y^{n+1})$. Hence

$$\sum_{i=1}^{n} C\{(1 + C_i - \lambda C_i)y^i\} + C(\lambda y^{n+1})$$

is a concave function of λ. Hence its minimum occurs at one of the end points of λ's range, that is, at

$$\lambda = 0 \quad \text{or} \quad \lambda = \min_{i=1,\ldots,n} \left(1 + \frac{1}{C_i}\right) = 1 + \frac{1}{C_j}$$

$$\text{for some} \quad j \epsilon \{1, \ldots, n\}$$

When $\lambda = 0$, then the $(n + 1)$th firm does not produce anything. When $\lambda = 1 + 1/C_j$, then the jth firm does not produce anything. In either case only n firms are left, producing the industry output more cheaply than when $\lambda = 1$ under which we have the original outputs $y^1, \ldots, y^{n+1}$. However,

PROPOSITION 14 (Raa and Fischer): *Declining ray average costs alone do not preclude the optimality of a number of firms larger than the number of products supplied by the industry.*

PROOF:
    The following is an example in which it is optimal to have three firms producing two commodities when ray average costs are (not strictly) declining and there are no fixed costs.[14] Let

$$y^l = \left(1 + \frac{\sqrt{3}}{3}, 2\right)$$

[14]Note that the addition of any positive fixed cost will make the ray average costs decline *strictly*, without affecting the example.

and, to simplify the argument (letting us deal with only three rays in output space) let C be such that production is relatively cheap along rays involving three particular output bundles

$$(y_2 \equiv 0, y_1 \equiv 0 \quad \text{and} \quad y_2 = \sqrt{3} y_1)$$

but prohibitively expensive along all other rays. In addition, let the cost function satisfy

$$C\left(\frac{y_2 \sqrt{3}}{3}, y_2\right) = 2y_2 \quad \text{for} \quad y_2 \geq 0$$

$$C(0, y_2) = \sqrt{3} y_2 \quad \text{for} \quad y_3 \geq 0$$

$$C(y_1, 0) = y_1 \quad \text{for} \quad y_1 \geq 1; \ \sqrt{3} - 1$$

$$< C\left(1 - \frac{\sqrt{3}}{3}, 0\right) < 1$$

$$C(y_1, 0) \quad \text{is linear for} \quad y_1 \epsilon \left[0, 1 - \frac{\sqrt{3}}{3}\right]$$

$$\text{and for} \quad y_1 \epsilon \left[1 - \frac{\sqrt{3}}{3}, 1\right]$$

Then y^l is produced more cheaply by

$$y^1 = (1, 0), y^2 = \left(\frac{\sqrt{3}}{3}, 1\right) \quad \text{and} \quad y^3 = (0, 1)$$

To show this, because of the linearity of C, it is sufficient to show that (y^1, y^2, y^3) is cheaper than

$$\left(\left(1 - \frac{\sqrt{3}}{3}, 0\right), \left(\frac{2\sqrt{3}}{3}, 2\right)\right)$$

and

$$\left(\left(1 + \frac{\sqrt{3}}{3}, 0\right), (0, 2)\right)$$

the two pairs of output vectors capable of producing y^l. Thus:

$$C(y^1) + C(y^2) + C(y^3) = 1 + 2$$
$$+ \sqrt{3} = 3 + \sqrt{3}$$

$$C\left(1 - \frac{\sqrt{3}}{3}, 0\right) + C\left(\frac{2\sqrt{3}}{3}, 2\right)$$
$$> \sqrt{3} - 1 + 4 = 3 + \sqrt{3}$$

$$C\left(1 + \frac{\sqrt{3}}{3}, 0\right) + C(0, 2) = 1 + \frac{\sqrt{3}}{3}$$

$$+ 2\sqrt{3} = 1 + \left(2\frac{1}{3}\right)\sqrt{3} > 3 + \sqrt{3}$$

REFERENCES

W. J. Baumol, "Scale Economies, Average Cost and the Profitability of Marginal-Cost Pricing," in Ronald E. Grieson, ed., *Essays in Urban Economics and Public Finance in Honor of William S. Vickrey*, Lexington 1976.

———, E. E. Bailey, and R. D. Willig, "Weak Invisible Hand Theorems on Pricing and Entry in a Multiproduct Natural Monopoly," *Amer. Econ. Rev.*, June 1977, *67*, 350–65.

——— and D. Fischer, "On the Optimal Number of Firms in an Industry," *Quart. J. Econ.*, 1977, forthcoming.

——— and Y. M. Braunstein, "Empirical Study of Scale Economies and Production Complementarity: The Case of Journal Publication," *J. Polit. Econ.*, 1977, forthcoming.

G. R. Faulhaber, (1975a) "Cross-Subsidization: Pricing in Public Enterprise," *Amer. Econ. Rev.*, Dec. 1975, *65*, 966–77.

———, (1975b) "Pricing Rules in Cooperative Markets," unpublished doctoral dissertation, Princeton Univ. 1975.

——— and E. E. Zajac, "Some Thoughts on Cross-Subsidization in Regulated Industries," paper presented at the International Conference in Telecommunications, England 1974.

G. Hanoch, "Homotheticity in Joint Production," *J. Econ. Theory*, Dec. 1970, *2*, 423–26.

———, "The Elasticity of Scale and the Shape of Average Costs," *Amer. Econ. Rev.*, June 1975, *65*, 492–97.

E. D. Lowry, "Justification for Regulation: The Case for Natural Monopoly," *Publ. Util. Fortnightly*, Nov. 8, 1973, *28*, 1–7.

P. Newman, "Some Properties of Concave Functions," *J. Econ. Theory*, Oct. 1969, *1*, 291–314.

J. C. Panzar and R. D. Willig, (1975a) "Economies of Scale and Economies of Scope in Multi-Output Production," unpublished paper, Bell Laboratories 1975.

——— and ———, (1975b) "Free Entry and the Sustainability of Natural Monopoly," unpublished paper, Bell Laboratories 1975.

R. A. Posner, "Natural Monopoly and its Regulation," *Stanford Law Rev.*, Feb. 1969, *21*, 548–643.

R. S. Seneca, "Inherent Advantage, Costs and Resource Allocation in the Transportation Industry," *Amer. Econ. Rev.*, Dec. 1973, *63*, 945–56.

W. W. Sharkey and L. G. Telser, "Supportable Cost Functions for the Multiproduct Firm," unpublished paper, Bell Laboratories 1977.

[3]

Contestable Markets: An Uprising in the Theory of Industry Structure

By WILLIAM J. BAUMOL*

The address of the departing president is no place for modesty. Nevertheless, I must resist the temptation to describe the analysis I will report here as anything like a revolution. Perhaps terms such as "rebellion" or "uprising" are rather more apt. But, nevertheless, I shall seek to convince you that the work my colleagues, John Panzar and Robert Willig, and I have carried out and encapsulated in our new book enables us to look at industry structure and behavior in a way that is novel in a number of respects, that it provides a unifying analytical structure to the subject area, and that it offers useful insights for empirical work and for the formulation of policy.

Before getting into the substance of the analysis I admit that this presidential address is most unorthodox in at least one significant respect—that it is not the work of a single author. Here it is not even sufficient to refer to Panzar and Willig, the coauthors of both the substance and the exposition of the book in which the analysis is described in full. For others have made crucial contributions to the formulation of the theory—most notably Elizabeth Bailey, Dietrich Fischer, Herman Quirmbach, and Thijs ten Raa.

But there are many more than these. No uprising by a tiny band of rebels can hope to change an established order, and when the time for rebellion is ripe it seems to break out simultaneously and independently in a variety of disconnected centers each offering its own program for the future. Events here have been no different. I have recently received a proposal for a conference on new developments in the theory of industry structure formulated by my colleague, Joseph Stiglitz, which lists some forty participants, most of them widely known. Among those working on the subject are persons as well known as Caves, Dasgupta, Dixit, Friedlaender, Grossman, Hart, Levin, Ordover, Rosse, Salop, Schmalensee, Sonnenschein, Spence, Varian, von Weiszäcker, and Zeckhauser, among *many* others.[1] It is, of course, tempting to me to take the view that our book is the true gospel of the rebellion and that the doctrines promulgated by others must be combatted as heresy. But that could at best be excused as a manifestation of the excessive zeal one comes to expect on such occasions. In truth, the immediate authors of the work I will report tonight may perhaps be able to justify a claim to have offered some systematization and order to the new doctrines—to have built upon them a more comprehensive statement of the issues and the analysis, and to have made a number of particular contributions. But, in the last analysis, we must look enthusiastically upon our fellow rebels as comrades in arms, each of whom has made a crucial contribution to the common cause.

Turning now to the substance of the theory, let me begin by contrasting our results with those of the standard theory. In offering this contrast, let me emphasize that much of the analysis rests on work that appeared considerably earlier in a variety of forms.

*Presidential address delivered at the ninety-fourth meeting of the American Economic Association, December 29, 1981. I should like to express my deep appreciation to the many colleagues who have contributed to the formulation of the ideas reported here, and to the Economics Program of the Division of Social Sciences of the National Science Foundation, the Division of Information Science and Technology of the National Science Foundation, and the Sloan Foundation for their very generous support of the research that underlies it.

[1]Such a list must inevitably have embarassing omissions—perhaps some of its author's closest friends. I can only say that it is intended just to be suggestive. The fact that it is so far from being complete also indicates how widespread an uprising I am discussing.

We, no less than other writers, owe a heavy debt to predecessors from Bertrand to Bain, from Cournot to Demsetz. Nevertheless, it must surely be acknowledged that the following characterization of the general tenor of the literature as it appeared until fairly recently is essentially accurate.

First, in the received analysis perfect competition serves as the one standard of welfare-maximizing structure and behavior. There is no similar form corresponding to industries in which efficiency calls for a very limited number of firms (though the earlier writings on workable competition did move in that direction in a manner less formal than ours).

Our analysis, in contrast, provides a generalization of the concept of the perfectly competitive market, one which we call a "perfectly contestable market." It is, generally, characterized by optimal behavior and yet applies to the full range of industry structures including even monopoly and oligopoly. In saying this, it must be made clear that perfectly contestable markets do not populate the world of reality any more than perfectly competitive markets do, though there are a number of industries which undoubtedly approximate contestability even if they are far from perfectly competitive. In our analysis, perfect contestability, then, serves not primarily as a description of reality, but as a benchmark for desirable industrial organization which is far more flexible and is applicable far more widely than the one that was available to us before.

Second, in the standard analysis (including that of many of our fellow rebels), the properties of oligopoly models are heavily dependent on the assumed expectations and reaction patterns characterizing the firms that are involved. When there is a change in the assumed nature of these expectations or reactions, the implied behavior of the oligopolistic industry may change drastically.

In our analysis, in the limiting case of perfect contestability, oligopolistic structure and behavior are freed entirely from their previous dependence on the conjectural variations of *incumbents* and, instead, these are generally determined uniquely and, in a manner that is tractable analytically, by the pressures of *potential* competition to which Bain directed our attention so tellingly.

Third, the standard analysis leaves us with the impression that there is a rough continuum, in terms of desirability of industry performance, ranging from unregulated pure monopoly as the pessimal arrangement to perfect competition as the ideal, with relative efficiency in resource allocation increasing monotonically as the number of firms expands.

I will show that, in contrast, in perfectly contestable markets behavior is sharply discontinuous in its welfare attributes. A contestable monopoly offers us some presumption, but no guarantee, of behavior consistent with a second best optimum, subject to the constraint that the firm be viable financially despite the presence of scale economies which render marginal cost pricing financially infeasible. That is, a contestable monopoly has some reason to adopt the Ramsey optimal price-output vector, but it may have other choices open to it. (For the analysis of contestable monopoly, see my article with Elizabeth Bailey and Willig, Panzar and Willig's article, and my book with Panzar and Willig, chs. 7 and 8.)

But once each product obtains a second producer, that is, once we enter the domain of duopoly or oligopoly for each and every good, such choice disappears. The contestable oligopoly which achieves an equilibrium that immunizes it from the incursions of entrants has only one pricing option—it must set its price exactly *equal* to marginal cost and do *all* of the things required for a first best optimum! In short, once we leave the world of pure or partial monopoly, any contestable market must behave ideally in every respect. Optimality is *not* approached gradually as the number of firms supplying a commodity grows. As has long been suggested in Chicago, two firms can be enough to guarantee optimality (see, for example, Eugene Fama and Arthur Laffer).

Thus, the analysis extends enormously the domain in which the invisible hand holds sway. In a perfectly contestable world, it seems to rule almost everywhere. Lest this

VOL. 72 NO. 1   *BAUMOL: CONTESTABLE MARKETS*   3

seem to be too Panglossian a view of reality, let me offer two observations which make it clear that we emphatically do not believe that all need be for the best in this best of all possible worlds.

First, let me recall the observation that real markets are rarely, if ever, perfectly contestable. Contestability is merely a broader ideal, a benchmark of wider applicability than is perfect competition. To say that contestable oligopolies behave ideally and that contestable monopolies have some incentives for doing so is not to imply that this is even nearly true of all oligopolies or of unregulated monopolies in reality.

Second, while the theory extends the domain of the invisible hand in some directions, it unexpectedly restricts it in others. This brings me to the penultimate contrast I wish to offer here between the earlier views and those that emerge from our analysis.

The older theoretical analysis seems to have considered the invisible hand to be a rather weak intratemporal allocator of resources, as we have seen. The mere presence of unregulated monopoly or oligopoly was taken to be sufficient per se to imply that resources are likely to be misallocated *within* a given time period. But *where the market structure is such as to yield a satisfactory allocation of resources within the period*, it may have seemed that it can, at least in theory, do a good job of intertemporal resource allocation. In the absence of any externalities, persistent and asymmetric information gaps, and of interference with the workings of capital markets, the amounts that will be invested for the future may appear to be consistent with Pareto optimality and efficiency in the supply of outputs to current and future generations.

However, our analysis shows that where there are economies of scale in the production of durable capital, intertemporal contestable monopoly, which may perform relatively well in the single period, cannot be depended upon to perform ideally as time passes. In particular, we will see that the least costly producer is in the long run vulnerable to entry or replacement by rivals whose appearance is inefficient because it wastes valuable social resources.

There is one last contrast between the newer analyses and the older theory which I am most anxious to emphasize. In the older theory, the nature of the industry structure was *not* normally explained by the analysis. It was, in effect, taken to be given exogenously, with the fates determining, apparently capriciously, that one industry will be organized as an oligopoly, another as a monopoly and a third as a set of monopolistic competitors. Assuming that this destiny had somehow been revealed, the older analyses proceeded to investigate the consequences of the exogenously given industry structure for pricing, outputs, and other decisions.[2]

The new analyses are radically different in this respect. In our analysis, among others, an industry's structure is determined explicitly, endogenously, and simultaneously with the pricing, output, advertising, and other decisions of the firms of which it is constituted. This, perhaps, is one of the prime contributions of the new theoretical analyses.

I. Characteristics of Contestable Markets

Perhaps a misplaced instinct for melodrama has led me to say so much about contestable markets without even hinting what makes a market contestable. But I can postpone the definition no longer. A contestable market is one into which entry is absolutely free, *and exit is absolutely costless.* We use "freedom of entry" in Stigler's sense, not to mean that it is costless or easy, but that the entrant suffers no disadvantage in terms of production technique or perceived product quality relative to the incumbent,

[2] Of course, any analysis which considered the role of entry, whether it dealt with perfect competition or monopolistic competition, must implicitly have considered the determination of industry structure by the market. But in writings before the 1970's, such analyses usually did not consider how this process determined whether the industry would or would not turn out to be, for example, an oligopoly. The entry conditions were studied only to show how the *assumed* market structure could constitute an equilibrium state. Many recent writings have gone more explicitly into the determination of industry structure, though their approaches generally differ from ours.

4 THE AMERICAN ECONOMIC REVIEW MARCH 1982

and that potential entrants find it appropriate to evaluate the profitability of entry in terms of the incumbent firms' pre-entry prices. In short, it is a requirement of contestability that there be no cost discrimination against entrants. Absolute freedom of exit, to us, is one way to guarantee freedom of entry. By this we mean that any firm can leave without impediment, and in the process of departure can recoup any costs incurred in the entry process. If all capital is salable or reusable without loss other than that corresponding to normal user cost and depreciation, then any risk of entry is eliminated.

Thus, contestable markets may share at most one attribute with perfect competition. Their firms need not be small or numerous or independent in their decision making or produce homogeneous products. In short, a perfectly competitive market is necessarily perfectly contestable, but not *vice versa*.

The crucial feature of a contestable market is its vulnerability to hit-and-run entry. Even a very transient profit opportunity need not be neglected by a potential entrant, for he can go in, and, before prices change, collect his gains and then depart without cost, should the climate grow hostile.

Shortage of time forces me to deal rather briefly with two of the most important properties of contestable markets—their welfare attributes and the way in which they determine industry structure. I deal with these briefly because an intuitive view of the logic of these parts of the analysis is not difficult to provide. Then I can devote a bit more time to some details of the oligopoly and the intertemporal models.

A. Perfect Contestability and Welfare

The welfare properties of contestable markets follow almost directly from their definition and their vulnerability to hit-and-run incursions. Let me list some of these properties and discuss them succinctly.

First, a contestable market never offers more than a normal rate of profit—its economic profits must be zero or negative, even if it is oligopolistic or monopolistic. The reason is simple. Any positive profit means that a transient entrant can set up business,

replicate a profit-making incumbent's output at the same cost as his, undercut the incumbent's prices slightly and still earn a profit. That is, continuity and the opportunity for costless entry and exit guarantee that an entrant who is content to accept a slightly lower economic profit can do so by selecting prices a bit lower than the incumbent's.

In sum, in a perfectly contestable market any economic profit earned by an incumbent automatically constitutes an earnings opportunity for an entrant who will hit and, if necessary, run (counting his temporary but supernormal profits on the way to the bank). Consequently, in contestable markets, zero profits must characterize any equilibrium, even under monopoly and oligopoly.

The second welfare characteristic of a contestable market follows from the same argument as the first. This second attribute of any contestable market is the absence of any sort of inefficiency in production in industry equilibrium. This is true alike of inefficiency of allocation of inputs, X-inefficiency, inefficient operation of the firm, or inefficient organization of the industry. For any unnecessary cost, like any abnormal profit, constitutes an invitation to entry. Of course, in the short run, as is true under perfect competition, both profits and waste may be present. But in the long run, these simply cannot withstand the threat brandished by potential entrants who have nothing to lose by grabbing at any opportunity for profit, however transient it may be.

A third welfare attribute of any long-run equilibrium in a contestable market is that no product can be sold at a price, p, that is less than its marginal cost. For if some firm sells y units of output at such a price and makes a profit in the process, then it is possible for an entrant to offer to sell a slightly smaller quantity, $y - \varepsilon$, at a price a shade lower than the incumbent's, and still make a profit. That is, if the price p is less than MC, then the sale of $y - \varepsilon$ units at price p must yield a total profit $\pi + \Delta\pi$ which is greater than the profit, π, that can be earned by selling only y units of output at that price. Therefore, there must exist a price just slightly lower than p which enables the entrant to undercut the incumbent and yet to earn at least as much as the incumbent, by eliminating the unprofitable marginal unit.

This last attribute of contestable equilibria —the fact that price must always at least equal marginal cost—is important for the economics of antitrust and regulation. For it means that in a perfectly contestable market, no cross subsidy is possible, that is, no predatory pricing can be used as a weapon of unfair competition. But we will see it also has implications which are more profound theoretically and which are more germane to our purposes. For it constitutes half of the argument which shows that when there are two or more suppliers of any product, its price must, in equilibrium, be exactly equal to marginal cost, and so resource allocation must satisfy all the requirements of first best optimality.

Indeed, the argument here is similar to the one which has just been described. But there is a complication which is what introduces the two-firm requirement into this proposition. $p < MC$ constitutes an opportunity for profit to an entrant who drops the unprofitable marginal unit of output, as we have just seen. It would seem, symmetrically, that $p > MC$ also automatically constitutes an opportunity for profitable entry. Instead of selling the y-unit output of a profitable incumbent, the entrant can now offer to sell the slightly larger output, $y + \varepsilon$, using the profits generated by the marginal unit at a price greater than marginal cost to permit a reduction in price below the incumbent's. But on this side of the incumbent's output, there is a catch in the argument. Suppose the incumbent is a monopolist. Then output and price are constrained by the elasticity of demand. An attempt by an entrant to sell $y + \varepsilon$ rather than y may conceivably cause a sharp reduction in price which eliminates the apparent profits of entry. In the extreme case where demand is perfectly inelastic, there will be no positive price at which the market will absorb the quantity $y + \varepsilon$. This means that the profit opportunity represented by $p > MC$ can crumble into dust as soon as anyone seeks to take advantage of it.

But all this changes when the market contains two or more sellers. Now $p > MC$ does always constitute a real opportunity for prof-

itable entry. The entrant who wishes to sell a bit more than some one of the profitable incumbents, call him incumbent A, need not press against the industry's total demand curve for the product. Rather, he can undercut A, steal away all of his customers, at least temporarily, and, in addition, steal away ε units of demand from any other incumbent, B. Thus, if A and B together sell $y_a + y_b > y_a$, then an entrant can lure away $y_a + \varepsilon > y_a$ customers, for ε sufficiently small, and earn on this the incremental profit $\varepsilon(p - MC) > 0$. This means that the entrant who sells $y_a + \varepsilon$ can afford to undercut the prevailing prices somewhat and still make more profit than an incumbent who sells y_a at price p.

In sum, where a product is sold by two or more firms, any $p > MC$ constitutes an irresistible entry opportunity for hit-and-run entry in a perfectly contestable market, for it promises the entrant supernormal profits even if they accrue for a very short period of time.

Consequently, when a perfectly contestable market contains two or more sellers, neither $p < MC$ nor $p > MC$ is compatible with equilibrium. Thus we have our third and perhaps most crucial welfare attribute of such perfectly contestable markets—their prices, in equilibrium, must be equal to marginal costs, as is required for Pareto optimality of the "first best" variety. This, along with the conclusion that such markets permit no economic profits and no inefficiency in long-run equilibrium, constitutes their critical properties from the viewpoint of economic welfare. Certainly, since they do enjoy those three properties, the optimality of perfectly contestable equilibria (with the reservations already expressed about the case of pure monopoly) fully justifies our conclusion that perfect contestability constitutes a proper generalization of the concept of perfect competition so far as welfare implications are concerned.

B. *On the Determination of Industry Structure*

I shall be briefer and even less rigorous in describing how industry structure is determined endogenously by contestability analysis. Though this area encompasses one of its most crucial accomplishments, there is no way I can do justice to the details of the analysis in an oral presentation and within my allotted span of time. However, an intuitive view of the matter is not difficult.

The key to the analysis lies in the second welfare property of contestable equilibria—their incompatibility with inefficiency of any sort. In particular, they are incompatible with inefficiency in the *organization* of an industry. That is, suppose we consider whether a particular output quantity of an industry will be produced by two firms or by a thousand. Suppose it turns out that the two-firm arrangement can produce the given output at a cost 20 percent lower than it can be done by the 1,000 firms. Then one implication of our analysis is that the industry cannot be in long-run equilibrium if it encompasses 1,000 producers. Thus we already have some hint about the equilibrium industry structure of a contestable market.

We can go further with this example. Suppose that, with the given output vector for the industry, it turns out that *no* number of firms other than two can produce at as low a total cost as is possible under a two-firm arrangement. That is, suppose two firms can produce the output vector at a total cost lower than it can be done by one firm or three firms or sixty or six thousand. Then we say that for the given output vector the industry is a *natural duopoly*.

This now tells us how the industry's structure can be determined. We proceed, conceptually, in two steps. First we determine what structure happens to be most efficient for the production of a given output vector by a given industry. Next, we investigate when market pressures will lead the industry toward such an efficient structure in equilibrium.

Now, the first step, though it has many intriguing analytic attributes, is essentially a pure matter of computation. Given the cost function for a typical firm, it is ultimately a matter of calculation to determine how many firms will produce a given output most efficiently. For example, if economies of scale hold throughout the relevant range and there are sufficient complementarities in the production of the different commodities supplied by the firm, then it is an old and well-known conclusion that single firm production will be most economical—that we are dealing with a natural monopoly.

Similarly, in the single product case suppose the average cost curve is U shaped and attains its minimum point at an output of 10,000 units per year. Then it is obvious that if the industry happens to sell 50,000 units per year, this output can be produced most cheaply if it is composed of exactly five firms, each producing 10,000 units at its point of minimum average cost.

Things become far more complex and more interesting when the firm and the industry produce a multiplicity of commodities, as they always do in reality. But the logic is always the same. When the industry output vector is small compared to the output vectors the firm can produce at relatively low cost, then the efficient industry structure will be characterized by very few firms. The opposite will be true when the industry's output vector is relatively far from the origin. In the multiproduct case, since average cost cannot be defined, two complications beset the characterization of the output vectors which the firm can produce relatively efficiently. First, since here average cost cannot be defined, we cannot simply look for the point of minimum average costs. But we overcome this problem by dealing with output bundles having fixed proportions among commodity quantities—by moving along a ray in output space. Along any such ray the behavior of average cost *is* definable, and the point of minimum ray average cost (RAC) is our criterion of relatively efficient scale for the firm. Thus, in Figure 1 we have a ray average cost curve for the production of boots and shoes when they are produced in the proportion given by ray OR. We see that for such bundles y^m is the point of minimum RAC. A second problem affecting the determination of the output vectors the firm can produce efficiently is the choice of output proportions—the location of the ray along which the firm will operate. This depends on the degree of complementarity in production of the goods, and it also lends itself to formal analysis.

We note also that the most efficient number of firms will vary with the location of the

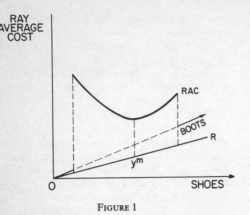

FIGURE 1

industry's output vector. The industry may be a natural monopoly with one output vector, a natural duopoly with another, and efficiency may require seventy-three firms when some third output vector is provided by the industry.

This, then, completes the first of the two basic steps in the endogenous determination of industry structure. Here we have examined what industry structure is least costly for each given output vector of a given industry, and have found how the result depends on the magnitudes of the elements of that output vector and the shape of the cost function of the typical firm. So far the discussion may perhaps be considered normative rather than behavioral. It tells us what structure is most efficient under the circumstances, not which industry structure will emerge under the pressures of the market mechanism.

The transition toward the second, behavioral, stage of the analysis is provided by the observation that the optimal structure of an industry depends on its output vector, while that output vector in turn depends on the prices charged by its firms. But, since pricing depends on industry structure, we are brought full circle to the conclusion that pricing behavior and industry structure must, ultimately, be determined simultaneously and endogenously.

We are in no position to go much further than this for a market whose properties are unspecified. But, for a perfectly contestable market, we can go much further. Indeed, the properties of perfect contestability cut

through every difficulty and tell us the equilibrium prices, outputs, and industry structure, all at once.

Where more than one firm supplies a product, we have already characterized these prices precisely. For we have concluded that each equilibrium price will equal the associated marginal cost. Then, given the industry's cost and demand relationships, this yields the industry's output quantities simultaneously with its prices, in the usual manner. Here there is absolutely nothing new in the analysis.

But what is new is the format of the analysis of the determination of industry structure. As I have already pointed out, structure is determined by the efficiency requirement of equilibrium in any contestable market. Since no such equilibrium is compatible with failure to minimize industry costs, it follows that the market forces under perfect contestability will bring us results consistent with those of our normative analysis. Whatever industry structures minimize total costs for the equilibrium output vector must turn out to be the only structures consistent with industry equilibrium in the long run.

Thus, for contestable markets, but for contestable markets *only*, the second stage of the analysis of industry structure turns out to be a sham. Whatever industry structure was shown by the first, normative, portion of the analysis to be least costly must also emerge as the industry structure selected by market behavior. No additional calculations are required by the behavioral analysis. It will all have been done in the normative cost-minimization analysis and the behavioral analysis is pure bonus.

Thus, as I promised, I have indicated how contestability theory departs from the older theory which implicitly took industry structure to be determined exogenously in a manner totally unspecified and, instead, along with other recent writings, embraces the determination of industry structure as an integral part of the theory to be dealt with simultaneously with the determination of prices and outputs.

At this point I can only conjecture about the determination of industry structure once we leave the limiting case of perfect contestability. But my guess is that there are no

8 THE AMERICAN ECONOMIC REVIEW MARCH 1982

sharp discontinuities here, and that while the industry structures which emerge in reality are not always those which minimize costs, they will constitute reasonable approximations to the efficient structures. If this is not so it is difficult to account for the similarities in the patterns of industry structure that one observes in different countries. Why else do we not see agriculture organized as an oligopoly in any free market economy, or automobiles produced by 10,000 firms? Market pressures must surely make any very inefficient market structure vulnerable to entry, to displacement of incumbents by foreign competition, or to undermining in other ways. If that is so, the market structure that is called for by contestability theory may not prove to be too bad an approximation to what we encounter in reality.

II. On Oligopoly Equilibrium

I should like now to examine oligopoly equilibrium somewhat more extensively. We have seen that, except where a multiproduct oligopoly firm happens to sell some of its products in markets in which it has no competitors, an important partial monopoly case which I will ignore in what follows, all prices must equal the corresponding marginal costs in long-run equilibrium. But in an oligopoly market, this is a troublesome concept. Unless the industry output vector happens to fall at a point where the cost function is characterized by locally constant returns to scale, we know that zero profits are incompatible with marginal cost pricing. Particularly if there are scale economies at that point, so that marginal cost pricing precludes financial viability, we can hardly expect such a solution to constitute an equilibrium. Besides, we have seen that long-run equilibrium requires profit to be precisely zero. We would thus appear to have run into a major snag by concluding that perfect contestability always leads to marginal cost pricing under oligopoly.

This is particularly so if the (ray) average curve is U shaped, with its minimum occurring at a single point, y^m. For in this case that minimum point is the only output of the firm consistent with constant returns to scale

and with zero profits under marginal cost pricing. Thus, dealing with the single product case to make the point, it would appear, say, that if the AC-minimizing output is 1,000, in a contestable market, equilibrium is possible if quantity demanded from the industry happens to be exactly 2,000 units (so two firms can produce 1,000 units each) or exactly 3,000 units or exactly 4,000 units, etc. But suppose the demand curve happens to intersect the industry AC curve, say, at 4,030 units. That is, then, the only industry output satisfying the equilibrium requirement that price equals zero profit. But then, at least one of the four or five firms in the industry must produce either more or less than 1,000 units of output, and so the slope of its AC curve will not be zero at that point, precluding either MC pricing or zero profits and, consequently, violating one or the other of the requirements of equilibrium in a perfectly contestable market.

It would appear that equilibrium will be impossible in this perfectly contestable market unless by a great piece of luck the industry demand curve happens to intersect its AC curve at 2,000 or 3,000 units or some other integer multiple of 1,000 units of output.

There are a variety of ways in which one can grapple with this difficulty. In his dissertation at New York University, Thijs ten Raa has explored the issue with some care and has shown that the presence of entry costs of sufficient magnitude, that is, irreversible costs which must be borne by an entrant but not by an incumbent, can eliminate the existence problem. The minimum size of the entry cost required to permit an equilibrium will depend on the size of the deviation from zero profits under marginal cost pricing and ten Raa has given us rules for its determination. He has shown also that the existence problem, as measured by the required minimum size of entry cost, decreases rapidly as the equilibrium number of firms of the industry increases, typically attaining negligible proportions as that number reaches, say, ten enterprises. For, as is well known, when the firm's average cost curve is U shaped the industry's average cost curve will approach a horizontal line as the

VOL. 72 NO. 1   *BAUMOL: CONTESTABLE MARKETS*   9

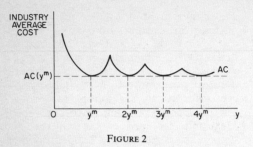

FIGURE 2

FIGURE 3

size of industry output increases. This is shown in Figure 2 which is a standard diagram giving the firm's and the industry's AC curves when the former is U shaped. As a result, the deviations between average cost and marginal cost will decline as industry output increases and so the minimum size of the entry cost required to preserve equilibrium declines correspondingly.

However, here I want to describe another approach offered in our book to the problem of existence which I have just described—the difficulty of satisfying simultaneously the zero-profit requirement and the requirement of marginal cost pricing. This second avenue relies on the apparently unanimous conclusion of empirical investigators of the cost function of the firm, that AC curves are not, in fact, characterized by a unique minimum point as they would be if they had a smooth U shape. Rather, these investigators tell us, the AC curve of reality has a flat bottom—an interval along which it is horizontal. That is, average costs do tend to fall at first with size of output, then they reach a minimum and continue at that level for some range of outputs, after which they may begin to rise once more. An AC curve of this variety is shown in Figure 3. Obviously, such a flat segment of the AC curves *does* help matters because there is now a *range* of outputs over which MC pricing yields zero profits. Moreover, the longer the flat-bottomed segment the better matters are for existence of equilibrium. Indeed, it is easy to show that if the left-hand end of the flat segment occurs at output y^m and the right-hand end occurs at ky_m, then if k is greater than or equal to 2 the existence problem disappears altogether, because the industry's AC curves will be horizontal for any output greater than y_m. That

is, in any contestable market in which two or more firms operate the industry AC curve will be horizontal and MC pricing will always yield zero profits. To confirm that this is so, note that if, for example, the flat segment for the firm extends from $y = 1,000$ to $y = 2,000$, then any industry output of, say, $9,000 + \Delta y$ where $0 \leqslant \Delta y \leqslant 9,000$ can be produced by nine firms, each of them turning out more than 1,000 but less than 2,000 units. Hence, each of them will operate along the horizontal portion of its AC curve, as equilibrium requires.

Thus, if the horizontal interval (y^m, ky_m) happens to satisfy $k \geqslant 2$, there is no longer any problem for existence of equilibrium in a contestable market with two or more firms. But fate may not always be so kind. What if that horizontal interval is quite short, that is, k is quite close to unity? Such a case is shown in our diagram where for illustration I have taken $k = 4/3$.

I should like to take advantage of your patience by dealing here not with the simplest case—that of the single product industry—but with the multiproduct problem. I do this partly to offer you some feeling of the way in which the multiproduct analysis, which is one of the hallmarks of our study, works out in practice.

Because, as we have seen, there is no way one can measure average cost for all output combinations in the multiproduct case, I will deal exclusively with the total cost function. Figure 4 shows such a total cost function for the single firm, which is taken to manufacture two products, boots and shoes.

Let us pause briefly to examine its shape. Along any ray such as OR, which keeps

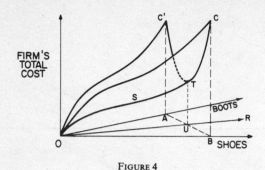

FIGURE 4

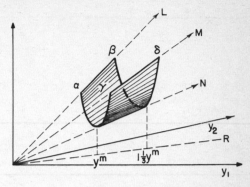

FIGURE 5

output proportions constant, we have an ordinary total cost curve, OST. With one exception, which I will note soon, I have drawn it to have the usual sort of shape, with marginal costs falling near the origin and rising at points much further from the origin. On the other hand, the trans ray cut above AB yields a cross section $C'TC$ which is more or less U shaped. This means that it is relatively cheaper to produce boots and shoes together (point U) than to produce them in isolation (point A or point B). That is, this convex trans ray shape is enough to offer us the complementarity which leads firms and industries to turn out a multiplicity of products rather than specializing in the production of a single good.

Now what, in such a case, corresponds to the flat bottom of an AC curve in a single product case? The answer is that the cost function in the neighborhood of the corresponding output must be linearly homogeneous. In Figure 5 such a region, $\alpha\beta\gamma\delta$, is depicted. It is linearly homogeneous because it is generated by a set of rays such as L, M, and N. For simplicity in the discussion that follows, I have given this region a very regular shape—it is, approximately, a rectangle which has been moved into three-dimensional space and given a U-shaped cross section.

Now Figure 6 combines the two preceding diagrams and we see that they have been drawn to mesh together, so that the linearly homogeneous region constitutes a portion of the firm's total cost surface. We see then that the firm's total cost does have a region in which constant returns to scale occur, and which corresponds to the flat-bottomed segment of the AC curve.

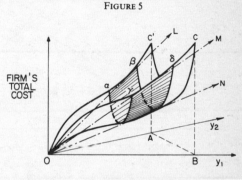

FIGURE 6

Moreover, as before, I have deliberately kept this segment quite narrow. Indeed, I have repeated the previous proportions, letting the segment extend from a distance y^m from the origin to the distance $1\frac{1}{3}y^m$ along any ray on the floor of the diagram.

Let us now see what happens in these circumstances when we turn to the total cost surface for the *industry*. This is depicted in Figure 7 which shows a relationship that may at first seem surprising. In Figure 7 I depict only the linearly homogeneous portions of the industry's cost surface. There we see that while for the firm linear homogeneity prevailed only in the interval from y^m to $1\frac{1}{3}y^m$, in the case of industry output linear homogeneity also holds in that same interval but, in addition, it holds for the interval $2y^m$ to $2\frac{2}{3}y^m$ and in the region extending from $3y^m$ to infinity. That is, everywhere beyond $3y^m$ the industry's total cost function is linearly homogeneous. In this case, then, we have three regions of local linear homogene-

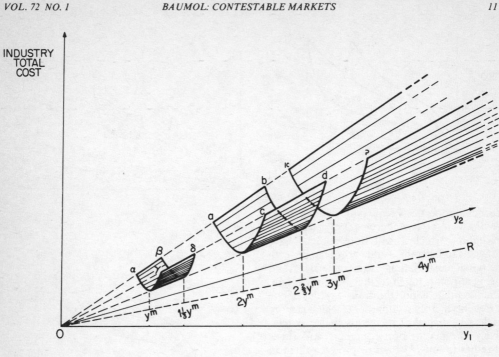

FIGURE 7

ity in the industry's cost function, $\alpha\beta\gamma\delta$, which is identical with that of the individual firm, the larger region *abcd*, and the infinite region *aleph beth*....

Before showing why this is so we must pause to note the implications of the exercise. For it means that even a relatively small region of flatness in the *AC* curve of the individual firm, that is, of linear homogeneity in its total cost function, eliminates the bulk of the existence problem for oligopoly equilibrium in a contestable market. The problem does not arise for outputs nearer to the origin than y_m because such outputs are supplied most efficiently by a monopoly which is not required to price at marginal cost in a contestable market equilibrium. The problem also does not arise for any industry output greater than $3y^m$ in this case, because everywhere beyond that marginal cost pricing yields zero profits. There are two relatively narrow regions in which no equilibrium is, indeed, possible, but here we may conjecture that the vicissitudes of disequilibrium will cause shifts in the demand relationships as changing prices and changing

consumption patterns affect tastes, and so the industry will ultimately happen upon an equilibrium position and remain there until exogenous disturbances move it away. Thus we end up with an oligopoly equilibrium whose prices, profits, and other attributes are determined without benefit of the conjectural variation, reaction functions, and the other paraphernalia of standard oligopoly analysis.

To complete this discussion of oligopoly equilibrium in a contestable market, it only remains for me to explain why the regions of linear homogeneity in the industry's cost function are as depicted in Figure 7. The answer is straightforward. Let $C(y)$ be the firm's total cost function for which we have assumed for expository simplicity that in the interval from y^m to $1\frac{1}{3}y^m$ along each and every ray, total cost grows exactly proportionately with output. Then two firms can produce $2y^m$ at the same unit cost, and three firms can produce $3y^m$ at that same unit cost for the given output bundle, etc. But by exactly the same argument, the two firms together, each producing no more than $1\frac{1}{3}y^m$, can turn out anything up to $2\frac{2}{3}y^m$ without affecting unit costs, and three firms can produce as much as $3\frac{3}{3}y^m$, that is, as much as $4y^m$. In sum, the intervals of linear homogeneity for the industry are the following:

  Interval 1: from y^m to $1\frac{1}{3}y^m$
  Interval 2: from $2y^m$ to $2\frac{2}{3}y^m$
  Interval 3: from $3y^m$ to $4y^m$
  Interval 4: from $4y^m$ to $5\frac{1}{3}y^m$
  Interval 5: from $5y^m$ to $6\frac{2}{3}y^m$

. . . .

That is, each interval begins at an integer multiple of y^m and extends $1/3$ y^m further than its predecessor. Thus, beyond $3y^m$ successive intervals begin to touch or overlap and that is why linear homogeneity extends everywhere beyond $3y^m$ as I claimed.[3]

There is one complication in the multiproduct case which I have deliberately slid over, feeling the discussion was already complicated enough. The preceding argument assumes implicitly that the firms producing the industry output all employ the same output proportions as those in the industry output vector. For otherwise, it is not legitimate to move outward along a single ray as the number of firms is increased. But suppose increased industry output were to permit savings through increased specialization. Might there not be constant returns with fixed output proportions and yet economies of scale for the industry overall? This problem is avoided by our complementarity assumption used to account for the industry's multiproduct operation—our U-shaped trans-ray cross section. This, in effect, rules out such savings from specialization in the regions where linear homogeneity also rules out savings from increased scale.

This, then, completes my discussion of oligopoly equilibrium in perfectly contestable markets, which we have seen, yields a determinate set of prices and outputs that is not dependent upon assumptions about the

nature of incumbent firm's expectations relating to entrants' behavior and offers us a concrete and favorable conclusion on the welfare implications of contestable oligopoly.

III. Intertemporal Vulnerability to Inefficient Entry

Having so far directed attention to areas in which the invisible hand manifests unexpected strength, I should like to end my story by dealing with an issue in relation to which it is weaker than some of us might have expected. As I indicated before, this is the issue of intertemporal production involving durable capital goods.

The analysis is far more general than the following story suggests, but even the case I describe is sufficiently general to make the point. We deal with an industry in which a product is offered by a single firm that provides it period after period. The equilibrium quantity of the commodity that is demanded grows steadily with the passage of time in a manner that is foreseen without uncertainty. Because of economies of scale in the production of capacity the firm deliberately builds some excess capacity to take care of anticipated growth in sales volume. But there is some point, let us say, $z = 45$ years in the future, such that it would be uneconomic to take further growth in sales volume into account in the initial choice of capacity. This is so because the opportunity (interest) cost of the capacity that remains idle for 45 or more years exceeds the savings made possible by the economies of scale of construction. Thus, after 45 years it will pay the firm to undertake a second construction project to build the added capacity needed to produce the goods demanded of it.

Suppose that in every particular period our producer is a natural monopolist, that is, he produces the industry's supply of its one commodity at a cost lower than it can be done by any two or more enterprises. Then considering that same product in different periods to be formally equivalent to different goods we may take our supplier to be an intertemporal natural monopolist in a multiproduct industry. That is, no combination of

---

[3] The reader can readily generalize this result. If the flat-bottomed segment for the firm extends from y^m to $y^m(1 + 1/w)$, where w is an integer, then there will be w regions of linear homogeneity in the industry cost function and it will be linearly homogeneous for any output $y \geqslant wy^m$.

VOL. 72 NO. 1   *BAUMOL: CONTESTABLE MARKETS*   13

two or more firms can produce the industry's intertemporal output vector as cheaply as he. I will prove now under a set of remarkably unrestrictive assumptions that despite its cost advantages, there exists no intertemporal price vector consistent with equilibrium for this firm. That is, whatever his price vector, his market will at some time be vulnerable to partial or complete takeover by an entrant who has neither superior skills nor technological superiority and whose entrance increases the quantities of resources used up in production. In other words, here the invisible hand proves incapable of protecting the most efficient producing arrangement and leaves the incumbent producer vulnerable to displacement by an aggressive entrant. I leave to your imaginations what, if anything, this says about the successive displacements on the world market of the Dutch by the English, the English by the Germans and the Americans, and the Americans, perhaps, by the Japanese.

The proof of our proposition on the intertemporal vulnerability of incumbents to entry that is premature from the viewpoint of cost minimization does require just a little bit of algebra. To keep our analysis simple, I will divide time into two periods, each lasting $z = 45$ years so that capacity in the first period is, optimally, just sufficient to satisfy all demand, but in the second, it requires the construction of added capacity to meet demand growth because, by assumption, anticipatory construction to meet growth more than z years in the future simply is too costly. Also for simplicity, I will assume that there are no costs other than cost of construction. Of course, neither this nor the use of only two periods really affects the argument in any way. My only three substantive assumptions are that demand is growing with time, that there are economies of scale, that is, declining average costs in construction, and that there exists some length of time, z, so great that it does not pay in the initial construction to build capacity sufficient for the growth in quantity demanded that will occur beyond that date.

The argument, like the notation, is now straightforward. Let y_t be output in period t,

p_t be price in period t, and $K(y)$ be the cost of construction of capacity sufficient to produce (a maximum of) y units per period. Here, both p_t and $K(y)$ are expressed in discounted present value.[4]

Then, by assumption, our firm will construct at the beginning of the first period capacity just sufficient to produce output y_1 at cost $K(y_1)$ and at the beginning of the second period it will produce the rest of the capacity it needs, $y_2 - y_1 > 0$, at the cost $K(y_2 - y_1)$.

The first requirement for the prices in question to be consistent with equilibrium is that they permit the incumbent to cover his costs, that is, that

$$(1) \quad p_1 y_1 + p_2 y_2 \geqslant K(y_1) + K(y_2 - y_1).$$

Second, for these prices to constitute an equilibrium they must protect the incumbent against any and all possible incursions by entrants. That is, suppose an entrant were to consider the possibility of constructing capacity y_1 and not expanding in the future, and, by undercutting the incumbent, selling the same output, y_1, in each period. Entry on these terms will in fact be profitable unless the prices are such that the sale of y_1 in each period does not bring in revenues sufficient to cover the cost, $K(y_1)$, of the entrant's once-and-for-all construction. That is, entry will be profitable unless

$$(2) \quad p_1 y_1 + p_2 y_1 \leqslant K(y_1).$$

Thus, the prices in question cannot constitute an equilibrium unless (2) as well as (1) are satisfied.

Now, subtracting (2) from (1) we obtain immediately

$$p_2(y_2 - y_1) \geqslant K(y_2 - y_1)$$

or

$$(3) \quad p_2 \geqslant K(y_2 - y_1)/(y_2 - y_1),$$

----

[4] That is, if p_1^*, p_2^*, represent the undiscounted prices, $p_1 = p_1^*, p_2 = p_2^*/(1+r)$, where r is the rate of interest, etc.

but, by the assumption that average construction cost is declining, since $y_1 > 0$,

$$(4) \quad K(y_2 - y_1)/(y_2 - y_1) > K(y_2)/y_2.$$

Substituting this into (3) we have at once

$$p_2 > K(y_2)/y_2$$

or

$$(5) \qquad p_2 y_2 > K(y_2).$$

Inequality (5) is our result. For it proves that any prices which satisfy equilibrium requirements (1) and (2) must permit a second-period entrant using the same techniques to build capacity y_2 from the ground up, at cost $K(y_2)$, to price slightly below anything the incumbent can charge and yet recover his costs; and that in doing so, the entrant can earn a profit.

Thus, our intertemporal natural monopolist cannot quote, *at time zero*, any prices capable of preventing the takeover of some or all of his market. Moreover, this is so despite the waste, in the form of replication of the incumbent's plant, that this entails. That, then, is the end of the formal argument, the proof that here the invisible hand manifests weakness that is, perhaps, unexpected.

You will all undoubtedly recognize that the story as told here in its barest outlines omits all sorts of nuances, such as entrants' fear of responsive pricing, the role of bankruptcy, depreciation of capital, and the like. This is not the place to go into these matters for it is neither possible nor appropriate here for me to go beyond illustration of the logic of the new analysis.

IV. Concluding Comments

Before closing let me add a word on policy implications, whose details must also be left to another place. In spirit, the policy conclusions are consistent with many of those economists have long been espousing. At least in the intratemporal analysis, the heroes are the (unidentified) potential entrants who exercise discipline over the incumbent, and who do so most effectively when entry is free. In the limit, when entry and exit are completely free, efficient incumbent monopolists and oligopolists may in fact be able to prevent entry. But they can do so only by behaving virtuously, that is, by offering to consumers the benefits which competition would otherwise bring. For every deviation from good behavior instantly makes them vulnerable to hit-and-run entry.

This immediately offers what may be a new insight on antitrust policy. It tells us that a history of absence of entry in an industry and a high concentration index may be signs of virtue, not of vice. This will be true when entry costs in our sense are negligible. And, then, efforts to change market structure must be regarded as mischievous and antisocial in their effects.

A second and more obvious conclusion is the questionable desirability of artificial impediments to entry, such as regulators were long inclined to impose. The new analysis merely reinforces the view that any proposed regulatory barrier to entry must start off with a heavy presumption against its adoption. Perhaps a bit newer is the emphasis on the importance of freedom of exit which is as crucial a requirement of contestability as is freedom of entry. Thus we must reject as perverse the propensity of regulators to resist the closing down of unprofitable lines of activity. This has even gone so far as a Congressional proposal (apparently supported by Ralph Nader) to require any plant with yearly sales exceeding $250,000 to provide fifty-two weeks of severance pay and to pay three years of taxes, before it will be permitted to close, and that only after giving two years notice!

There is much more to the policy implications of the new theory, but I will stop here, also leaving its results relating to empirical research for discussion elsewhere.

Let me only say in closing that I hope I have adequately justified my characterization of the new theory as a rebellion or an uprising. I believe it offers a host of new analytical methods, new tasks for empirical research, and new results. It permits reexamination of the domain of the invisible hand, yields contributions to the theory of

VOL. 72 NO. 1   *BAUMOL: CONTESTABLE MARKETS*   *15*

oligopoly, provides a standard for policy that is far broader and more widely applicable than that of perfect competition, and leads to a theory that analyzes the determination of industry structure endogenously and simultaneously with the analysis of the other variables more traditionally treated in the theory of the firm and the industry. It aspires to provide no less than a unifying theory as a foundation for the analysis of industrial organization. I will perhaps be excused for feeling that this was an ambitious undertaking.

REFERENCES

Bain, Joe S., *Barriers to New Competition*, Cambridge: Harvard University Press, 1956.

Baumol, William J., Bailey, Elizabeth E., and Willig, Robert D., "Weak Invisible Hand Theorems on the Sustainability of Multiproduct Natural Monopoly," *American Economic Review*, June 1977, *67*, 350–65.

_____, Panzar, John C., and Willig, Robert D., *Contestable Markets and the Theory of Industry Structure*, San Diego: Harcourt Brace Jovanovich, 1982.

Bertrand, Jules, Review of *Théorie Mathematique de la Richesse* and *Récherches sur les Principes Mathématiques de la théorie des Richesses*, *Journal des Savants*, 1883, 499–508.

Cournot, A. A., *Researches into the Mathematical Principles of the Theory of Wealth*, New York: A. M. Kelley, 1938; 1960.

Demsetz, Harold, "Why Regulate Utilities?," *Journal of Law and Economics*, April 1968, *11*, 55–65.

Fama, Eugene F. and Laffer, Arthur B., "The Number of Firms and Competition," *American Economic Review*, September 1972, *62*, 670–74.

Panzar, John C. and Willig, Robert D., "Free Entry and the Sustainability of Natural Monopoly," *Bell Journal of Economics*, Spring 1977, *8*, 1–22.

ten Raa, Thijs, "A Theory of Value and Industry Structure," unpublished doctoral dissertation, New York University, 1980.

Part II
Essays in Welfare Theory

This section is characterized primarily by the wide range of the issues in welfare economics to which it devotes itself. These span the role of diminishing and increasing returns as symmetric obstacles to Pareto optimality and competitive equilibrium, Ramsey pricing in general and in the pricing of public goods in particular, pricing over time for efficiency in intertemporal allocation of resources, and application of the new superfairness theory to exchange and the rationing of scarce commodities.

The first article, which I consider the most fundamental in the section, has, in my view, not attracted the attention it deserves relative to some of my other writings. It explores some of the foundation issues in the optimality analysis of welfare economics, and makes clear the central role of a variety of elements which hitherto may have seemed peripheral and of secondary significance. Indeed, I feel that without them the logic of the optimization issue cannot be understood fully.

The three most important of these items are variability in the number of firms in the economy, diminishing returns to scale and Ramsey pricing for the economy.

In some of the standard general equilibrium analyses of optimality and its relation to competitive equilibrium it is assumed either that the number of enterprises is fixed and given as an exogenous datum, or that returns to scale are constant. It is shown in the first article in this section that the former premise underlies the asymmetry of the conclusion that diminishing returns do *not* interfere with the ability of the competitive mechanism to assure Pareto optimality, while increasing returns do prevent optimality from being achieved by competition. The reason is straightforward. Diminishing returns, as we know, mean that universal marginal cost-pricing must yield total revenues that inevitably exceed total costs. This constitutes a surplus in the economy as a whole that must inevitably accrue to someone—who will thereby automatically be paid more than the marginal cost of producing the input he supplies. In particular, if the surplus accrues to firms in the form of economic profit we can expect new firms to be opened for business, because the reward to the owner of a new enterprise will exceed the cost of its formation. However, there is no way in which this process can bring about an equilibrium in the number of firms in the economy because the expansion in the number of firms cannot eliminate the difference between total cost and total revenue for the economy as a whole so long as diminishing returns remain present.

The point is that unless there is a product whose supply is *absolutely* inelastic and all of society's revenue surplus goes to the suppliers of that product, the fact that some suppliers necessarily receive a surplus on their products is certain to lead to output quantities that are not optimal.

The general implication is that if the economy is to achieve an optimum through parametric prices, then at the optimal output vector the economy's production frontier must be (at least) locally linearly homogeneous. For, as we know, the optimal parametric prices must be equal to marginal costs, and those prices will be incompatible with zero economic profits if the homogeneity condition is violated by either diminishing or increasing returns.

More than that—in such circumstances a competitive general equilibrium will also be impossible for similar reasons. For then either some prices must not equal marginal costs or economic profits cannot be zero (or both), and either of these precludes competitive equilibrium.

This same discussion also puts to rest the notion that Ramsey pricing is an artificial intrusion upon the market mechanism necessitated by unwillingness of the authorities to provide the subsidies (or taxes) necessary to permit total revenue to equal total costs under a regime of marginal cost pricing. Where the optimal point is not characterized by local linear homogeneity, as we have just seen, marginal cost pricing cannot work, at least so long as lump sum taxes (positive or negative) are not a real option. It is shown here that in these circumstances Ramsey prices are those that yield as high a level of welfare as can be achieved by *any* set of parametric prices. These Ramsey prices will, of course, not achieve as high a level of welfare as that offered by an unconstrained social optimum, and in that sense they are indeed second best; but they *are*, nevertheless, best in the sense that *no* other set of fixed prices can do any better.

A major lesson of Ramsey theory is that if absence of constant returns to scale, or fiscal needs of government, or any other such requirement calls for taxes which lead to a deviation between the price of at least one of the economy's outputs and its marginal cost, then, in general, efficiency requires *all* prices in the economy to deviate from their corresponding marginal costs.

There follow immediately two implications for standard welfare theory which so far seem to have escaped general notice. The first is that under Ramsey pricing the magnitude of the standard Pigouvian tax also must be modified from its Paretian (marginal cost) level. Since the Pigouvian tax is neither more nor less than a price upon use of social resources that would otherwise be made available without (adequate) charge, such a tax, along with all other prices, requires a Ramsey adjustment whenever economic efficiency requires such an adjustment anywhere in the economy. For example, in the special circumstances in which Ramsey prices satisfy the much-noted inverse elasticity formula, it follows that the optimal Pigouvian tax upon an activity that generates a detrimental externality must equal the resulting marginal social damage *plus a percentage surtax that is inversely proportionate to the elasticity of demand for the product of that activity.*

A second and related application of these observations about Ramsey theory relates to the pricing of public goods. This is the subject of the second article in this section, whose coauthor is Janusz Ordover. For well-known and legitimate reasons the received wisdom calls for zero pricing for the use of public goods. By the definition of a public good, the marginal cost of accommodating an additional user of such a good is zero. Then any positive price that leads to a reduction in use of that good below its zero-price usage level appears necessarily to constitute a wasted opportunity to benefit someone at no cost to society.

Ramsey analysis shows that this conclusion is not as valid, generally, as it appears to be. If nonconstant returns to scale in production of the entire economy or fiscal requirements for the public sector call for a deviation from $p=mc$ anywhere in the economy, then, as I have noted, efficiency requires the magnitude of that distortion to be kept within bounds in any one sector, and, instead, for smaller price distortions to be instituted throughout the economy. *This requirement encompasses public goods along with all other outputs.*

In particular, in a world where the Ramsey rule follows the inverse elasticity formula, if commodity i is a public good, so that $mc_i=0$ (for added *consumption* of the good), then the

Ramsey rule becomes

$$k/E_i = \frac{P_i - mc_i}{P_i} = P_i/P_i = l \text{ or } E_i = k.$$

where E_i is the price elasticity of demand for i. In other words, it requires any two public goods, i and j, to be priced so that each is used to such a degree that $E_i = E_j$. In any event, it is clear that in such cases a nonzero price for public goods will generally be required for efficiency.[1]

The third paper in this section examines the defining characteristics of public goods and concludes that they really are simply an amalgam of scale economies and externalities properties. That is, the impediments to optimality in resource allocation that are a consequence of the presence of public goods are really no different from those caused by scale economies and externalites. Moreover, I conclude that in practice cases which at first sight seem to constitute good approximations to the case of pure public goods turn out to be impure to a significant degree. The nature of these impurities, I believe, helps us to understand more fully the nature of the public good concept.

The fourth paper in this section could as easily have been fitted into the section of this book devoted to contestability. The paper deals with the requirements of efficiency in intertemporal prices and their relationship to economic depreciation of a capital stock. In that sense the subject of the paper is normative: it examines how interperiod price patterns should be selected if they are to avoid intertemporal resource misallocation. The analysis comes out with surprisingly explicit and concrete rules and analytical methods. But here, as in other areas, the efficiency requirement of perfect contestability transforms normative properties into behavioural ones. Since in a perfectly contestable market equilibrium is incompatible with inefficiency, we expect in such a market to encounter behaviour that tends to conform perfectly with efficiency requirements.

Depreciation is a topic that seems never to have fitted comfortably into the corpus of economic analysis, even in the literature of capital theory. Instead, it seems more at home in the domain of accountants, tax authorities and rate regulators. Still, those persons also speak of something they call 'economic depreciation' which the accountant's depreciation figures are allegedly designed to approximate. The depreciation calculation is intended to serve three apparently mildly related roles (tax avoidance aside): first, it is designed to provide funds just equal to the cost of replacement for a piece of equipment when the time for replacement arrives, second, it is intended to reflect the decline of either the productive or earning power of the equipment that occurs over the course of a given period of time, and, third, it is intended to serve as a guide to pricing or, rather, as an element that enters into the price calculation.

The fourth article in this section brings these three strands together explicitly. It makes the obvious point that the choice of a stream of depreciation earnings sufficient to replace an item of equipment is equivalent to the choice of a stream of prices for the products of that equipment, prices sufficiently in excess of concurrent expenditures to yield the selected depreciation accruals. This at once brings the matter into the terrain familiar to economists, for it asserts that depreciation decisions and pricing decisions are merely two different guises of the same choices. Moreover, it tells us that if there exists an optimal set of prices there must also exist a counterpart in the form of an optimal stream of depreciation accruals. Finally, defining economic depreciation as the decline per period in the present value of the stream of future net revenues to be yielded by the equipment over its remaining life, it is clear that this is tautologically the same as that period's depreciation accrual. It is the revenue earned in that period by the equipment's products minus the costs incurred on their behalf—in short, it is the net revenue of the equipment which, by the end of the period, will already have been obtained by the firm and will, consequently, no longer be part of its future revenue stream, as it was at the period's beginning.

The analysis uses a direct extension of the Kuhn-Tucket procedures for the calculation of optimal peak-off peak prices. The analogy is clear; both problems deal with optimal intertemporal price relationships. One typically concerns itself with different hours of the day, the other with different years in the life of a machine, but for the mathematics that makes absolutely no difference. The only significant difference arises out of the fact that equipment loses its powers of production over the course of the years of its lifetime, but not with the passage of hours of the day.

In the end there emerge surprisingly explicit formulae which show how optimal depreciation and intertemporal pricing are affected by the real interest rate, the rate of inflation, the rate of cost saving technical progress and the rate of deterioration of the equipment.

I should add that my work on the subject is based on ideas that emerged from a long conversation with Ralph Turvey, and draws heavily upon the writings of Stephen Littlechild and R. Rees.

Finally the section ends with an article based on the fairness theory associated with Foley, Schmeidler, Varian, Kolm and others. Since I am about to publish a separate book on the subject[2] I view this paper, in contradistinction to some of the other articles in the present volume, as a presage of my future work rather than a record of its past.

The main conclusion I derive from the papers that constitute this section is that there is still an enormous amount of territory to be explored in welfare theory. Platitudinous though this conclusion may sound, it is rendered substantive by specific lacunae in the work included. For example, in the paper on intertemporal pricing it is deliberately assumed that returns to scale in the construction of equipment are constant. This is done to avoid the Ramsey issues and the other complications which arise when there are economies or diseconomies of scale. Since writing this piece, further research by Panzar, Willig and myself has shown how serious those complications can be,[3] but we are far from having mastered them.

The outlines of the work that remains to be done in application of fairness theory is much less clear, but its magnitude is obvious. In short, if nothing else, the gaps in my writings here can perhaps be viewed charitably as a repository of opportunities for future writers.

Notes

1. Other analogous Ramsey modifications of standard welfare theoretic results obviously arise immediately. For example, the classical result on efficient peak-off peak pricing requires off-peak users to cover only the marginal operating (nonfixed capital) costs of serving them, so that, where this conclusion is valid, efficient off-peak user revenues will include no contribution toward the cost of capacity construction. We see now that where efficiency requires a Ramsey adjustment in most prices of the economy this result is no longer valid—off-peak prices can be expected to exceed marginal operating costs and, thereby, to help cover the cost of construction of capacity.

2. *Toward Application of Fairness Theory* (Cambridge, Mass.: MIT Press, 1985) (forthcoming).
3. See Baumol, W. J., Panzar, J. C. and Willig, R. D. *'Contestable Markets and the Theory of Industry Structure',* (San Diego: Harcourt Brace Jovanovitch, 1982) Chs. 13 and 14.

[4]

Quasi Optimality: The Price We Must Pay for a Price System

William J. Baumol

Princeton and New York Universities

The paper argues that, in the absence of lump-sum payments, a Pareto optimum is achievable by marginal-cost pricing and/or competitive equilibrium only when the boundary of the social production set happens to be linearly homogeneous near that optimal solution. Thus, contrary to widespread belief, both diminishing and increasing returns can be incompatible with achievement of optimality via parametric prices. Generally, the best that any set of fixed prices can achieve is the Ramsey solution constrained by Walras's law. The resulting welfare loss is the price society must pay for using a price system to allocate resources.

This paper offers five main results important for our understanding of welfare theory.

1. In the absence of lump-sum payments, an optimum is achievable by marginal-cost pricing and/or competitive equilibrium when and only when the boundary of the social production set happens to be linearly homogeneous in the neighborhood of that optimal solution.[1] Thus, though there is a significant theoretical difference between the

---

I am grateful to Elizabeth Bailey, Dietrich Fischer, Thijs ten Raa, and Hugo Sonnenschein for their valuable suggestions, and to the National Science Foundation and the Sloan Foundation for their support of the research.

[1] Strictly speaking, this result is correct if the boundary of the production set happens to be twice differentiable at the optimal point. Otherwise, the optimum may lie at a vertex of the production set and matters grow slightly more complicated. If we construct a smooth approximation to the boundary of the production set at that point, then if that approximation is sufficiently close, our results will all apply to it without further modification. Moreover, the condition is not quite sufficient by itself. Global as well as local characteristics of the production set can cause problems for the competitive solution.

[*Journal of Political Economy*, 1979, vol. 87, no. 3]
© 1979 by The University of Chicago. 0022-3808/79/8703-0003$01.86

problems in the two cases, contrary to a widely held view, diminishing returns as well as increasing returns in the social production set can be incompatible with the achievement of optimality via competitive prices (or any other parametric prices, for that matter).

2. Walras's law constitutes a budgetary requirement which unavoidably constrains resource allocation under any fixed prices, unless they are supplemented by lump-sum payments.

3. In the long run, direct lump-sum payments are not possible. However, in the case of diminishing returns, rents may serve the purpose.

4. Generally, the best that any set of fixed prices can achieve is the Ramsey (1927) solution,[2] whose welfare yield is constrained by Walras's law.

5. The Ramsey solution will generally be inferior to a true optimum. The resulting welfare loss is the price that society must pay for relying on a price system to allocate its resources.

In brief, the reason diminishing returns also cause problems for competitive equilibrium in the long run is that such an equilibrium requires prices to be set equal to marginal costs and that, we know, must yield positive economic profits. Unless the number of firms is for some reason assumed unchangeable, entry will be induced. If returns diminish everywhere, the number of firms must continue to expand indefinitely. There simply can be no equilibrium in the number of firms and, hence, there can be no equilibrium. Put in a different way, once one departs from the assumption, widely used in general equilibrium models, that the number of firms is simply fixed,[3] one can no longer take the difference between value of output and cost of inputs to be paid out to shareholders as a pure (lump-sum) rent. The economy, as it were, ends up with a rent payment fund—but there may be no one to whom it can be paid without upsetting any possible equilibrium.

I. Preliminary Remarks: Welfare Status of the Ramsey Optimum

It is often suggested that society is forced to accept constrained Pareto and Ramsey prices instead of a true optimum only because narrow-

[2] Elsewhere, Bradford and I (Baumol and Bradford 1970) have described quasi-optimal or Ramsey prices as the set of prices that yields the (Pareto) optimal departures from marginal costs, when that optimum must satisfy a budget constraint. That is, they are the least welfare-damaging deviations from marginal-cost prices that permit the supplier to cover his costs or to meet some other total profit requirement. There are standard formulas that give the values of these Ramsey prices, which have played an increasingly important role in the literature of welfare theory, regulatory economics, and the theory of public finance.

[3] For a general equilibrium analysis which avoids this premise, see Novshek and Sonnenschein (1978). A bit more will be said on this issue later.

580   JOURNAL OF POLITICAL ECONOMY

minded legislators refuse subsidies to firms with scale economies to cover any losses that would result from marginal-cost pricing. It is implied that in the absence of this artificial constraint, it would be possible to institute a regime of universal marginal-cost pricing, with any resulting deficits covered by subsidy and any abnormal profits taxed away.

Recently, this conclusion was disputed by Bradford and me (Baumol and Bradford 1970). We argued that for the economy as a whole the budget constraint is not an artificial requirement, but is, rather, an inescapable feature of the economy's monetary flows. For example, if all production sets exhibited scale economies, under marginal-cost pricing every firm would require a subsidy. But a subsidy must come from somewhere. If it is financed by taxes, these must be taxes on economic activities of one sort or another. If we can rule out lump-sum taxes as a figment of the theorists' imagination, the taxes must be added to the before-tax prices which had been set equal to marginal costs, obviously forcing after-tax prices to depart from marginal costs after all. Because after-tax prices *do* have to satisfy the economy-wide budget constraint, we are, ultimately, back at the Ramsey problem, that of selecting the after-tax prices that are Pareto optimal, subject to the inescapable budget constraint for the economy.

In the following pages it will be shown by counterexample that the Ramsey solution is not strictly optimal. In some ultimate sense the economy is capable of doing better. On the other hand, marginal-cost pricing (the Hotelling [1938] principle) is not a better solution. Indeed, the same counterexample will be used to show that it is not even feasible, in general. We will see that, in the absence of lump-sum taxes, in a world of scale economies it will lead consumers to demand, ex ante, more than the economy can produce, though Walras's law will prevent them from making these demands effective. The reverse will hold under diminishing returns.

Thus, the welfare loss required by the acceptance of the Ramsey solution is generally unavoidable under any standard price system in which the individual decision maker treats prices as fixed parameters whose values are beyond his control, and where those prices are not discriminatory.

II. Walras's Law as the Ramsey Constraint for the Economy

We may note first in what sense the budget constraint of the Ramsey analysis is an unavoidable feature of the price mechanism. By a parametric price system I mean an economic arrangement under which the net revenue function for any individual or for the economy is a hyperplane, with net revenues being obtained either by the sale or purchase of some good or service at a fixed price or by a transfer of income from some individuals to others. The net revenue function for the economy as a whole, then, must take the form

$$\sum_i \sum_j p_i z_{ij} + \sum_j t_j = k,$$

where p_i = the price of commodity i; z_{ij} = the net quantity of commodity i supplied by individual j (where $z_{ij} < 0$ if j is a net demander of i); t_j = the net transfer payment received by individual j.

By definition, for society as a whole we must have $\sum t_j \equiv 0$, that is, any transfer receipt must be offset by a transfer payment. Moreover, if we posit that in the absence of all economic activity, that is, if all $z_{ij} = 0$, net receipts must be zero, it follows that the net revenue hyperplane must go through the origin, so that we must have $k = 0$. Thus, under a parametric price system, the net revenue function for the economy must take the form

$$\sum_i \sum_j p_i z_{ij} = 0. \qquad (1)$$

I will refer to this as Walras's law relationship, which, we will see, serves as the constraint generally leaving the Ramsey prices as the economy's best parametric pricing option.

III. A Trivial Model: The Optimum Optimorum

To make clear just how scale economies and diseconomies for the economy affect the analysis, we turn to an example whose triviality contributes to its transparency. Despite its triviality, this example will suffice to prove:[4] (*a*) that the Ramsey solution is not, in general, as good as the *optimum optimorum,* and (*b*) that the marginal-cost pricing solution is not, in general, feasible. The simple example will also indicate why things work out the way they do. I will leave a fuller and more general discussion until later in the paper.

Let us assume that there is a single consumer who owns the one resource (call it labor) that is used in making the economy's only product. The consumer derives his income from the sale of his resource but owns no shares in the firm. The firm and the government are operated by (nonhuman) agents who do not consume anything themselves.[5] We will also select particular and simple forms for the

---

[4] Shlomo Maital has called my attention to the old Yiddish proverb: "For example is not a proof." But, of course, a counterexample can indeed be a disproof! More important, it will be obvious that nothing depends upon the characteristics of the counterexample provided here, except the simplicity of the calculations.

[5] We adopt this queer assumption to preserve the simplifications permitted by a single consumer, so that no Pareto-optimality complications need arise. This consumer, however, cannot be the owner of the firm if any exchange is to take place, i.e., if pricing is to be a real issue, as it must be for the Ramsey solution to apply.

consumer's utility function and the firm's production relationships to permit us to obtain explicit numerical solutions. We use the following notations and assumptions: r = quantity of resource not used in production (leisure); y = output of the produced commodity;

$$u = ry = \text{the utility function,} \tag{2}$$

$y^{0.5} + r = 3$, the resource availability constraint
[with the implicit production function $y = (3-r)^2$]. $\tag{3}$

This is clearly a case of scale economies, and the increasing returns produce the curvature of the production frontier shown in curve *AB* in figure 1. We will now proceed by calculating successively (and comparing), first, the true *optimum optimorum* (which in our one-consumer economy is the unique Pareto optimum); second, the Ramsey solution; and finally, the result of an attempt to impose marginal-cost pricing (after taxes).

The true optimum is obtained by maximization of utility function (2) subject to resource constraint (3). We have the Lagrangian yr +

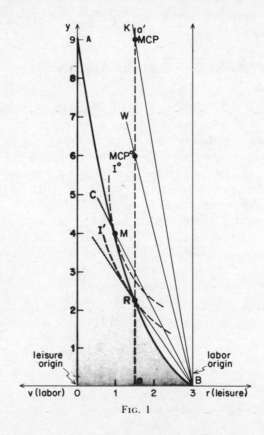

Fig. 1

$\lambda(3-y^{0.5}-r)$, yielding first-order conditions:

$$y = \lambda$$
$$r = 0.5\lambda y^{-0.5}. \tag{4}$$

By (4) we have

$$r = 0.5y^{0.5}. \tag{5}$$

Substituting (5) into (3) we obtain $y^{0.5} + 0.5y^{0.5} = 3$, or $y^{0.5} = 2$. Hence, by (5) the *optimum optimorum* is given by $y^M = 4$, $r^M = 1$, that is, by point M in figure 1.

At that point the production frontier is tangent to consumer indifference curve I^0 (which by [2] is a rectangular hyperbola).

Now, consider the consumer's budget (income) constraint

$$py + r = 3, \tag{6}$$

which for any value of p must go through the point at which $y = 0$, $r = 3$ (point B in the diagram). Thus, the corresponding price line must go through point B (the labor-output origin), that is, the consumer may choose to sell none of his resource and keep all of it for himself.

If the consumer's income constraint is to be satisfied at the optimum, M, then p must be chosen so that the consumer's price line is BMC. But in that case the price line is not tangent to indifference curve I^0 at M. In short, M is not an equilibrium point at any product price.

We conclude that, because of the curvature of the production frontier, there is no price p at which the economy can achieve its optimum and yet satisfy the consumer's budget requirement.

Another way to see this is to observe that the consumer's price-consumption (offer) curve does not intersect the production frontier at the optimal point M. To show this, we must digress briefly to examine the equilibrium of the consumer. The result will also be helpful to us throughout the discussion of our numerical example. As usual, we assume that the consumer maximizes the value of his utility (2), subject to his income (budget) constraint (6), giving the Lagrangian $yr + \alpha(3-py-r)$ with first-order conditions $r = \alpha p$ and $y = \alpha$. Eliminating α, we have $r = yp$.

Substituting this into the consumer's budget constraint (6), we obtain at once $2r = 2py = 3$, or

$$r = 1.5 \qquad y = 1.5/p. \tag{7}$$

We see from (7) that in our trivial numerical example the offer curve is the vertical line aa' in figure 1, satisfying the condition $r = 1.5$. Obviously, that offer curve does not intersect the production frontier

584   JOURNAL OF POLITICAL ECONOMY

at the optimal point M, so that there exists no product price yielding M as the market solution.

IV. The Ramsey Solution in the Simple Model

We now compare the optimum with the Ramsey solution, which is found by maximizing the consumer's utility function (2) subject to the resources requirement (3) and the Walras's law budget constraint[6]

$$py - (3-r) = 0 \tag{8}$$

or, by (3), $py - y^{0.5} = 0$, or

$$p = y^{-0.5}. \tag{9}$$

In this trivial example, with these two constraints there is in fact nothing to maximize—the constraints, together with the consumer's behavior rules, suffice to determine the unique equilibrium point.[7]

The Ramsey solution point is the intersection of the vertical offer curve aa' given by (7) with the production frontier. This is obtained by substituting into (7) the value of p in (9), which was obtained from the budget constraint and the production function. We have $y = 1.5/y^{-0.5}$, or $y^{0.5} = 1.5$, yielding the Ramsey solution (by [7]) $r^R = 1.5, y^R = 2.25$, $p^R = 2/3$.

This is represented by point R in figure 1, where the price line is tangent to indifference curve I'. Compared to the true optimum, this clearly constitutes a real loss in welfare. Thus, our simple example is sufficient to prove:

PROPOSITION 1: The Ramsey solution is not generally as desirable as an unconstrained optimum.

Nevertheless, the Ramsey point is the best point that can be ob-

---

[6] Note that this Walras's law budget constraint (8) is the special case of the Walras's law expression (1) with two commodities, y and r (leisure), with respective prices p and unity, and with r^*, the available quantity of the single resource, equal to 3. Since there is only one consumer in our model, that person's budget constraint (8) must, of course, be the same as the budget constraint for the economy, (6). Note also that it is Walras's law which requires both budget constraints, (6) and (8), to go through the point $(r,y) = (3,0)$, i.e., point B in fig. 1, since this is a point at which money flows in the economy just balance out.

[7] The problem is that for a nontrivial Ramsey solution one must have at least two outputs in addition to leisure. In the single-output case the Ramsey price must equal average cost since that is the only price, p^*, which satisfies the budget constraint $p^*y = $ total cost. It is only in the case where there are $n \geq 2$ outputs that Ramsey pricing comes into its own, using a Pareto optimization procedure to determine relative outputs and the corresponding relative prices. Dietrich Fischer has constructed an illuminating numerical example of such a case, having all the properties displayed here with the aid of our more transparent single-output example. Fischer's discussion is available on request.

tained through the standard price mechanism with its parametric and nondiscriminatory prices, that is, it is the best point (indeed, in this case, the only point) of tangency between an indifference curve and a price line through B that lies on the production frontier.

V. Marginal-Cost Prices in the Simple Model

We may now usefully examine what would happen if the (nonhuman) government in our economy were preprogrammed to offer a Hotelling solution, decreeing that the economy's one manufactured good be offered at a price equal to its marginal cost, the government then attempting to absorb the resulting deficit of the increasing-returns producer of that good. Measuring everything in wage units as before, we clearly have, from (3), $C = y^{0.5} + r$, so

$$\partial C/\partial y = 0.5y^{-0.5} = p, \qquad \partial C/\partial r = 1. \tag{10}$$

Thus the marginal-cost price of r is still unity. Substituting the value of p given by (10) into the consumer's equilibrium conditions (7), we obtain $yp = 0.5y^{0.5} = 1.5$. That is, with marginal-cost pricing the consumer will demand

$$y^C = 9, \ r^C = 1.5, \text{ (and price will be } p^C = 1/6), \tag{11}$$

represented by point MCP in figure 1. Clearly this point is just not feasible.

Note that the slope of the price line, BK, here is $-1/p = -9/1.5 = -6$. That is not the same as the ratio of the marginal costs at optimal point M with coordinates $y^M = 4$, $r^M = 1$, where by (10) $\partial C/\partial y = 1/4$. That is, in (11) we have set price equal to relative marginal cost at the point corresponding to consumer equilibrium, not equal to relative marginal costs at the optimal point. If we were instead to adopt the "optimal-marginal-cost price," $\partial C/\partial y = p^{C^o} = 1/4$, by (7) the quantities demanded would satisfy, instead of (11), $r = py = y/4 = 1.5$ or $r^{C^o} = 1.5$, $y^{C^o} = 6$, represented by point MCP^o in figure 1. This point, too, is clearly not feasible. Thus, we have proved:

PROPOSITION 2: Universal marginal-cost pricing will not, generally, yield an optimal allocation of resources.

Of course, points MCP and MCP^o are only ex ante solutions. Neither of them can be achieved ex post. Their impossibility can be ascribed either to their violation of the production constraints or to the nonhuman government's attempt to circumvent Walras's law. For that financial constraint is binding even upon the government, which cannot absorb the industry's deficit by any act of magic. It can, of course, cover the deficit by taxing the consumer, that is, by taxing his

586   JOURNAL OF POLITICAL ECONOMY

purchases of the commodity or his sale of resources, in which case it effectively rejects marginal-cost prices (after taxes) and the quest for optimality then returns to the Ramsey problem. Or alternatively, it can rely upon a market-clearing mechanism for the elimination of the contradictions inherent in our ex ante solutions. But then prices must deviate once more from their marginal costs—a process of inflation will absorb the chimerical excess of consumer purchasing power and thereby bring commodity flows into their inevitable compliance with the dictates of Walras's law.

VI. The Diminishing-Returns Case

It is easy to illustrate that problems precisely analogous to those we have just been observing arise in the case of diminishing returns, though we will note later that it is easier in theory to repair the damage in the diminishing-returns case. The only basic difference is that now marginal-cost pricing yields a consumer equilibrium point which falls inside the possibility frontier rather than outside it, as was the case where scale economies were present. That is, under diminishing returns, the equilibrium point will be inefficient (not using resources fully) rather than infeasible.

Our trivial example is easily turned into a diminishing-returns case by replacing our production function (3) with

$$y^2 + r = 9. \tag{12}$$

There is no need to repeat the arithmetic of our four solutions, which is precisely the same as before. They are shown in figure 2, in which, as before, $M, R, MCP,$ and MCP^o, respectively, represent the *optimum optimorum,* the Ramsey solution, the marginal-cost pricing solution, and the "optimal" marginal-cost pricing solution, that is, the solution obtained when prices are set equal to marginal costs as calculated at the optimal point M. As before, the consumer's offer curve is a vertical line aa', this time at $r = 4.5$.

We see immediately our basic results, the deviation between the Ramsey solution point and the true optimum, as well as the deviation between the marginal-cost pricing solutions and the production frontier.

VII. Local Linear Homogeneity Necessary (and Normally Sufficient) for Optimality of Marginal-Cost Pricing

All of the problems we have discussed disappear when the production function is homogeneous of degree one, throughout. But that is a stronger condition than we need for the purpose. A necessary and

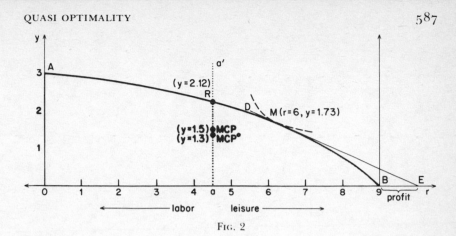

FIG. 2

sufficient condition is that the production function be linearly homogeneous in the neighborhood of the optimal point. That is to say, at the optimal point all of the coordinates and all of the first partial derivatives of the production function must be the same as those of a linearly homogeneous function through that point. In that case, we have the following (assuming that the pertinent second-order conditions are satisfied):[8]

PROPOSITION 3: Assuming differentiability, if and only if at the optimal solution point the production function is locally linearly homogeneous, (a) the *optimum optimorum* will be attainable via a set of fixed (parametric) prices, (b) the optimal prices will each be equal to their corresponding marginal costs, and (c) the Ramsey prices will be marginal-cost prices. That is, all of the solutions we have been discussing will collapse into one.

[8] No rigorous and general proof of the "if" portion of proposition 3 will be provided since, unlike most of the other propositions of this paper, it cannot be proved by counterexample, and since it involves some fairly complex problems in general equilibrium analysis which have been dealt with by Arrow (1951) and Debreu (1951). The basic idea is that if the relevant functions are twice differentiable, an optimum will be attainable via a set of fixed input and output prices if and only if the hyperplane $H = \Sigma p_i y_i - \Sigma w_k v_k$ (where p_i and y_i are the price and quantity of output i and w_k and v_k are the price and quantity of input k) is a separating hyperplane of the production set and the set of points preferred to or indifferent to the optimal point. Since H is obviously linearly homogeneous, if the boundary of the production set is twice differentiable at the optimal point, it must be tangent to H at that point and, hence, locally linearly homogeneous there. The argument is very similar to that of the discussion of fig. 3 which follows.

However, as has been pointed out to me by Thijs ten Raa, local linear homogeneity may not be sufficient for proposition 3. If elsewhere in the production set there are scale economies sufficiently great, no separating hyperplane may be possible and then competition will once again be incapable of achieving the optimum. Thus, in fig. 3, if the production frontier is BA' rather than BA it is clear that no separating hyperplane is possible.

588   JOURNAL OF POLITICAL ECONOMY

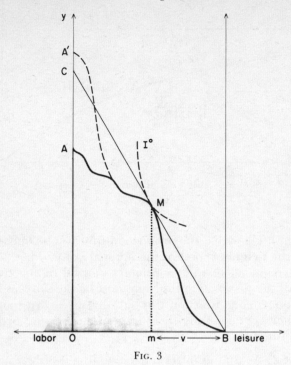

FIG. 3

Before entering into a generalized discussion of this proposition, it will be useful to indicate why it works, with the aid of our single-output case and its associated diagram.

Figure 3 shows an odd-shaped production frontier BMA. Point M is, again, the *optimum optimorum*—the point of tangency between the production frontier and an indifference curve, I^0. However, M is drawn so that the budget line BC through M happens to be tangent to the production frontier (and the indifference curve) at that point. Obviously, this is the necessary and sufficient condition (assuming differentiability) for point M to be attainable by a system of fixed prices, that is, for the offer curve to contain M.

I will show now that this tangency between the budget line and the production frontier will occur if and only if the production function is (locally) linearly homogeneous at M. For this purpose let v represent labor used up in the production process, so that $v = r^* - r =$ total available labor supply minus leisure. Then in the diagram, point B on the horizontal axis represents the available labor supply, r^*, and v is measured leftward from point B. Thus, at point m on the horizontal axis corresponding to optimal point M, we have $r = Om$, $v = mB$, and so, by the tangency of CB and the production frontier at point M, the marginal product of labor must satisfy $dy/dv = y/v$ or $dy/y = dv/v$. This is, clearly, the requirement for constant returns to scale: A given percentage increase in input use, dv/v, yields exactly the same percentage increase in output, dy/y, so homogeneity holds at M if and only if the slope of the production frontier there is equal to the slope of the budget line through that point.[9]

Thus, at least in the two-variable case, we see that local linear homogeneity is indeed the necessary and sufficient condition for proposition 3 to hold. Note that there is no a priori restriction upon the shape of the indifference curves to lead to any presumption that the optimal point will in fact fall at a spot such as M in figure 3, where the production frontier happens to be linearly homogeneous.

One observation that follows from all this is the special circumstances that are required for competitive equilibrium to produce its vaunted optimality results. We see now, subject to some qualifications which will appear later, that such a competitive optimum cannot occur if the production frontier contains no points that are locally linearly homogeneous. In particular, in a world in which either diseconomies or economies of scale prevail throughout, we see that a competitive solution could not be optimal even if it were possible. But even if the production frontier is locally linearly homogeneous somewhere, the optimum need not fall there, and therefore need not be attainable by competition. It will fall there only if consumer preferences happen to select that particular output vector, and there is no a priori reason to expect this to be so.

VIII. Euler's Theorem and the Infeasibility of Marginal-Cost Pricing

Let us consider next why marginal-cost pricing produces infeasibly large demands in the case of scale economies and demands inadequate to use up the available resources in the case of scale diseconomies.

All of this is the obverse of what we have learned from Euler's theorem, which tells us, at least where a production function is homogeneous of some degree, that if there are local economies of scale in the production process, total receipts of producers at marginal-cost prices will fall short of their costs, that is, their payments to inputs. If this occurs throughout the economy, the economy's budget constraint will be violated. More than that, it means that if the suppliers of inputs spend all their earnings, the economy simply will not offer a supply of

---

[9] A geometric interpretation gives us the same result more directly. Treating B as the origin in (y,v) space, the budget line BC is obviously the graph of a linearly homogeneous function. Hence it will be tangent to the production frontier at M if and only if the frontier is linearly homogeneous in the neighborhood of M.

goods sufficient to use up their outlays. Producers will, in effect, be unable to redeem their input payments by exchanging them for goods at the announced prices. That is why marginal-cost pricing in this case leads to an infeasible point of consumer equilibrium. The reverse obviously holds where there are diseconomies of scale.

We will now prove that this budget constraint must be violated by the presence of scale economies and diseconomies, in precisely the directions we would expect from Euler's theorem. Consider the total cost function $C(y_1, \ldots, y_n, w_1, \ldots, w_m) = \Sigma w_k v_k$, where w_k is the price of input k and v_k is the quantity of that input utilized. Here $C(\cdot)$ is obviously the standard dual cost function of the economy's production set.

Next we define the production set to exhibit local scale economies (diseconomies) if, starting from an efficient input-output combination, a small proportionate increase in all input quantities permits a greater (less) than proportionate increase in all output quantities.

More formally, let $y_1', \ldots, y_n', v_1', \ldots, v_m'$ be a point on the efficient boundary of the production set, and select a small value $b > 0$, setting $dv_k = bv_k'$, all k. Then local scale economies are present if there exists a $b^* > b$ such that $(y_1^*, \ldots, y_n^*, v_1^*, \ldots, v_m^*)$ is in the production set, where $v_k^* = (1 + b)v_k', y_i^* \geq (1 + b^*)y_i'$ (all k, i). An analogous definition holds for diseconomies of scale. We may now prove:

PROPOSITION 4: At a point of local scale economies, a set of prices equal to marginal input costs will yield a value of output less than the cost of producing it (including cost of capital and wages of entrepreneurs) and will violate the economy's budget constraint (Walras's law).

PROOF:[10] Writing $dv_k = bv_k', dy_i \geq b^*y_i', b^* > b$, we have from our cost function

$$dC = \Sigma(\partial C/\partial y_i)dy_i \geq b^*\Sigma(\partial C/\partial y_i)y_i' = b^*\Sigma p_i y_i' \qquad (13)$$

if $p_i = \partial C/\partial y_i$, that is, prices are set at marginal costs. But we also have, holding input prices constant, $dC = \Sigma w_k dv_k = b\Sigma w_k v_k' = bC$. Comparing our two expressions for dC, we have at once $b^* \Sigma p_i y_i' \leq bC$ or

$$\Sigma p_i y_i' \leq (b/b^*)C < C = \Sigma w_k v_k'. \text{ Q.E.D.} \qquad (14)$$

Obviously, a similar proof holds for the case of diseconomies.

Now, comparing (14) with the economy's budget constraint (1), we see at once that (14) violates the (Walras's law) constraint where scale economies (diseconomies) are present. We see also from (14) that

---

[10] The argument goes beyond the usual analysis in avoiding any assumption of homogeneity or even homotheticity.

marginal-cost prices leave excess purchasing power in the hands of consumers, permitting them to seek to purchase more than the quantity vector of outputs that has been produced. Clearly, the reverse is true in the case of diseconomies of scale. Similarly, where and only where the production function is locally linearly homogeneous will the economy's budget constraint be satisfied by marginal-cost pricing, and the purchasing power of input suppliers will just suffice to buy the available outputs.[11]

IX. Implications for Competitive Equilibrium

Obviously marginal-cost pricing is not the only victim of this discussion. Competitive equilibrium with its zero profit requirement is also an impossible solution under (14) or the corresponding expression under diminishing returns to scale. In other words, the competitive solution, instead of being the universal solution of the welfare-maximization problem, may also break down as soon as the social production frontier fails to exhibit locally constant returns at an optimal solution point.

The problem, as we have seen, is this: Under pure competition with all products sold at their marginal costs, the budget constraint will be violated under diminishing returns to scale. Inputs will simply not receive income sufficient to buy the available output.

What appears to be the simple way out is to permit a residual income earner, the entrepreneur, who under diminishing returns earns, in the form of supernormal profit, the value of residual product (i.e., value of total product minus payment to inputs). But this does not get us out of the difficulty, for two interrelated reasons:

a) We no longer have a marginal-cost pricing solution. To see this, suppose additional entrepreneurs can be trained at graduate business schools at $25,000 each. Then, in a pure marginal-cost pricing solution, an entrepreneur can be paid only the annual equivalent of this amount and no more. To give him the residual product is an automatic violation of universal marginal-cost pricing. This is no mere definitional quibble, because, by the second best theorem, there is no special virtue in a regime of partial marginal-cost pricing.

b) More important, unless the stock of potential entrepreneurs is zero elastic, this solution is inconsistent with any equilibrium. It is inconsistent with any stationary number of firms. For, if diminishing returns prevail throughout, there must always be a residual product

---

[11] This argument demonstrates the "only if" portion of the first two parts of proposition 3. The third part is the well-known result that where marginal-cost pricing satisfies the budget constraint the Ramsey solution and the marginal-cost pricing solution will coincide.

592   JOURNAL OF POLITICAL ECONOMY

under marginal-cost pricing. But, then, if entrepreneurs are paid more than the marginal cost of their training, (perfectly competitive) graduate business schools must expand in number without limit!

Thus, from a general equilibrium point of view the problem of competitive equilibrium is similar under universally decreasing and under universally increasing returns. The difficulty of equilibrium under increasing returns is not merely that the firm makes losses. There are also deeper problems, precisely the other side of the coin of the decreasing returns case. First, under either universally increasing or diminishing returns, a finite number of firms consistent with competitive equilibrium cannot persist. Second, in either case, full marginal-cost pricing must violate Walras's law. In the increasing returns case, as was noted earlier, if firms price at marginal cost before taxes and receive subsidies to cover their deficits, the taxes to pay for those subsidies (by the inviolable budget constraint) must come from somewhere, and so after-tax prices cannot possibly equal marginal costs. We have just seen the guise this same problem takes where returns are diminishing. Thus, in both cases, competitive equilibrium is not compatible with the Walras's law constraint, and in both cases the constraint must prevail.

One may well wonder, then, how the standard literature is able to arrive at its well-known conclusion that all Pareto optima are competitive solutions and vice versa, even where production sets are strictly convex (i.e., returns to scale are diminishing). There are, in fact, several alternative sets of assumptions under which this result will hold. How satisfactory they are the reader will have to judge.

The first, as we have noted, takes the number of firms to be absolutely fixed. In that case the supply of entrepreneurship can be interpreted to be absolutely inelastic. But where either supply of or demand for *any* item is absolutely price inelastic, the Ramsey solution will automatically do the trick—for, as is easily proved, the Ramsey formula then requires that every item (except the one with zero elasticity) be priced precisely at its marginal cost. The Ramsey formula then automatically sets the price of the inelastic item at whatever level is necessary to meet the budget constraint since, by its zero elasticity, no price deviation from marginal cost for that item can cause any distortion in the amount of it that will be sold. The deviation between that price and the corresponding marginal cost becomes, in effect, a lump-sum tax or subsidy. In particular, with the supply of firms zero elastic, if returns are diminishing, those firms will earn a positive profit and all other goods and services will be priced at marginal cost under the Ramsey solution. This will automatically also be the optimal solution even though entrepreneurship obtains returns more than covering its marginal cost. For since its supply is assumed absolutely

QUASI OPTIMALITY   593

inelastic, such excessive payments cannot possibly induce a misallocation of resources. Of course, one can argue that this just assumes away
the problem of pricing and optimal resource allocation by simply
wishing into existence a residual distortion-proof sector of the economy.[12]

A second approach to the matter assumes implicitly that at some
small but finite output level firms no longer experience diseconomies
of scale so that at this least-cost output the firm's cost function is
locally linearly homogeneous. In addition, this approach assumes that
firms are then perfectly replicable without rising costs. Then, a process of expansion of outputs by sheer multiplication of enterprises
must yield a social production set which is a cone—it must be characterized by constant returns to scale. Since this is the condition under
which pure competition and marginal-cost pricing work, all is well,
the standard optimality results are rescued. But note that this is
accomplished by precluding diminishing returns, both for the firm
and for society. That is, once again it solves the problem by assuming
it away.

A third, and far more attractive, approach to the matter has been
called to my attention by my colleague, Hugo Sonnenschein. Suppose
diminishing returns in the social production set are attributable to
nonreplicability of firms. Rather, firms are taken to differ in efficiency
because inputs are heterogeneous in quality and available inputs of
any particular quality are absolutely fixed in supply. Then, if demand
shifts outward, entry by successively less efficient firms will be induced, and rents to superior inputs will constitute the lump-sum
payments needed to make the competitive equilibrium payments possible. Here again, for this solution to work, Euler's theorem tells us
that the firms must exhibit locally constant returns at the equilibrium
point since otherwise the rent payments will not add up to the required amount. But despite constant returns for individual enterprises, we now end up with diminishing returns in the social production frontier and an optimal competitive solution.[13] This is, of course,

[12] Analogous simplifying assumptions occur in many parts of the literature. While
often fully justified by their convenience for analysis, they can also be seriously misleading when extended without caution. A relevant example occurs in the literature on
two-part tariffs which are sometimes taken to solve the problem of unprofitability of
marginal-cost pricing in the presence of scale economies. The notion is that one can
achieve full Pareto optimality by imposing upon, say, electricity users an inescapable
connection charge just sufficient in magnitude to prevent a deficit and then supplying
as much electricity to customers as they want at a price equal to marginal cost. But this
arrangement is optimal only if the connection charge leads no customers to give up
using electricity. If demand for connections is not exactly zero elastic, optimality
requires equality between the connection charge and the marginal cost of connection,
and that price will, in general, not keep the supplier's losses to zero.
[13] The next section describes the geometry of this solution.

594   JOURNAL OF POLITICAL ECONOMY

the Ricardian model, and the brilliance of the construct is thus once again confirmed.

There is no doubt, then, that the problem can be dealt with in diminishing-returns cases, if these returns do take one of the forms just assumed. However, before leaping to the conclusion that there is no problem, several observations are pertinent:

1. The two preceding models take the equilibrium of the firm to be characterized by locally constant returns to scale. If the firm's production set exhibits diminishing returns throughout, there can indeed be no equilibrium involving any finite number of firms. Such firms will always produce a return exceeding the marginal cost of their creation, and the economy must constantly move toward an infinite number of enterprises, each of zero size.

2. Diminishing returns to society may indeed be attributable to limited supplies of heterogeneous inputs. But they need not arise only from this source. For example, they may obviously be caused by externalities, which make the cost of operation of a firm dependent upon the total number of firms in operation. If, for example, firms are sources of pollution which reduces worker efficiency, this clearly can cause diminishing social returns even though added firms are perfect duplicates of their predecessors. Similarly, if some sort of communication or other forms of coordination are required among some proportion of the firms in operation, the resulting combinatorial activities must involve costs which rise disproportionately with their number (even if at a diminishing rate). This combinatorial problem may very well be a significant source of diminishing returns in practice.

The point is, one cannot simply assume that the social production frontier must be linearly homogeneous in the absence of obstacles to the replication of firms. But then, as we have seen, we encounter all the problems for the achievement of a Pareto optimum which are the focus of this paper.

We may also note, as an incidental result:

PROPOSITION 5: If there exists no Pareto optimal allocation of resources at which the production set is locally linearly homogeneous, then there exists no allocation of resources that is compatible with competitive equilibrium.

This proposition is a trivial consequence of two well-known results: (1) that at a competitive equilibrium the production set is locally linearly homogeneous,[14] and (2) that (in the absence of externalities) a competitive equilibrium is always Pareto optimal.

[14] See the mathematical appendix to Hicks (1963). The argument is easy to express in diagrammatic terms. The input cost function is $c = \Sigma w_k r_k$, where w_k is the unit price of

QUASI OPTIMALITY 595

But a more explicit way of showing this in terms of our simple models may be more illuminating. A competitive equilibrium requires the consumer's (community's) budget line to be tangent simultaneously both to the production boundary and to a consumer (community) indifference curve. For if it is not tangent to the former, producers will not be in equilibrium, while if it is not tangent to the latter, consumers will not be in equilibrium. This, in simplistic terms, is tantamount to the standard requirement for competitive equilibrium that the budget hyperplane serve as a separating hyperplane between the production set and the set of points preferred to or indifferent to the equilibrium point.

But, say, where returns are diminishing (fig. 2) the separating hyperplane, DE, at the optimal point, M, will not go through point B as the Walras's law condition (1) requires. That is, someone must receive income which represents neither a transfer nor the sale of resources at a fixed price. But where the firm is also subject to diminishing returns, these earnings amount to a positive profit to firms representing the difference between the value of output and the (lower) cost of inputs. As we have seen, while this may occur, it cannot possibly be a competitive equilibrium. No matter how large the number of firms, still more will enter, and that can scarcely be considered a state of equilibrium.

X. Evaluation

One of our central conclusions is that with fixed nondiscriminatory prices one simply does not, in general, have the option of ignoring the budget constraint, decreeing a regime of universal marginal-cost prices and covering the deficits by subsidy. Marginal-cost prices may simply promise the consumer more than the economy can offer because they violate the (Walras's law) rules of the price system.

Under these circumstances, there are four alternative avenues for public policy if it is concerned with optimality of resource allocation:

1. Ramsey pricing with its attendant loss in potential welfare.[15]
2. Lump-sum payments along with "optimal-marginal cost prices,"

---

input k and r_k is the quantity of that input used. This cost function is clearly linearly homogeneous, indeed it is a hyperplane through the origin in input space. At a competitive equilibrium this cost hyperplane must be tangent to the production hypersurface (with output measured in units whose equilibrium price is one). Hence the latter must be locally homogeneous of first degree, i.e., all its derivatives at that point must be the same as those of a linearly homogeneous function.

[15] It is perhaps suggestive that in the multiproduct example constructed by Dietrich Fischer the percentage welfare loss from substitution of the Ramsey solution for a true optimum is relatively small. The losses generated by marginal-cost pricing in the absence of a lump-sum transfer are considerably larger.

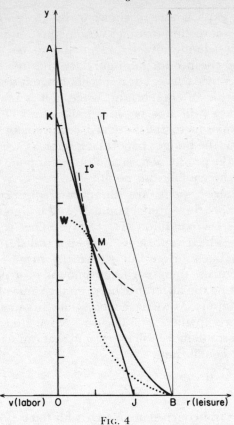

FIG. 4

as given by the slope of the price line, BT (fig. 4). The lump-sum payments will shift the consumer's budget line until, with the total payment equal to BJ, the new budget line, JK, achieves tangency with the production possibility locus (and the tangent indifference curve) at the *optimum optimorum, M*. Of course, if no one can find any way to arrange a lump-sum payment this approach falls to the ground. We have seen that the conventional welfare analysis, implicitly, uses this way of dealing with the problem by taking the number of firms to be fixed exogenously, so that profits, in effect, become a lump-sum receipt which affect no economic decisions; but this is hardly a solution we can accept as a description of reality. We have also seen that if firms exhibit constant returns to scale in equilibrium, but there are socially diminishing returns because of limited quantities of inputs of given quality, then Ricardian rents can serve as the required lump-sum payments.

3. Variable prices to the consumer which can be described by a price-response function $p = P(y,r)$. His price line is then no longer

linear. In that case one can, in theory, design the price line cleverly to start out at *B* and curl about to achieve a tangent with the production frontier at optimal point *M*, avoiding tangencies at all other points (curve *BW* in fig. 4).[16] Such a price system may, however, lose the beautiful automatic properties given to the standard price mechanism by the invisible hand. The resource allocator takes on more than the task of the ideal central planner, for he must first determine the true optimum and then calculate an appropriate price-response function which may very well have to be different for every consumer. The mind does, indeed, boggle at this prospect.

4. Finally, we have the possibility: Central planning and direct control of outputs that impose optimal output vector, *M,* upon the economy. There is no point in reentering here the discussion of the pros and cons of this approach.

XI. On the Possibility of Lump-Sum Taxes or Subsidies

We have seen that the possibility of lump-sum payments plays a key role in the discussion. As we know, marginal-cost pricing can work, in theory, with the aid of lump-sum taxes (where scale economies predominate in the economy) or lump-sum subsidies (where diseconomics predominate).

A lump-sum payment may be defined as a payment which has absolutely no influence upon behavior anywhere in the economy. In principle, this may occur in one of two ways: First, if there exists any activity which is perfectly price inelastic then it can, by definition, be taxed or subsidized without any consequences. Second, the amount of the payment may be set in a way which is totally independent of any individual's behavior, and so, since no one can do anything to change the amount of his payment, its incentive effects will be zero.

I have already considered the former in my discussion of rents. I shall now argue that the latter, to which I will refer as a pure lump-sum payment, is, in the long run, not possible either in practice or even in principle. That is, I will argue that it is, in principle, impossible to design taxes and subsidies which really do have the required zero incentive effects, except, perhaps, for a limited period of time.

A pure lump-sum payment must be a fixed tax upon (or subsidy to) each individual, regardless of wealth or income (provided it must also be paid by the person's estate in case of suicide—as insurance companies found, to their regret, at the onset of the Great Depression). We may note first that such a payment raises serious equity issues. For

---

[16] For an analogous suggestion in another context, see Klevorick (1966). On nonlinear prices as a means to increase welfare, see, e.g., Faulhaber and Panzar (1976), Goldman, Leland, and Sibley (1977), and Willig (1978).

example, where diseconomies predominate, what is required is an annual payment to consumers, perhaps an equal amount to each person, or an amount that is randomly determined. This will inevitably be regressive—the "head payment" must benefit a Rockefeller as much as it does the poor (at least in terms of expected value, if the payments are assigned randomly).[17]

However, even subsidies so determined (or their counterpart taxes) will not be the pure lump-sum payments we are seeking because they must inevitably serve as a subsidy for large families—as an incentive to births. For if they are not offered to the newborn, the entire system must break down in one generation, while if they do, they must act as an incentive to population growth, a consequence which, in the long run, may prove neither minor nor very desirable. Thus, if economic inducements have any effect upon the rate of increase of population, it follows that such taxes and subsidies cannot be lump sum after all.[18] Since a perfect inelasticity assumption seems no more plausible here than elsewhere in the economy, we may conclude that:

PROPOSITION 6: Pure lump-sum payments are impossible in the long run.

XII. Concluding Comment

The simple general-equilibrium models of this paper have shown us the relationship between a Ramsey allocation and one that is truly optimal, as well as the reasons the Ramsey solution is the best one can hope for in an economy controlled by a system of fixed and nondiscriminatory prices and in which lump-sum payments are not possible either for political reasons or because there simply is no way to design them.

Pure competition can bring us to a truly optimal solution only if at that solution the budget constraint for the economy happens to be satisfied. Indeed, if there exists a purely competitive equilibrium it

[17] This is not quite true. The payments can, for example, be set on the basis of family income the year before the system goes into effect—i.e., payments can be determined on any basis which individuals can no longer affect. However, from then on one must either turn to an equal or a randomized basis of apportionment, or, alternatively, one must adhere to the original tax rates, based on historic income or wealth of the taxpayer, forcing formerly wealthy persons to continue to pay their high taxes even if they become indigent.

[18] It will not do the trick for government to try to compensate for a predominance of, say, diseconomies in the private sector by expanding governmental activities which offer scale economies. The requirements of optimal resource allocation predetermine the magnitude of each government activity as well as that of each activity in the private sector. It can surely not help in the achievement of an optimum for the government to engage in nonoptimal activities just as a means to prevent nonoptimal decisions in the private sector.

QUASI OPTIMALITY 599

must necessarily satisfy the budget constraint. For pure competition does require the firm's production function to be locally homogeneous of first degree at the equilibrium point, and this guarantees that marginal-cost prices will just suffice to cover total cost.

Looked at another way, what the analysis has shown is that, if at every Pareto optimal point the economy's production set happens to exhibit either (local) scale economies or diseconomies, then without lump-sum payments there is no way in which an ordinary price system can lead the economy to any such optimum. The second-best Ramsey solution will then be the best that is achievable with the aid of a standard pricing approach.

References

Arrow, K. J. "An Extension of the Basic Theorems of Classical Welfare Economics." In *Proceedings of the Second Berkeley Symposium on Mathematical Statistics and Probability*. Berkeley: Univ. California Press, 1951.

Baumol, W. J., and Bradford, D. F. "Optimal Departures from Marginal Cost Pricing." *A.E.R.* 60 (June 1970): 265–83.

Debreu, Gerard. "The Coefficient of Resource Utilization." *Econometrica* 19 (July 1951): 273–92.

Edgeworth, F. Y. *Papers Relating to Political Economy*. London: Macmillan, 1925.

Faulhaber, G. R., and Panzar, J. C. "Optimal Two-Part Tariffs and Self Selection." Mimeographed. Holmdel, N.J.: Bell Laboratories, 1976.

Fischer, Dietrich. "Comparison of Resource Allocation Mechanisms in an Economy with Two Goods: Some Numerical Examples." Discussion Paper no. 77-20, New York Univ., Dept. Econ., Center Appl. Econ., November 1977.

Goldman, M. B.; Leland, H. E.; and Sibley, David S. "Some Qualitative Properties of Non-Uniform Prices." Mimeographed. Holmdel, N.J.: Bell Laboratories, 1977.

Hicks, J. R. *The Theory of Wages*. 2d ed. London: Macmillan, 1963.

Hotelling, Harold. "The General Welfare in Relation to Problems of Taxation and of Railway and Utility Rates." *Econometrica* 6 (July 1938): 242–69.

Klevorick, Alvin. "The Graduated Fair Return: A Regulatory Proposal." *A.E.R.* 56 (June 1966): 477–84.

Novshek, William, and Sonnenschein, Hugo. "Cournot and Walras Equilibrium." Mimeographed. Research Memorandum no. 224, Princeton Univ., Econometric Res. Program, February 1978.

Ramsey, Frank. "A Contribution to the Theory of Taxation." *Econ. J.* 37 (March 1927): 47–61.

Willig, R. D. "Pareto-Superior Nonlinear Outlay Schedules." *Bell J. Econ.* 9, no. 1 (Spring 1978): 56–69.

[5]

ON THE OPTIMALITY OF PUBLIC-GOODS PRICING WITH EXCLUSION DEVICES

WILLIAM J. BAUMOL and JANUSZ A. ORDOVER*

It is a standard doctrine that the optimal price to consumers of a pure public good is zero because, by definition, there is no cost to anyone if that good serves an additional user. This is true *even if exclusion from the use of the good is easy*, so that a nonzero price is a practical possibility. So long as the good possesses the property HEAD calls 'supply jointness', or which some of us have elsewhere called 'undepletability', it would seem that a zero price for the good is desirable if somehow it can be made available at that price.

It will be argued here, however, using the RAMSEY theorem on quasi-optimal pricing, that a zero price is normally *not* Pareto optimal for such a quasi-public good, *i.e.*, one for which supply jointness holds but exclusion is possible. That is, it will be suggested that resource allocation may benefit by the imposition of positive prices for public goods in cases where such prices are collectable.

This may imply that there is more to be gained that might otherwise have been suspected from the supply of these goods by private firms or other organizations outside the public sector. Suppose a private firm can adopt some device that permits it to exclude potential beneficiaries from the use of the public good and is therefore able to charge a price for its services. Since it is claimed here that a nonzero price is (quasi) optimal, may it not follow that a profit seeker can in such a case supply a public good on remunerative terms and do so at prices consistent with optimal resource allocation?

* Princeton and New York Universities and New York University, respectively. This paper was read at the Annual Meeting of the American Economic Association, Dallas, Texas, December 1976. Our research was sponsored by a grant from the Office of Science Information Services of the National Science Foundation.

WILLIAM J. BAUMOL AND JANUSZ A. ORDOVER

We will see that while profitable supply is indeed possible in such a case, the prices that a private supplier is likely to charge will differ in rather interesting ways from the quasi-optimal price levels.

Since the cost function will play a critical role throughout this paper, it is useful to begin with a few comments about its form. If we take $y_1, \ldots, y_m$ to be the numbers of users of m excludable public goods (*e.g.*, scientific journals), as defined here and $x_1, \ldots, x_n$ to be associated quality variables, *e.g.*, number of pages in the different journals), then the total cost functions, $C(\cdot)$, for the production of this set of outputs is given by

$$C(y, x) = C(y_1, \ldots, y_m, x_1, \ldots, x_n) \tag{1}$$

with

$$C_i = \partial C/\partial y_i = 0 \text{ and } C_j = \partial C/\partial x_j > 0, \ (\forall y_i, x_j \neq 0) \tag{2}$$

Clearly $\partial C/\partial y_i$ is the marginal cost of supplying an additional unit of ith good. In many instances, we can assume that the number of users, v_i, of the ith public good depends not only on the relevant prices but also on x_i. For example, the intensity of use of a scientific journal surely depends, *ceteris paribus*, on the 'quality' of that journal[1]. In the next section we derive quasi-optimal prices taking the output vector, x, as already determined.

I. THE RAMSEY THEOREM: BRIEF REVIEW

The RAMSEY Theorem (1928) on quasi-optimal pricing indicates the pattern of prices that will yield the best (Pareto optimal) allocation of resources when the optimum is constrained by a budgetary condition[2]. One of its several variants proved in the literature [see, *e.g.*, BAUMOL and BRADFORD (1970)] asserts that since, in general, marginal cost pricing will be inconsistent with the budget constraint, the quasi-optimal difference between price and marginal cost for a particular output, i, is

1. See SPENCE (1975) for an extensive discussion, albeit in a rather different context.
2. See ORDOVER and WILLIG (1976) for another application of this approach to the pricing of excludable public goods.

6

ON THE OPTIMALITY OF PUBLIC-GOODS PRICING

$$p_i - C_i = -v(R_i - C_i) \qquad (3)$$

where v is a Lagrange multiplier and R_i and C_i are, respectively, the marginal revenue and marginal cost of good i. This result indicates that where marginal-cost pricing does not bring in enough revenue to cover the budgetary constraint then prices must deviate from marginal costs. The set of deviations that satisfies the constraint and yet minimizes the misallocation of resources resulting from the differences between prices and marginal costs are those given by (3).

The form of the RAMSEY theorem that has in fact received most wide-spread attention is a special case which is not universally valid, but holds only when all the pertinent cross-elasticities of demand are zero. In that case it can be proved that

$$(p_i - C_i)/p_i = k/E_i \qquad (4)$$

where E_i is the price elasticity of demand of commodity i. This last result asserts that quasi-optimality requires the percentage deviation of price from marginal cost $(p_i - C_i)/p_i$, to vary inversely with elasticity of demand. This conclusion has a simple intuitive explanation. It asserts that if prices must be raised above marginal costs in order to meet a budgetary requirement, then the largest such rises must be instituted for those products whose demands will suffer the smallest consequent distortion from their otherwise optimal levels, *i.e.*, for those items whose demands are most *in*elastic.

II. THE INEVITABILITY OF THE BUDGET CONSTRAINT

Returning to our excludable public good with its zero cost of additional users, it is obvious immediately that a marginal-cost price (*i.e., a zero price,* $p_i = \partial C/\partial y_i = 0$) for the use of such a good, i, will not cover its total production cost. A budgetary constraint then usually enters the issue in an obvious manner. For even if the good is supplied by the public sector it is often an article of public policy to require the consumers of such goods to cover their costs.

The imposition of such a budget constraint may well be considered an artificial requirement – an interference with optimal resource

7

WILLIAM J. BAUMOL AND JANUSZ A. ORDOVER

allocation which arises only because legislators are slavishly devoted to accounting conventions. That is, it may be argued that in such a case the public would be served better by a subsidy program which permits the public good to be priced at its (zero) marginal cost.

However, it is easy to show that, in general, this inference is not valid. To bring the reason out clearly, let us deal with a polar case – that in which the n commodities in the economy all happen to be public goods. Then, obviously every good should be subsidized, according to the preceding argument. That is, each output should be priced at zero (marginal cost) and the deficits should all be made up by the public treasury. However, the funds for these subsidies must ultimately derive from some source outside the government, *i.e.*, from taxes. Since lumpsum taxes are a figment of the welfare economists' imagination, these must be taxes upon *some* good or service, perhaps on labor (income). In that case each such good will be sold at an after-tax price which is *not* equal to zero, after all. Thus the budget constraint turns out ultimately to be inescapable and marginal-cost prices unimplementable. Whether we consider the matter in terms of optimal taxation or quasioptimal pricing, we are always brought back to the same question – what departures from marginal cost prices are required for optimal resource allocation?

III. REQUIREMENTS FOR PARETO OPTIMAL PRICING OF PUBLIC GOODS

Necessary conditions for the quasi-optimal prices for these public goods now follow directly from (2), and (3). Writing R_i for $\partial R/\partial y_i$, *etc.*, we obtain

$$p_i = - v R_i \text{ or } p_i/p_k = R_i/R_k \tag{5}$$

for any two public goods, i and k.

The relationship is illustrated in *Figure 1* which shows the demand and marginal revenue curves for two public goods 1 and 2, which are subject to a common budget constraint. Suppose the price for item 1 is p_{1a} at which price is twice the corresponding marginal revenue. ($A_1 = 2B_1$). Then the quasi-optimal price of item 2 must be p_{2a} which is also twice its corresponding marginal revenue. However,

ON THE OPTIMALITY OF PUBLIC-GOODS PRICING

Figure 1

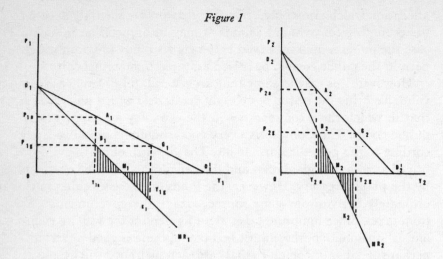

these will not be the true quasi-optimal prices for two reasons (only one of which *necessarily* applies in this case):

i. The total revenue from the two goods at these prices may or may not cover the total cost of the public goods. Suppose, for example, that the total revenue (the sum of the areas, $Oy_{1a}B_1D_1 + Oy_{2a}B_2D_2$, under the two marginal revenue curves) turns out to be insufficient for the purpose. In that case both equilibrium points must move closer to the revenue-maximizing outputs at which the marginal revenue curves cut the horizontal axes. However, in any such move the relative prices must continue to satisfy (5) as p_{1a} and p_{2a} do.

ii. Suppose now that the total revenue *does* just suffice to satisfy the budget constraint at prices p_{1a} and p_{2a}. Then there will generally be a lower pair of prices to the right of the revenue-maximizing points which bring in the same total revenue as before and which also satisfy (5). For example, in our linear case, two prices which obviously satisfy (5) are p_{1g} and p_{2g} at which $p_1 = -R_1$ and $p_2 = -R_2$. (It is not difficult to show that p_{1g} and p_{2g} yield, respectively the same total revenues as p_{1a} and p_{2a})[3].

3. This can either be proved geometrically by observing that y_{1a} and y_{1g} must divide OD'_1 into three equal parts, noting the congruence of the shaded triangles, or it can be shown algebraically, using expression (6) setting $p(y_{1a}) = 2R_1(y_{1a})$ and $p(y_{1g}) = -R_1(y_{1g})$.

9

WILLIAM J. BAUMOL AND JANUSZ A. ORDOVER

These lower prices will obviously be closer to the zero marginal costs for these public goods than are p_{1a} and p_{2a}. For a concrete illustration assume again that the two demand curves are the linear so that we have $(i = 1,2)$

$$p_i = a_i - b_i y_i \quad R_i = d(a_i y_i - b_i y_i^2)/dy_i = a_i - 2b_i y_i \qquad (6)$$

If C is the total cost of the public goods we have the two requirements for quasi optimality:

$$\frac{p_1}{p_2} = \frac{a_1 - b_1 y_1}{a_2 - b_2 y_2} = \frac{a_1 - 2b_1 y_1}{a_2 - 2b_2 y_2} = \frac{R_1}{R_2} \qquad (7a)$$

and the budget constraint

$$C = p_1 y_1 + p_2 y_2 = a_1 y_1 - b_1 y_1^2 + a_2 y_2 - b_2 y_2^2 \qquad (7b)$$

Relation (7a) can be shown by cross multiplication and elimination to reduce simply to

$$a_2 b_1 y_1 = a_1 b_2 y_2 \text{ or } y_2 = (a_2 b_1/a_1 b_2) y_1 \qquad (8)$$

which shows that the quasi-optimal value of y_2 will vary monotonically with that of y_1. When substituted into the budget equation, this yields a quadratic equation in y_1:

$$C = a_1 y_1 - b_1 y_1^2 + (a_2^2 b_1/a_1 b_2) y_1 - (a_2^2 b_1^2/a_1^2 b_2) y_1^2$$

which is usually satisfied by two values of y_1, and hence two values of y_2, p_1 and p_2. The quasi-optimal values in these pairs of solutions are those corresponding to the higher value of y_1. By (8) this also necessarily gives us the higher value of y_2 (and by the negative slope of the demand curves) the lower of the pairs of values of p_1 and p_2.

In the case where cross elasticities are zero (as in our diagrammatic and linear algebraic illustrations) we can write a substitute expression for (5) based on the inverse elasticity formula (4) rather than on (3). Setting $C_i = 0$ in (4), we obtain

10

ON THE OPTIMALITY OF PUBLIC-GOODS PRICING

$$p_i/p_i = 1 = k/E_i$$

$$E_i = E_w \text{ for all pairs of public goods } i \text{ and } w$$

(9)

In the linear case this tells us immediately that all sets of quasi-optimal equilibrium points must divide the tangents to their demand curves proportionately, since it will be recalled from MARSHALL's geometric argument that the ratio of the two segments of such a tangent gives the elasticity at any point along a demand curve[4].

4. We can also prove the following:

Proposition. Given *linear* demand curves in two markets, I and II, let outputs y_1 and y_2 in the respective markets be such that $p_1/R_1 = p_2/R_2$ and that they yield total revenues R_I and R_{II}. If y_1' and y_2' *also* yield, respectively total revenues R_I and R_{II}, then the corresponding prices and marginal revenues must satisfy $p_1'/R_1' = p_2'/R_2'$.

Proof. Let the demand curve and marginal revenue in market i satisfy (6). Then we have:

$$p_i - R_i = b_i y_i \qquad (f.1)$$

Equality of total revenue at outputs y_i and y_i' requires

$$a_i y_i - b_i y_i^2 = a_i y_i' - b_i (y_i')^2$$

or

$$a_i (y_i - y') = b_i [y_i^2 - (y_i')^2] = b_i (y_i - y_i')(y_i + y_i')$$

That is,

$$a_i/b_i = y_i + y_i' \text{ or } y_i' = (a_i/b_i) - y_i \qquad (f.2)$$

so that by (f. 1),

$$p_i' = a_i - b_i y_i' = a_i - b_i [(a_i/b_i) - y_i] = b_i y_i = p_i - R_i$$

and by (f. 2),

$$R_i' = d(a_i y_i' - b_i y_i'^2)/dy_i' = a_i - 2 b_i y' = a_i - 2 b_i [(a_i/b_i) - y_i]$$

$$= - a_i + 2 b_i y_i = - R_i$$

Thus,

$$p_i'/R_i' = - (p_i - R_i)/R_i = 1 - p_i/R_i$$

It follows that if $p_1/R_1 = p_2/R_2$ then $p_1'/R_1' = p_2'/R_2'$.

Since, as shown in the text, because of the quadratic character of the relationship there are no more than two solutions to the quasi-optimality problem in this linear case, y_i and y_i' are the only solutions to our problem.

11

WILLIAM J. BAUMOL AND JANUSZ A. ORDOVER

IV. PROVISION OF PUBLIC GOODS BY A
PROFIT-MAXIMIZING SUPPLIER

Once exclusion devices have been imposed there is no reason why public goods need be supplied by a government agency. A private firm can charge prices for its services and make a profit in the process. It is easy to see what will happen in this case and to determine how the prices will differ from their quasi-optimal values.

In this case the necessary condition for an (interior) profit maximum[5] $C_i = R_i$, becomes (because for our public good $C_i = 0$):

$$R_i = 0 \text{ or } E_i = 1$$

The reason is clear. With all costs effectively fixed (so far as volume of usage is concerned) the supplier will maximize his profit by maximizing his total revenue. In this case sales and profit maximization collapse into a single objective.

In terms of *Figure 1* the profit-maximizing supplier will always end up at outputs M_1 and M_2 where the marginal-revenue curves cut the horizontal axes. Prices will be above their quasi-optimal levels unless maximal total revenues produce no return over total costs. If the budget constraint calls for a total revenue below its maximal level, revenue can be reduced from its maximum either by an increase or a decrease in all prices and, as we have seen, it is the latter which will constitute the quasi-optimal prices.

It should be noted that *while the prices charged by the profit maximizing supplier of a public good will be undesirably high, they need not be worse from the point of view of resource allocation than the zero prices that are traditionally recommended.* That is, the giving away of goods for which a price ought to be charged does not necessarily lead to a better use of resources than the prices charged by a profit maximizer.

---

5. Obviously it is being assumed here that the supplying firm is a monopolist. It is difficult to see how it could be otherwise with all marginal costs zero (average cost declining steadily throughout). In this case surely competition is neither sustainable nor desirable, except, perhaps, if the products can usefully be differentiated. *Cf.* however, OAKLAND (1974).

12

ON THE OPTIMALITY OF PUBLIC-GOODS PRICING

V. PROVISION OF PUBLIC GOODS BY A PRIVATE
NON-PROFIT GROUP

A third group of organizations involved in the supply of public goods, particularly in the dissemination of information, is made up of private non-profit institutions. Notable is the activity of the professional associations, which issue journals, sponsor publication and distribution of books and engage in other such activities.

Relatively little work has been done in the construction of models of the behavior of this type of firms but for our purposes this task cannot be avoided. We will see that several approaches suggest themselves readily and that may permit some inferences about the welfare implications of the resulting price behavior.

We will consider three prototypes of behavior which can be described as:

a) organizational quasi-optimization;
b) physical volume maximization;
c) membership maximization.

The first of these simply amounts to the adoption of a set of prices that are quasi-optimal in two restricted senses: i) they take into account the budgetary requirements only of the non-profit organization supplying the public good; ii) they consider the welfare of some limited set of individuals, *e.g.*, members of the organization. In this model we assume, perhaps rather implausibly, that the officers of the organization understand either instinctively or from experience the requirements of quasi-optimality. They set out to maximize benefits to the members of the organization subject to the requirements for its financial viability.

In that case all the formal requirements of quasi-optimal pricing will be satisfied. That is, pricing will necessarily satisfy equation (3) and the budget constraint so that, if the situation is characterized by the appropriate concavity-convexity conditions, the unique set of quasi-optimal prices for the organization will be employed. This would seem to suggest that an organization that behaves in accord with the model we are discussing will produce results that are socially quasi-optimal. But this is not necessarily so because of the parochial

13

WILLIAM J. BAUMOL AND JANUSZ A. ORDOVER

basis for its calculations, considering only its own costs and the interests of its membership.

It is tempting to argue that where membership in such an organization is completely unrestricted and frictions are nonexistent, the conflict between the objectives of the organization and those of society as a whole will disappear. For everyone whose welfare is affected by the decisions of the non-profit organization will presumably join it to protect his own interests. If entry into the organization is unrestricted, then the Lagrangian maximand for the organization will have precisely the same form as that in the Pareto-optimality analysis of the RAMSEY problem, and it will yield what are formally the same necessary conditions for quasi-optimality (5). However, the correspondance may still be illusory. True, freedom of entry into the organization may make the ordinal welfare function of its members correspond to that of society. However, there seems to be no reason for its profit (zero-loss) constraint to be the same as that of society. The costs that the organization must cover are only a portion of those which society must cover and the maximum yielded under such a parochial constraint may be as far from the social optimum as a set of tolls for a number of bridges which are designed to make each bridge self-supporting.

The outputs of a non-profit organization may not consist entirely of consumers' goods. Some of its products may be used by firms – *e.g.*, the information provided by chemical journals may be helpful in corporate research and medical journals are intended to be useful to doctors who are also private entrepreneurs. It should be noted that, if taxes on rents are truly lump sum, *i.e.*, if all activity levels in the economy are truly inelastic with respect to such taxes[6], RAMSEY theory appears to require all such rents to be taxed away to help defray any shortfall in revenues *vis-à-vis* total cost. This is brought out most dramatically by the inverse – elasticity condition (4) of RAMSEY analysis. The reason, of course, is that such taxes will help to meet the profit constraint without producing any distortion in resource allocation.

6. In an unpublished paper (1975), FELDSTEIN has recently questioned this premise. One device that can be used to tax rents is the licence fee; see STIGLITZ and DASGUPTA (1971) and DASGUPTA and STIGLITZ (1972).

14

ON THE OPTIMALITY OF PUBLIC-GOODS PRICING

In a world of perfect competition, including competition among non-profit organizations, the fact that the organization is supplying producers' rather than consumers' goods would be irrelevant, and optimality for the organizations would also correspond to optimality for society and would also automatically satisfy a zero-profit constraint. But in reality such organizations are not competitors and it is then quite natural to assume that the organizational goal will be to maximize the total profits, *i.e.*, producers' surplus of *its* members, subject to the budget constraint, whereas society's goal is to maximize the sum of consumer and producer surpluses. Thus the nonprofit organization behaves as if it were a profit maximizing monopoly which can not only select its output level but also the vector of prices (w_r) of the inputs it supplies to others subject to the constraint that

$$\sum w_i x_i = C$$

We obtain the important proposition that if a nonprofit organization prices its products so as to maximize profits of its members then it cannot be expected to charge socially optimal prices.

We come now to the second and analytically the most interesting of the behavioral models for a nonprofit organization. The pattern we now consider is also a rather plausible one – a case in which the managers of the nonprofit organization consider their products sufficiently beneficial to make it desirable to maximize their usage within the limits imposed by the organization's budgetary constraint. Where several products are supplied, if $y_1, \ldots, y_n$ are the quantities of the usage levels of its various outputs, and $w_1, \ldots, w_n$ are the respective weights assigned to them by the group, the organization's goal becomes maximization of $\sum w_i y_i$ subject to the budget constraint $\sum p_i y_i = M$. This yields the Lagrangian

$$L(\cdot) = \sum w_i y_i + v(\sum p_i y_i - M) \tag{10}$$

Rather than dealing directly with prices, it is more convenient to determine the optimal output vector, y^0, which in turn determines, through the inverse demand functions, the optimal price vector, p^0. Thus, differentiating with respect to quantities, we obtain the obvious requirement

15

WILLIAM J. BAUMOL AND JANUSZ A. ORDOVER

$$w_i + v R_i = 0 \text{ or } w_i/w_k = R_i/R_k \ \forall i, k \tag{11}$$

The similarity of the requirement to the RAMSEY condition (5) is striking. What (11) suggests, in fact, is that the behavior of our output-maximizing organization will be quasi-optimal if the weights, w_i, are chosen to be equal to the corresponding quasi-optimal prices, p_i. Of course, there seems to be little if any reason to expect such a set of equalities to hold, *i.e.*, for such an organization to know, much less care, about the RAMSEY prices as evaluators of its outputs.

It is easy to show that, at the optimum (as at the RAMSEY solution) marginal revenues must turn out to be negative for those outputs that are assigned positive weights[7], $w_i > 0$.

We can translate (11) directly into the following form which brings the optimal prices into the calculation explicitly:

$$w_i = -v\left[p_i + \sum_j \left(\frac{\partial p_j}{\partial y_i} y_j \right) \right] \ \forall i \tag{12}$$

As a more convenient substitute for the concept of cross-elasticity of demand, let us define the *flexibility* of the inverse-demand function as[8]

$$\Phi_{ji} = (\partial p_j / \partial y_i) \ (y_i / p_j)$$

---

7. For if we write our constraint as $R = \Sigma p_i y_i > M$, the KUHN-TUCKER conditions turn out to include:

$$w_i + v R_i \leq 0 \quad y_i (w_i + v R_i) = 0 \quad \forall i$$
$$R = \Sigma p_i y_i \geq M \quad v(R - M) = 0$$
$$v \geq 0$$

The first of these conditions tells us immediately that $v \neq 0$ since otherwise all $w_i \leq 0$, *i.e.*, all outputs must be accorded nonpositive weights. It follows that with $w_i > 0$ and $v > 0$ we must have $R_i \leq -w_i/v < 0$, as was to be proved. It also follows by the second equation that since $v > 0$, we must have $R = M$, *i.e.*, the constraint must be effective at an optimum.

8. Note that despite the similarity of the expressions, Φ_{ij} is not, in general, the reciprocal of E_{ji}, the cross elasticity of demand between products i and j, since in elasticities other *prices* are held constant while in flexibilities it is other *output quantities* that are not permitted to vary.

16

ON THE OPTIMALITY OF PUBLIC-GOODS PRICING

Using this concept (12) yields the following convenient expression for optimal prices:

$$\frac{p_i}{p_k} = \frac{w_i}{w_k} \frac{1 + \sum_j (p_j y_j / p_k y_k)\, \Phi_{jk}}{1 + \sum_j (p_j y_j / p_i y_i)\, \Phi_{ij}} \quad \forall i, k \tag{13}$$

where the summations may be interpreted as weighted sum of the Φ_{ji}, with the (non-negative) weights given by relative expenditures on products j and i. In particular, where all demands are independent, so that $\Phi_{ji} = 0$ for $i \neq j$ and $\Phi_{ii} = -1/E_{ii}$, where E_{ii} is own elasticity of demand for product i, the last relationship becomes

$$\frac{p_i}{p_k} = \frac{w_i}{w_k} \frac{1 - 1/E_{kk}}{1 - 1/E_{ii}} \tag{14}$$

which seems to bear some resemblance to the well-known RAMSEY *formula* (4) that relates quasi-optimal prices inversely to elasticities of demand. However, some care must be exercised in the interpretation of (13) and (14). For example, a quick glance at these equations suggests, counter intuitively, that quasi-optimal prices will vary directly with the weights, that is, that an increase in the value that the organization places on the physical volume of its output i, the higher should be the price it should adopt for the good and hence, presumably, the smaller the quantity it should sell. However, a simple exercise in comparative statics with our Lagrangian (10) shows that $\partial y_i / \partial w_i > 0$, as intuition leads us to expect[9].

9. We have the first-order conditions

$$w_i + v R_i = 0 \quad \forall i$$
$$R - M = 0$$

Differentiating totally, assuming $dw_1 > 0$, $dw_i = 0$ $i \neq 1$, we have

$$v \sum R_{1j}\, dy_j + R_1\, dv = - dw_1$$
$$v \sum R_{ij}\, dy_j + R_i\, dv = 0 \quad (i = 2, \ldots, n)$$
$$\sum R_i\, dy_j = 0$$

Writing H for the bordered Hessian of the system and H_{11} for the cofactor of the element in the first row and column, we obviously have our result,

$$\partial y_1 / \partial w_1 = - H_{11}/H > 0$$

WILLIAM J. BAUMOL AND JANUSZ A. ORDOVER

This result tells us that with an increase in w_i there must be off-setting changes in the Φ_{ji} so that p_i will normally decrease, contrary to what (13) and (14) seem to suggest. In particular, writing (14), in accord with (12), as

$$p_i = - w_i/v \, (1 - 1/E_{ii})$$

we note that in an optimal solution (since we have already shown that marginal revenue, R_i, must be negative) E_{ii} must be less than unity. Consequently, if the demand curve is negatively sloping then the value of v must rise and that of E_{ii} must decline sufficiently, when there is a rise in w_i, to be consistent with a net decrease in p_i.

For our purposes, however, the main conclusion that emerges from this model of the organization that seeks to maximize the magnitude of its (weighted) outputs, is that the resulting behavior seems to be able to lay little claim to anything resembling maximization of welfare.

We come, finally, to our third model of organizational behavior. Our analysis has abstracted from the important distinction between members and nonmember users (buyers) of organizational output. In fact, we assumed implicitly that anyone could become a member of a nonprofit organization simply by purchasing the organization's output, in however small a quantity. Yet in reality many nonprofit organizations discriminate in prices between member and non-members, perhaps in an effort to increase the size of their member-ship. Indeed, maximization of its membership may be viewed as an independent objective of a nonprofit organization. One method of price discrimination involves a higher usage price to nonmembers, an extreme case being that in which this price is infinite. To become a member one pays a membership fee which is set in conjunction with user charges for its products so as to maximize the membership and which entitles members to all regular publications and services of the group perhaps at a low or even a zero price. If the prices of the organization's products to its members do turn out to be very low, this method may seem to approximate the zero usage charge usually recommended for pure public goods; but it is more properly viewed as a degenerate two-part tariff in which the flat fee is high and the user charge is (near) zero. The substance of the distinction is that a flat fee can inhibit use just as effectively (though in a somewhat

18

ON THE OPTIMALITY OF PUBLIC-GOODS PRICING

different pattern) as a normal price. It may even be a stronger deterrent to use. If a professional association issues two periodicals to all its members, someone who really wants only one of these may be deterred from obtaining either of them if the membership fee is sufficiently high to cover both their costs. This suggests another way one can regard this sort of payment arrangement – as a tie-in sale, in which the potential purchaser is prevented from obtaining one of a set of items without at the same time acquiring the others.

VI. CONCLUDING COMMENT

The results of the discussion are, in brief, that quasi-optimality in the supply of quasi public goods (*i.e.*, public goods for which exclusion is possible) is in general not guaranteed by any of the forms of distribution described – supply by private enterprise, by nonprofit organizations pursuing a variety of different objectives, or (perhaps most surprisingly) by a public organization that distributes the services at the zero price usually recommended for public goods. It follows that in such a case there seems to be little welfare-theoretic ground favoring the one form of distribution over the others. Perhaps it suggests that policy makers are justified in a case-by-case approach, examining in each instance how much of a welfare loss is incurred, say, by supply through private firms, in order to determine whether public intervention and financing is appropriate.

REFERENCES

BAUMOL W.J. and BRADFORD D.F.: 'Optimal Departures from Marginal Cost Prices', *American Economic Review*, Vol. 60 (1970), June.

FELDSTEIN M.: 'The Surprising Incidence of a Tax on a Pure Rent: A New Answer to an Old Question'. HIER Discussion Paper, No. 424, Harvard University, 1975.

OAKLAND W.H.: 'Public Goods, Perfect Competition, and Under-Production', *Journal of Political Economy*, Vol. 82 (1974), September.

ORDOVER J.A. and WILLIG R.: 'On the Optimal Provision of Journals *Qua* Excludable Public Goods', (Manuscript) June 1976.

RAMSEY F.: 'A Contribution to the Theory of Taxation', *Economic Journal*, Vol. 37 (1927), March.

WILLIAM J. BAUMOL AND JANUSZ A. ORDOVER

SPENCE M.: 'Product Selection, Fixed Costs, and Monopolistic Competition', IMSSS Technical Report, No. 157, Stanford University, 1975.

STIGLITZ J. E. and DASGUPTA P.: 'Differential Taxation, Public Goods, and Economic Efficiency', *Review of Economic Studies*, Vol. 38 (1971), April.

SUMMARY

Contrary to standard welfare analysis, we show the Pareto-Optimal price of a public good is usually *not* zero, though, by definition, the marginal cost of additional users *is* zero. Since society must somehow pay the total cost of a public good, its Paretian price must satisfy RAMSEY's theorem on optimal pricing under a budget constraint. A zero price for a public good may be further from the optimum than that of a profit-maximizing monopolist, or a nonprofit organization pricing to cover its costs. Several pricing models for nonprofit organizations (such as learned societies) are offered. These include models of organizations whose objective functions are (i) maximization of the welfare of their members or (ii) maximization of the sales of their services (*e. g.*, number of subscribers to their journals) or (iii) maximization of number of members. It is shown that none of them will generally produce Pareto-Optimal results.

ZUSAMMENFASSUNG

In diesem Artikel wird gezeigt, dass, entgegen herkömmlicher Wohlfahrtsanalyse, der paretooptimale Preis eines öffentlichen Gutes in der Regel *ungleich* Null ist, obwohl, definitionsgemäss, die Grenzkosten eines zusätzlichen Nachfragers *gleich* Null sind. Da die Gesellschaft die gesamten Kosten eines öffentlichen Gutes auf irgendeine Weise tragen muss, hat der Paretopreis RAMSEYS Theorem der optimalen Preissetzung unter einer Budgetrestriktion zu genügen. Ein Preis von Null für ein öffentliches Gut kann weiter entfernt vom Optimum sein als derjenige eines gewinnmaximierenden Monopolisten oder als der kostendeckende Preis einer nicht-gewinnorientierten Unternehmung. Es werden mehrere Preissetzungsmodelle für nicht-gewinnorientierte Unternehmen (wie zum Beispiel wissenschaftliche Gesellschaften) dargestellt. Betrachtet werden Modelle für solche Organisationen, deren Zielfunktionen die folgenden sind: (i) die Maximierung der Wohlfahrt ihrer Mitglieder, (ii) die Maximierung der verkauften Dienstleistungen (zum Beispiel Zahl der Zeitungsabonnenten) oder (iii) die Maximierung der Mitgliederzahl. Es wird gezeigt, dass im allgemeinen keines dieser Modelle zu paretooptimalen Ergebnissen führt.

RÉSUMÉ

Les auteurs de cet article démontrent que, contrairement aux conclusions de l'analyse classique du bien-être, le prix optimum d'un bien public n'est généralement *pas* égal à zéro, bien que, par définition, le coût marginal des usagers addi-

ON THE OPTIMALITY OF PUBLIC-GOODS PRICING

tionnels soit, *lui*, égal à zéro. Puisque la société doit, d'une façon ou d'une autre, payer le coût total d'un bien public, son prix Parétien doit remplir les conditions du théorème de RAMSEY sur la fixation optimale des prix sous une contrainte budgétaire. Un prix égal à zéro pour un bien public peut être plus éloigné de l'optimum que celui d'un monopoleur maximisant son profit, ou d'une organisation à but non lucratif établissant un prix qui couvre ses frais. L'article présente plusieurs modèles de fixation des prix pour les organisations à but non lucratif (comme les sociétés savantes, par exemple). Citons parmi ceux-ci les modèles destinés aux organisations dont les fonctions objectifs sont: 1) la maximisation du bien-être de leurs membres, ou 2) la maximisation des ventes de leurs services (par exemple le nombre d'abonnés à leurs publications), ou encore 3) la maximisation du nombre de leurs membres. L'article démontre que, dans aucun de ces cas l'on obtient des résultats conformes à l'optimum de Paréto.

21

[6]

The Public-Good Attribute
as Independent Justification for Subsidy

By W. J. Baumol*

The economic literature generally recognizes four different grounds on which it may be possible to justify government subvention of a particular activity:

i) that the activity produces a public good;

ii) that the activity generates beneficial externalities;

iii) that the activity has scale economics and cannot be priced at marginal cost without losing money; and,

iv) that the output is consumed by lower income groups or others who deserve government support.

I will suggest in this paper that the public good argument is not as straightforward as it is usually considered. In particular, I will first suggest that most of the standard examples of pure public goods are in fact, somewhat impure. Second, I will show that an "impure public good" (that is, a mixed case) is in fact, a combination of a scale economies problem and/or an externality, so that the (partial) public-good property by itself does not offer an independent ground for government support. This is not a mere quibble about words. Rather, it affects the nature of the evidence that must be provided before one can claim to have a legitimate economic basis for government subsidy. For example, in seeking to justify government support for the publication of technical and scientific journals, it has been argued that subsidy is called for by the public-good characteristics of the product, which may seem obvious on their face. But once this argument disappears, it becomes necessary to show either that such publication generates beneficial externalities, or that it involves scale economies and that marginal-cost pricing is the best principle to use in charging for them. But evidence for either or both of these assertions is quite another kettle of fish.

* The author is Professor of Economics, Princeton and New York Universities. The author is extremely grateful to the Division of Science Information, of the National Science Foundation whose grant to his study on Scale Economies and Public Good Attributes of Information Transfer, greatly facilitated the preparation of this paper. Some of the results in this paper draw upon W. J. Baumol and J. A. Ordover, "Public Good Properties in Reality: The Case of Scientific Journals," paper delivered before The Annual Meeting of the American Society of Information Science, San Francisco, 1976.

2   INTERMOUNTAIN ECONOMIC REVIEW

The Standard Characterization of Public Goods: Brief Review

A pure public good is usually defined in terms of two characteristics:

i) *Supply jointness or nondepletability;* meaning that, at least within a significant range, once the good is supplied to *anyone, it requires no additional resources for its benefits to be enjoyed by additional persons.*

ii) *Non-Excludability;* meaning that persons cannot be prevented from consuming the good or, rather, from enjoying its benefits. In particular, they can enjoy these benefits without paying anything for them.

The usual definition takes supply jointness to be the defining characteristic of a public good, while non-excludability is judged, on the basis of (casual) observation, to be a frequent concomitant of supply jointness.[1]

To complete this brief review, we may note that supply jointness is normally used to argue that a zero price *should* be charged for a public good (on grounds of Pareto optimality) since the marginal cost of an additional beneficiary is zero. The non-excludability characteristic is used to argue that in fact, no private firm will be *able* to charge a positive price for the good since anyone is able to enjoy its benefits without paying for them. Consequently, private enterprise will be unable to supply non-excludable public goods.

We may also note the Bowen-Samuelson necessary condition for the optimal supply of a pure public good, which requires:

(1) the *sum* of the marginal benefits to all users of a public good must equal the marginal cost of the good.

A moment's thought shows why this condition must hold instead of the usual optimality requirement for a pure private good, namely:

(2) the marginal benefit to any consumer, *alone* must equal the marginal cost of the private good.

For, by definition, the supply of an additional unit of a public good can benefit many persons simultaneously, and so it will be worthwhile to produce this additional unit if the sum of those additional benefits exceeds the corresponding additional cost.

The Near-Universal Impurity of Public Goods

We rarely expect in practice to encounter unadulterated examples of polar categories. Thus, it is hard to find examples of industries that are perfectly competetive, or firms that are pure monopolies. In the same way, no one will really be surprised that public goods rarely are perfectly pure. But we must first confirm this suspicion, leaving it until later to argue that for analytic purposes, near purity of a public good may make little more sense than "near virginity" of an individual!

---

[1] For an excellent discussion, see J. G. Head [4].

Dealing with the issue of exclusion first, let me argue that this is never an immutable property of a particular good, but rather that it is almost always a function of the time and resources the supplier is willing to devote to it. For the skillfull shoplifter, there is no good so private that he can always be excluded from enjoying it without payment. Clearly, the more surveilance the shopkeeper arranges for, the more nearly his goods will approximate exclusion. At the other end of the spectrum, similar observations hold for most standard examples of public goods. TV broadcasting, one such illustration, is a clear case in point. Scrambling and other devices can be used to prevent individuals from receiving broadcasts without paying for them. Failure to do so represents a conscious decision by the supplier or the regulatory agency, not a technological property of the service. Similarly, toll gates can permit a supplier to charge the beneficiary for the removal of snow from a road. Even defense of the individual or his property can be charged for, as has been demonstrated amply by organized crime's profitable supply of protection (which does in fact, often protect shopkeepers from petty criminals whose activities have not been authorized by "the organization"). It is difficult to think of any good or service for which some degree of excludability cannot be achieved by a supplier who puts his mind to it, and is not hampered in his task by constraints imposed by legislation or regulation.

The situation in the case of pure supply jointness is not quite analogous. A supplier cannot normally choose the degree of supply jointness of his product by deciding how much to spend for the purpose. Depending on the nature of the product and the state of technology, there will be some minimum expenditure which must be incurred in supplying the product to an additional consumer. Either this marginal cost will be zero (in which case, the item will be a pure public good), or it will be positive, and the degree of impurity of the public good will then presumably be judged by the magnitude of this marginal cost.[2]

Once again, it is difficult to think of cases where the pure supply-jointness condition is fulfilled perfectly, i.e., in which absolutely no resources need be expended in order to permit an additional individual to benefit from them. Standard public-good examples such as the broadcast of a television program or the discoveries produced by a research program will illustrate the point. The recipients of a TV broadcast must pay for electricity and for the TV sets themselves, if the emission is to reach them. Manufacturers who benefit from an idea for a new product may incur no additional re-

---

[2] Actually, this is somewhat of an oversimplification. What will be a large marginal cost for one product (say a dollar for an additional banana) will clearly be a small marginal cost for another (say, an automobile). We must therefore compare the absolute marginal cost of supplying an additional user to some other magnitude before we can hope to judge whether it is large or small. In a single-product firm we can perhaps compare marginal and average cost. But in a multiproduct firm, average cost is not even defined unless we mean by it the average *variable* cost of the item in question.

search cost in turning out the new good, but without the other associated inputs, the idea would do them little good.

One can argue that the marginal resource cost involved in serving another consumer in the broadcast example is relatively *small* in comparison with the initial cost of the broadcast. Indeed, it is plausible that this will be true of a variety of items usually considered to be public goods. But the point is that such cases can no longer be considered to involve *pure* public goods.

Sometimes, moreover, the costs of serving an additional user turn out to be surprisingly large. For example, in the study which led to the writing of this paper, it was estimated that the (long-run) marginal cost to a library of permitting an additional reader to check out a book from closed stacks (and then return it) probably exceeds $1.50, and thus constitutes a substantial proportion of the cost of the book. The time required for library employees to get the book, record its withdrawal and return, and the work of shelving easily total the amount indicated. Adding to this the wear and tear upon the volume, it becomes obvious that the marginal cost of an additional user is far from zero.

Imperfect Supply Jointness as a Case of Fixed Costs

If I am now granted, for the sake of argument, that the marginal resource cost of serving an additional user is rarely if ever precisely zero, what, then, is the significance of this observation? To permit us to deal with the two public-good issues separately we will assume in the discussion of this section that the goods in question pose no exclusion problems.

In connection with the allocation of resources, the difficulty posed by such an imperfect supply-jointness case is that, if one desires to supply the good at a price equal to its marginal cost, then the sale of the commodity is likely to incur a loss. For its marginal cost, by assumption, is small in comparison with the total cost of supplying the item. But that is precisely what plagues the optimal provision of any good whose production involves a (relatively large) fixed cost. Such a commodity, if produced by a single-product supplier, will (unless average costs are rising for other reasons) have a marginal cost that is below average cost and so, as is well known, marginal cost pricing will generally yield losses to the supplier in the fixed-cost case as well.

The similarity of the resource allocation problem in the two cases is hardly coincidental. For, by saying that a broadcast incurs a low cost in serving an additional consumer we have asserted, in effect, that it is nothing more than a product with a high fixed cost (the cost of programming and transmission) and a low marginal cost (the cost of serving an additional viewer). The same is obviously true of any other public good whose marginal cost is non-zero.

In other words, it would seem that impure public goods are simply goods whose production has a large fixed cost component and for which there is a comparatively low marginal cost (in the sense of the cost of serving another customer rather than the cost of providing another unit of physical product).

Perhaps more important, there is no analytical difference between the case of fixed costs and the case of impure public goods of the sort we are now discussing. Both will tend to subvert pure competition because they are likely to be characterized by declining average costs in the single-product case as well as its equivalent in the multiproduct case. Both will tend to be offered for sale only at prices that exceed their marginal costs, since otherwise the supplier will be unable to make ends meet. In short, both will give rise to all of the allocative problems which we usually associate with the presence of scale economies.

It may also be noted, incidentally, that they will both have the same sort of (second-best) Pareto-optimal prices which are constrained to permit the supplier to meet his costs. These prices, which were first discovered by Frank Ramsey in 1927, represent the optimal departures from marginal cost pricing when prices are required to satisfy the constraint that the producer earn some specified amount (say, zero, i.e., the normal return on his capital). But it is easy to show that if *all* prices are really to be Pareto optimal subject to the budget constraint, then the prices of public goods must follow exactly the same pattern and obey the same rules as do those of ordinary fixed-cost products.[3] Thus, in no essential do we find any difference between goods with high fixed costs and goods with imperfect supply jointness, i.e., impure public goods.

Digression: Public Goods, Fixed Costs and Sunk Costs

Any readers who are now convinced that (aside from issues of non-excludability) there is no difference between commodities which are public goods and commodities with heavy fixed costs, may well wonder why one observes so many products with heavy fixed costs in private industry. After all, we tend to think of public goods as goods whose production cannot or should not be left to the private sector. Yet it would seem that the automobile industry, aircraft production, telecommunications transmission, and many other industries do have large fixed costs, which, it has been claimed, makes them equivalent to public-good producers.

Part of the confusion, as we will note in the next section, arises from the issue of excludability, which we have so far ignored. If consumers cannot easily be excluded from the enjoyment of a good, so that it is difficult to charge a price for it, then it is indeed true that one cannot expect private industry to supply it. This will, however, be true whether it is characterized by scale economies or diseconomies, whether it does or does not have the property of supply jointness.

---

[3] For more on this subject, see Baumol and Ordover [2].

6   INTERMOUNTAIN ECONOMIC REVIEW

However, there is a second observation which helps to explain the high number of *apparently* near public goods offered by the private sector. For most industries which are alleged to have high *fixed* costs, in fact, only have heavy *sunk* costs, i.e., costs which are *temporarily* unchangeable because their current values are determined by an earlier decision.

To make clear the distinction between a fixed and a sunk cost, consider a single-product firm which has a long-run cost function that is linear. That is, for this firm,

total cost = a+by,

where y is the quantity of its output. Here, *a* is a true fixed cost. Like the research cost underlying a new product, it does not decline even in the long run, if the number of users decreases.

The reverse is true of a sunk cost. Suppose a company has built a huge plant with a capacity of producing a million units of product per year. If demand for the product falls to 10 thousand per year, the original plant will be built at a fraction of the cost of replacement of the larger factory.

The difference between fixed and sunk costs is easily illustrated by comparison of the production relations of a railroad and an assembly line. Car production *can* be carried out on a small scale with a commensurate reduction in total cost of plant. If the price of petroleum were to skyrocket to a point where only a market for a few hundred cars a year remained, huge assembly lines would soon disappear. Cars might be hand tooled, albeit at a rather high cost per vehicle. But the industry's *total* equipment cost would be reduced to miniscule proportions relative to its level today. In sum, the equipment cost of an assembly line is sunk, not fixed.

On the other hand, if a railroad is to run between New York and Chicago, there is a minimum outlay on track and roadbed which must be incurred even if the trains run virtually empty. The service can be discontinued altogether. But even in the longest of long runs, it cannot be turned into a negligible amount, if the amount of service is to be positive.

Thus, one must regard the textbook aphorism, that in the long run all fixed costs become variable, with strong reservations. Sunk costs do become variable in the long run, but fixed costs only become variable to the extent that they can be escaped if the activity they serve is no longer carried on.

Non-Excludable Goods as Externality Generators

Returning now to the characteristics of public goods, let us reconsider the issue of non-excludability. Before, we dealt with goods that offer imperfect supply jointness for which exclusion is possible, so that the supplier is able to sell them at a positive price. Now let us reverse this procedure and ignore the issue of supply jointness.

What, then, is the significance of the fact that when certain goods are supplied to some individuals, it is difficult to prevent others from benefitting also? The question itself supplies its own answer: the supply of such goods in some way generates beneficial externalities. After all, that is what we mean by the term. A beneficial externality is a case where an economic activity incidentally benefits others who are not direct parties to the process — neither sellers nor buyers of the product.

In short, any beneficial externality involves an imperfectly excludable service to the beneficiary, and any imperfectly excludable output, *per se,* generates an externality. Hence, the allocative problems which concern us (as a result of imperfect excludability) are precisely the same as those that concern us in the case of beneficial externalities. We fear that if the activities are left to private industry, their outputs will tend to be undesirably low — if any output is supplied at all.

Impure Public Goods and the Bowen-Samuelson Optimality Condition

It remains for us to investigate whether we can rescue public goods as a distinctive category with the aid of the Bowen-Samuelson condition (1), which is often taken to be the property of public goods most significant for theoretical analysis. I will show in this section that, where public goods are impure, the formula loses much of its convenient simplicity. Moreover, I will show that public goods are not the only items to which such a formula applies. Thus, it would seem to follow that the Bowen-Samuelson condition, important though it is, does not serve to restore the character of a distinctive property to the public-goods concept.

Where marginal costs are not zero, it is clear that the Bowen-Samuelson formula requires modification. First, a moment's thought indicates that the marginal cost of serving any additional user must be equalled or exceeded by its marginal benefit to the customer (as measured by his willingness to pay — i.e., his marginal rate of substitution between the good and money). Second, the sum of these benefits to all consumers together must equal the sum of the marginal cost of producing the item *plus* the sum of the marginal costs of providing them to the individual consumers. Not surprisingly, the simple formula (1) is replaced by a multiplicity of conditions, which are a hybrid between the necessary conditions for optimality in the supply of private and public goods.

The Bowen-Samuelson condition on the pure public-goods case follows from the premise that the quantity produced of any public goods automatically enters the utility function of each and every individual in the economy. As a consequence, in contrast with the case of a private good, when one differentiates the Lagrangian expression for the Pareto-optimality problem with respect to the quantity of a pure public good, the sum of the marginal utilities of all individuals in the community enters the resulting first-order conditions.

But D. Levhari and others have recently shown, using a similar argument, that the same sort of relationship occurs whenever there is a decision that (potentially) affects every consumer. For example, a decision by a firm to improve, say, the durability of its product must affect the utility level of every actual buyer of that good and perhaps even those of potential buyers. The Pareto-optimality requirement is an identical twin of the Bowen-Samuelson condition: the sum of the marginal benefits to all affected consumers must equal the marginal cost of the quality improvements.

It is noteworthy, though, that while such a decision on product quality must satisfy an optimality condition like that of a pure public good, it does not follow that private enterprise is likely to select a non-optimal product quality — as one fears in the case of the output of a pure public good. On the contrary, one would expect, under pure competition, that the market will offer precisely the right durability of product and the right degree of any other quality attribute. The reason, of course, is that the products do permit exclusion and so consumers can normally be required to pay for each and every unit they obtain. Higher quality must permit a sufficient increase in price and/or a sufficient increase in sales volume to make up for the incremental cost of the increase in quality. And that is precisely what is required for optimality in the allocation of resources among product quality and other uses.

Thus we see that the resource allocation problem caused by the presence of pure public goods cannot be attributed to the fact that they satisfy the Bowen-Samuelson formula. Rather, the problem stems from the difficulty of exclusion; that is, on our interpretation, from the externality they generate which, as has long been known, is a very real source of resource misallocation.

On Justification of Government Subsidy

I conclude from the preceeding discussion, that in seeking to use public-good properties to argue for public subsidy of a particular activity, it is necessary to show that the activity in question is characterized by scale economies — at least in the neighborhood of the pertinent output levels. That is, the assertion that the activity is a public good does not constitute an independent ground for government financing (an assertion that is easier to document than the externality or scale economies properties).

A bit more detail about the illustration with which I began this paper will bring the point out more clearly. A few years ago, several colleagues and I began a study of the principles of government support of scientific and technical journals, with the presumption that a case for such support would be easy to make. We reasoned by analogy with the public-good properties of research, assuming that a similar property would extend to the journals which report the results of this research.

The facts soon disabused us of this presumption. As already indicated, we found that the marginal cost of additional library use was hardly negligible. The cost of supplying individually owned copies to individual users was, predictably, even higher — though not nearly as much higher as one might have supposed. Thus, the evidence made it very difficult for us to consider journal supply or journal usage as exhibiting supply jointness to any significant degree.

More than that, we failed to turn up any evidence of significant exclusion problems. True, photocopying of articles has grown increasingly frequent, even in disregard of any legal presumption about "fair use" that may apply. It is also true that journals are often stolen from libraries or mutilated. Yet the fact is that the more popular journals do *not* find it difficult to sell copies to individual subscribers, and that many that are less popular continue to find a market among libraries at prices that do cover their production costs.

To analyze the subvention issue, one is then left with the task of investigating whether the supply of journals involves externalities or scale economies. The scale economies issue is not beyond systematic study — though it does involve a difficult process of data gathering, statistical study and analysis. Yale Braunstein and I [1] have so far been able, in a few cases, to provide empirical evidence of the presence of scale economies and some associated phenomena; but as yet, there is little reason to believe that their domain extends beyond the few publishers whose data we have analyzed. In short, the hypothesis that journal publication involves scale economies is far more difficult to confirm than one often believes to be true in the case of public goods.

Empirical evidence of the presence of externalities is far more difficult, still. Since it now seems clear that we are going to find little evidence of serious non-excludability in the case of scientific journals, evidence of beneficial externalities in the publication of scientific journals will have to be more indirect and subtle in character. For example, one will have to show that by reading a scientific journal, an individual incidentally benefits others in a way that the market mechanism cannot easily capture. To give a far-fetched illustration, if journal reading increases the likelihood that the reader will take measures to immunize himself against communicable diseases, then, others who might otherwise have caught them from him will benefit incidentally. But more realistic externalities of that sort are in many cases hard to think of, much less document. For example, despite all of the discipline's contributions to human knowledge and to man's understanding of his antecedents, it does not seem easy to think of any such indirect externality that one can safely attribute to the reading of an archeological journal.

References

1. W. J. Baumol and Y. Braunstein, "Empirical Study of Scale Economies and Production Complementarity: The Case of Journal Publication," *J. Polit. Econ., 85,* Oct. 1977, 1037-48.

2. W. J. Baumol and J. A. Ordover, "On the Optimality of Public Goods Pricing With Exclusionary Devices," *Kyklos, 30,* 1977, 36–46.

3. H. R. Bowen, *Toward Social Economy,* New York 1948.

4. J. G. Head, "Public Goods and Public Policy," *Pub. Fin., 3,* 1962, 197–222.

5. F. Ramsey, "A Contribution for the Theory of Taxation," *Econ. J., 37,* March 1927, 47–61.

6. P. A. Samuelson, "The Pure Theory of Public Expenditures," *Rev. Econ. Statist., 36,* Nov. 1954, 381–89.

[7]

Optimal depreciation policy: pricing the products of durable assets

William J. Baumol

Professor of Economics
Princeton University and
New York University

Depreciation policy is analyzed from the point of view of optimal inter-temporal resource allocation. Because depreciation determines the time pattern of prices of the product of an asset it affects the timing of demands. Models extended from peak-load pricing theory are used to determine rules for depreciation that are consistent with economic efficiency of asset utilization. They show how technological progress, inflation, maintainance cost patterns, user costs, and other related elements should affect depreciation. The role of forecasting is considered and it is shown that in certain circumstances prediction becomes virtually unnecessary for optimal depreciation decisions.

■ Perhaps in part because economic analysis has provided little guidance in the area, depreciation practices have become so heavily entangled in accounting conventions and in tax consequences that the economic logic of the concept has all but vanished. One tends to think of a firm's depreciation policy simply as a means to obtain a tax advantage.

In this paper it will be shown that the economics of depreciation goes much deeper than this. One can define depreciation policies that are optimal from the point of view of society; that is, depreciation rules which make for most efficient utilization of resources and which do not, in general, coincide with those that simply minimize tax payments. We will see, however, that where taxation does not distort depreciation policies, under plausible conditions the profit-maximizing firm will find it in its own interest to adopt the socially optimal depreciation rules.

This paper constitutes an attempt to provide a few crude theoretical models which, it is hoped, will shed some light on the general subject, though they make no pretense at being suitable for direct application as they stand. The first section undertakes to define economic depreciation and to explain what is meant by an optimal depreciation policy; after that we turn to the specification of the amount to be recovered. Then some principles of optimal depreciation policy will be enunciated and derived from the models. Finally, some special depreciation rules will be obtained for the case in which the firm must add to its capacity in each and every decision period.

In essence, what we seek is an expression for long-run marginal cost where we define

long-run marginal cost for year t

= marginal operating cost$_t$ + economic depreciation payment$_t$,

= short-run marginal cost$_t$ + economic depreciation payment$_t$.

As usual, if average costs *of investment* are declining, prices *equal* to marginal cost will not yield revenues sufficient for the company to cover its capital and operating costs. In that case, it will clearly be necessary to set prices *above* long-run marginal cost as just defined. It must be emphasized that the assumption of constant costs implicit in our discussion refers only to the purchase or construction of the firm's physical capital equipment, and not to its operations as a whole. The company's production process may exhibit economies or diseconomies of scale without affecting the analysis of depreciation payments. For these payments to add up to the cost of the equipment we require only the far weaker assumption that if one machine costs the firm p dollars then 23 machines will cost it $23p$ dollars, so that the average and marginal cost *of machines* will be the same. Then, since the present values of the depreciation payments for each machine, as determined by the model, are guaranteed to sum to the marginal cost of the equipment, they will also equal the unit cost of the machine, as the definition of the depreciation concept requires.

■ Economists have tended to cede the area of depreciation to the accountants not only because they were unwilling to raise a dispute over squatter's rights, but also because much of the economic literature has, as a matter of fact, managed to get along without explicit recourse to the concept. The economist is primarily concerned with decision-making, and looked at in this way, depreciation is relevant primarily, if not exclusively, for the investment decision.

But even here the literature has managed to evade much use of the notion.[1] Calculations on the desirability of investment in an asset have been conducted in terms of the discounted present value of the associated streams of prospective costs and revenues (or with the aid of some substitute concept such as the marginal efficiency of investment). The investment decision criterion is easily formulated in these terms: Acquire an asset if the discounted present value of its expected returns exceeds the present value of its costs, including the cost of the capital tied up in the asset. At no point in this formulation is it necessary to make use of any explicit depreciation rule, because at no intermediate point in the life of the asset is it necessary to calculate its residual value.

However, implicit in the preceding discussion there reside at least two concepts of depreciation:

(1) The idea of residual value is itself a depreciation concept. That is, given an asset whose initial value is A_0, we may try to determine its remaining economic value, A_t, after t years have passed since its acquisition. In this case the year's loss in value, $A_{t-1} - A_t$, may be termed its depreciation in year t. A_t is itself generally taken to be equal to the discounted value at date t of the asset's remaining net returns.[2]

1. Why economic depreciation?

---

[1] See, e.g., Friedrich and Vera Lutz, *The Theory of Investment of the Firm*, Princeton, N. J.: Princeton University Press, 1951.

[2] In a letter, Ralph Turvey writes, "In speaking of A_t as 'the discounted value of the remaining net returns,' . . . it is necessary to distinguish between (a) the loss the firm would suffer if the asset vanished and output consequently fell and (b) the loss it would suffer if the asset vanished but the time-stream of output was not altered. (a) means less revenue, (b) means more costs. The latter corresponds

(2) There is a second economic depreciation concept which is our primary concern here and which, as we will see later, turns out to be closely related to the preceding concept. When an asset is purchased, it is expected that future revenues will repay investors for putting their funds into the asset.[3] However, given the present value of the asset's costs, there may be many alternative revenue streams, each of which can give investors their required returns. The choice of depreciation policy may then be defined as the selection of one of these *intertemporal patterns of prices* which will yield one of the revenue streams adequate to compensate investors. In these terms, an accelerated depreciation policy, for example, may be defined as one that yields a disproportionate share of the cost of the asset during the earlier years of its existence.

It should now be clear in what sense one depreciation policy may be better than another. One set of intertemporal patterns of product prices may yield a better allocation of resources (or higher profits) than another. We will define the optimal depreciation policy as that which results in a most efficient use of resources.

It should be observed that the depreciation decision, thus defined, is itself vital for the choice of investment program. That is, whether or not the acquisition of a particular asset will turn out to be a profitable move depends on the time pattern of prices selected for its products. One pattern of prices (i.e., one depreciation rule) may permit the investment to be acquired and utilized profitably, while with another depreciation principle the same asset may not be worth its cost.

The purpose of the paper can then be described as follows: We seek to determine a set of depreciation rules which permits the firm to cover the cost of (added) capacity in its pricing decisions in such a manner that if the firm equates supply and demand at the resulting set of prices it will produce an optimal intertemporal pattern of investment in capacity and in the usage of that capacity. Thus the analysis simultaneously determines three sets of magnitudes for each period: the firm's investment outlays, the prices of the products in whose production the capital is utilized, and the depreciation payments on these investments.

The point is that there is a duality relationship between the optimal investment program and the optimal pricing (depreciation) policy. This interrelationship underlies the Kuhn-Tucker analysis of the problem that follows. In terms of recent capital theory, the depreciation payments become the standard neoclassical rentals, the

---

to the dual of output capacity. . . . Your [two] depreciation . . . concepts coincide if the cost approach is used in both cases as I think it should be." I'm not sure I fully understand this argument. However, it seems to me that the opportunity value of a machine is the *minimum* loss to which the firm would be subjected by its disappearance, which might well involve changes in both costs and revenues. The proper interpretation of the dual, of course, depends on the choice of objective function, whether it involves maximization of total profits or total revenues, or minimization of the costs of producing a specified output vector. Only in the latter case is the cost concept the dual of capacity.

[3] To avoid confusion with the preceding definition and with the accounting concept, Ralph Turvey has suggested the term "amortization" as a substitute for "depreciation." See Turvey's "Marginal Cost," *Economic Journal*, Vol. LXXIX (June 1969), pp. 282–99. Ultimately, the ideas in this paper can be traced to Turvey's article.

optimal depreciation figure being the optimal rental charge for the use of the capital equipment.

These are all *ex ante* planning concepts and represent the magnitudes appropriate for the choice of an investment program. However, they also give us the *ex post* information needed for accounting purposes. If, after the equipment is purchased and installed, matters have developed as anticipated when the decision was under consideration, the optimal depreciation charges as calculated then become the optimal depreciation components for pricing decisions now.

■ We have then defined the depreciation decision as the choice of a stream of prices that permits recovery of a firm's investment in an asset. As it stands, this statement still suffers from at least one ambiguity; for it does not specify exactly what it is that is to be recovered. Granted, the sum to be replaced is the initial investment. But in a changing world in which costs and prices are not stationary, it is not immediately obvious how large a sum after the passage of *t* years is equivalent to some given initial outlay.

2. What amount should depreciation recover?

Obviously, we will want to discount the future sum to equate its present value to the initial outlay. But further adjustment may be required if improving technology reduces the cost of replacement of the asset at the end of its life and if inflation works in the contrary direction and simultaneously depreciates the currency received in repayment.

In these circumstances there are (at least) three candidates for the amount to be recovered:

(1) The replacement cost of the asset (which in a world of improving technology may well be below the initial cost of the asset),

(2) The initial dollar cost of the asset, and

(3) A number of dollars that, at the time they are received, is equivalent in purchasing power to the initial cost of the asset (which, in an economy whose prices are rising, will exceed the initial dollar outlay).

Of course, each of these is taken to include an amount sufficient to provide a return on the investor's capital. In the remainder of our discussion this will be taken for granted; that is, cost will always be taken to include the cost of capital.

For the firm to keep its physical capital intact, i.e., for it to suffer no loss in its productive capacity, all that needs to be recovered is the first of the three amounts, the asset's replacement cost. This will obviously enable it to replace the investment with its equivalent in productive ability when the appropriate time comes.

However, from the point of view of the investor, if no more than replacement cost is returned the entire asset purchase can turn out to be a mistake. That is, the investment decision will have been worth his while only if at the end he receives back his initial purchasing power plus compensation for the use of his funds.[4]

---

[4] This implies that there exist alternative uses of funds which are capable of preserving purchasing power and yielding a return. Indeed, the cost of capital *is* the return that the investor could obtain by using it elsewhere. It is the opportunity cost of his funds.

Furthermore, it seems rational *from the point of view of society* that an investment be undertaken only if it is expected to offer at least this return. For if consumers of the goods or services to be produced with the aid of the investment are unwilling to pay *in real terms* the opportunity cost of obtaining the asset in question, then construction of the asset by definition represents a wasteful use of resources.

We conclude, then, that if no mistake has been made in planning the investment, the return provided by depreciation payments on the asset will be adequate to meet the last of the three preceding criteria. That is, it will return funds whose discounted value, after correction for changes in the price level, is equivalent to the cost of the investment. This may or may not be equal to the replacement cost of the asset.

3. Optimal depreciation rules: the simplest case

■ We turn now to the central issue in this paper, the depreciation rules that will secure an optimal allocation of resources. Here the literature is rather sparse.[5] However, a seminal article by Littlechild has effectively given order to the entire discussion,[6] and most of the conclusions in this paper will follow Littlechild's line of reasoning.

In all of the models that follow, it is assumed that investments are divisible; that is to say, there is no minimum size of outlay required to achieve an expansion in plant. This is clearly unrealistic, but it does not cause any fundamental problems for the analysis.

It is also assumed, implicitly, that there is a constant average investment cost, i.e., that the construction of 50 radio towers costs exactly ten times as much as the acquisition of 5 towers. If this is not true, pricing at the long-run marginal cost as defined will cover only the *marginal* cost of the investment, and a revenue constraint will have to be added to make certain that the firm does not suffer a loss on its investment. Such a revenue requirement complicates the mathematics but causes no fundamental problem for the analysis. The nature of the revenue constraint will of course then determine the nature of the deviations of prices from long-run marginal costs.

The analysis can implicitly take account of the important role of taxation for optimal depreciation policy because taxes can be taken to enter the cost function. It may ultimately prove helpful to bring out the effects of taxes more clearly, but for now, in order to preserve some degree of simplicity this is not done.

Let us begin with the simplest possible case, that in which the asset has a fixed life and does not decrease in productivity with the passage of time, but suddenly becomes valueless, like the one-horse shay. Assume also that the price level remains constant, that the cost of replacement of the asset remains unchanged over time, and that it is equal to the initial cost of the item.

[5] See, e.g., Edgar O. Edwards and Philip W. Bell, *The Theory and Measurement of Business Income*, Berkeley, Calif.: University of California Press, 1961. See also the brief discussion in the Turvey paper referred to previously and in the writings cited there.

[6] S. C. Littlechild, "Marginal Cost Pricing with Joint-Costs," *Economic Journal*, Vol. LXXX (June 1970), pp. 223–35. As Littlechild himself points out, some of his results are implicit in previous discussions in capital theory. Thus see, e.g., K. J. Arrow, "Optimal Capital Policy, the Cost of Capital, and Myopic Decision Rules," *Annals of the Institute of Statistical Mathematics*, Vol. XVI, Nos. 1–2, Tokyo (1964), pp. 21–30.

In that case the rules for optimal pricing, and hence for depreciation policy, that emerge from the mathematics are easily described:

(1) During any years in which there is unused capacity, the long-run marginal cost of the firm's output should cover only operating costs (i.e., in such a period, it is equal to short-run marginal cost) and includes absolutely *no* contribution towards depreciation.[7]

(2) During the years when the asset is used to capacity, the depreciation charge should be determined by the demand function, and consumers should be charged that price which just induces them to purchase the item's capacity output. The difference between that price and marginal operating cost will constitute the depreciation payment for the period in question.

(3) It will be shown presently as a theorem that, if the cost of the asset is fixed and independent of the number of units of capacity purchased by the firm, the depreciation payments just described will add up precisely to the cost of the asset, i.e., they will provide *just* the right amount of depreciation to cover the marginal cost of the investment.

The rationale for the first two rules is easily described. For this purpose it is useful to think of the depreciation problem as an intertemporal peak-load pricing problem. The years in which the asset is used to capacity are the peak periods. It follows that during the earlier "off-peak" years, increased use of the asset is always desirable so long as marginal operating costs are covered. That is precisely why no contribution to depreciation is exacted then. However, once demand is able to reach capacity, price becomes the rationing device which equalizes the quantity demanded and the amount of output the asset is able to produce. This is essentially the reasoning behind our two rules of optimal depreciation. The third rule—which assures us that the funds collected in this way will happen to be adequate (except in the cases mentioned in the preceding footnote)—will be derived in the next section.

The irrationality of a depreciation policy that demands the same contribution toward the cost of an asset in periods of heavy and of light usage is not too dissimilar in character from the curious commuter discounts which, in effect, make it cheapest to travel through tunnels or over bridges precisely at the times of day when they are most crowded. Both practices simply serve to compound the congestion and contribute nothing toward increased utilization at times when unused capacity is available.

4. Derivation of the rules for the simplest case

■ This section will describe the mathematical analysis that underlies the preceding discussion. The asset in question will be taken to last n periods. Capacity can be added by the firm (i.e., more such assets can be bought) during any period. We use the following notation:

p_t = present value of anticipated price of output during period t,

x_t = quantity of output during t,

y_t = output capacity of assets acquired during t,

---

[7] This assumes that there exists no price at which demand during this period will suffice to utilize the capacity fully and cover the marginal operating cost.

$i_t =$ capacity in period t of assets purchased before period 1,

$c(x_1, \ldots, x_n) =$ present value of total operating costs,

$g(y_1, \ldots, y_n) =$ present value of total capital costs, including maintenance costs, and

$u(x_1, \ldots, x_n) =$ an (unspecified) money measure of total utility of outputs. To deal with the profit-maximizing firm we need merely interpret this as a total revenue function. We will note presently what modifications this requires in the analysis.

The objective is then to maximize *net* benefit (consumers' utility minus capital and operating costs of output), i.e., to maximize

$$u(x_1, \ldots, x_n) - c(x_1, \ldots, x_n) - g(y_1, \ldots, y_n)$$

subject to the production capacity constraints

$$
\begin{aligned}
x_1 &< y_1 + i_1 \\
x_2 &\leq y_1 + y_2 + i_2 \\
&\cdot \cdot \cdot \cdot \cdot \cdot \cdot \cdot \cdot \cdot \\
x_n &\leq y_1 + \cdots + y_n + i_n
\end{aligned}
\tag{1}
$$

all $x_t \geq 0,\, y_t \geq 0$.

By the Kuhn-Tucker theorem, we obtain the following Lagrangian expression:

Maximize

$$
\begin{aligned}
L = u(x_1, \ldots, x_n) &- c(x_1, \ldots, x_n) \quad g(y_1, \ldots, y_n) \\
&+ \lambda_1(y_1 + i_1 - x_1) + \lambda_2(y_1 + y_2 + i_2 - x_2) \\
&\qquad + \cdots + \lambda_n(y_1 + \cdots + y_n + i_n - x_n).
\end{aligned}
$$

Assuming that some output is sold in each period (all $x_t > 0$), this yields the following first-order conditions:

$$\frac{\partial L}{\partial x_t} = \frac{\partial u}{\partial x_t} - \frac{\partial c}{\partial x_t} - \lambda_t = 0. \tag{2}$$

In addition, since by assumption our asset is bought in the first period so that $y_1 > 0$, we have

$$\frac{\partial L}{\partial y_1} = -\frac{\partial g}{\partial y_1} + \lambda_1 + \cdots + \lambda_n = 0. \tag{3}$$

Last, we have the Kuhn-Tucker conditions

$$\lambda_t \frac{2L}{2\lambda_t} = \lambda_t(y_1 + \cdots + y_t + i_t - x_t) = 0. \tag{4}$$

Let us now eliminate the undefined utility function from our analysis by noting that for the usual reasons[8] $\partial u / \partial x_t = p_t$ (marginal utility equals price). Hence, substituting into (2) we obtain

$$p_t = \frac{\partial c}{\partial x_t} + \lambda_t. \tag{5}$$

---

[8] Strictly speaking, this implies the absence of externalities of consumption. Note that we are dealing here not with an "absolute marginal utility" but with a marginal utility measured in money terms. i.e., with the marginal rate of subsitution between x and money, which is, of course, equal to p_z/p_m, where $p_m = 1$ is the "price" of money.

This states that the optimal price in period t is equal to the marginal operating cost of output in that period plus a supplementary payment, λ_t, which may be interpreted as the depreciation component (i.e., the contribution toward capital outlays) per unit of output purchased in period t.

Now we note from (4) that in a year in which output is not up to capacity, i.e., in which $y_1 + \cdots + y_t + i_t > x_t$, we must have $\lambda_t = 0$, i.e., in that year there will be a zero depreciation charge. This is the first of the depreciation rules of the preceding section. Equation (5) now is readily interpreted as our second depreciation rule: In peak capacity years, price equals marginal operating cost plus depreciation payment.

Finally, from (3) we have

$$\lambda_1 + \cdots + \lambda_n = \partial g / \partial y_1 , \tag{6}$$

that is, the sum of the depreciation payments per unit of output and, therefore, per unit of capacity, during the n year life of y_1, the asset purchased in period 1, will equal $\partial g / \partial y_1$, the marginal cost of an additional unit of capacity. This is the last portion of our optimal depreciation result described in the preceding section.

All of the preceding results are essentially affected in only one respect if instead of maximization of social welfare we consider maximization of the profits of the firm. As already noted, in this case we need merely interpret $u(x_1, \ldots, x_n)$ to be total revenue, and our maximand $u(x_1, \ldots, x_n) - c(x_1, \ldots, x_n) - g(y_1, \ldots, y_n)$ then obviously represents the firm's total profit. This leaves unchanged every one of our equations except (5) in which the product price, p_t, appears. For except where price is fixed and independent of the size of output we now have, in general,

$$u_t \equiv MR_t \neq p_t ,$$

where $u_t = \partial u / \partial x_t \equiv MR_t$ is the marginal revenue of output x in period t.

However, it is not implausible that for a wide variety of products elasticity of demand does not change very rapidly over time. If as an approximation we take the elasticity, E_t, to be constant over time, then, by the standard relationship

$$MR_t = p_t(1 - 1/E_t) ,$$

we conclude that prices and marginal revenues will vary proportionately from period to period. In that case, (5) and all subsequent relationships which contain p_t will be affected only by multiplication of p_t by a constant. In terms of relative interperiod prices absolutely nothing will have changed. The firm will then find it most profitable to set relative prices and depreciation rates exactly as is required for maximization of the social welfare.

Let us now digress briefly to see how maintenance cost is taken into account in this analysis. Suppose that our asset does gradually show its age in one respect: its maintenance cost increases as it grows older. Implicitly we have already taken this possibility into account. The capital cost function $g(y_1, \ldots, y_n)$ includes both the initial and future costs contributed by added capacity. Since the acquisition of

y_1 units of capital adds to future maintenance costs, the discounted value of these costs must clearly constitute a component of the cost function g. However, it is useful to bring this out explicitly. Let M_t be the discounted present value of maintenance cost in period t of all equipment acquired since the initial period. Then under suitable assumptions (essentially, neglecting the interdependence of maintenance outlays in various periods) we can write

$$g(y_1, \ldots, y_n) = I(y_1, \ldots, y_n) + M_1(y_1)$$
$$+ M_2(y_1, y_2) + \cdots + M_n(y_1, \ldots, y_n),$$

where I represents the discounted present value of investment outlays, i.e., the cost of installing all of the firm's new equipment during the n periods. Then, writing g_1 for $\partial g / \partial y_1$, etc., we have

$$g_1 = I_1 + \sum_{t=1}^{n} M_{t1}. \tag{7}$$

Now let R_{t1} be the actual dollar outlay in period t whose discounted value is M_{t1} so that $(1 + r)^t M_{t1} = R_{t1}$. Assume that the maintenance cost of an added unit of y_1 grows at rate s each time the equipment ages one year, so that

$$R_{t+11} = (1 + s)R_{t1} \equiv vM_{t1},$$

or

$$M_{t+11} = \frac{1 + s}{1 + r} M_{t1} \equiv vM_{t1} \quad \left(\text{writing } v = \frac{1 + s}{1 + r}\right).$$

Substituting this into (7), we obtain

$$g_1 = I_1 + M_{11}(1 + v + \cdots + v^{n-1}) = I_1 + M_{11}\frac{1 - v^n}{1 - v}.$$

Hence, we can rewrite (6) as

$$I_1 + M_{11}\frac{1 - v^n}{1 - v} = I_1 + M_{11}(1 + v_1 + \cdots + v^{n-1}) = \lambda_1 + \cdots + \lambda_n,$$

which shows how the optimal depreciation payments, $\lambda_1, \ldots, \lambda_n$, increase both with M_{11}, the initial value of maintenance cost for an increment in capital, and with v, the rate of growth in that cost as the equipment ages.

Exactly the same sort of substitution can be used in the remainder of our discussion to bring maintenance into the analysis explicitly. Since it only complicates the exposition without adding any new insights, this will not be done. Instead, the maintenance payments will remain implicit in $g(y_1, \ldots, y_n)$. It need only be remarked that in later models, in which machines wear out gradually but never disappear altogether, there is no finite machine life n. In that case, to assure convergence of the series $1 + v + v^2 + \cdots$ we obviously require

$$v = \frac{1 + s}{1 + r} < 1, \text{ i.e., marginal maintenance costs must grow no faster}$$

than the discount rate, or else the cost incurred by installing a piece of equipment would clearly not be finite.

■ Let us now take into account the possibility that the asset will decrease in net productivity with the passage of time, partly because of aging and partly with wear and tear which is the result of usage (user cost).[9] We can introduce the first of these elements into our calculation by assuming that the asset whose capacity was y_1 in the initial period only has a capacity $y_1(1 - k)$ in the next period and a capacity $y_2(1 - k)^2$ the period after that, etc. User cost may be represented by a reduction in capacity in period t given by $w_t(x_1, \ldots, x_{t-1})$. Then our constraints (1) must be replaced by

$$x_1 \leq y_1 + i_1$$
$$x_2 \leq (1 - k)y_1 + y_2 + i_2 - w_2(x_1)$$
$$\cdots \cdots \cdots \cdots \cdots \cdots \cdots$$
$$x_t \leq (1 - k)^{t-1}y_1 + (1 - k)^{t-2}y_2 + \cdots + y_t + i_t - w_t(x_1, \ldots, x_{t-1})$$
$$\cdots \cdots \cdots \cdots \cdots \cdots \cdots$$

5. Further results: inflation, technological change, deterioration and user cost

Observe that the set of constraints is no longer finite since, with our present assumptions, an asset need never wear out completely if the user cost is sufficiently small. After t periods of aging, its capacity (neglecting user cost) will be reduced to $(1 - k)^t y$, which only approaches zero asymptotically. We then have as our Lagrangian

$$L = U - g - c + \sum_{s=1}^{\infty} \lambda_s[i_s - x_s - w_s(x_1, \ldots, x_{s-1})$$
$$+ \sum_{j=1}^{s} (1 - k)^{s-j}y_j] .$$

One consequence for our analysis follows immediately, for (5) is now replaced by

$$p_t = \frac{\partial c}{\partial x_t} + \lambda_t + \sum_{s>t} \lambda_s \frac{\partial w_s}{\partial x_t} . \tag{8}$$

This states that optimal price must include in its capital costs a payment for the marginal user cost of the output in question. The last term in (8) represents that marginal-user cost. It is the sum over all future years of the reduced output of all assets resulting from their use in producing x_t, that is, the sum of the $\partial w_s/\partial x_t$, each such future output loss valued at its λ_s, where this is the amount the public is willing to pay towards depreciation (i.e., for increased capacity) in that period. This will be zero in any period in which the firm's assets are not used to capacity. Note that to cover output losses in later peak periods a user cost must be paid in any period t, even if in period t itself the firm does not use its assets to capacity so that $\lambda_t = 0$.

The required modification in conditions (4) will not affect the analysis and will therefore not be specified here. However, we will presently require the revised (general inequality) form of condition (3) which now becomes[10]

$$\frac{\partial g}{\partial y_t} \geq \lambda_t + (1 - k)\lambda_{t+1} + (1 - k)^2\lambda_{t+2} + \cdots \tag{9}$$

---

[9] This section and the first part of the following section are essentially a slight modification of Littlechild's work.

[10] From (9) it follows directly that in this model, too, the sum of the depreciation payments on the output produced by a unit of equipment is equal to the marginal cost of that equipment. For suppose the unit of equipment is purchased

or

$$\lambda_t \leq \frac{\partial g}{\partial y_t} - (1 - k)\lambda_{t+1} - (1 - k)^2\lambda_{t+2} + \cdots.$$

6. Special depreciation rules when capital is added each period

■ We will now derive some remarkably simple depreciation rules that apply only in the special case where demand grows so rapidly that the asset is used to capacity in the period in which it is installed, and a new asset will be needed in each succeeding period. We will derive such rules for each of our two models. First, we continue with the more complex model of the preceding section. Since by assumption $y_t > 0$ in every period, (9) becomes an equation rather than an inequality. Comparing this equation (9) for period t with the corresponding equation for period $t + 1$, we obtain at once as an expression for the present value of the depreciation payment

$$\lambda_t = \frac{\partial g}{\partial y_t} - (1 - k)\frac{\partial g}{\partial y_{t+1}}. \tag{10}$$

Equation (10) can perhaps be considered the fundamental relationship in the model in which the productivity of equipment declines with age at a constant rate. Its interpretation helps to explain the logic of the entire analysis. Suppose output increases by dx_1 units above current capacity. This means that capacity in period one will have to be increased by $dy_1 = dx_1$ units at a cost $(\partial g/\partial y_1)dy_1$. However, since in the following period $(1 - k)dy_1$ units of this new capital will still be available, this will permit a corresponding reduction in next period's construction program, yielding a saving in that period of $(1 - k)dy_1(\partial g/\partial y_2)$.

Following Turvey (*loc. cit.*) we may in this case define the long-run marginal investment cost of output as the capital cost it incurs in this period minus the investment cost it saves in the following period, i.e., for $dx_1 = dy_1 = 1$, this marginal cost is $\partial g/\partial y_1 - (1 - k)\partial g/\partial y_2$, and, for any period t, this marginal capital cost is given by the right-hand side of (10). Thus (10) tells us that in the current model, assuming capital is purchased every period, the optimal depreciation charge, λ_t, is equal to the marginal capital cost of output in period t. Similarly, we may now interpret (8) to state that price should equal long-run marginal cost, which is equal to the sum of marginal operating cost, $\partial c/\partial x_t$, marginal investment cost, λ_t, and marginal user cost.

So far the analysis has all been expressed in terms of discounted present value. Since investments and prices are all expressed in current dollars, it will be useful to translate some of the above relationships into current dollars to explicitly examine how they are influenced by the discount rate and other relevant parameters. For this purpose, let r be the discount rate and let v_t be the value of $\partial g/\partial y_t$ expressed in dollars of period t so that

$$\frac{\partial g}{\partial y_t} = \frac{v_t}{(1 + r)^{t-1}}$$

in period t. Then the sum of the discounted depreciation payments on its outputs is $\lambda_t + \lambda_{t+1}(1 - k) + \lambda_{t+2}(1 - k)^2 + \cdots$. But since $y_t > 0$ we know that (9) must be an equation, so that these depreciation payments will then equal $\partial g/\partial y_t$, the marginal cost of y_t.

and[11]

$$\lambda_t = \frac{\mu_t}{(1+r)^t},\tag{11}$$

where μ_t is the number of dollars of depreciation accumulated in period t. By substitution of expressions (11) into the depreciation equation (10), we obtain

$$\mu_t = (1+r)^t \lambda_t = v_t(1+r) - (1-k)v_{t+1}.\tag{12}$$

Now, by the definition of $\partial g / \partial y_t$ and (11) we see that v_t is the marginal dollar cost of capacity in period t. Suppose that because of technological progress the real marginal cost of a unit of capacity is decreasing at the annual rate h, but because of price inflation this is (at least) partly offset by a rise in money cost at rate m per year. We then have

$$v_{t+1} = (1+m-h)v_t.\tag{13}$$

Substitution of (13) into (12) gives

$$\mu_t = v_t(1+r) - v_t(1-k)(1+m-h),$$

so that multiplying through and dropping the terms mk and $-kh$, which are presumably small,

$$\mu_t \cong v_t(r-m+k+h),\tag{14}$$

or if we wish to put the matter in terms of the real rate of interest $r^* = r - m$, we obtain

$$\mu_t \cong v_t(r^* + k + h).\tag{14'}$$

This rule, it must be emphasized once again, is valid only if growth is sufficiently rapid for capacity to be reached in each period so that $y_t > 0$ for every t.

The derivation of a similar depreciation formula for our simplest-model with fixed (n-year) asset life (Section 4) is, curiously, a bit more difficult. For this purpose, we utilize equation (3) to obtain

$$\frac{\partial g}{\partial y_1} = \lambda_1 + \cdots + \lambda_n$$

$$\frac{\partial g}{\partial y_2} = \lambda_2 + \cdots + \lambda_{n+1},$$

so that, subtracting, we have

$$\lambda_1 = \frac{\partial g}{\partial y_1} - \frac{\partial g}{\partial y_2} + \lambda_{n+1}.\tag{15}$$

These variables are all expressed in terms of present value. To replace them by variables representing actual dollar magnitudes for the period in question we again utilize expressions (11), substituting them into (15) to obtain

$$\mu_1 = v_1(1+r) - v_2 + \mu_{n+1}(1+r)^n.$$

---

[11] This defines the period so that the investment outlay, v_t, is made at its beginning while the depreciation, μ_t, is collected at the end of the period. Consequently, to obtain the corresponding present values at the initial period $t = 1$, we divide the former by $(1+r)^{t-1}$ and the latter by $(1+r)^t$.

If we assume replacement cost to decrease by a fixed proportion each period, we have

$$v_{t+1} = v_t(1 - h) \tag{16}$$

which, when substituted into the preceding equation, yields

$$\mu_1 = v_1[1 + r - (1 - h)] + \mu_{n+1}/(1 + r)^n$$
$$= v_1(r + h) + \mu_{n+1}/(1 + r)^n . \tag{17}$$

Since equation (17) applies for any initial period, we have for an asset purchased in period $n + 1$ exactly the same sort of equation:

$$\mu_{n+1} = v_{n+1}(r + h) + \frac{\mu_{2n+1}}{(1 + r)^n},$$

and, since by (16) $v_{n+1} = v_1(1 - h)^n$, the preceding expression becomes

$$\mu_{n+1} = v_1(1 - h)^n(r + h) + \frac{\mu_{2n+1}}{(1 + r)^n} \tag{17'}$$

and, similarly,

$$\mu_{2n+1} = v_1(1 - h)^{2n}(r + h) + \frac{\mu_{3n+1}}{(1 + r)^n}, \quad \text{etc} . \tag{17''}$$

Substituting successively from (17') into (17) to eliminate μ_{n+1} and then from (17'') to eliminate μ_{2n+1}, etc., we obtain the series

$$\mu_1 = v_1(r + h)\left[1 + \left(\frac{1 - h}{1 + r}\right)^n + \left(\frac{1 - h}{1 + r}\right)^{2n} + \cdots\right]$$

which, by the formula for the sum of a geometric series, becomes

$$\mu_1 = v_1 \frac{(r + h)}{1 - \left(\dfrac{1 - h}{1 + r}\right)^n}$$

Similarly, for any period t, since r, h, and n are independent of t,

$$\mu_t = v_t \frac{(r + h)}{1 - \left(\dfrac{1 - h}{1 + r}\right)^n}. \tag{18}$$

This is the general expression for the calculation of depreciation payments from the model with fixed (n-year) asset life.[12]

---

[12] In equation (14') for depreciation payments in our other model we found that, at least as an approximation, the term m disappeared from the expression. That is, the depreciation payment μ_t was shown to depend on the rate of increase in the price level, m, only through its effects on v_t, the cost of purchasing an additional unit of capacity in period t. A similar result is easily shown to hold here. Define the real annual reduction in investment cost h^*, and the real rate of interest r^*, respectively, as

$$h^* = h + m \quad \text{and}$$
$$r^* = r - m .$$

Substituting into (18) gives

$$\mu_t = v_t \frac{(r^* + m + h^* - m)}{1 - \left(\dfrac{1 - h^* + m}{1 + r^* + m}\right)} \leqq v_t \frac{(r^* - h^*)}{1 - \left(\dfrac{1 - h^*}{1 + r^*}\right)},$$

as was to be shown.

■ Equations (14) and (18) are the basic rules determining for our two models an optimal depreciation policy if new investments occur in every period. It will perhaps be helpful to discuss them further in more intuitive terms. Equation (14′), which is easier to interpret than (14), states that μ_t, the depreciation component of price in period t, should be proportional to v_t, the dollar cost per unit of added capacity in that period. Obviously, the ratio between the two is required by (14′) to vary directly with h, the annual rate of reduction in the replacement cost of the asset resulting from improved technology, and with k, the rate of decrease in net productivity of the asset. It also varies directly with the real rate of interest, r^*. Finally, it varies directly with m, the annual rate of increase in the price level, since v_t is raised correspondingly above v_{t-1}.

Intuitively, the rationale of the relationship is easily described. Technological changes that reduce costs of assets with the passage of time make it desirable that demands be postponed until less expensive equipment becomes available. Hence, the optimal current depreciation charge is increased by a rise in the value of h as a means to discourage current demand. Similarly, a high real discount rate, r^*, calls for postponement of investment since it makes a future investment less expensive relative to an earlier investment, and so, like a high value of h, a high r^* increases optimal depreciation charges. Rapid deterioration in the productivity of an asset (a high value of k) and higher prices (higher m) simply mean that more money must be collected each year of its life to cover the cost of the asset.

Turning now to a brief discussion of (18), the rule for the model with fixed asset life, we show that for this model (18) is the only depreciation rule that (a) permits payments to decrease in proportion with the rate of fall of the replacement cost of the asset, and (b) permits the original cost of the asset to be recouped by depreciation payments over its n-year life. In accord with (16), the replacement cost of the asset is assumed to fall at a constant percentage rate, $(1 - h)$, so that v_t, the cost of the asset in period t, will be

$$v_t = v_0(1 - h)^t .$$

Therefore, since by assumption (a) depreciation payments are to be proportional to replacement costs, we must have

$$\mu_t = \mu_0(1 - h)^t . \tag{19}$$

To show that (19) and (18) are identical, we must now prove that

$$\mu_0 = v_0 \frac{(r + h)}{1 - \left(\dfrac{1 - h}{1 + r}\right)^n} . \tag{20}$$

Utilizing assumption (b), we obviously require

$$v_0 = \text{sum of discounted depreciation payments}[13]$$

$$= \sum_{t=0}^{n-1} \mu_0 \frac{(1 + h)^t}{(1 + r)^{t+1}} = \sum_{t=0}^{n-1} \frac{\mu_0}{1 + r}\left(\frac{1 - h}{1 + r}\right)^t$$

---

[13] This assumes once again that the depreciation payment in period t occurs at the end of period t so that, e.g., the present value of the first depreciation payment will be $\dfrac{\mu_0}{1 + r} = \mu_0 \dfrac{(1 + h)^0}{(1 + r)}$.

which, by the usual formula for a finite geometric series,

$$= \frac{\mu_0}{1+r} \frac{1 - \left(\dfrac{1-h}{1+r}\right)^n}{1 - \dfrac{1-h}{1+r}}$$

$$= \mu_0 \frac{1 - \left(\dfrac{1-h}{1+r}\right)^n}{(1+r) - (1-h)} = \mu_0 \frac{1 - \left(\dfrac{1-h}{1+r}\right)^n}{r+h},$$

so that

$$\mu_0 = v_0 \frac{(r+h)}{1 - \left(\dfrac{1-h}{1+r}\right)^n},$$

which is equation (20), as was to be shown. Thus we conclude that (18) is the only depreciation formula which permits annual depreciation payments to fall proportionately with the replacement cost of the asset.

8. Some remarkable properties of the solution

■ The solution of the depreciation problem that has been described seems reasonable enough in terms of economic principles. For the economist its only surprising property is the fact that the depreciation payments called for by the calculation do add up, automatically, to the marginal cost of capacity even though that was not imposed in advance as a requirement for the solution. The reason they do so becomes clearer if we look at the sum of the depreciation payments, $\Sigma\lambda_t$ or $\Sigma(1-k)^t\lambda_t$, as the total rental values of the investments, as we interpreted them at the beginning of the discussion. Obviously, if the investment program is optimal its marginal cost, $\partial g/\partial y_t$, *must* be equal to its total rental per unit; for otherwise it would pay either to increase or to decrease the quantity of investment.

There are (at least) three other noteworthy properties of the solution, the first two perhaps of interest primarily for pure economics. The third characteristic, which Arrow has called the myopic property, may be important for application as well.

The first of these three properties is the fact that the λ_t, the depreciation payment in period t, is equal to the marginal net social yield of added capacity in period t. That is, the unit depreciation payment in any period is equal to the marginal productivity of added capital in that period. This is, of course, what neoclassical analysis should lead us to expect: that, optimally, an input will be paid its marginal yield, and that is how we conclude that the λ's are the rental values of the equipment in question. The proof of the property follows at once when we recognize that the λ_t, the Lagrange multipliers of the Kuhn-Tucker maximand, are necessarily the structural variables of the dual program. Since, as is well known, the dual variables are the marginal yields corresponding to the inputs of the primal problem, we have the first of the three results.

The second of our solution properties is equally easy to derive. It states that the two apparently independent definitions of the depreciation problem with which we began our discussion are *both* satisfied by our solution. Specifically, it will be recalled that the economic depreciation problem can be defined as the answer to one or the other of the following questions: (a) How much has the economic value of a given piece of equipment decreased in the period in question? (b) During the period, what is the (optimal) payment to be charged to consumers toward recovery of the cost of the equipment, over and above its marginal operating cost? In this paper we have obviously addressed ourselves to the latter of these questions, and our solution may at first glance appear to have no necessary relevance for the former. However, once having selected a set of consumer prices that satisfies our second question it is easy to show that the first is easily answered, at least for a *marginal* unit of capacity, and that the answers to the two questions then coincide. For we have decided to charge during the lifetime of the equipment (to deal with the simplest case for ease of exposition) a stream of prices given, according to (5), by $p_t = \partial c/\partial x_t + \lambda_t$. The net gain from the marginal unit of output is then $p_t - \partial c/\partial x_t = \lambda_t$. Hence the marginal value of a unit of capacity with a life of n years added in period t is (since the λ_t are all present values)

$$v_t = \lambda_t + \lambda_{t+1} + \lambda_{t+2} + \cdots + \lambda_n.$$

By the next period, the residual value of that piece of equipment will have fallen to $v_{t+1} = \lambda_{t+1} + \cdots + \lambda_n$. Consequently, the amount by which the value of the marginal unit of equipment will have declined in period t is precisely

$$v_t - v_{t+1} = \lambda_t,$$

i.e., it is exactly equal to the period t depreciation payment calculated in answer to the optimal depreciation problem. Thus, so long as the revenue requirement is met by prices given by (18) the two interpretations of depreciation turn out to be identical. Where, in addition, a revenue requirement must be imposed on the analysis, prices will presumably be different from long-run marginal costs, and so the two answers will no longer be identical.

Finally, we turn to the so-called myopic property of the solutions. This property, which Arrow attributes to Marglin, to Champernowne, and to Kurahashi,[14] applies in the special case where some equipment is purchased in successive periods, i.e., when $y_t > 0$ and $y_{t+1} > 0$. In that case *it becomes totally unnecessary to forecast more than one period* in determining depreciation or long-run marginal cost. Moreover, in that case, the depreciation figure can be determined simply from the cost of the equipment in the current period, v_t, and the next succeeding period, v_{t+1}, from the calculated rate of loss of physical productivity of the equipment, k, and the discount rate, r. This follows at once from (10) and (11). From these we calculate immediately our *long-run* marginal cost figure

$$\frac{\partial c}{\partial x_t} + \lambda_t = \frac{\partial c}{\partial x_t} + \frac{\mu_t}{(1+r)^t} = \frac{\partial c}{\partial x_t} + \frac{v_t}{(1+r)^{t-1}} - (1+k)\frac{v_{t+1}}{(1+r)^t}.$$

This is *the* correct long-run value of marginal cost, since it includes both the marginal operating cost and the period's assigned contribution toward capital replacement.

---

[14] See Arrow, *op. cit.*

The rules given by (12), (14), and (18) are called "myopic" because they permit capital depreciation to be calculated correctly with the aid of a forecast extending only over one period and not over the entire life of the equipment. Moreover, they do not refer to some average of one-year cost differences but to the actual difference in cost between this year and the next. For example, if, because of technological progress, costs of equipment decline 5 percent per year on the average, but this year happens to be particularly slow on innovation so that equipment cost is going down at a rate of only 2 percent, the latter is the correct figure to use in the myopic formulas for *long-run* marginal cost!

The reason the rules work has already implicitly been explained. If a radio tower is going to have to be built next year anyhow, the marginal cost of constructing one today is simply the added cost of producing it one year earlier, all other decisions remaining unchanged. After that (say in the third year), since the tower would have been in existence in any case, it makes no difference whether it is built today or next year. That is, in computing the marginal cost of its construction today, we perform the calculation (total present and future cost of building it today) minus (total present and future cost of doing so next year) plus (cost of replacing that portion which decays from this year to the next), and since any associated third-year cost is contained in each of the three terms in parentheses, it simply cancels out in subtraction. All that remains after subtraction is the cost difference over the one-year period beginning today, clearly $\partial g/\partial y_t - (1 - k)\partial g/\partial y_{t+1}$, the right-hand side of equation (10).

The myopic decision rules can be helpful in practice because, where they apply, they can simplify the calculation of marginal costs and depreciation charges. Unfortunately, the condition for their applicability is somewhat more demanding than it may seem at first glance. It is not enough for the company as a whole to buy new equipment every period. That equipment must all be substitutable (tomorrow's transmission tower must serve the same sort of purpose as today's) not only in the general nature of its function but also in the particular customers it is capable of serving. The theorems apply along a busy telephone route where volume grows so quickly that at least one new radio tower must be built every period. But a new tower in Oklahoma today and a new tower in Maine next period will not serve the purpose, simply because the former cannot act as a substitute for the latter. The Oklahoma tower is not just a slightly older piece of equipment capable of carrying traffic in Maine.

If this condition, the construction of new substitutable towers each period, does not hold, the myopic depreciation rules (14) and (18) need not be valid as they stand. In that case we may have to employ instead conditions such as (9) in which all relevant future periods must be considered in the depreciation calculation. However, if, rather than every period, a new tower has to be added, say, every four periods, the myopic depreciation rules will still hold in somewhat modified form. Equations (14) and (18) will now apply not to the depreciation payment in a single period but to the sum of the four depreciation payments between two successive substitutable investments, as is readily seen by going through our analysis for a longer super-period consisting of four of our basic periods. In this case, forecasts four periods into the future will be needed to calculate the depreciation payment.

However, since the decision period for a public utility, the period during which prices are not expected to change, may well be of the order of magnitude of 3–5 years, in such a growing firm the conditions for direct applicability of the myopic decision rules may well be valid for a substantial portion of its operations.

■ This note has attempted to examine systematically the economic logic of depreciation, and has sought to describe rules for a socially optimal depreciation policy. With the aid of an analysis contributed largely by Littlechild, it has been possible to do so on at least a preliminary basis. Like all results derived from purely abstract models, the rules obtained in our analysis must be handled with care and used only with attention to the practicalities. Yet the rules derived, though some of them may run counter to conventional notions, really seem reasonable on careful reflection. At least they do have more to be said for their rationale than the arbitrary choice of a purely traditional accounting convention. Indeed, the results of the analysis may themselves help to choose among accounting procedures.

9. Concluding comments

Finally, a technical note. If it transpires that marginal asset cost is not equal to unit asset cost, then the third result of Section 3 no longer guarantees that the depreciation charges given by (14) or (18) will suffice to cover the cost of the asset. In that case, it is necessary to adjoin to our model an explicit revenue requirement constraint assuring that adequate depreciation funds will be collected. But then we are back at the rules for welfare maximization subject to a revenue constraint, and the Ramsey-Boiteux theorems[15] for optimal departures from marginal cost pricing. These propositions indicate how prices can be set to produce optimal resource utilization when it is necessary to meet a revenue requirement determined by regulation or by some other means. If marginal cost pricing does not yield enough revenue to cover capital costs, these rules call for prices that exceed marginal costs. The pattern of prices is designed to minimize the distortion of consumer choice, and so it generally calls for the highest prices relative to marginal costs for those items whose demands are most inelastic, i.e., whose demands will be least affected by higher prices. If, in fact, the demands for the firm's products are not changing rapidly with the passage of time this means that the optimal prices for all periods should exceed marginal costs by the same percentage, so that the prices indicated by the expressions in this paper would simply all be raised by the same percentage. However, note once again that so long as the cost of purchasing equipment is simply proportionate to the number of units of equipment bought, even this adjustment will be unnecessary. Our depreciation rules will then cover the equipment costs precisely.

We conclude by observing once again that this paper has provided several technical constructs which, hopefully, will illuminate an important practical problem but which do not pretend to provide a

[15] See Frank Ramsey, "A Contribution to the Theory of Taxation," *Economic Journal*, Vol. XXXVII (March 1927), and M. Boiteux, "Sur la gestion des Monopoles Publics astreints à l'équilibre budgétaire," *Econometrica*, Vol. 24 (April 1956).

neatly prepackaged set of answers to it. If it is applied to regulated industries, the analysis should not be taken to prejudge such critical issues as the rate base on which to calculate the revenue requirement for a regulated firm or the degree of disaggregation of its services which should be used as a basis for its pricing. Rather, the objective has been to take these decisions as given by whatever means happen to apply, and to determine on that basis the values of long-run marginal costs (the depreciation payments) that provide for an optimal allocation of resources.

[8]

Applied Fairness Theory and Rationing Policy

By WILLIAM J. BAUMOL*

In the past few years, several economists, notably Duncan Foley, Hal Varian, E. A. Pazner and David Schmeidler, have produced a novel analytical theory of *fairness* in the distribution of resources, in contradistinction to the efficiency of their allocation. This work is primarily philosophical in orientation, being concerned primarily with the logical underpinnings of an analysis of fair division, rather than with its application. Here, I offer a nontechnical introduction to the subject, providing a few new results about the construction. But this is only a preliminary to an attempt to show how fairness theory can be used to study policy, employing the issue of rationing of commodities as an illustration.

Persons who design public policy are, typically, at least as concerned with issues of equity as with allocative efficiency. The economist's influence is therefore impeded by his inability to deal with issues of fairness in applied problems. Fairness theory, perhaps for the first time, provides an analytic instrument for the purpose. Inevitably, it must, of course, rest upon value judgments as well as observable relationships. But what is remarkable about fairness theory is that both the behavioral relationships and the value judgments on which it is based are, essentially, those used in the standard welfare analysis of resource allocation. In both, the basic data are consumer preferences and production relationships, and in both the basic value judgment is that the desires of the affected individuals, rather than those of some superior arbitrator, must count.

Our illustrative policy issue—the rationing of commodities—has reemerged with the fuel

problem. Here, I will examine the choice between two points-rationing arrangements, under which consumers are each issued a fixed number of ration points, redeemable at a fixed "points price," P_g, per gallon of gasoline, or at another coupon price, P_h, per gallon of heating oil, etc. The consumer is thereby subjected to a second budget constraint expressed in ration points rather than money. Economists have suggested that the efficiency of such a rationing system can be improved if it is accompanied by a "white market," in which consumers with unwanted ration coupons can sell them to others at a market-clearing (money) price. I will show that while there is a valid *efficiency* argument favoring the white market arrangement over one in which the sale of ration coupons is prohibited, fairness analysis yields a presumption that goes the other way. This may provide some justification for the apparently widespread suspicion of the fairness of white markets among noneconomists.

I. Foley's Criterion of Fairness

Fairness theory can be considered a straightforward extension of the standard algorithm for fair division of a homogeneous cake between two individuals: I cut, you choose. The theory becomes much more interesting when there are several commodities to be divided (the cake is not homogeneous) and tastes are not identical. Suppose, for example, that one side of the cake is covered preponderantly by chocolate chunks and the other by raisins and person 1, the cutter, likes chocolate and has no particular love for raisins while the reverse is true of the chooser, 2. Then 1 will find it advantageous to cut the cake so that one slice contains most of the chocolate and the other, most of the raisins.[1]

*Princeton University and New York University. I am grateful to the National Science Foundation for its support of the research reported here. Portions of this paper were first delivered as the Harry Johnson Memorial Lecture before the Association of University Teachers of Economics in Durham, England.

[1]There is an interesting strategic issue here. The cut will be very different in the case where A is sure of B's preferences and that in which he is very uncertain about

640   THE AMERICAN ECONOMIC REVIEW   SEPTEMBER 1982

Now, 2 can be expected to pick the raisin slice because it offers her more than half the total utility of the cake, *in her own estimation*. But by doing so, she leaves 1 with the chocolate side of the cake which yields him more than half the utility of the cake, in his own estimation. I call such a distribution superfair—for it offers each participant *more* than the minimum bundle of goods necessary to yield a distribution that is subjectively "fair" to that individual. The following definitions slightly modify the terminology of previous writers:

Definition 1. Envy. A distribution,[2] *i*, of *n* commodities is said to involve envy by individual 2 of the share obtained by individual 1 if 2 would rather have Y_{1i}, the bundle of commodities received by 1 under this distribution, than Y_{2i}, the bundle the distribution assigns to 2.

Definition 2. Fairness. A distribution is fair if it involves no envy by any individual of any other.

Definition 3. Strict Superfairness. A distribution is strictly superfair if each participant receives a bundle which is strictly preferred by that individual to the bundle received by anyone else, that is, if his holdings could be reduced (in the case of divisibility) without giving rise to envy.[3]

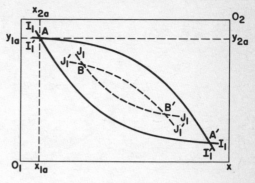

FIGURE 1

II. Graphics of Superfairness

Since we are dealing with the division of fixed bundles of commodities, the Edgeworth box diagram will serve as our basic tool. Most of the literature deals with the case of *m* persons and *n* commodities, but for convenience in graphing it is obviously appropriate to deal with a world of two persons, 1 and 2, and two goods, *X* and *Y*.

Locus $I_1 I_1$ in Figure 1 is simply an arbitrarily selected indifference curve of individual 1, as in the standard Edgeworth diagram. However, $I_1' I_1'$ is *not* one of individual 2's indifference curves. Rather, $I_1' I_1'$ is simply the mirror image of $I_1 I_1$—it is $I_1 I_1$ redrawn so that $I_1' I_1'$ relates to 2's origin, O_2, in exactly the same way that $I_1 I_1$ rates to O_1. This upside-down version of 1's indifference curve enables us to judge 1's evaluation of what 2 receives at a particular point in the box, as the concept of envy requires.

Now consider points *A* and *A'*, the intersection points of our two renderings of the same indifference curve. The distribution represented by *A* must leave individual 1 indifferent between what *A* gives to him and what *A* gives to individual 2. For 1 receives

---

them. This issue has been dealt with by Vincent Crawford (1977), but here it only complicates the discussion unnecessarily.

[2] In this article I deal only with the distribution of a fixed bundle of outputs—the case of exchange, for which superfairness analysis is known to be far more tractable than it is in cases in which production is involved. For further discussion of the problems that arise when production is part of the issue, see Pazner and Schmeidler (1974) and Varian (1974, 1975).

[3] One of the referees of this paper asks, cogently, "so long as it is assumed, as it is here, that preferences are strictly selfish, who *cares* about fairness? The economist is here in the position of the utilitarian advising people who... do not care about others, that total welfare will be maximized by the equal distribution of income." But, surely, there is more to the matter. Selfish people are selfishly worried that they may be treated unfairly, and they may, consequently, insist on rules of fairness. That is what the cake division game is all about. A rule of fairness is a sort of insurance arrangement which selfish people accept to make sure they will not be mistreated, and pay for it by providing assurance to others that

they, too, will not be mistreated. Rawls' social contract interpretation of fairness is no more dependent on altruism of the members of society than is Foley's fairness theory, which we are discussing here. Both deal with, in effect, an insurance program for those who do not come out on top.

VOL. 72 NO. 4   *BAUMOL: APPLIED FAIRNESS THEORY*   641

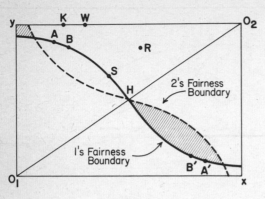

FIGURE 2

the bundle $A_1 = (O_1x_{1a}, O_1y_{1a})$, lying on his indifference curve I_1I_1; while 2 receives $A_2 = (O_2x_{2a}, O_2y_{2a})$ which lies on $I_1'I_1'$, the same indifference curve of individual 1 as A_1 does. Hence, 1 must be indifferent between A_1 and A_2 and so point A must involve no envy by person 1 of 2's commodity bundle. Consequently, point A is an allocation that is just *marginally* fair from the viewpoint of individual 1. The same is obviously true of A'. Thus we say that points A and A' lie on person 1's *fairness boundary*. We can obtain two more such points from a second indifference curve, J_1J_1, of individual 1 yielding boundary points B and B'. Continuing in this way we trace out all of individual 1's fairness boundary (Figure 2), that is, the borderline between distributions which 1 considers unfair and those he considers more than fair.

In exactly the same way we can construct 2's fairness boundary, from her indifference curves and their mirror images. This boundary is also shown in Figure 2.

It is now easy to see how superfair solutions can arise. Assuming (as I will throughout) that neither individual is sated in either good, then any point such as R, above and/or to the right of 1's fairness boundary, must be more than fair to him. For there must then exist points such as S on the fairness boundary which offer 1 less (or at most as much) of each good as R, and which offer 2 more (no less) of each good. Hence, since S is marginally fair to 1, R must

be more than fair to him. Similarly, any point below 2's fairness boundary must be more than fair to her. Consequently, any point in a region which lies, simultaneously, above 1's fairness boundary and below that of person 2 (the shaded regions in Figure 2) must represent a superfair distribution.

III. Properties of the Fairness Boundaries

We can derive several properties of fairness boundaries.

PROPOSITION 1: *If each individual's preferences are continuous, they depend only on the quantities received by him, and if nonsatiety holds everywhere, the fairness boundary must* (a) *contain the midpoint, H, of either diagonal of the box;* (b) *its portion to the left of H must be the inverted mirror image of its portion to the right of H. That is, if (x^*, y^*) gives the dimensions of the box (i.e., x^* is the available quantity of x, etc.) and point $A \equiv (x, y)$ on the boundary lies to the left of H, then the symmetric image point $A' \equiv (x^* - x, y^* - y)$ must lie on the boundary to the right of H;* (c) *the boundary must have a negative slope everywhere.*[4]

Properties (a) and (b) follow trivially:

PROOF:

(a) At midpoint H, each individual receives exactly the same bundle as the other and so each must be indifferent between his own bundle and the other person's.

(b) By the construction of the boundary, if A lies on 1's boundary, person 1 must be indifferent between his bundle (x, y) and 2's bundle $(x^* - x, y^* - y)$. Hence, he must remain indifferent if the bundles are interchanged, so A' must also lie on 1's boundary.

(c) Let $(x_1, y_1)(x_2, y_2)$, respectively, be 1's and 2's possessions at point A on 1's fairness boundary; and let $(x_1 + \Delta x_1, y_1 + \Delta y_1)$, $(x_2 - \Delta x_1, y_2 - \Delta y_1)$ be their respective holdings at point $A + \Delta A$ on the boundary. If U^1 is 1's utility function, then, by defini-

---

[4] This characteristic was pointed out to me by Dietrich Fischer.

tion of the fairness boundary, we must have

(1) $U^1(x_1, y_1) = U^1(x_2, y_2)$,

(2) $U^1(x_1 + \Delta x_1, y_1 + \Delta y_1)$

$\quad = U^1(x_2 - \Delta x_1, y_2 - \Delta y_1)$.

Taking $\Delta x_1 > 0$, if the slope were nonnegative, so that $\Delta y_1 \geq 0$, then by nonsatiety

$$U^1(x_1 + \Delta x_1, y_1 + \Delta y_1) > U^1(x_1, y_1),$$

$$U^1(x_2 - \Delta x_1, y_2 - \Delta y_1) < U^1(x_2, y_2),$$

which together with (1) contradict (2). Thus, if $\Delta x_1 > 0$ we must have $\Delta y_1 < 0$, and the boundary's slope must be negative.

Next, we turn to existence of the fairness boundary.

PROPOSITION 2: *Where the individual's utility function and hence the indifference map is everywhere continuous, and the individual is not sated in the commodities, the fairness boundary must extend to the edges of the Edgeworth box. The fairness boundary will then always exist. In particular, in the two-commodity case it will extend continuously from some point, K, on the upper or left-hand edges of the Edgeworth box, through the midpoint to the point K' symmetric with K on the lower or right-hand edges.*

PROOF:

As we have seen, the midpoint, H, will always lie on the fairness boundary. By continuity, the boundary must always also exist in a neighborhood of H. Next, note (Figure 2) that individual 1's origin O_1 must be unfair to him because there individual 1 gets nothing and the goods all go to other parties. By the nonsatiety assumption 1 will envy the parties who do get goods. Analogously, O_2, the opposite origin, must be more than fair to 1 in his own opinion. As one moves along the boundary of the Edgeworth box from O_1 coming steadily closer to O_2, the degree of envy of individual 1 must decline steadily. By continuity, there must be some intermediate point, K, on this path at which 1 is

indifferent between what is assigned to him and what is assigned to that other individual who in 1's opinion is most favored. By definition, K must lie on 1's fairness boundary.

Next, draw in a ray from O_1 to *any* point, such as W, which lies on the northeast boundary $O_1 y O_2$ of the box to the right of K; then by the same argument as before, a marginally fair point must lie somewhere on ray OW. The remainder of Proposition 2 follows immediately by the continuity assumption, and the symmetry property of the fairness boundary.

IV. Properties of the Regions of Superfairness

We see that the set of (nonstrictly) superfair distributions must contain H, but it is generally not symmetric about H. Given one such region to the right of H, the symmetric region to the left of H will never be superfair since in the former, 1's fairness boundary must lie below 2's so that in the latter, 2's fairness boundary must lie above 1's (Figure 2).

We also see that the superfair regions may be disconnected and may contain portions of the axes. Thus we obtain

PROPOSITION 3: *The superfair region will generally not be located symmetrically within the Edgeworth box and it may not be convex or a single connected set of points.*

Next, let us discuss the existence of strictly superfair solutions. It was remarked earlier that their existence is ascribable to differences in tastes. Indeed, it is easy to show

PROPOSITION 4: *If both individuals have identical preferences, then their fairness boundaries must coincide and so there can be no region of strictly superfair solutions, for such a region must lie between the two curves.*

The proof is obvious. If point A lies on 1's fairness boundary yielding basket A_1 to 1 and A_2 to 2, then, by definition, 1 must be indifferent between A_1 and A_2. But, with identity of tastes, the same must be true of 2 so that A must also lie on 2's fairness boundary.

VOL. 72 NO. 4   *BAUMOL: APPLIED FAIRNESS THEORY*   643

Thus, differences in tastes are necessary for the existence of strictly superfair solutions. The geometry also suggests a related sufficient condition.

PROPOSITION 5: *If, in the neighborhood of H, the two fairness boundaries have continuous first derivatives which are, however, different from one another, then some strictly superfair solutions must exist.*

PROOF:

If at H the slopes of the two boundaries are not identical, they must intersect there. Then 2's boundary must lie above 1's boundary either immediately to the right of H or to the left of H (but not both). There, any point between the two boundaries must be strictly superfair.

To interpret this economically, note that the slope of the fairness boundary is a sort of marginal rate of substitution. As in (1) and (2), for individual 1 it is $\Delta y_1/\Delta x_1$, where Δx_1 and Δy_1 are the increments in individual 1's holdings which change their utility to him by exactly the same amount that they change the utility to him of the bundle received by individual 2. Thus, if both individuals' fairness boundaries have the same slopes, both must have the same relative valuations of the two goods at the margin throughout the neighborhood in question. It is in this sense that tastes must differ in order for the sufficient condition for the existence of superfair solutions to be satisfied.

We come next to a fundamental theorem which seems first to have been discovered by Schmeidler and Menachaim Yaari. It deals with the relationship between Pareto optimal solutions and solutions that are superfair. Specifically, it tells us that among the available solutions to a problem involving the distribution of a *fixed* stock of commodities among a fixed number of individuals there will always be at least one solution which is at the same time superfair (though not necessarily strictly superfair) and Pareto optimal. To see why this is so, consider an initially equal distribution of all goods (point H). If the contract curve happens to contain H, the result follows since H is fair by definition.

Assume next that the contract curve does not go through H and consider the intersection point L of the two individuals' offer curves that begin from H, as in the usual international-trade diagram. Then the standard proof shows that L must lie on the contract curve. But L must also be superfair because at the prices given by the slope of the common price line each individual has the same range of choices available. Letting L_1 and L_2 be the bundles chosen by 1 and 2 at L (where, by construction, the two bundles add up to the available quantities of the two goods), 1 thus reveals a preference for L_1 over L_2 and the reverse is true for 2. Consequently, L is necessarily superfair as well as Pareto optimal. Thus, we have a result now well known in the fairness literature:

PROPOSITION 6: *In the exchange of fixed quantities of n commodities among m individuals, there always exists at least one Pareto optimal solution which is superfair.*

V. Multistage Superfairness

While all distributions represented by points within a superfair region are superfair, some are more superfair than others. In Figure 3 let the shaded area be a region of superfair distributions with B_1B_1 and B_2B_2 the fairness boundaries. Consider point V, the tangent point between B_2B_2 and 1's indifference curve, I_1, the highest of 1's indifference curves within the region of superfair distributions. Then any distribution represented by a point just below and to the left

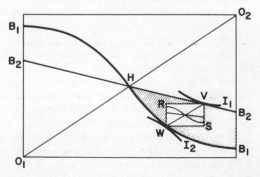

FIGURE 3

of V clearly is (marginally, but strictly) superfair. The same is true of any point just above and to the right of W, the point of tangency of $B_1 B_1$ with 2's indifference curve, I_2. But the former offers individual 1 much more than is in his view necessary to give him a fair share while it offers virtually no such surplus to 2; the reverse is clearly true of point W. Obviously, in some sense, points just above W are "superfairer" to 2 and points just below V are "superfairer" to 1. In that sense, an intermediate point seems "more superfair," the interests of both parties considered, than is either a point near W or one near V.

The example of the cutting of a nonhomogeneous cake should bring out the source of the issue. Suppose one-quarter of the cake is covered with chocolate chunks and the opposite quarter with raisins, with the remainder of the cake having neither. Suppose that chocolate-lover 1 is indifferent between the quarter of the cake having the chocolate and the remaining three quarters of the cake, and that the reverse is true of raisin-lover 2. Then any division of the cake which gives 1 the chocolate-covered quarter and bit more is strictly superfair, and the same is true of any division of the cake which gives 2 the raisined quarter and a bit more, since in neither case will either of the parties wish to exchange with the other. But it would seem that a fairer and better distribution yet would result if the cake were cut in half with the half containing all the chocolate and no raisins going to 1 and the remainder going to 2. Such a solution is, however, arbitrary. It returns us to the problems of interpersonal comparison with which one can deal in practice in a rough and ready manner, but which is quite unsatisfactory as a basis for analysis. What if 1 likes chocolate more than 2 likes raisins? Indeed, what does that mean and how does one measure the difference in intensity of feeling? And what is the implication for the fairest of superfair divisions of the cake? The entire approach is obviously unsatisfactory analytically, though, I repeat, not always insoluble in practice.

We can, however, do something to narrow the issue analytically. Perhaps the search for any one distribution which is fairest of all is ultimately a quest for a nonexistent phantom —there is no perfectly just price and no perfectly fair distribution. Then, the best we can hope for is to rule out those distributions which are in some respect demonstrably *un*fair. From this point of view, the fact that we are left with a range of choices is not in itself unsatisfactory. What is unsatisfactory is the possibility that the region of superfair distributions as so far traced out may be discomfortingly large, and permit discomforting asymmetries in terms of the preferences of the individuals. However, there is a simple iterative replication of our superfairness analysis which may enable us to narrow that range of choice as much as we like, at least in principle.

The procedure is readily illustrated with the aid of Figure 3. Consider the rectangle $RVSW$ whose northeast corner is V, individual 1's most desired superfair distribution, and whose southwest corner, W, is the superfair distribution most preferred by 2. Any point inside that box represents a redistribution of the surplus, between maximal satisfaction to 1 with just marginal fairness to 2 at the one extreme, and the opposite situation at the other. But the choice among the distributions in rectangle $RVSW$ may itself be treated as an issue of fair division, and it can in its turn be analyzed with the aid of the instruments described here.

Thus, we can consider $RVSW$ to be an interior Edgeworth box containing the indifference curves of 1 and 2 over the redistributions represented by points in the box. We can use our previous construction to trace out regions of superfair distributions within that box. If individual 1's optimal superfair point lies above and to the right of W, the optimal superfair point of 2, as is not unlikely, then by the negative slope of the fairness boundaries all of subbox $RVSW$ will lie inside the shaded region of superfairness, and so the (shaded) superfair distributions within the interior Edgeworth box must obviously also lie within the original superfairness region. Thus, the second stage of such a superfairness analysis will have narrowed the range of solutions which we consider most meritorious on equity grounds. If this narrowing is considered insufficient, the process

VOL. 72 NO. 4   BAUMOL: APPLIED FAIRNESS THEORY   645

can be repeated, carrying the multistage fairness analysis through as many rounds as we desire.

Once again, the cake-cutting example helps to explain the multistage superfairness calculation. Suppose we assign to 1 the quarter-cake covered with chocolate which is most important to him, and assign to 2 the quarter covered with raisins that is most important to her. That guarantees fairness to each party, since there is no slice of the remainder that either prefers to what he or she receives. Let us, therefore, examine what has so far been assigned to neither of them and consider it the surplus still to be divided between them (with *any* division of the surplus being "fair" by our criterion). But if the surplus in turn is divided by 1 cutting and 2 choosing, or vice versa, that will be a superfair division, representing the second stage of our superfairness algorithm.

The iterative process I have just described can, in principle, narrow the region of superfair distribution, and may reduce it considerably at each step, as is suggested by Figure 3. Indeed, by repeating it a substantial number of times with the successive Edgeworth subboxes each nested within its predecessor in the manner just described, we would appear to approach a limit point.[5] The significance of that point is another matter. Should it in some sense be considered the

"most superfair" point of all? Does it lie on the contract curve? Does it have any other interesting properties? These are all issues which must be left for future research.

VI. Rationing: Application of Superfairness Theory

As an exercise designed to illustrate the applicability of superfairness analysis to concrete issues, I will discuss what the theory tells us about the equity of the several rationing methods. Specifically, I will deal with two rationing procedures: 1) *pure points rationing* in which individuals are each assigned fixed numbers of ration points (their points incomes) which they can use to "buy" the rationed commodities at a fixed (parametric) point price for each commodity; 2) *rationing with salable points*, the case in which the individual pays for goods with both points

---

program

   min k_i subject to

$$U^i(k_i y_{i1},...,k_i y_{in}) \geq U^i[y_{w1}+(1-k_i)y_{i1}$$

$$/(m-1),...,y_{wn}+(1-k_i)y_{in}/(m-1)]$$

$$(\forall w \neq i); 0 \leq k_i \leq 1.$$

Step 3. Let y_j^* be the total quantity of commodity j available. We know that in the initial distribution, y^h,

$$\sum_{w=1}^{m} y_{wj} = y_j^*.$$

Therefore, $y_j^{**} \equiv y_j^* - \sum_{w=1}^{m} k_w y_{wj} \geq 0$, since $k_w \leq 1$.

Then repeat the previous steps, this time distributing the nonnegative residual quantities, y_j^{**}, rather than the initial quantities y_j^*, among the m individuals.

This process can be repeated as many times as we desire. In essence, step 1 is designed, simply, to give us a feasible solution that is superfair and which can be used as an initial point. Step 2 is designed to reduce *each* individual's initial allocation to a point he considers minimally fair, and it is done in such a way that a nonnegative quantity of each commodity is guaranteed to be left over. It is this nonnegativity property that permits the calculation to be repeated. The preceding discussion suggests how other portions of our graphic discussion that are not contained in the previous literature can be generalized to a multiplicity of goods and consumers.

---

[5] The limit-point result was suggested to me by James Mirrlees. It is easy to devise an analogous algorithm for an exchange process involving m persons and n commodities. Any such algorithm is designed to reduce the region of superfair solutions sequentially, at each step removing some subsets of points that are "less superfair" than those that remain. It should be clear that such a process will not be unique. The following is an example of such a process:

Step 1. Calculate the market exchange solution which would result if all m individuals were given equal incomes, i.e., if the initial point were H and all voluntary exchanges were permitted. We have already seen that the resulting distribution $y^h = (y^1,...,y^m)$ must be Pareto optimal and superfair. Here y^i is the vector of quantities of the n goods accruing to individual i.

Step 2. For each individual, i, calculate the minimal value of the parameter $k_i \leq 1$ such that $k_i y^i$ remains fair to i if all of the quantities $(1-k_i)y^i$ are divided equally among all $m-1$ remaining persons. That is, letting U^i be the utility function of person i and y_{ij} the quantity of good j going to i in distribution y^h, one solves the

646   THE AMERICAN ECONOMIC REVIEW   SEPTEMBER 1982

and money, and is free to purchase or sell points for money.

On efficiency grounds the literature generally considers pure points rationing to be superior to fixed rations, and considers rationing with salable points to be still better.[6]

I will show that

a) With pure points rationing any market-clearing equilibrium solution will be superfair.

b) In general, the equilibrium under rationing with salable points need not be fair.

Thus, there will be cases in which the equilibrium with salable ration points will be inferior in terms of the fairness criterion to the case where sale of points is prohibited, even if the former arrangement is superior in terms of resource allocation, something which is itself not as clear as usually assumed.

VII. Points Rationing with Unsalability of Ration Coupons

Points rationing involves the payment of money as well as points in exchange for goods. Each rationed commodity has its money price determined by market forces, as well as its points price determined by the authorities, *both* of which must be paid by the consumer. As has long been recognized, this makes the individual consumer's decision problem one involving maximization of utility subject to *two* linear constraints: the money budget inequality and the points budget inequality.

Since the analysis is most pertinent to a case involving inflationary pressure, it is useful to assume that the two parties represented in our Edgeworth box have, between them, more than enough money to purchase the available quantities of the two outputs. This means that individuals 1 and 2's price lines will not coincide. They will have the same slopes since, in the absence of price discrimination, they will face the same relative prices. However, with 1 the individual whose origin is the lower left-hand corner of the box, 1's price line, P_1P_1, will lie above

[6] Of course, economists have recognized that an equity issue is involved here. See, for example, Tobin's classic survey (1952).

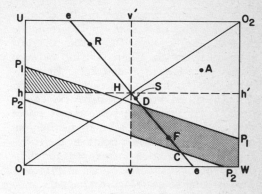

FIGURE 4

and to the right of 2's price line, P_2P_2 (Figure 4), meaning that the two together can, at current prices, afford to buy more than the available quantities of the two goods. Notice that the two together cannot afford to end up at a point (such as A) that lies above P_1P_1 (or one that lies below P_2P_2). While 2 has the money to pay for the quantities of X and Y assigned to her by point A (because it lies nearer to her origin than her price line), 1 cannot get to A since it lies above his price line. Thus, the two parties can only afford to get to points lying on or between their price lines.

We can now see easily what happens if the authorities decide to impose points rationing. As we know, this amounts to the introduction of a new points price line, ee, which cuts through point H of equal division. An equilibrium point must now satisfy both the monetary and the budget constraints. That is, it must lie on ee and, as we have just seen, on or between the two monetary price lines P_1P_1 and P_2P_2. This leaves us with only the line segment DC of ee that lies between P_1P_1 and P_2P_2. No other point in the diagram is consistent with the constraints.

But this is true only at the relative points prices whose ratio is equal to the slope of points price line, ee. If the authorities select other points prices, the points price lines will rotate through H. The feasible price lines will range from a vertical price line, vv', along which the points price of Y divided by the points price of X equals zero, to horizontal price line hh', along which the reciprocal of that price ratio is zero (Figure 4).

As the points price line rotates counter-clockwise from vv' to hh' in Figure 4, the feasible line segment DC covers the two shaded regions in Figure 4 lying between money price lines P_1P_1 and P_2P_2. Thus, under points rationing a particular distribution can be attained only if it satisfies two conditions: (*i*) if there exist some points prices that clear the market at that distribution, and (*ii*) the equilibrium point on the corresponding points price line happens to fall in one of the two shaded regions in Figure 4. That is, suppose *ee* in Figure 4 happens to be the points price line that clears the market. If a position such as R or S on that line is the points equilibrium, the arrangement will not work because individual 1 will lack an amount of money sufficient to get to the purchases he would like to make with the ration points in his possession. Only if the equilibrium happens to fall at a location such as F on line segment DC on *ee* will the points rationing clear the market.

But this is not the end of the story. If the candidate equilibrium point corresponding to a particular points price line such as *ee* is not feasible financially because consumers do not all have enough money to make the required purchases, then unsold goods will remain on the market and prices will fall. This will change the slopes of the money price lines. More important, it will shift each individual's price line further from his (her) origin, as the purchasing power of the associated money balance rises. Under a regime of price flexibility this will continue until a market-clearing solution becomes possible. That is, after the money price changes have taken place, we may expect the points equilibrium solution to be feasible—to be represented by a point such as F rather than R or S, as rising purchasing power of money increases the distance between the money price lines P_1P_1 and P_2P_2 and, consequently, the feasible region between them. But the market-clearing equilibrium point need not, in fact, lie on the points price line, *ee*.

For the magnitude of the market-clearing price reductions depends on the tightness of the rationing scheme. In principle, it is possible to provide each consumer with so large a points budget relative to the points price of

each good that consumption by the wealthy is reduced only slightly, and that of the poor remains sufficiently constrained by their money price lines, and yet markets are exactly cleared after price adjustments. This can occur only if the supply of points is more than sufficient by itself, to permit purchase of the available quantities, that is, if, in terms of the diagram (in analogy with the money price lines), there are two parallel points price lines (symmetric about point H) each permitting the person to whom it pertains to buy more than half the available stock of goods.

In the analysis I assume points rationing to be sufficiently tight to prevent such an anomaly. Indeed, I make the rather stronger assumption that the parameters of the rationing arrangement are chosen to satisfy the following tightness criterion:

Definition. A rationing arrangement is tight if it offers a total number of rationing coupons just sufficient to purchase the individual stock of goods and that induces no individual to buy a vector of goods so large that others absolutely cannot afford to purchase that same vector should they desire to do so.[7]

Equilibrium under such a tight rationing arrangement will then work most admirably. As we will now see, it will clear the market, it will eliminate all inflationary pressure, it will be Pareto optimal and it will be superfair. We know it will clear the market because it places both persons at a common position in the Edgeworth box. We know that by making excess money supplies useless, it will stop the inflation, at least in the prices of the two rationed commodities, since neither individual will have any ration points left over to bid for more. Each person's money constraint becomes essentially ineffective, with

---

[7] In reality we normally expect this condition to be satisfied, but only because just a small subset of the available goods is rationed. If only, say, gasoline and sugar are rationed, almost anyone will be *able* financially to buy the maximal amounts to which he is entitled, even if he does not choose to do so. It is only the *ability* to make this purchase that the tightness premise assumes. But the presence of unrationed goods itself creates an analytical problem which will be noted later.

the points price line the only effective constraint. We know that the solution will be Pareto optimal, because with money no longer an effective constraint upon either party, the equilibrium is tantamount to a market-clearing equilibrium under a single pair of prices— the pure points prices of the two goods. And we know from standard analysis that such an equilibrium point must lie on the contract curve.

Finally, the superfairness follows from Schmeidler and Yaari's argument for the existence of a solution that is simultaneously fair and efficient. The points rationing scheme simply amounts to the establishment of an artificial price line, *ee*, which goes through the point of equal distribution, *H*. This artificial price line is just a substitute for the market price line. The only basic difference between the two is that the market price line would presumably not have contained the equal distribution point, *H*. Now, since points price line *ee* goes through *H*, it must offer identical purchase opportunities to both parties—since they have identical points incomes and face identical points prices. But, unless they end up at point *H*, because of the negative slope of the points price line any equilibrium point on *ee* will give *different* bundles of goods to the two parties. Since by the assumption that rationing is tight, each has had the option of purchasing without increased points expenditure the combination that goes to the other party but has not chosen to do so, each reveals a preference for his own commodity bundle as against the other person's. Therefore, on the usual premises of revealed preference theory, the distribution must be fair, indeed, *strictly* superfair.[8] From all this we

conclude

PROPOSITION 7: *Tight points rationing will generally be able to produce a market-clearing equilibrium which is Pareto optimal and superfair.*

VIII. Rationing with Salability of Points

I now come to a variant of points rationing which has recommended itself more strongly to many economists. The idea is to create, along with points rationing, an organized market in which points can be bought and sold at a price that equates their supply and demand. It is argued that the result must be Pareto optimal and that it must constitute a Pareto improvement over the equilibrium when ration coupons are not salable since all trades of ration points for money must be voluntary and so, as usual, there must be mutual gains from the trade.

I will note first that this argument is not necessarily valid; that is, we will see that it is false under rather plausible assumptions. Second, I will show that even where the argument *is* valid the resulting equilibrium may well be inferior to the unsalable points equilibrium on the fairness criterion. We may observe that the gains from trade argument for the Pareto superiority of salability of points is valid only if such sales do not generate a detrimental externality in the form of what may be described as a loss of the feeling of fairness in the system. Suppose that most people consider it unfair for the wealthy to be able to get more than their "fair share" of rationed goods. Given the opportunity, a large majority of the public might choose to vote to prevent everyone (including themselves) from participating in such sales. Yet once such sales become legal, so that the wealthy will be able to get additional points on the market, an opponent of the arrangement gains nothing by withholding his own surplus points from the market. Certainly he obtains gains from such trades, if legal trades will take place in any event. But his gains may be greater still if the market for points is eliminated altogether. The problem is that other persons' sales of ration points create detrimental externalities

---

[8]However, if there are some unrationed goods in addition to the two rationed items represented in the diagram, matters are more complicated. Obviously, there is then no reason for the entire consumption bundles of the different consumers to constitute a superfair distribution. Indeed if, as is to be expected, rationing prevents the rich from spending as much as they wish on the rationed items, it may increase their relative consumption of other goods. Thus, the conclusion that the pure points solution is necessarily superfair represents a rather myopic view of the matter.

by offending (nearly) everyone's sense of fairness. Here, as usual, the market is unable to cope with such externalities problems, and the resulting gains from trade, like the Pareto optimality of the resulting free-market solution, can be purely illusory.[9]

Before we are able to use our fairness criterion to examine the fairness of the equilibrium under salability of points, we must first characterize that equilibrium. When points can be bought and sold freely, the two constraints that characterize normal points rationing are effectively reduced to a single constraint. For then money and ration points simply become two different forms of purchasing power which can be transformed into one another at the current market price of points. One can see this clearly by writing out the relevant constraints.

Since we can easily generalize our argument, let there be n commodities and q individuals and let

$x_{a,b}$ = the quantity of commodity A obtained by individual B,

x_a = the quantity of commodity A available to the economy,

p_a = the market price of A,

c_a = the number of ration points required to buy a unit of A,

m_b = B's money income,

z = the number of ration points issued per person,

z_b = the number of points bought (sold) by B, and

p_z = the market price of a ration point.

Then individual B's money and points constraints are, respectively,

$$(3) \quad \sum_{a=1}^{n} p_a x_{ab} + p_z z_b = m_b (b=1,...,q);$$

$$(4) \quad \sum_{a=1}^{n} c_a x_{ab} = z + z_b.$$

Multiplying the ration points constraints (4) by p_z and adding the result to money constraint (3), we obtain the one effective

constraint for individual B,

$$(5) \quad \sum_a (p_a + p_z c_a) x_{ab}$$
$$= p_z z + m_b (b=1,...,q),$$

where, following Becker, we may describe $p_z z + m_b$ as individual B's full income, that is, it represents m_b, the money available to him directly as well as the money value of the points issued to him, $p_z z$. This full income can be disbursed among the available goods in any way the individual desires. Each unit of good A he buys, costs him p_a in money and c_a in ration points, each worth p_z dollars on the market. Thus each unit of A effectively costs $p_a + p_z c_a$ (the "full price" of A). For any two goods X and Y, the slope of the individual's money price line (3) is obviously $-p_x/p_y$, that of the points constraint line (4) $-c_x/c_y$, and that of the full-income line with salable ration points is

$$(6) \quad -(p_x + p_z c_x)/(p_y + p_z c_y).$$

Clearly (6) will lie between the slope of the money price line and the points budget line. It will equal the former when the price of points, p_z, is zero, and will approach the latter as p_z approaches infinity. Similarly, for any two individuals R and S, relative purchasing power will obviously change from m_r/m_s to

$$(7) \quad (m_r + p_z z)/(m_s + p_z z).$$

We may conclude at once

PROPOSITION 8: *Salability of points amounts to a partial equalization of the real incomes of the individuals. The greater the money value of $p_z z$, the points issued per person, relative to the available money incomes, the greater the equalization that will occur.*

However, so long as the number of ration points issued and their market price both remain finite, as is normally to be expected, a regime of rationing via salable points will amount only to a partial equalization of incomes, as indicated by (7), along with a modification of relative prices towards the

---

[9]Note the analogy to the argument of Richard Titmus (1971) against a market for blood. This argument occurs in my 1952 volume, pp. 130–34, 205 (second edition).

ratios decided upon by the authorities, in accordance with (6). We have seen from (7) that the greater the total money value of the ration points issued, the nearer the solution will be to that under pure points rationing, since the less the share the initial endowments of money income will have in the individual consumer's full income. However, there will generally be a maximal value of the ration points, which cannot achieve full equality, and which corresponds to the issue of some finite ("intermediate") number of points. For, obviously, the issue of a sufficient number of ration points to make them absolutely redundant will drive their price and, hence, their total market value to zero.

How, then, do we evaluate the outcome of pure points rationing with a market in ration coupons? Assuming away the externalities problem raised at the beginning of this section, the result will obviously be Pareto optimal since it involves free exchange at the nondiscriminatory and fixed "full" prices $r_a = p_a + p_r c_a$. But will the result be equitable?

We have seen that under points rationing, equilibrium can only occur somewhere on the contract locus and at a point that lies in a region of superfair distributions. In the complete absence of rationing of any sort, if the market is competitive, the solution will also lie somewhere on the contract locus, but, in general, this equilibrium need not be fair. With salability of ration points and in the absence of externality problems, we know from (7) that the distribution of real income will be intermediate between that under pure points rationing and that under the free-market solution without rationing, both of which lie on the contract curve if markets are competitive. Consequently, if over the relevant range the contract locus is everywhere single valued and continuous in every variable, the solution S_s under salability of ration points will be intermediate between the superfair solution S_p under pure points rationing and the solution S_c yielded by a competitive market without rationing. But we know that with sufficient inequality S_c must lie outside the region of superfairness, since this is true of each individual's origin. Obviously, then, the salable ration points solution, S_s, which will also be somewhere on the contract

curve, can be expected to lie closer to the superfairness region than S_c. But, like S_c, S_s may not lie within it.[10]

PROPOSITION 9: *Under rationing with resalability of points, the solution may be fair but need not be so. It can be expected to lie closer to a region of superfair solutions than the free-market solution without rationing.*

IX. Concluding Remarks

While this paper has dealt with many issues related to a variety of forms of rationing, its primary purpose has not been to provide another analysis of rationing. Rather, its goal has been to show that the fairness criterion is operational—that it can be applied to concrete problems and that with its aid one can derive results which are not all obvious in advance. Of course, rationing was selected for that purpose because, of all economic equity issues, it seems to lend itself most readily to this sort of approach.

Something else that emerges is the impression that the views of noneconomists on the subject of rationing, at least sometimes, have

---

[10]One can prove by counterexample that the white market solution, S_s, need not be superfair. For simplicity, consider a perfectly symmetrical two-good, two-person case with $x^* = y^* = k$ the (same) available quantities of the two goods, and the two persons having the identical utility functions $u^i = x_i y_i$, $i = 1, 2$. Then the fairness boundaries must satisfy

$$U^i(x_i, y_i) = U^i(k - x_i, k - y_i)$$

or
$$x_i y_i = (k - x_i)(k - y_i);$$

that is (multiplying out and simplifying),

$$x_1 + y_1 = k \text{ and } k - x_1 + k - y_1 = k,$$

for individuals 1 and 2, respectively. These two boundaries clearly coincide. Therefore, the entire superfairness region is the straight line $x + y = k$. By symmetry, the contract curve must be the 45° line $y = x$. Thus, there is only one free-market equilibrium point which is superfair: the midpoint, H.

Here, if income is divided unequally to *any* degree between the two persons they must end up at some point on the contract locus other than H, for at H their real incomes *must* be equal. Moreover, since by Proposition 8 the issue of ration points with a free market in the coupons only equalizes income partially, it follows that the resulting equilibrium point will also not be superfair.

VOL. 72 NO. 4   *BAUMOL: APPLIED FAIRNESS THEORY*   *651*

a basis more solid than some of the discussions in our literature would seem to imply. For example, salability of ration points does not turn out to be the unmixed blessing we sometimes suggest it to be, and "the common man" is shown to have reason for suspecting its fairness.

All in all, then, fairness analysis represents a breakthrough which may permit us to begin to deal in rational terms with the equity issues raised so often by policymakers, which we have so often been forced to evade.

Of course, it cannot be claimed that the fairness approach is "value free"—but neither is the allocative efficiency sort of advice which has not troubled our consciences much in the past. And, like our allocative-efficiency work, fairness analysis rests as much on the judgments and preferences of the individuals affected as it does on our own.

REFERENCES

Baumol, William J., *Welfare Economics and the Theory of the State*, London: Longmans Green, 1952: 2d edition, Cambridge: Harvard University Press, 1965.

Crawford, Vincent, "A Game of Fair Division," *Review of Economic Studies*, June 1977, *44*, 235–47.

Foley, Duncan, "Resource Allocation and the Public Sector," *Yale Economic Essays*, Spring 1967, *7*, 45–98.

Pazner, E. A. and Schmeidler, David, "A Difficulty in the Concept of Fairness," *Review of Economic Studies*, July 1974, *16*, 441–43.

Schmeidler, David and Yaari, Menachaim, "Fair Allocations," unpublished paper, 1974.

Titmus, Richard M., *The Gift Relationship: From Human Blood to Social Policy*, New York: Pantheon Books, 1971.

Tobin, James, "A Survey of the Theory of Rationing," *Econometrica*, October 1952, *20*, 521–53.

Varian, Hal R., "Equity, Envy and Efficiency," *Journal of Economic Theory*, September 1974, *9*, 63–91.

_____, "Distributive Justice, Welfare Economics, and the Theory of Fairness," *Philosophy and Public Affairs*, Spring 1975, *4*, 223–47.

Part III
Towards Application

The five papers that compose this section of the book are far less homogeneous in their themes than those of any other part of the volume. They range from regulation and antitrust and hence, from intimate relation with contestability theory, to an exercise in macroeconomics dealing with the Phillips curve. There is one paper on urban economics and one on the pitfalls of using, in the analysis of real issues, dual values derived from linear models when the underlying reality is nonlinear, even to a relatively small degree.

Since the materials relating to the first of the papers in this part of the book that I will offer in this introduction are rather lengthy I will leave that discussion and my remarks on the related second paper until last.

The third paper in the section provides a supply-side model of the economic difficulties that have beset many of the cities of the non-Soviet industrialized countries during the second half of the twentieth century.[1] I suggest that while in the nineteenth century the city could be regarded as a particularly efficient mechanism for manufacturing activity, by the end of World War II a variety of developments in transportation and other economic areas had transformed the city into a distinctly inferior arrangement for the purpose. It follows that our cities can be expected to have to adjust to a new and smaller-sized equilibrium suited to the more restricted set of activities that are most efficiently conducted in such an entity. I conclude that much of the difficulty besetting the cities is a transition problem and that the unrest and anger that have emerged from their slums represent the frustration inevitable when individuals are lured into remaining in the cities, which offer them no jobs, by a cheap (but deteriorating) stock of housing destined for ultimate abandonment and by ill-conceived policies such as housing rehabilitation programmes that undertake the impossible task of turning back the clock, instead of easing the process of transition by facilitating migration of surplus urban labour toward the new job locations.

The next article deals with the much-maligned Phillips curve. It has now become fashionable to assert that, at least in the long run, there is no analytical relationship such as the curve depicts, that is, no menu of policy choices representing a tradeoff between inflation and unemployment. Instead, it is said, there exists in any period, a 'natural rate of unemployment' and any attempt to achieve an unemployment rate lower than this will indeed fuel inflation, but must fail to stimulate employment.

I am not convinced. True to my Keynesian training, I believe that suitable policy measures can cut employment, certainly for substantial periods, and that they can be expected to yield an inflation rate inversely related to the equilibrium employment level. My paper, originally contributed to a volume in honour of Professor Phillips (whom I knew at the London School of Economics), undertakes to construct a formal and explicit model showing how such a stable long-run Phillips curve can arise. I am told, incidentally, that the volume was shown to Professor Phillips as he was dying and that he said he was very pleased by it.

The last paper in this section is focused on the use of linear programming models in development planning; but the point it makes is more general. Dual values are often proposed as indicators of the relative seriousness of the various constraints that circumscribe a decision maker and of the relative priorities that should be assigned to the loosening or elimination of those constraints (e.g. what capital (capacity) expansion projects have the greatest urgency?).

While nonlinear programming computation procedures *are* widely available, the statistical data required to construct the relevant (numerical) nonlinear programme is often difficult to come by and well beyond the resources of the model builder. As a result, while virtually all circumstances of reality are characterized by at least *some* degree of nonlinearity, many studies in development planning and other applications of mathematical programming employ what the investigators believe to constitute linear approximations to the true underlying relationships.

However, the paper shows that such approximations are more than a little dangerous. The slightest degree of nonlinearity can cause vast quantitative *and qualitative* differences between the true dual values and those emerging from the linear calculations. In particular, such a linear calculation has an inherent tendency to absolve a large number of constraints from any responsibility for preventing the objective function from attaining a value higher than it does, when in reality the constraints thus alleged not to be binding in fact are a serious drag upon the objective function and consequently may urgently require the planner's attention. In short, the paper shows that in such cases a linear calculation may easily be worse than no calculation at all, and that linearization therefore is a surprisingly dangerous game.

Next, I turn (out of order) to the second paper in this section of the book, which is an entry into the now rather extensive literature on the proper criterion to determine the borderline between 'predatory' and 'nonpredatory' pricing. Here, predatory prices may be defined, roughly, as prices which involve a sacrifice of profits by the firm that adopts them and which will produce a positive profit yield in the long run *only* if they drive some competitors from the field or prevent the entry of some rivals, thereby permitting the firm in the future to raise prices above what they would otherwise have been, by an amount and for a period more than sufficient to make up for the initial incremental losses. Professors Areeda and Turner of the Harvard Law School inaugurated the modern literature on the subject in their classic article[2] proposing, first, that a price be judged not to be predatory if it is at least equal to the corresponding short run marginal cost and, second, that average variable cost be considered an acceptable proxy for short run marginal cost if data on the latter are unavailable or their acquisition is impractical.

I still accept their cost criterion (with some minor modifications) as a reasonable test, and as the best that is available if cost is used as the test of acceptability of a price. However, there is a second side of the matter constituted by the sequence of events and their timing. Does the firm cut prices just when entry threatens or just after it occurs? Does it rescind the price cut just after the entrant leaves the arena? If so, is there not a marked predatory odour, even if price never falls below short run marginal cost? Accordingly, I propose that any incumbent firm which cuts prices after entry occurs be required to bear the burden of proving that any price increases within, say, five years after the entrant withdraws are justified by changes in costs or other exogenous developments.

Two remarks are in order here. First, it can be argued that adoption of this rule, which I call 'quasi permanence of price reductions', renders redundant any cost test of predatoriness such as that proposed by Areeda and Turner. For if the firm knows it will have to live with its price cuts for some considerable period it will surely avoid any reductions which bring the pertinent prices below the corresponding costs and hence incur a protracted sacrifice of profits.

Second, in a subsequent and justly noted article[3] Joskow and Klevorick (independently) advocated a proposal which, as they point out, is essentially equivalent to mine. Their exposition, however, rightly emphasizes that the appropriate associated procedure should involve two steps: first, in any hearings in which a firm is accused of predatory pricing, the judicial authority should investigate whether the industry is clearly effectively competitive (or contestable). If so, the investigation should be dropped immediately and the defendant exonerated. But if the firm fails the test of competitiveness the second step becomes appropriate, with the accused firm being required to assume the burden of proof described in my article. Though in footnotes I had implicitly already concurred with the two-stage procedure proposed by Joskow and Klevorick, I readily acknowledge that my remarks on the subject were unacceptably terse and obscure. In other words, I enthusiastically endorse their two-stage formulation of the proposal.

Turning at last to the first of the articles in this section, I note that it was my Presidential Address at the Eastern Economic Association. It deals with two issues arising in markets in which absence of contestability and the simultaneous presence of monopolistic elements render price regulation appropriate. First, it considers the criteria suitable for use in the imposition of ceilings upon the monopolists' prices—a subject which has received surprisingly little attention in the literature. Here I advocate what has come to be called the stand-alone cost test—requiring that no group of customers be charged prices higher than they would have to pay in a competitive market to an entrant who undertook to supply those customers alone. The logic of this principle is described in the paper. It is noteworthy that the stand-alone cost rule has since been proposed before a number of regulatory agencies and at least one of them has committed itself to it, at least in principle.

The rule, so far as I know, was first formulated by Gerald Faulhaber. He does point out, rather generously, that it appears in (more or less) explicit form in something I had written much earlier. But I still remember my surprise when this was pointed out—since I had no inkling that I had produced any such rule at the time I wrote the paper and recognized none of its implications, even any whiff of attribution to me is quite unjustified.

The second part of the paper deals with the other side of price regulation, the use of floors on prices as means to prevent predation and cross subsidy. This introduces the justly-noted Areeda-Turner rule, which is now accepted by a considerable body of court opinion.

In this connection it may be pointed out that the Areeda-Turner rule as originally formulated used several terms which were unclear to economists. In subsequent correspondence I asked Professor Areeda just what he and his coauthors meant by them. Since the associated issues are rather significant I reproduce the pertinent portions of our letters (which are made public here for the first time).[4] I have also made several insertions in my letter (in parenthesis) for expository clarity.

August 14, 1980

Professor Phillip Areeda
Harvard Law School
Cambridge, MA 02138

Dear Professor Areeda:

Thank you very much for your letter of July 30 . . . I will try to answer your questions about my article and if I may, will return a few questions of my own on several minor points that are not clear to me in your pathbreaking paper . . .

1. Just how do you define short run marginal costs (SRMC)? Do you use the term as it is sometimes employed before regulatory agencies to mean long run marginal cost minus the cost of the marginal requirements of durable capital? Or do you instead use it the way it is employed in technical economic writings to mean the relatively high cost of expanding output by one unit if time is too short to make money-saving adjustments in capital stock? Note that used the first way, SRMC < LRMC, while used the other way, for an increment in output from an output level optimally adjusted to the firm's capital stock SRMC > LRMC.

2. In a multiproduct firm suppose the price of product X is cut but still exceeds its marginal cost. However, because of cross elasticity with product Y the firm loses business in the market for Y. As a result, the net marginal revenue from the cut in price of X (after deduction of lost Y revenue) is less than the marginal cost of X. Does the price cut pass the Areeda-Turner test? In other words, is the Areeda-Turner test equivalent to the 'burden test' which requires the *net* marginal (incremental) revenue of X to exceed its marginal (incremental) cost?

3. How do you define the average variable cost of product Z? Specifically, suppose a firm that already produces products X and Y decides to add Z to its product line. To do so it must buy a $1000 adapter for the equipment it already uses to produce X and Y and, in addition, pay $4 for labor and raw materials for each unit of Z supplied. If 100 units of Z is supplied, is your average variable cost $14=($1000/100)+$4 or is it simply $4? In other words, do you include or exclude the cost of any fixed cost equipment that must be *added* to produce the item? (If so, the average cost of Z is equivalent to what has been called its 'average incremental cost') . . .

Sorry this letter has gotten so long. With very best regards,

Sincerely,

William J. Baumol

November 13, 1981

Dear Professor Baumol:

Without burdening you with the tedious details, let me simply apologize for my record delay in responding to your three questions.

(1) Is the relevant SRMC for my purposes equal to (1) LRMC minus marginal durable

capital or (2) incremental costs when time is too short to make money saving adjustments in capital stock? There may not be a single answer.

Most predatory pricing cases involve defendants operating with a given plant and not constructing or planning to construct a new one. As a first approximation for SRMC in that situation, I look to the defendant's incremental costs in its existing capital situation, and thus tend to use the second or 'technical' definition. Projected costs with a new capital arrangement would not seem relevant for the firm not planning such construction and the LRMC that was assumed at the time the existing plant was built would not be readily knowable to a court and does not seem relevant to the firm's present pricing decisions. For defendants operating at less than optimal output with existing plants, moreover, the technical definition also seems appropriate and will be less than LRMC (unless technology has improved greatly since the existing capital was built).

Of course, even with a given capital stock, the defendant's SRMC could be very much higher for incremental output produced with much overtime than with added employees operating otherwise idle equipment. I would think that the relevant SRMC should allow for the later adjustment and need not be confined to the most immediate and extremely short run jump in output.

More complex would be the case where the challenged price calls forth additional demand for the firm's product which can be satisfied in the short run by high-cost output beyond the firm's optimal level but which would later be satisfied by the construction of new equipment which could then be operated with lower labor-materials inputs and use depreciation (see III below) than the existing equipment pressed beyond its optimal output. A price that failed to cover full unit cost with the new equipment, which approximates LRMC, would not seem justifiable. Suppose, however, that the challenged price covered that amount but fell below the temporary high operating cost (after, say, hiring new employees) of existing equipment. I am tempted to say that such a price is not justifiable.

(II) Should the defendant's revenue from product X be reduced by the net revenues lost by the defendant on substitute product Y as a result of its price reduction on X? No.

First, no such adjustment would be made if the two products were made entirely by different firms. Second, the health of rival X producers is ordinarily unaffected by the decline in Y sales. (If all or most producers make both products, one might consider both products together the relevant product line, but rivalry would not be impaired so long as the product line as a whole remains profitable.) With each product considered separately, so long as the price cut does not push the price of X below its marginal cost and so long as the diminished volume of Y does not result in costs above the price of Y, the Areeda-Turner rule would not be violated.

(III) What is the defendant's AVC of producing 100 units of Z when it can do so with a $1,000 adapter and labor-material costs of $4.00 per unit (for a total outlay of $1,400)? You compare it to a rival firm which can supply 100 units for a total outlay of $1,200 (let's say all labor and material without any capital so that AVC=$12).

If the adapter is exhausted after 100 units, the AVC is $14 per unit. This presents no special problem under the A-T definition which includes use depreciation as a variable cost. In that event the rival is more efficient and could not be excluded by the A-T AVC rule. (Also includable would be the use depreciation, if any, of any plant and equipment involved in X-Y production—in your example—that is attributable to the defendant's Z production.)

If the adapter never wears out, unit use depreciation would be $1,000 divided by the number of units that would be produced over time by the continuing firm. (We assume that it is a continuing firm becuse it is being charged with seeking a monopoly.) If the adapter is added so that the defendant can produce 125 units of Z, the total resource cost for the defendant ($\$1,000+(125\times\$4)$) would equal that for the rival ($125\times\$12$). For a greater output, the defendant would be more efficient . . .

With thanks for your letter, and best wishes.

Sincerely,

Phillip Areeda

Notes

1. Of course, what I describe here is inevitably only one side of the matter. I make no attempt to deal with such important topics as the racial issues which have surely contributed to the problems of urban areas, and ignore pertinent arguments of my own, such as the cost disease model, which asserts that urban services such as elementary education and police protection are inherently resistent to increases in productivity and, hence, tend to rise in cost faster than the general price level, thus raising special financial difficulties for municipal governments. *See* my 'Macroeconomics of Unbalanced Growth: The Anatomy of Urban Crisis', *American Economic Review*, vol. 57, June 1967, pp. 415–26.
2. Areeda, Phillip and Turner, Donald, 'Predatory Pricing and Related Practices under Section 2 of the Sherman Act', *Harvard Law Review*, vol. 88, 1977, p. 869ff.
3. Joskow, Paul and Klevorick, Alvin, 'A Framework for Analyzing Predatory Pricing Policy', *Yale Law Journal*, vol. 89, Dec. 1979, pp. 213–70.
4. I am grateful to Professor Areeda for permission to reprint the letter. Some of the issues are also discussed in Areeda, Phillip E., *Antitrust Law* 1982 Supplement (Boston: Little, Brown) pp. 145–56.

[9]
Minimum and Maximum Pricing Principles for Residual Regulation

WILLIAM J. BAUMOL*

Princeton and New York Universities

Recent moves toward abolition of regulation of prices in a number of industries bring with them some concern about the desirability of complete elimination of all constraints upon the price-setting process. Though many of the industries involved are actually or potentially highly competitive, none of them can by any stretch of the imagination be said to approximate a state of atomless perfect competition. As a result, at least some of the prices which can be expected to emerge from their markets, if unimpeded by government interference, may well not exhibit the optimality properties described by our theoretical models of perfect competition. Is it not possible, then, *in those markets in which there is little or no competition* that some of the resulting prices will, in some sense, be "too high" or even "too low"? This suggests that one should consider the possibility of giving deregulated firms power to select their own prices, but constraining that freedom by a floor and a ceiling in markets in which competition is extremely weak.

In raising this issue I should not be misunderstood to be raising doubts about the desirability of deregulation. I continue to be a strong supporter of deregulation of air, rail, and truck transportation, and there are no doubt other regulated economic activities that will serve the public far more effectively when their pricing decisions are freed from government control. More specifically, by examining reasonable criteria for the residual regulation of price floors or ceilings I am not implying that the adoption of such constraints will serve the general welfare. There are very strong arguments which suggest that the heavy efficiency costs of the regulatory procedures needed to oversee any such residual rules may far outweigh their benefits. Here I am merely inquiring whether there is *any* analytic basis for the formulation of such rules and, if so, to describe the nature of such rules. But, as will be seen, I have not succeeded in attaining even this limited objective. For while I believe that the rules I will describe are fully defensible in terms of the underlying theory, most of them are clearly too complicated to be used as they stand. Reasonable compromises and approximation procedures will be required to permit their employment in practice.

The rules which emerge from the discussion will not be entirely unfamiliar. They are certainly related to some of the results that emerge from the marginal analysis and the theory of optimal pricing. However, their primary basis will not be the usual one—the rules of efficiency in resource allocation. While it is unusual in economics, equity rather than efficiency will serve as the main foundation for those principles, though I will show that they do promote economic efficiency as well.

*Presidential Address, Eastern Economic Association; Boston, May 1979.

I am extremely grateful to the National Science Foundation and the Sloan Foundation whose support greatly facilitated the preparation of this paper.

236   EASTERN ECONOMIC JOURNAL

1. Previous Discussions of Price Floor Criteria

Let us begin by turning for guidance to earlier discussions of minimum and maximum pricing rules. An unsophisticated but intelligent observer would naturally expect the most of these to be devoted to price ceilings designed to prevent the use of monopoly power to gouge consumers, for surely that is the immediate danger to the public welfare threatened by market power. It is therefore curious but not inexplicable that the vast preponderance of regulatory and antitrust pricing cases, and almost all of the pertinent discussions, have been devoted to limitation of price *reductions* rather than price *increases*.

There is a very simple explanation for this anomaly. A seller's high prices are likely to be harmful to his *customers*, but his low prices are apt to harm his *competitors*. The competitors (who themselves are often giants of industry) are in a far better position to organize an effective protest than are the consumers. Inscribing on their banners, "fairness in competition," "prevention of predatory pricing" and other equally persuasive mottos, they have not only succeeded in making headway among regulators, but they have even managed to provide an aura of respectability to their self-interested attempt to shield themselves from the rigors of competition. "It always is and must be the interest of the great body of the people to buy what they want of those who sell it cheapest," wrote Adam Smith. "The proposition is so very manifest, that it seems ridiculous to take any pains to prove it; nor could it ever have been called in question, had not the interested sophistry of merchants and manufacturers confounded the common sense of mankind" [1776, p. 461].

Two interrelated issues are cited by those who hold that floors upon the prices charged by firms with some degree of market power

are needed. First, it is maintained that without such floors there is nothing to prevent one group of a seller's customers from benefiting at the expense of another. If the seller has market power he may, on this view, be tempted to sell, say, one of his products at a loss, and make up for it by a suitable overcharge of other customer groups. This issue is usually referred to as *cross subsidy* of one product's customers by another's. The second issue involves the relation between the seller and his competitors. We are told that the firm will wish to sell some of its products below cost if by this means potential entrants can be deterred from opening for business in that field or current competitors can be prevented from growing or even be forced to leave the market. A variety of pejorative terms are used to describe this sort of practice, "predatory pricing" or "destructive pricing" being adjoined to cross subsidy, though until recently no one seems to have attempted to offer a definition for either term. As one of our leading courts has remarked,

The use of the term "predatory" to describe conduct violative of the antitrust laws has left much to be desired. This court has noted, the term probably does not have a well-defined meaning in the context it was used, but it certainly bears a sinister connotation. [U.S. Court of Appeals, 10th Circuit, 1977]

Implicit in discussions of concepts such as predatory pricing are somewhat elusive concepts like "intent" which in practice are not easy to measure or perhaps even to define. But many of the discussions seem to adopt or at least to flirt with the notion that a scarlet letter should be affixed to any price which lies below some floor regarded as the boundary of the region of cross subsidy. A price higher than that borderline is considered acceptable on that score, while a price below that floor stands condemned, at least in the absence of unusual exonerating circumstances.

Almost all commentators agree that in

designing such a floor a critical role must be assigned to the cost of the product whose price is in question. The problem, however, is which cost datum should be assigned this determinant role, and just how that cost figure should be used in the calculations process. Three basic approaches have been considered. They may be called the full-cost test, the marginal-cost pricing test, and the test of net-incremental contribution. The meaning of the first two may seem self-evident, though we will see as we discuss them that this appearance is deceptive. The third is rather less familiar and will later be described somewhat more carefully.

2. Full-Cost Price Floors

Full cost, alias fully allocated costs, alias fully distributed cost, is a concept closely associated with the more routine procedures of the accountants. The basic idea underlying its use as a standard for pricing is that a price below that cost level must condemn the supplier to a financial loss. In a single-product firm full cost is merely a synonym for average combined cost, that is, it is equal to the sum of total fixed and variable cost divided by output. Since that cost figure is calculated so as to include a normal rate of return on capital, pricing in this way means that the firm should earn normal competitive profits on its investment, no more and no less.

Even in the single-product firm of the elementary textbook there are some flies in this ointment. For wishing does not always make things so. As early as 1900 Gustav Cassel pointed out that a rise in the price of a commodity in an attempt to get it up to the full cost of current output will reduce the quantity sold and that this in turn can lead to a rise in the full cost figure itself. He tells a tale of a railroad whose average cost is a decreasing function of output and whose price initially is below full cost. Successive attempts

to raise price to the full cost level only lead to successive reductions in volume of traffic, each accompanied by such a rise in full cost that the supplier is saddled with greater and greater losses. Thus, he concludes, full-cost pricing is not the guarantee against loss that it seems to be.[1]

However, the really serious problems that beset full-cost pricing arise in a multi-product firm, that is, in any firm one can expect actually to encounter in the real world. In any such firm some expenditures (the salaries of its officers, if nothing else) are inevitably expended on behalf of several of the company's products simultaneously, with no identifiable portion of such expenditures being attributable to any one of the products.[2]

Now, to calculate on a rational basis the average or "full" cost of any one product in such a firm it is necessary to be able to do the

[1]That is, he concludes that it may not be possible for losses to be eliminated by *raising* price to full cost as though full cost were an invariant figure. In his parable, Cassel has the management of the firm learn by experience, finally deciding to reduce price drastically, which simultaneously attracts many new customers and reduces average cost, and then the firm does at last manage to make a profit.

[2]This is not means to deny that *some* portion of such common costs will be economically attributable to a firm's individual products. For example, if on launching a particular product the firm hires an additional vice president, his cost is clearly attributable to that product alone. Even in more complicated cases partial attribution is possible in principle. Suppose, for example, that a trucking firm takes on the transportation of a product, X, which it did not carry before. Suppose, moreover, that X is never carried by itself but is always transported in mixed truckloads. But if, as a result of the increase in traffic, the firm adds three trucks to its fleet, even though these trucks also carry only mixed loads, their cost must be entirely attributable to product X (assuming there are no offsetting changes in the use of other inputs). Nevertheless, there will always or almost always remain a residue of common costs which is unattributable to any individual product *because the magnitude of this residue is unaffected by the quantity of any product supplied or sold,* or even by the decision to inaugurate the supply of a particular product. Such unattributable common costs can constitute a very substantial proportion of a firm's total costs.

238   EASTERN ECONOMIC JOURNAL

impossible, to divide up the firm's total cost so that each of its products is assigned its *appropriate* share. But unattributable common costs are precisely what their name implies: they are simply unattributable to particular products on any sensible economic basis. At this point accounting conventions undertake to come to the rescue. Using admittedly arbitrary procedures for the apportionment, total supplier costs are simply divided up among the firm's different products. These accounting rules are not uncontested, because there is so much to be gained or lost by the choice of apportionment criterion. If a railroad line carries three products—steel, feathers, and platinum—the steel shippers can be relied upon to fight against the use of weight as a basis for assigning "cost responsibility." The feather shippers will combat the use of volume for that purpose, and the platinum shippers will fight tooth and nail against market value as the criterion of cost allocation.

Most economists have long been passionate in their rejection of the full-cost pricing criterion. There are many reasons for the strength of our feelings on this matter of which only three will be mentioned here: the arbitrariness of the criterion, the resource misallocation it is likely to produce, and its tendency to undermine the competitive process at the consumer's expense.

Of course, everyone recognizes that arbitrary decisions are sometimes unavoidable and that arbitrariness can occasionally be superior to complete indecision. Perhaps the most irritating practice of full-costers in this regard is their propensity to adopt cosmetic procedures which give the allocation process a spurious appearance of rationality. Costs of common facilities are allegedly allocated on the basis of the "relative use" of those facilities by different products. But this veneer is easily stripped away. The preceding railroad example shows how different the results of the

calculation can be, depending on whether weight, volume or market value is used as the criterion determining the relative use of the roadbed and tracks by the different goods transported along it. The appearance of reasonableness imparted by a "relative use" criterion only increases the danger of full-cost procedures because it lulls its advocates and even some uncommitted observers into overlooking the arbitrariness of the calculation and the very serious consequences which can result from the choice of allocation procedure.

The likelihood that full-costing will produce a misallocation of resources follows at once from its arbitrariness. There is obviously not the slightest reason to expect that the prices emerging from a full-costing process will bear the slightest resemblance to those we know to be necessary for efficiency in resource utilization. Whether one deals with the Hotelling rule (1938), or the Ramsey rule (1927), or any other optimality principle, it is clear that marginal rather than fully distributed cost is involved in the relevant test. Prices based on fully distributed costs will almost certainly be inconsistent with efficiency in resource use and so they will be harmful to the general welfare. Some reservations which will emerge in the next section must be expressed about this argument. But no such doubts need be felt about the remaining argument against full-costing and its substantial handicap upon efficiency which the discussion will point out.

In practice, the role of fully distributed cost has been a burning regulatory issue because competitors of the firm under attack almost inevitably use it to claim that the prices of the products in direct competition with their own are noncompensatory—that they are financed by cross subsidy. In this way, fully distributed cost is normally used as a protectionist instrument preventing buyers from benefiting from price reductions which suppliers are willing to offer them.[3] Competitors battle for a high floor under the regulated firm's prices in order to make life easier for themselves. Since the rules of full costing are arbitrary, the results can always be skewed, deliberately or unconsciously, to maximize the competitive handicap imposed upon the regulated firm, and one can generally rely upon the complaining competitor to try to do so.[4] Regulators are regularly persuaded to bow to this position in the belief that, unless such a full cost floor is imposed to protect competitors, they will be unable to survive. But thereby, in protecting inefficient competitors who could not otherwise fend for themselves, the regulators obviously succeed only too well in undermining the competitive process. Customers are forced to pay prices higher than they otherwise would, ostensibly in their own best interests! The extreme distaste shown by most economists for the full cost arguments is, thus, not very difficult to explain.

3. Marginal Cost Criteria

The notion that price should be permitted to be set as low as marginal cost seems to

---

[3]It can be argued with considerable justice that the public will gain little from such a price reduction if it is offered only so long as the competitor remains in operation and is promptly withdrawn once that competitor is driven from the field. But, surely, the proper cure for this disease is prevention of the subsequent price rise, rather than prohibition of the initial price reduction. Elsewhere (1978) I have proposed a criterion of predatory pricing which is based on this view.

[4]Their advocacy of such full-cost prices is often buttressed by a fallacious argument which implies that marginal cost is inevitably lower than average, i.e., "full" cost. Of course, this view could not get by the examination in a freshman economics course but it is instructive to observe how it is presented. Its advocates imply that marginal cost is not the first derivative of total cost but that it is what may be described as a partially distributed cost, from which all common costs and perhaps all capital costs have simply been omitted. To defend themselves from this charge some advocates of the marginal cost criterion have been driven to emphasize *long-run* marginal cost which, of course, must include all marginal capital costs.

follow in an obvious way from the principles of welfare economics. As every economist knows, optimality of resource allocation, as achieved under pure competition, requires the prices of all commodities to be set equal to their respective marginal costs. It would seem an easy inference that any rule which prevents prices from reaching marginal costs is an indefensible source of inefficiencies.

Economists have long flirted with this sort of argument, though the position most of them have ended up with is somewhat different. Their conclusion nevertheless remains altogether marginalist in logic, as we will soon see.

Most recently the marginal-cost pricing criterion has been espoused, with considerable influence upon the judicial process, by two eminent lawyers, Professors Phillip Areeda and Donald Turner. In a widely cited article [1975]—which deals, actually, with antitrust law rather than regulation—they took the position that no price which equals or exceeds short-run marginal cost should be considered predatory. Conversely, they assert, any price which falls below short-run marginal cost can be presumed to be predatory. They note, in addition, that in practice, it will sometimes be difficult to estimate the value of short-run marginal cost, and that in these circumstances average variable cost can be used as an acceptable proxy. Thus, the Areeda-Turner criterion effectively approves of any price that can be shown to exceed either of these cost figures, or both. This criterion has, in the past few years, been cited with approval by a growing number of courts.[5] The Areeda-Turner position is extremely attractive despite the questions I will raise about their arguments. Among the reasons I find the rule attractive is my belief that the adoption of *any*

---

[5]See, for example, Pacific Engineering v. Kerr-McGee [1977]; Inglis and Sons Baking Co. v. ITT Continental Baking Co. [1978]; and Janich Bros., Inc. v. American Distilling Co. [1977].

such testable criterion is an enormous contribution to the general welfare; without it decision makers must act without knowing whether they will be running afoul of the law, and the resulting indecisions, delays and needless litigation are enormously wasteful.[6] Moreover, I shall argue later that in proposing the adoption of a test based on average variable cost, Areeda and Turner have done better than they thought. Rather than being only a poor cousin of marginal cost, average variable cost turns out to be a very reasonable criterion in its own right.[7]

One can complain that the Areeda-Turner discussion seems never to have explained

clearly why it advocates the use of short-run rather than long-run marginal cost. In fact, the authors seem never to have defined precisely what they mean by the terms "short-run marginal cost"[8] or "average variable cost." We will see later the nature of the ambiguity in the latter concept.

But the main fault one can find with the Areeda-Turner discussion of their position is the basis on which they choose to espouse it. They argue the desirability of marginal-cost pricing on the welfare theoretic grounds which I have already mentioned. Unfortunately, there are at least three critical weaknesses in this position. First, the second-best

---

[6]This conclusion is viewed with considerable suspicion by a number of observers who argue that the social desirability of any particular pricing pattern must be judged, in ways which cannot be specified completely, in terms of the circumstances of each case, and that there are too many ways in which pricing freedom can be misused to permit the adoption of any simple criterion of legality. On this see, e.g., Scherer (1976). In reaching this conclusion I believe these commentators have not adequately weighed the costs and benefits of an *undefined* criterion of illegality in pricing.

[7]As a matter of fact, if one is merely looking for an approximation to marginal cost, it should often be possible to do better than average variable cost. We know, for example, that when costs decline with output marginal costs must lie below average variable costs, and such qualitative information can help us to narrow down the zone of ignorance about the true marginal cost figure. As this was being written, a court decision appeared which seems to have taken a fairly similar view, concluding that in the case in question the use of average variable cost to evaluate a price was illigitimate because there were special reasons in that instance for believing ???

[8]There seems to be some confusion about the relation between short and long-run marginal cost. It seems to be believed rather widely that short-run marginal cost will normally be the lower of the two, on the ground that it contains no investment outlays or returns on capital because these are fixed in the short run. But this conclusion about the relative size of the two costs is generally not true. As a matter of fact, short-run *total* cost will normally be higher than its long-run counterpart. A simple example will make this clear. Suppose a shift in the demand curve leads a firm to expand output by hiring overtime labor at a cost of $10 per unit of output. The increase in demand seeming more or less permanent, the firm decides to invest in additional equipment as a substitute for the overtime labor. Why does it do so? Obviously, the explanation must be that the machines

incur a cost *below* the $10 per unit corresponding to the overtime labor. This is the explanation of the act of legerdermain whereby long-run total cost includes capital outlays omitted from the short-run figure, and yet manages to be the lower of the two. This relation will hold generally, since capital will be purchased only if it is the more economical means to do the job.

The reason short-run total costs are at least as high as the long-run figures is that short-run costs correspond to an investment commitment based on a particular expected output level, y^*. If demand turns out to be just sufficient to elicit this level of output, short and long-run total costs will coincide. But if output turns out to be larger (smaller) than y^* the plant selected will be uneconomically large (uneconomically small) and so short-run total cost for that actual output must be larger than it would be if the firm were operating in the long run, meaning that it had full freedom of choice in plant design.

From this we can now deduce the relationship between short and long-run marginal costs. Figure 1 depicts the pattern of short and long-run costs that has just been

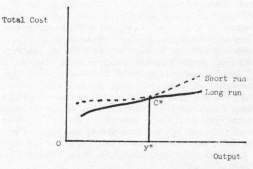

Figure 1

theorem reminds us that there is no necessary advantage to satisfaction of some Pareto-optimality conditions while others are being violated. If prices are, say, above marginal costs in some sectors of the economy, it is not necessarily beneficial to bring prices into equality with marginal costs in the remainder. Indeed, one can easily see how a misallocation of resources will be produced in this way, with an excessive proportion of society's resources devoted to products whose demand has been stimulated by marginal cost prices, and an undesirably low proportion of the community's resources consequently going to the remainder of the economy. Second, welfare economics says nothing about the desirability of setting prices *temporarily* equal to marginal cost and then re-raising them above marginal cost after competitive pressures have declined. Yet such an intertemporal price pattern is perfectly compatible with the Areeda-Turner criterion. Third, whatever can be said on welfare grounds for the desirability of prices *equal* to marginal cost, there seems little particular allocative virtue to prices set at some *unspecified* level higher than marginal costs. Yet the Areeda-Turner

criterion is impartial in its approval both of prices equal to and prices which exceed marginal costs.[9]

None of this is in any way meant to imply that the Areeda-Turner price floors are indefensible. The point simply is that while price floors, appropriately chosen, may help to promote efficiency, *any* price floor is simply too coarse an instrument to be able by itself to achieve optimality in resource allocation.

4. Compensatory Pricing: Incremental Cost and Revenue

Since the 1880s economists have been proposing, at least by implication, the use of incremental cost, a close relative of marginal cost, in the setting of price floors. Incremental cost may be defined as the addition to the firm's total cost by a specified change in the output of each of the firm's products. Thus, marginal cost is simply the limiting case of incremental cost as the change in question approaches zero. Obviously, a similar definition applies to revenues.

However, here I will use incremental cost and revenue in a more restricted manner, to refer to what has been described as the incremental cost (revenue) *of an entire product*. This is the difference in the total cost (revenue) of the supplier of some specified vector of outputs and the corresponding total cost (revenue) of its output, if the one item whose price is in question were reduced to zero. I will be using two different incremental cost (revenue) concepts which are best described symbolically.

Let x = the quantity of some commodity X;

y = the corresponding vector of outputs of all the firm's other products, Y;

$y + \Delta y$ = the vector of outputs of Y which would be demanded if

---

described, with y^* the output level for which current plant was designed. As one can see, several relationships emerge: i) If the total cost curves are differentiable they must be tangent at output y^*, so that at this output level short-run and long-run marginal costs must be equal. ii) For outputs slightly above y^* short-run marginal cost must exceed long-run marginal cost, while the reverse must be true for outputs slightly below y^*. iii) For outputs far from y^* we cannot, in general, say which of the marginal cost figures is the larger, though *if curvatures do not change* the short-run figure will be higher for all $y > y^*$ and the long-run figure will be higher for $y < y^*$. Intuitively, the reason SRMC > LRMC for $y > y^*$ is that expansion of output beyond y^* is handicapped in the short run by inadequate plant size, so that expensive substitute inputs, such as overtime labor, will be required to make it possible. On the other hand, where $y < y^*$ the usual story about excess capacity and the consequently low cost of expansion becomes valid.

I am deeply grateful to Robert Willig and Gerald Faulhaber for correcting a serious error in my discussion of this issue in an earlier draft.

[9]Similar points are made by Williamson [1977].

242   EASTERN ECONOMIC JOURNAL

output of X were reduced to zero as a result of complementarity or substitution;

$C(x, y)$ = the total cost function.

Then we may define:

Gross Incremental Cost of X =
$$C(x, y) - C(0, y) \quad (1)$$

Net Incremental Cost of X =
$$C(x, y) - C(0, y + \Delta y). \quad (2)$$

Gross and net incremental revenues are defined as the obvious analogues of (1) and (2).

It is then proposed to test the adequacy of the price of product X by checking whether it equals or exceeds the corresponding average incremental cost, i.e., the incremental cost divided by output. Since the (gross) incremental revenue of X at price P_x is simply $P_x x$, if the price of X equals or exceeds its (gross) incremental cost, the total incremental revenue of X must obviously exceed its incremental cost; that is, if

$$P_x \geq [C(x, y) - C(0, y)]/x \quad (3)$$

then

$$P_x x \geq C(x, y) - C(0, y). \quad (4)$$

This price is then said to be compensatory, or to involve no cross subsidy, on the grounds that under these circumstances the revenues contributed by purchasers of X must at least cover the costs imposed upon the supplier in the course of serving them.

Indeed, particularly where the firm's profits are effectively constrained by some ceiling, as they are intended to be under rate-of-return regulation, there is more to the argument. A price of X which satisfies this rule can be shown to be Pareto-superior, from the viewpoint of all affected customers, to any higher prices which would cause the firm to lose all (or a substantial proportion of) the customers for product X. Thus, suppose the

test criterion (4) is passed as a strict inequality. Then customers of X must be making a net contribution to company profits. But if the prices, P_y^*, of goods in the vector y were otherwise enough to bring profits up to the ceiling, this revenue contribution of product X must put the company over the top. The firm must then reduce the prices of product Y to a level we represent by the vector P_y in order to comply with the ceiling. That is, let P_x^* be a price which drives customers of X from the market; then at any lower price, P_x, which satisfies (3) as an inequality and thus attracts the corresponding demand for X, consumers of Y must also benefit as their prices are reduced from P_y^* to p_y.

This argument goes back at least to the 1880s (Hadley, 1886, Chapter 6; Alexander, 1887, pp. 2–5, 10–11; and Ackworth, 1891, Chapter 3; see also Lewis, 1949, p. 20ff., for an excellent discussion). It is fundamentally valid, though, as we shall see, at least in principle it does require some amendments as it stands. But before coming to these, several observations are in order.

First, this is not primarily an argument based on grounds of efficiency of resource allocation. Rather, it is founded first and foremost on considerations of distributive equity among different groups of the supplier's customers. The test is intended to assure that the customers of each product bear the costs imposed by them and do not shift any portion of these costs to buyers of other company products. In other words, by implication, each customer group then bears its contribution to total company costs. Moreover, since such prices pass a test of Pareto improvement it follows that the gains from such pricing policy are shared among the company's customers.

Second, while I have emphasized the interpretation of the incremental-cost criterion as a test of fairness, its role as an inducement of efficiency must not be overlooked. For if price were to violate the rule it would exclude potential entrants who are more efficient producers of the product in question. For if AC^m and AC^e are, respectively, the unit incremental costs of the incumbent and the potential entrant, then the item should at least partly be supplied by the entrant if $AC^e < AC^m$. However, if the incumbent's price is $p^m < AC^e$, then this (cross-subsidized) price will obviously exclude the more efficient producers of the item.[10] Thus, the incremental cost floor is a necessary condition for economic efficiency.

Third, we may note that the incremental cost test is directly related to the second Areeda-Turner criterion—the comparison of price with average variable cost. For it is natural to define[11] average variable cost as the right side of expression (3), that is as the amount per unit of X by which the firm's total cost varies as a result of the decision to supply x units of X. Then (3) or (4) become identical with the average-variable-cost test of Areeda and Turner. We conclude that, far from being defensible only as some sort of approximation to the ideal marginal-cost criterion, there are strong grounds for advocating the average variable cost test as something with validity of its own. Note also that, as I have indicated earlier, this view provides a foundation for the Areeda-Turner test quite different from the

one they themselves offer, one which I believe is considerably stronger than theirs.

Let us turn next to the ways in which it has more recently been proposed to amend the incremental cost criterion. Here two such modifications will be described. First, it has been proposed that the test require a comparison not between *gross* incremental cost and revenues but between their *net* counterparts. That is, from the revenue contributed by X one should subtract any revenues lost by other company products as the result of the availability of X, if the two goods happen to be substitutes. The reverse is proposed in the case where they are complements, and similar adjustments for cross elasticity effects are suggested on the cost side. The argument for this position is self evident. Product X should be credited with all revenues it contributes directly or indirectly and debited with any indirect revenue losses it causes, and the same is true on the cost side. Along this line, it is easy to show that the Pareto improvement argument is valid for the incremental cost test only if net cost and revenue figures are used in carrying out the test. For suppose that the price of X were to satisfy the gross criterion but fail the net test. Then a moment's thought confirms that the company's net profits will actually be reduced by the supply of product X and so, under an overall profit ceiling, consumers of its remaining products, Y, may well be required to make up the deficiency.

The second amendment that has been proposed (see Faulhaber, 1975) is that compensatory pricing of product X is not proved if *only* P_x is shown to satisfy the criterion

net incremental revenue $\geq$

net incremental cost. (5)

Rather, to show that their prices are compensatory, it is held necessary to show that each and every product of the company, taken

---

[10] I am indebted to Robert Willig for this observation. See also W. A. Lewis [1947], p. 22ff.

[11] This definition seems first to have been formulated by Panzar and Willig [1976]. It is not absolutely certain that Areeda and Turner want to define average variable cost in this way. Suppose there is a product-specific fixed cost incurred in supplying X; for example, suppose X represents the delivery of oil by pipeline to a particular city and that this requires the construction of an extension to the company's pipeline system leading directly into that community. Then this investment outlay is clearly incurred exclusively on behalf of X and by either definition (1) or (2) it constitutes part of its incremental cost. On the other hand, on the grounds that a "fixed cost" cannot be considered "variable" it might be decided, quite inappropriately, to exclude this construction outlay from the average cost.

separately *and in combination,* also satisfies criterion (5). If the firm produces X, Y and Z, each alone must satisfy (5); but in addition this must be shown for the four combinations: (X, Y), (X, Z), (Y, Z) and (X, Y, Z). The reason is, once more, made clearest by example. Suppose X and Y are the only two goods shipped along a particular railroad route which is constructed and maintained specifically for the purpose. Then the incremental track construction cost of product X by itself will be zero since that track must, in any event, be built if any Y is to be transported along the route. Similarly, the incremental track construction cost of Y must also be zero. However, if the two products each were to contribute revenue just sufficient to pay for their own incremental costs nothing would be available for replacement of track, and accordingly it would make little sense to describe that set of rates as compensatory. In this view it follows that, in order to pass an appropriate test of compensatory pricing, the incremental revenue of each product and every combination of products must contribute net incremental revenues which equal or exceed the corresponding net incremental costs, including the cost of any associated incremental capital *and the normal rate of return* on that incremental capital.

This definition will also prove relevant later when we turn to a discussion of an appropriate maximum price criterion. We may also note that the preceding test must be passed by the totality of the firms' products, i.e., in terms of our three-product example it requires that the incremental revenue of all three company products, X, Y and Z, together cover their total incremental cost. This last requirement implicitly assures us that the prices of the firm's products cover all of the company's costs including a normal return to its capital. If, in addition, these returns are constrained to be no higher than the normal yield of capital, this amounts to assurance that the firm's price vector yields revenues that just exactly cover its total costs and bring in what regulators sometimes call a "fair rate of return."

It may even be maintained as a result, albeit somewhat perversely, that these prices correspond to a full allocation process. But, of course, it is only so in retrospect. No accountant has been asked to perform the voodoo rites involved in assigning the unassignable costs. Rather, the price-setting process, as constrained by the market, has yielded a set of prices which, together, cover total costs. If, as a matter of aesthetics, one then wishes to allocate company costs in proportion to the revenues yielded by those prices, it is possible to maintain that the result constitutes a full allocation of costs and that the prices are consistent with that full allocation. Anyone who derives pleasure from such an exercise should of course not be deprived of it.

This completes my discussion of appropriate criteria for price floors, should these be considered desirable either for regulated or deregulated industries. It must only be added that the last criterion, the compensatory pricing test, seems to be the preferable criterion in terms of theory. In practice one must, of course, be prepared to compromise when such a test imposes unreasonable and unrealizable data and calculation requirements. I once wrote of the desirability of *optimally imperfect* decision criteria which balance off the cost and feasibility of a more demanding decision process against its benefits. Clearly, granted the desirability of any such criterion, one which is usable in practice will be preferable to one which is not. The main task before us, then, is the design of reasonable approximations to the ideal criterion of compensatory pricing which do not impose impossible or even excessive demands upon those who want to use them.

5. Toward a Reasonable Criterion for Price Ceilings

Though common sense would seem to suggest that in the presence of market power price ceilings are rather more to the point than price floors, I will have much less to say about the former than I did about the latter. In part, this is because so much less analysis seems to have been devoted to appropriate criteria for the setting of ceilings; in part it is a result of the inherent difficulty of the problem.

One way to get around its difficulties is simply to follow the dictates of Ramsey theory, requiring each regulated price to be set at a level that maximizes consumers' and producers' surplus subject to a profit constraint. One might, for example, just require prices, as an approximation, to obey the famous inverse-elasticity rule, under which the percentage deviation between price and marginal cost is inversely proportionate to the elasticity of the demand for the item in question.

In practice this solution will not do; first, because, as we have already noted, if applied only to a small subset of the economy's prices it loses its welfare-theoretic standing. More important, the immediate objective of deregulation is to broaden management's range of freedom in making economic decisions, not to narrow it further, let alone extinguish it altogether. One is therefore led to seek a permissible range within which management can exercise its judgment in setting price, but beyond which it will not be permitted to go in markets in which competition is ineffective. It can be argued that by permitting this degree of freedom, and by making the bounds of the permissible range as specific and observable as possible, one contributes to the scope and incentives for the exercise of aggressive entrepreneurship.

What then can one propose as an appropriate upper bound upon price? The one criterion which seems to have been suggested rests upon Faulhaber's concept of stand-alone cost. The (average) stand-alone cost of a particular service is the minimum amount per unit it would cost to provide if it were offered by a single-product supplier. That is, it is the amount the customers would have to pay if they were, in effect, to secede from their implicit association with the buyers of the supplying firm's other products.

It is to be noted that a price equal to stand-alone cost does deprive the customer of any share in the economies of scope[12] derived from simultaneous production of the other items in the firm's product line. But like the price floors we have discussed, its justification rests primarily (but not exclusively) on an equity principle—the view that it is unfair to extract more from a customer group than it would cost that group to serve itself.

Here we must be careful to distinguish two interpretations of stand-alone cost which so far have implicitly been confused in my discussion. One way to measure stand-alone cost is in terms of what it would cost *the current supplier* to provide the product in question after divesting itself of all other items in its product line. The second interpretation is the cost of serving the customers if they were to form *their own* company in competition with the existing firm. An example will bring out the distinction. Suppose a railroad carries several different goods over a route through the only mountain pass between the origin and destination, so that any alternative route would be prohibitively expensive. Here the second stand-alone cost of one of the freight items, that of an (imaginary) rival carrier, is obviously far greater

---

[12]For the original source and fullest discussion of this concept, see Panzar and Willig [1976] or [1978].

than the first stand-alone cost figure corresponding to the transportation of the one good by the existing railroad.[13]

It should be obvious that if this railroad were permitted to charge a price equal to the higher of the two stand-alone costs it would derive enormous profits attributable exclusively to the monopoly power it holds by having preempted the mountain pass. Clearly, in this case, the second stand-alone criterion is unacceptable.

But there are other cases in which it is to be preferred. Suppose the current supplier is inefficient and that a new firm could supply the affected customer group at a far lower cost. Surely there is no reason the incumbent firm, which by hypothesis possesses market power, should be permitted to extract the costs of its inefficiency from its customers.

It would seem to follow that, in principle, the appropriate stand-alone cost figure is the lower of the two.

Granted, for the sake of argument, the acceptability of the stand-alone criterion, whose logic as an inhibitor of monopoly profit is indicated by the preceding mountain-pass example, let us turn last to the measurements it requires. This is obviously no trivial issue since it refers to a hypothetical arrangement which almost certainly will never have been observed in fact. The multiproduct firm simply will not have been observed, at least in recent history, providing any of its products in isolation, and so there will exist no data permitting a direct calculation of stand-alone cost.

One obvious possibility is an engineering calculation, attempting to obtain by simulation an estimate of what would be required to supply one product alone. There are obvious questions about the reliability of such a calculation which the engineers themselves are the first to emphasize. Its cost is also likely to be enormous.

There is a second way of going about this calculation which follows directly from the test of compensatory pricing. Here, the crucial result is due to Faulhaber, who proved that a firm which earns no more than a normal return on its capital overall is guaranteed to earn no more than its stand-alone cost from the sale of a particular item, if it is also true that the prices of all other products are compensatory in the sense defined in the preceding section. In other words, the firm can prove that it is not exceeding the stand-alone ceiling over the price of product X by showing that it is earning normal profits in total, and that the prices of its remaining products, Y, Z, ..., are compensatory.[14]

The intuitive reason for this result is not difficult to describe. If a firm earns more than the stand-alone cost of item X (including a normal return on the capital involved), then X must, by definition, be contributing more than normal profits to the firm. This must then manifest itself in (at least) one of two ways: it must result in greater than normal profits for the firm overall, or some other product or products of the firm must yield enough of a loss to offset the excessive profit brought in by item X. Thus, violation of the stand-alone ceiling on the price of X will always be accompanied either by an observable supernormal profit rate for the entire firm or by noncompensatory net prices for some of its other products. That, of course, is

---

[13]Of course, if there really were a rival, so that the mountain pass had an alternative user, it would carry a rent, and the incumbent's cost average would disappear. I deliberately deal with the case in which this is not so in order to be able to consider the appropriate criterion for cases in which the two stand-alone costs *do* differ.

[14]This is not quite true if we define the proper ceiling as the *lower* of the two stand-alone costs defined before. Since the data in the calculation described in Faulhaber's theorem apply only to the firm whose price is being tested, the stand-alone figure provided by the calculation refers to the cost if product X were to be supplied by itself but by the firm which now also produces items Y, Z, ...

precisely what the Faulhaber theorem asserts.

It follows immediately that a ceiling based on stand-alone cost is required for efficiency and not just for equity. For we saw earlier that noncompensatory prices lead to inefficiency by preventing the entry of more efficient firms. Thus, we conclude now, violation of the stand-alone ceiling means that the firm must either be earning profits that are inefficiently large and must involve a misallocation of resources (unless the earnings are pure rent) or it must involve uncompensatory and, hence, inefficient prices of some other products.

The preceding explanation of the Faulhaber theorem was deliberately loosely phrased, but it is easy to provide a simple proof for the case of the two-product firm to give the flavor of the argument.

Suppose the firm produces exactly two goods X and Y, that P_x, the price of X, is compensatory, and that the firm's revenues just cover its overall costs, including its cost of capital. I will prove that then the price of Y cannot exceed the stand-alone ceiling.

Compensatory pricing of X requires by (5) and (2) that net incremental revenue of $X = (p_x x + P_y y) - [P_x 0 + P_y(y + \Delta y)] \geq$ net incremental cost of $X = C(x, y) - C(0, y + \Delta y)$, or

$$P_x x - P_y \Delta y \geq C(x, y) - C(0, y + \Delta y). \quad (6)$$

But if the firm is earning only its normal return, then

$$P_x x + P_y y = C(x, y). \quad (7)$$

Subtracting (6) from (7), we have:

$$P_y(y + \Delta y) \geq C(0, y + \Delta y) \quad (8)$$

which proves immediately that the total revenue that would be produced by price P_y if X were not supplied (so that the demand for Y would rise to $y + \Delta y$) is no greater than the

(stand-alone) cost of $y + \Delta y$. But that is precisely what it was intended to show.

This, then, completes my discussion of an appropriate ceiling formula for products over which the residually regulated firm still retains some market power. No doubt, further analysis of the subject is still needed urgently. But the economic logic of the proposed stand-alone criterion seems clear, and its intimate connection with the criterion of compensatory pricing is one of its attractive features.

6. Concluding Remarks

In a sense, the preceding discussion may be characterized as an attempt to do something economists have with good reason attempted to avoid—to provide some substantive content to the discredited concept of "just price." But, as I have said elsewhere, while there may be no unique price which can unequivocally be declared "just," it may be possible to determine ranges of prices all of which we will agree to be unjust. It is in this spirit that I have sought to deal with floors and ceilings, implicitly using them to define a range of intermediate prices each of which is to be considered acceptable in the weak sense that there appears to be no reasonable way to show it to be unjust.

I must end as I began, by protesting that it has not been my objective to advocate the desirability of price floors and ceilings, even for a small subset of markets in a deregulated industry in which there is no effective competition. The social costs of the associated regulatory process may or may not be justified by the likely benefits. But whatever one's judgment on this score, it seems clearly desirable, *if* price regulation is to be preserved, to minimize the administrative and resources cost of the process by spelling out the approved range of freedom of entrepreneurial decisions and making as specific as possible the boundary between acceptable and objectionable conduct. That has been the primary purpose of this paper.

References

Ackworth, W. M. *The Railways and the Traders.* London, 1891.

Alexander, E. P. *Railway Practice.* New York, 1887.

Areeda, Phillip and Donald Turner. "Predatory Pricing and Related Practices under Section 2 of the Sherman Act." *Harvard Law Review,* 88 (February 1975), 697–733.

Baumol, W. J. "Quasi-Permanence of Price Reductions—A Policy for Prevention of 'Predatory Pricing'." Forthcoming (1978).

Cassel, Gustav, "The Principles of Railway Rates for Passengers." *International Economic Papers,* No. 6 (   ). Translated from *Archiv für Eisenbahnwesen,* 1900.

Faulhaber, G. R. "Cross-Subsidization: Pricing in Public Enterprise." *American Economic Review,* 65 (December 1975), 966–77.

Hadley, A. T. *Railroad Transportation.* New York and London, 1886.

Hotelling, Harold. "The General Welfare in Relation to Problems of Taxation and Utility Rates." *Econometrica,* 6 (July 1938), 242–69.

Lewis, W. A. *Overhead Costs.* London, 1949.

Panzar, John and Robert Willig. "Economies of Scale and Economies of Scope in MultiOutput Production." Bell Laboratories Economics Discussion Paper (1976).

_____ . "Economies of Scope, Product-Specific Economies of Scale and the MultiProduct Competitive Firm." Bell Laboratories Economics Discussion Paper (1978).

Ramsey, Frank. "A Contribution to the Theory of Taxation." *Economic Journal,* 37 (March 1927), 47–61.

Scherer, F. M. "Predatory Pricing and the Sherman Act: A Comment." *Harvard Law Review,* 89 (1976), 869–90.

Smith, Adam. *The Wealth of Nations* (1976), Cannan (ed.). New York: 1937.

Williamson, Oliver E. "Predatory Pricing: A Strategic Welfare Analysis." *Yale Law Journal,* 87 (1977), 284–340.

U.S. Court of Appeals, 10th Circuit. 551 F. 2d 790, *Pacific Engineering and Prod. Co. v. Kerr-McGee Corp.* (February 28, 1977).

U.S. Court of Appeals, 9th Circuit. 570 F. 2d 856, *Janich Bros., Inc. v. American Distilling Co.* (1977).

U.S. District Court, Northern District of California. No. C-71-1906, SW, *Inglis and Sons Baking Co. v. ITT Continental Baking Co.* (October 2, 1978).

[10]

Quasi-Permanence of Price Reductions: A Policy for Prevention of Predatory Pricing

William J. Baumol*

> *The use of the term "predatory" to describe conduct violative of the antitrust laws has left much to be desired. This court has noted, "The term probably does not have a well-defined meaning in the context it was used, but it certainly bears a sinister connotation."[1]*
>
> *Pricing is predatory only where the firm foregoes short-term profits in order to develop a market position such that the firm can later raise prices and recoup lost profits.[2]*

While no one has succeeded in providing a satisfactory definition of the term "predatory pricing," the issue is real and important. Arceda and Turner,[3] Scherer,[4] and Williamson[5] have made substantial contributions in their analyses of the issue and in their formulation of criteria for use in the evaluation or prevention of predatory behavior.

This Article seeks to go one step further, both in the discussion of the problem and in the formulation of such a criterion. I will propose a simple rule that enjoys significant optimality properties with respect to economic efficiency. Equally important, the rule is rela-

* Professor of Economics, Princeton and New York Universities. I am grateful to the Sloan Foundation and the National Science Foundation, whose grants greatly facilitated the preparation of this article.

1. Pacific Eng'r & Prod. Co. v. Kerr-McGee Corp., 551 F.2d 790, 795-96 (10th Cir.), *cert. denied*, 434 U.S. 879 (1977) (quoting Telex Corp. v. I.B.M. Corp., 510 F.2d 894, 927 (10th Cir.), *cert. dismissed*, 423 U.S. 802 (1975)).

2. Janich Bros. v. American Distilling Co., 570 F.2d 848, 856 (9th Cir. 1977), *cert. denied*, 439 U.S. 829 (1978).

3. *See* Areeda & Turner, *Predatory Pricing and Related Practices under Section 2 of the Sherman Act*, 88 HARV. L. REV. 697 (1975).

4. *See* Scherer, *Predatory Pricing and the Sherman Act: A Comment*, 89 HARV. L. REV. 869 (1976).

5. *See* Williamson, *Predatory Pricing: A Strategic and Welfare Analysis*, 87 YALE L.J. 284 (1977).

The Yale Law Journal   Vol. 89: 1, 1979

tively easy to administer, permits full and fair competition by both entrants and established firms, and encourages enduring, rather than temporary, price cutting, in order to serve consumers' interests over the long-run. In short, I believe that the proposed approach offers substantial advantages: consumer benefits; the stimulation of true competition; efficiency of resource allocation; and greater effectiveness of antitrust and regulatory policy. The proposal, it should be noted, is not intended to be a substitute either for regulation or for antitrust programs, but rather to be a new instrument for both of these. It is intended not to replace market forces, but to permit those forces to work more effectively.

Much of the discussion of rules for the prevention of predatory pricing has focused on economists' *static* analysis of allocative efficiency and the maximization of consumers' and producers' surplus. However, this static analysis of the issue of predatory behavior, illustrated, at its best, by the Areeda-Turner approach,[6] is inadequate, not because such analysis is irrelevant, but because it draws our attention away from some of the most pressing issues that are involved.

The problem has recently been dramatized by the entry of Laker Airlines into the transatlantic passenger air-travel arena with a great reduction in fares. Predictably, established firms quickly sought permission to respond by matching and, in fact, offering better terms than Laker's. The obvious alternatives for policymakers who had to pass on the applications seemed uniformly distasteful:

a) Rejection of the competitors' responsive proposals would have been tantamount to granting a protective shield to Laker, the first step toward establishment of a cartel in which effective competition is prevented by public policy, even though the survival of each "competitor" is artificially preserved. This is an invitation to inefficiency and, ultimately, to poor customer service and perhaps to higher prices.

b) Approval of the proposed responses carried the danger that established firms would have succeeded in driving Laker out of the market and that the low fares offered by the established carriers would have been withdrawn after the competitive threat had passed.

In such a case the regulator finds himself confronted with the choice between Scylla and Charybdis, apparently with no safe middle course. Neither the creation of a cartel nor the sanctioning of the destruction of the entrant is an appealing prospect. Both are incompatible with effective competition and neither serves the long-run interests of consumers.

6. *See* Areeda & Turner, *supra* note 3, at 703-20.

Predatory Pricing

Williamson has identified the nub of the problem in his emphasis on the intertemporal aspect of the situation.[7] The difficulty is that a firm seeking to prevent entry by others need not confine itself to a single price move. Instead, it may choose to cut price temporarily when entry occurs, raising price again after the threat recedes, or it may undertake a more complex sequence of price changes, responding step by step to each change in an entrant's decisions. The resulting threat to competition and to the general welfare is not a function of the relationship between prices and costs, but rather a matter of the responsiveness of pricing to changing competitive developments.[8] Thus, it seems appropriate to look beyond the Areeda-Turner test, which evaluates matters solely in terms of the relation between the established firm's prices and its marginal costs or average variable costs.

It should be noted that even those courts that have been most unqualified in their support of the Areeda-Turner test have expressed the same reservation.[9] As one court stated:

7. *See* Williamson, *supra* note 5, at 289-304.

8. In addressing the problem of predatory pricing, Williamson has proposed a set of rules, the basic component of which is the stipulation that "Dominant firms that expand their (demand adjusted) output in the face of new entry will be deemed to be engaged in predatory behavior—even if the resulting market price exceeds the dominant firm's average variable cost." Williamson, *supra* note 5, at 334. The object of the rule is to prevent the incumbent firm from forestalling entry by flooding the market when competition threatens. Moreover, if the incumbent cannot expand its output, it cannot maintain a low price because doing so would only cause demand to exceed supply and thus make it easier for the entrant to establish itself by serving the unsatisfied demand on favorable price terms analogous to the high black-market prices that accompany shortages under rationing. Williamson observes that a demand forecast must be used to set the admissible level of output for the dominant firm; in a growing market the incumbent must be permitted to increase output along with market demand, but no faster. *Id.* at 305. Williamson believes that the need for such a forecast should not pose a serious problem. *Id.*

One clear advantage of the Williamson proposal is the incentive it provides for anticipatory expansion of output by the incumbent; consumers receive the advantages of lower prices and increased volume well before entry threatens. On the other hand, if entry nevertheless does occur, the rule prevents it from serving the purpose for which it is normally advocated: under the rule, entry cannot force competitive price reductions upon the incumbent. Furthermore, Williamson's rule inhibits price wars among large incumbent firms, who are constrained, in effect, to retain their initial market shares, at least for the immediate post-entry period. In addition, in an industry expanding rapidly as a result of a recent innovation, the Williamson rule well may run into difficulties in selecting an output constraint to impose upon the innovator. Moreover, the required demand forecast may not be as simple and objective a process as Williamson suggests.

I am grateful to Professor Dennis Mueller of the University of Maryland for suggesting some of the preceding ideas to me.

9. *See, e.g.,* Janich Bros. v. American Distilling Co., 570 F.2d 848, 856 (9th Cir. 1977), *cert. denied,* 439 U.S. 829 (1978); Hanson v. Shell Oil Co., 541 F.2d 1352, 1358 (9th Cir. 1976), *cert. denied,* 429 U.S. 1074 (1977); International Air Indus., Inc. v. American Excelsior Co., 517 F.2d 714, 723 (5th Cir. 1975), *cert. denied,* 424 U.S. 943 (1976); Murphy Tugboat Co. v. Crowley, 454 F. Supp. 847, 854 & n.8 (N.D. Cal. 1978); Weber v. Wynne, 431 F. Supp. 1048, 1059 (D.N.J. 1977).

The Yale Law Journal   Vol. 89: 1, 1979

> To demonstrate predation, [the plaintiff] had to show that the prices charged by [the defendant] were such that [the defendant] was foregoing present profits in order to create a market position in which it could charge enough to obtain supranormal profits and recoup its present losses.[10]

While ostensibly expressing adherence to Areeda-Turner, the court is in fact demonstrating its concern over the intertemporal issue, which unavoidably involves considerations going beyond the atemporal Areeda-Turner test.

I. Quasi-Permanence of Responsive Price Reductions

So far it has been assumed implicitly that the dilemma of the policymaker, illustrated by the Laker case, permits only two possible reactions: either the erection of a protective umbrella over the entrant or freedom for the established firm to raise and lower prices subject only to cost constraints. But there is a third possibility: the established firm can be left free to cut prices in order to protect its interests, without being permitted to *reraise* those prices *if the entrant leaves the market* or if the firm wants to subsidize price cuts of other products that are then threatened by competition. In short, such price reductions can be made quasi-permanent.

A. *The Proposed Rule*

The quasi-permanence of price reduction proposal can be readily illustrated by the Laker parable.[11] Suppose established firms had been told they could reduce their own fares as far as they wished, subject only to some sort of cost floor. But suppose the established firms had also been informed that if Laker should cease to operate, they would not be permitted to withdraw these low rates in the future except in response to independent changes in costs and market demands.[12] Under such an arrangement, the established firm would

---

10. Hanson v. Shell Oil Co., 541 F.2d 1352, 1358 (9th Cir. 1976), *cert. denied*, 429 U.S. 1074 (1977).

11. Civil Aeronautics Board Commissioner Elizabeth E. Bailey has suggested that the Laker case is in fact a poor example for the proposed principle since the airline industry is potentially very competitive because of low entry costs. Telephone conversation with Elizabeth E. Bailey, October 1978 (notes on file *Yale Law Journal*). If upon deregulation, with full freedom of entry and exit, the airlines prove to be effectively competitive, then nothing can be gained by pricing that is predatory. In such a case, quasi-permanence will be an unnecessary encumbrance upon the market mechanism.

12. If the entrant is alive and well, there seems no reason to prevent the established firm from rescinding a price cut unless the price is raised to help the incumbent counter another price cut by an entrant. After all, such a rise in the established firm's price can only be to the advantage of the entrant.

4

Predatory Pricing

be put on notice that its decision to offer service at a low price is tantamount to a declaration that this price is compensatory, and thus, that it can be expected, in the absence of exogenous changes in costs or demands, to offer the service at this price for the indefinite future.[13]

The consequences are clear. A quasi-permanent pricing arrangement does not raise a protective umbrella over the entrant; the established firm is left free to respond.[14] However, it will no longer be free to respond without fear of long-term repercussions. The established firm only will adjust its price if the value of the resulting competitive gain exceeds the long-run cost of a permanent reduction in price. True competition is thereby unleashed,[15] and the consuming public is offered the rewards accompanying a durable price reduction.[16] Moreover, the chances of the entrant's survival are increased; he can expect to survive if his costs are at least as low as those of the established firm—that is, if he is entitled to survive on the merits of his relative efficiency. Thus the intertemporal side of the problem

13. Although it may appear that the Williamson proposal is very similar in its effects to those of quasi-permanence of price reductions, in fact, the two proposals are very different. Williamson proposes that a ceiling be set on the output of the established firm when entry occurs. As a result, market price may not fall as much as it might have otherwise. The same may be true of the price reduction that will occur under quasi-permanence. But there the similarity ends. Under the Williamson proposal, many output and price choices are, in effect, forbidden to the firm. Under quasi-permanence there are no such prohibitions unless the prices fail a test of cross subsidy. *See* p. 10 *infra.* Moreover, under the Williamson proposal, price can rise again, if and when the entrant leaves the market, so that consumers may receive no long-term price benefit. That, of course, is precisely what quasi-permanence prohibits. Furthermore, there are additional advantages for quasi-permanence in terms of allocative efficiency. *See* pp. 24-25 *infra.*

14. Note, however, that the firm is not permitted to readjust a price upward in order to permit a cut in the price of another product threatened by a new price reduction by an entrant. The established firm is thus inhibited in responding, move by move, to each price change by the entrant. Rather, it must choose carefully the prices it originally adopts in response to entry, taking into consideration possible future moves by the entrant. This requirement that the firm adopt a price strategy appropriate to deal with future price moves by the competitor is what forces the established firm to adopt prices that promote economic efficiency.

15. That is, competition results to the degree permitted by scale economies and other influences making for monopolistic elements within the industry. Obviously, if monopolistic influences are not a relevant problem, the industry is not an appropriate subject for antitrust measures. Thus, the entire issue leading to the quasi-permanence proposal does not arise. If, for example, an industry is obviously composed of a number of small firms, none of which has sufficient market power to make the industry an oligopoly, the firms' pricing decisions need not be subject to the quasi-permanent pricing rule.

16. In economics jargon, the quasi-permanence principle will promote "X-efficiency," in that it forces firms to prevent waste, to search for innovation, and to avoid the "laziness" that a protective price umbrella encourages. *See* Leibenstein, *Allocative Efficiency vs. 'X-Efficiency,'* 56 AM. ECON. REV. 392 (1966). This type of efficiency is different from the efficiency in resource allocation usually addressed by economists. I also make a strong claim, however, for quasi-permanence as an instrument to promote efficiency in resource allocation. *See* pp. 10-24 *infra.*

is dealt with; if the entrant's costs are lower than those of an established firm, but the latter chooses to undercut him nevertheless, it will be left with the burden of a continuing drain upon company profits even when no competitive advantage from the low prices remains.[17] Managements of established firms will surely think twice before entering upon such a commitment.[18]

B. *Practical Issues in Implementing the Rule*

Several practical issues must be addressed in considering the application of the proposed rule. How can permanence of price cuts be enforced in an inflationary world? What if the established firm makes a mistake in its price calculation? How can such a principle be used in antitrust policy?

Inflation and other autonomous changes in costs and market de-

---

17. The claim that ambiguity arises because of the likelihood that after some time has passed it will become difficult to distinguish the entrant from an established firm causes no difficulties for the proposed principle; an entrant should be subject to the same rule as the incumbent. If Laker succeeds in driving Pan Am out of its market, it, too, should not be free to raise its fares at will. Thus, while the discussion has emphasized the special role of the entrant, the quasi-permanence pricing rule should apply to any firm whose low prices are suspected of having driven its competitor from the field, whether or not that competitor was a recent entrant.

18. It should be pointed out that Areeda and Turner did consider the problem raised by temporary price reductions and considered several means of dealing with it, including the quasi-permanence rule. Areeda & Turner, *supra* note 3, at 708-09. They concluded that they could find "no satisfactory method of control." *Id.* at 707. While the quasi-permanence rule was "perhaps the most feasible," *id.* at 708, Areeda-Turner later indicated that they "were inclined to reject it." Letter from Professor Donald F. Turner to Professor William J. Baumol, Sept. 28, 1978 (on file *Yale Law Journal*). Among their reasons were the following: (1) the difficulty of adapting the rule to changing market conditions—such as rising costs and shifting demand—a subject to which I will return in the next section; (2) the possibility that the rule might "have adverse effects on the established firm's incentive to reduce price in response to entry"; and (3) the certainty that the rule would "put the courts into a 'quasi' price regulatory role—which they have regularly shunned and for good reasons." *Id.*

Clearly, Areeda and Turner are right in arguing that the rule will inhibit price cutting to some degree. But the object of the quasi-permanence rule, like that of the Areeda-Turner rule, is precisely to inhibit price cutting that is legally and economically unacceptable. The quasi-permanence rule does so by encouraging firms to cut prices only when they believe they can live with the consequences, even after the entrant has departed. A price cut that the incumbent cannot afford to retain is neither "honestly industrial" nor likely to improve resource allocation. Finally, I agree that examining price adjustments to ensure that they are justified by changing costs or shifting demands involves the courts in a quasi-regulatory role. However, this chore is no more demanding than is the task assigned the courts by Areeda-Turner. In a multiproduct firm, comparison of price with marginal cost or average variable cost is a matter of technical economics that has long been a major preoccupation of our regulatory agencies. I also argue that the proposed criterion involves calculations less exacting than it may appear to require. *See* p. 7 *infra.* But any sensible criterion for determining predatory conduct inevitably involves difficult considerations that the courts or the regulatory agencies can avoid only by refusing to address the issue.

Predatory Pricing

mands pose no insuperable problem for the administration of the
proposed program. Of course, the established firm that has instituted
a price cut of fifty percent should be permitted to adjust that price
upward when, for example, there is a five percent rise in fuel prices.
But the firm should only be permitted a rise that brings in additional
revenue sufficient to cover the rise in fuel cost, starting from its new,
low price. Such an independent rise in costs does not justify or neces-
sitate the elimination of all restraints upon price increases by the
established firm. It should still be held to the stipulated arrangement: its underlying price cut is permanent, with adjustments permitted only when the firm can demonstrate they are required by
autonomous changes such as subsequent inflation.[19]

   At first blush this would seem to put the courts in the position
of regulatory agencies, requiring them to undertake delicate calculations comparing price and cost increases in order to evaluate the ap-
propriateness of the former in light of the magnitude of the latter.
This appearance is deceptive, however, because courts need not determine what precise price increase is called for by a particular rise
in costs. All that is necessary is to verify that the two are similar in
order of magnitude so that there are no grounds for believing that
the firm has used a five percent rise in costs as an excuse for rescinding a fifty percent price cut. That is, under a quasi-permanence rule,
the incumbent firm should be expected to provide convincing evidence that any price rise that takes place after the withdrawal of
an entrant was of the same order of magnitude as the cost change
that led to the increase. Price changes attributable to other exogenous changes such as shifts in demand should also be required to
be supported by evidence that they are appropriate in general magnitude. However, they need not be tested on the basis of any knife's-
edge criterion of ideal pricing that would require precise evaluations
of demand elasticities, marginal costs, or other economic variables,
the magnitudes of which would be difficult to estimate.

   The case of miscalculation by the established firm is another
matter. In the free market it is always the stockholders who bear
the penalties of miscalculations by management. This is appropriate
because otherwise the firm would have little incentive to take into
account the risks of its decisions. The proposed rule should con-

---

   19. Under the proposed arrangement the firm would still be free to change its prices
in response to any changes in the pertinent economic variables with the exception of
the specified changes in the state of competition in the market. The point is that the
burden will be on the firm to show that any price change was a response to a pertinent
economic development other than the exit of a competitor.

The Yale Law Journal   Vol. 89: 1, 1979

stitute no exception to this principle. If management makes an ill-advised price cut on the basis of erroneous cost estimates, stockholders should bear the resulting losses.[20] Otherwise it would be too tempting to undercut entrants on the basis of calculated "miscalculations."

Of course it will be difficult politically and practically to hold the established firm permanently to price levels that subject it to a continuing financial drain. Therefore, it may be impractical to require the price cut to be literally permanent, even in the absence of autonomous changes in costs or market demands. That is why the policy is termed "quasi-permanent" pricing; a specified, finite period, perhaps on the order of five years, will no doubt suffice to achieve its goals. The choice of time period is, of course, a matter to be worked out in light of experience and considerations of practicality.[21]

A regulated firm is most easily subjected to a policy of quasi-permanence of any reductions in prices it undertakes in response to entry. Since its rate revisions are always subject to regulatory approval, a price cut made in the presence of recent entry or the threat of entry can be approved only on the condition that upward revisions be precluded for a stipulated and substantial period, except as required by demonstrable autonomous changes. Thus the proposal is entirely consistent with continued regulation of certain industries and should not be interpreted as a substitute for it.

The proposed rule can also be applied to an industry that is not subject to rate regulation. Areeda and Turner have proposed that prices below marginal or average variable costs should constitute evi-

---

20. A possible exception is a firm subject to rate-of-return regulation whose profit ceiling prevents stockholders from obtaining any gains from a felicitous managerial decision. Here symmetry, as a condition of fairness, may call for stockholders to be protected from managerial miscalculations as a counterpoise to the arrangement that prevents them from benefiting from a particularly fortunate managerial act.

21. In the final analysis, the choice of any particular period will be arbitrary to some degree. However, this is true of other proposals as well. *See, e.g.*, Williamson, *supra* note 5, at 296 (the output-restriction rule should be imposed for a "period from twelve to eighteen months [because that is ordinarily] sufficient to allow the entrant to realize cost economies and establish a market identity"). The period must be sufficiently long to bear significant weight in the pricing calculations of the incumbent firm and to offer significant benefits to its customers, but it must not be so long as to threaten to strangle that firm because of actions that have become ancient history. While in theory it may be desirable to vary the period from case to case depending on the circumstances of the individual firms involved, in practice this should be avoided. One of the great benefits of the Areeda-Turner rule is an injection of a clear and uniform standard into an arena previously characterized by vagueness and uncertainty. The economic costs of indecision by those who cannot judge whether a contemplated act will run afoul of the law are high. Adoption of a clear and uniform standard is desirable wherever that is possible without intolerable consequences.

8

Predatory Pricing

dence of illegal behavior under the antitrust laws.[22] Williamson has proposed the same for increases in excess of trend in an established firm's output following entry of new firms into the industry.[23] Surely, a similar arrangement can apply to the proposal that a price cut following entry or the threat of entry not be withdrawable.[24] Should a firm being sued under the antitrust laws be accused of violating this principle, the burden would be on that firm to provide convincing evidence that the price increases being challenged were justified by cost increases or by other autonomous developments.[25]

C. *On the Role of Supplementary Cost Tests*

It is necessary to consider whether a policy of quasi-permanence of price reductions requires supplementation by a set of cost criteria designed to ensure that prices never be set unacceptably low and, if so, just what cost test is appropriate. Even Williamson, whose basic antipredation rule is a maximum-output restriction that does not mention price directly, feels it appropriate nevertheless to supplement this rule with a cost test.[26] A case can be made for the proposition that no such cost test is really needed under a policy of quasi-permanent price reductions by arguing that the principle can be left to take care of the problem automatically. The reasoning is simply that a noncompensatory price will be very costly to the firm

22. *See* Areeda & Turner, *supra* note 3, at 712-13, 716-18.
23. Though an oversimplification of Williamson's position, this characterization is sufficient for our discussion. *See* Williamson, *supra* note 5, at 297-99.
24. This clearly means also that the firm should not withdraw the low-priced product from the market after the rival exits. I do not suggest, of course, that the quasi-permanence principle should be applied retrospectively to acts undertaken before the proposal was offered.
25. This shifting of the burden of proof is common in antitrust litigation. For example, under the Robinson-Patman Act, 15 U.S.C. §§ 13-13b, 21a (1976), three affirmative defenses are available to rebut a prima facie case of price discrimination: meeting competition, cost justification, and changing market conditions. *See* F. Rowe, Price Discrimination under the Robinson-Patman Act 207-329 (1962).
26. Williamson's use of the term "average total cost," *see* Williamson, *supra* note 5, at 321-22, 332, injects some ambiguity into his proposal. By average total cost, he surely does not mean fully allocated cost, which is a mare's nest of arbitrary calculations parading as substantive information. In reality, the single-product firm is probably nonexistent, and it is normally impossible to define, much less to measure, the average cost of any output of a multiproduct firm because of the difficulty of subdividing nonincremental common costs. Williamson, of course, is well aware of all this. Consequently, I assume that when he requires the price of a good in the long-run to exceed its "average total cost," he defines the latter to mean the average incremental cost of the product including any fixed cost outlays required to provide the item. That is, the average incremental cost of product X is defined as total company cost minus what the total cost of the company would be in the absence of production of X, all divided by the quantity of X being produced. Total costs refer to those that would prevail in the long-run with the output combinations specified.

if it cannot be rescinded after it has served to deter entrants; therefore, quasi-permanence of price reductions attaches to the setting of a price below cost an automatic penalty sufficient to make the established firm voluntarily avoid predatory pricing.

This argument, however, may leave some observers uncomfortable: they may well believe that the management of a very profitable firm may prefer, even for long periods, to use some of the profits contributed by other outputs as a source to subsidize socially unacceptable low prices of products threatened by entry. Some analysts maintain that some managements prefer the quiet life sufficiently to sacrifice a substantial amount of profit in order to protect themselves from the competition of entrants. Whether or not this is likely to happen in practice is a matter for empirical investigation. But whatever the outcome of such a study, it may be prudent to have available, as it were, a stand-by cost test to determine whether a particular price has been set so low as to require the product to draw cross subsidies from other outputs of the same supplier. Thus, policymakers may want to supplement a policy of quasi-permanence of price reductions with a test like the Areeda-Turner test to determine whether a particular price involves cross subsidy. This would avoid injustice both to the entrant and to the purchasers of those products of the established firm that are the potential source of cross subsidy.

II. Economic Efficiency, Stationary Limit Pricing, and Quasi-Permanence of Price Reductions

Different proposals addressed to the problem of predatory pricing have been evaluated on the basis of their ability to promote allocative efficiency. Areeda-Turner, using the tools of economic analysis, conclude that their pricing rule will have desirable efficiency consequences.[27] Williamson counters by arguing that his output-restriction rule will perform still better.[28] But neither Williamson nor Areeda-Turner are able to claim that their proposal is consistent with the requirements of allocative efficiency.

In contrast, a quasi-permanence pricing policy is similar to a policy —known as stationary limit pricing—that can be shown to pass at least the theoretical tests of allocative efficiency. Stationary limit pricing refers to a policy under which the established firm adopts a single

27. *See* Areeda & Turner, *supra* note 3, at 709-12; Areeda & Turner, *Williamson on Predatory Pricing*, 87 YALE L.J. 1337, 1338-45 (1978).
28. *See* Williamson, *supra* note 5, at 306-12.

10

Predatory Pricing

set of prices designed to protect it to the extent possible from the incursions of entrants and leaves those prices unchanged (or changes them only because of exogenous developments such as rises in input prices). Such a policy is distinguished from responsive limit pricing, under which the established firm seeks to frustrate entry by continually readjusting its prices to meet each move of an entrant.

Although quasi-permanent pricing is not identical with stationary limit pricing, it is sufficiently similar that it approximates the optimality properties enjoyed by stationary limit pricing. However, demonstration of the efficiency benefits of such a pricing scheme rests upon a body of economic analysis that is quite new and unfamiliar in its approach. For this reason, and because this literature is potentially useful for antitrust analysis, I digress at this point to provide a relatively nontechnical summary of some of its results.[29] Using this material, I will be able to demonstrate the desirable properties of stationary limit pricing and quasi-permanent pricing.[30]

A. *Weak Invisible Hand Theorems*

1. *Criteria of Natural Monopoly*

Generally, an industry is said to be a natural monopoly if production by a single firm is the cheapest way to produce the combination of outputs supplied by the industry. One of the conclusions of the new analysis is that if an industry is *not* a natural monopoly, that is, if several firms can produce its output at least as cheaply as one, then a policy of stationary limit pricing will be impossible for an incumbent monopolist. Thus, no fixed prices will exist that can be adopted by the monopolist's firm that can cover its costs and yet prevent the entry of competitors.

Because the concept of natural monopoly is at the heart of the issue, our discussion must begin with an examination of some of the properties of a natural monopoly. The notion of natural monopoly al-

29. Section IIA provides a relatively theoretical analysis of the efficiency properties of the quasi-permanence principle and can be omitted by the reader uninterested in economic theory. However, the theory is pertinent to a number of issues in antitrust law.

30. The discussion is formulated in terms of pricing by a monopoly firm; however, most of the conclusions also apply to oligopolies. Since most issues of predatory pricing arise in oligopolistic rather than competitive industries, the extension of the analysis to the oligopoly case is a pressing matter. Unfortunately, as is well known, the oligopoly case has not proved nearly as amenable to analysis as that of pure monopoly. It is, therefore, perhaps a bit of luck that the following propositions can, in general, be shown to be valid for the oligopoly case. The exceptions are Propositions I and II, which clearly refer only to monopolies.

11

The Yale Law Journal   Vol. 89: 1, 1979

ways has been associated loosely with the phenomenon of economies of scale, which exist when an x percent expansion in all input quantities (an expansion to scale) is capable of yielding an expansion in output that is greater than x percent. However, one of the basic theorems of the new analysis of natural monopoly is that the presence of scale economies is neither necessary nor sufficient for an industry to be a natural monopoly.

To show what conditions are directly relevant, we must turn to the definition of the concept itself. As we have already noted, an industry is said to be a natural monopoly at some given level of its output if that output combination can be produced more cheaply by a single firm than it can be by any multiplicity of different firms. When this is true, the cost relationship is said to be *subadditive,* meaning that the cost of total output (if all produced together by one firm) is less than the sum of the costs of producing it in any separate portions by different firms.

Thus, if an industry is a natural monopoly, then more resources will be required to produce its output if it is broken up into smaller firms. It is to be noted that this way of looking at natural monopoly comes closer to a commonsense view of the matter than does the notion of economies of scale. Subadditivity is, in itself, not a very complex or sophisticated notion, though its analysis is relatively complicated.

The following theorem[31] establishes what observable conditions are sufficient to prove that an industry is a natural monopoly, that is, that its cost structure is subadditive:

Proposition I:

> *Two pieces of evidence are* together *sufficient to prove that an industry is a natural monopoly as defined:*
> i) average costs decline *when all outputs increase by any given percentage (e.g., if a five percent increase in* all *the firm's outputs causes only a four percent increase in its total costs),*[32] *and ii)* the production of the different outputs supplied by the firm is

31. For a formal statement and proof, see Baumol, *The Proper Cost Tests for Natural Monopoly in a Multiproduct Industry,* 67 AM. ECON. REV. 809 (1977).

32. Note that economists agree that one cannot define the behavior of average costs generally in a multiproduct firm, because average cost is defined as total cost divided by total output; in a multiproduct firm, output can be totaled only by adding apples and oranges. However, in the special case where one is interested in what happens when all outputs increase or decrease by precisely the same percentage, there is no such problem because the quantity of any one of the products can then serve as a perfect index of the quantities of all other goods.

Predatory Pricing

complementary *(that is, if the firm produces two items A and B, the cost of producing A and B together is less than that of producing them separately).*[33]

The first of these requirements corresponds roughly to economies of scale, though it is not quite as tough a requirement: a firm that does not have scale economies may, nevertheless, have average costs that decline when all outputs are increased by the same percentage. The second requirement is related to what have been termed "economies of scope,"[34] economies imparted not by the size of output of any one product of the firm but by the sheer number of different items it produces simultaneously. The role of these concepts is clarified by considering, in turn, the consequences of violation of our two conditions.[35] First, consider what is implied by violation of re-

33. More technically, the cost of producing, for example, 50 units of A together with 50 units of B is less than the average of the cost of producing 100 units of A all by itself or the cost of producing 100 units of B all by itself.

The two conditions just stated are not equivalent to subadditivity, however. Although the satisfaction of these two conditions implies subadditivity and hence natural monopoly, the converse is not true; subadditivity is a weaker concept. These two conditions are essential, however, for several crucial results that will be described below. *See* p. 22 *infra.*

34. *See* Panzar & Willig, Economies of Scale and Economies of Scope in Multi Output Production (1975) (Bell Laboratories working paper).

35. Several graphs may make clearer the substance of Proposition I. Figure 1 simply shows the range of outputs of two products of an industry, call them cars and trucks.

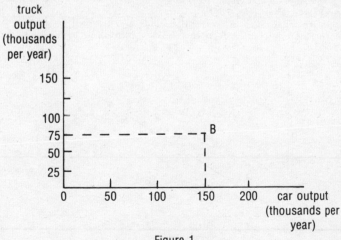

Figure 1
A Point in Output Space

The Yale Law Journal   Vol. 89: 1, 1979

quirement (i): suppose average costs were not to decrease when output expanded proportionately. This would mean that two firms each producing half the outputs of a monopoly firm would have unit

For example, point B in the figure indicates that the industry is producing an output of 150,000 cars and 75,000 trucks per year. Figure 2 is a three-dimensional diagram in

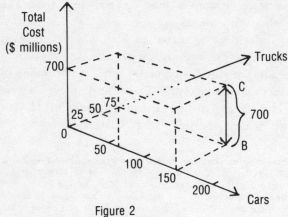

Figure 2
A Point on the Cost Surface

which a third axis has beeen added to the two axes in Figure 1. The third axis indicates how many dollars are required to produce any combination of cars and trucks depicted in Figure 1. For example, point B in Figure 2 represents again the production of 150 cars and 75 trucks (the thousands henceforth will be omitted). Then the length of the vertical line BC above point B will indicate the cost of producing output combination B, in this case $700 million per year. If such a total cost figure is determined for every output combination in the graph, the locus of all those points will constitute what is called a cost surface. *See* note 37 *infra* (Figure 9).

Next, observe what happens when all outputs are increased or decreased proportionately. In Figure 3, point A represents a 33⅓% increase in both outputs over point

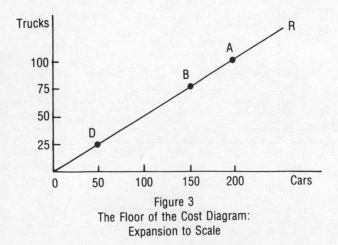

Figure 3
The Floor of the Cost Diagram:
Expansion to Scale

Predatory Pricing

costs no higher than the monopolist's. Therefore, society would lose nothing (in terms of costs) by breaking the monopoly into a set of smaller firms, each with a minireplica of the monopolist's product line.[36] Next, consider the implication of violation of requirement (ii): suppose the firm's outputs were not complementary in production, so that it was as cheap (or cheaper) to produce them in isolation as to make them together. Then, society would lose nothing if the (multiproduct) monopoly were to be broken up into a set of more spe-

---

B (200 rather than 150 cars and 100 rather than 75 trucks). Similarly, it is obvious that point D represents a $66\frac{2}{3}\%$ reduction in both outputs. All three points lie along the same straight line through the origin, OR. A straight line through the origin is called a ray, and one can prove that any equal percentage expansion or contraction of every output must involve a movement along a single ray. (Proof: if $y =$ number of trucks and $x =$ number of cars, then always expanding or contracting y and x by the same percentage means that y and x must satisfy $y/x = k$ (constant) or $y = kx$. That is the standard equation of a straight line through the origin.) We now can examine in the next two footnotes the two sufficient conditions for natural monopoly that are given in Proposition I.

36. We first examine *Condition (i)* of Proposition I. *Condition (i)*: Average costs must decline when all outputs increase by the same percentage. We have just seen that an equal percentage increase in both outputs is represented by a movement along a ray in Figures 1 and 3. We now will see in a three-dimensional diagram analogous to Figure 3 what happens to costs as a result of such a change. Figures 4 and 5 both show shaded cross

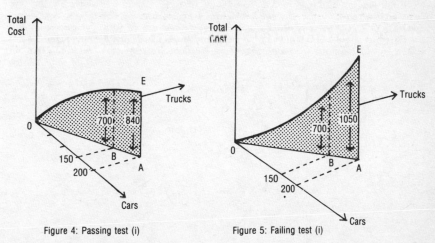

Figure 4: Passing test (i)   Figure 5: Failing test (i)

sections OAE of the area under the cost surface; Figure 4 satisfies condition (i) while Figure 5 violates it. How do we know this? First, note that our cross sections are taken above a ray because we are investigating the cost effects of equal percentage changes in all outputs. In Figure 4 we see, for example, that when we move from B to A, so that a $33\frac{1}{3}\%$ increase occurs in both outputs, total cost rises by only 20%, from $700 to $840. Clearly, average cost must be declining. On the other hand, in Figure 5, the same percentage increase in outputs from B to A raises total cost by 50% from $700 to $1,050. Thus, average cost must be rising, as all outputs increase by the same percentage; condition (i) of Proposition I is violated.

The Yale Law Journal   Vol. 89: 1, 1979

cialized firms.[37] Therefore, only if both conditions (i) and (ii) can be proved to be valid for a particular industry can we be sure that the industry is a natural monopoly:

37. Next we examine *Condition (ii)*: Figures 6 and 7 show corresponding situations

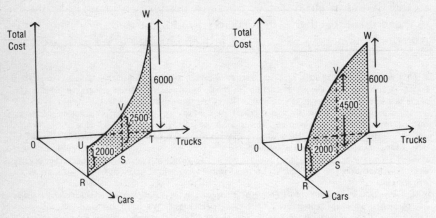

Figure 6: Passing test (ii)   Figure 7: Failing test (ii)

for condition (ii) of Proposition I: economies of scope. Here, we take cross sections more or less perpendicular to those in Figures 4 and 5, because we are now comparing the costs of specialized production (cars alone or trucks alone) with the cost of multi-good production (non-zero output of both cars and trucks). In Figure 8, point R on the car axis represents production of automobiles alone (point R represents the production of

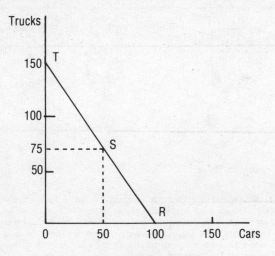

Figure 8:
The Floor of the Cost Surface:
Specialized and Nonspecialized Production

Predatory Pricing

There is a second important feature of tests to determine whether an industry is a natural monopoly:

Proposition II:

To prove that an industry is a natural monopoly it is not sufficient to provide evidence that the two requirements of Proposition I are satisfied at the current output levels of the industry or the largest firms. These two requirements must be satisfied also at all smaller output levels.

100 cars and zero trucks). For the same reason, point T on the truck axis represents specialized production of trucks alone. On the other hand, an interior point (a point not on either axis), such as S, represents non-zero production of both items. For example, midpoint S on the line connecting R and T represents the production of 50 cars and 75 trucks—exactly half as many cars as at R plus half as many trucks as at T. Returning to Figure 6, we see now why we have drawn a cross section above the line RST from Figure 8. We see that the production of 150 trucks by itself costs $6,000 (point W) (000's omitted). The production of 100 cars costs $2,000 (point U), but the production of the combination 50 cars and 75 trucks costs $2,500 (point V), which is less than the $4,000 average of the two types of specialized production. Thus, in Figure 6, multi-good production is relatively inexpensive, as is required for economies of scope (Condition (ii) of Proposition I). By contrast, in Figure 7, where the costs of specialized production are the same as in Figure 6, multi-good production at point S costs $4,500, which is more than the $4,000 average of the two specialized output costs. Thus, a cost relationship like that in Figure 7 fails Condition (ii). The shapes shown in Figures 5 and 7 are typical of cost relationships that fail the natural monopoly test, while the shapes shown in Figures 4 and 6 are typical of those that pass it. Finally, in Figure 9, both characteristics are combined to show the shape of the entire cost surface typical of an industry that can be classified as a natural monopoly.

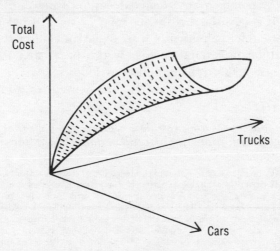

Figure 9
A Cost Surface Satisfying
Proposition I

The Yale Law Journal   Vol. 89: 1, 1979

To determine whether an industry is a natural monopoly, by the definition, one must examine whether it is cheaper to have production carried out by one large firm or by several medium-sized ones or, perhaps, even by many, very small ones. To decide this one must know not only about the cost of operation of the large firm, but also about the operating costs of a medium-sized and of a small firm.[38]

2. *Pricing and Entry in a Natural Monopoly*

The propositions described above permit us to examine the issues of pricing and entry that are our primary concern. We begin with a fundamental definition:

> *A set of prices of a monopoly firm is said to be* sustainable *against entry if at those prices the monopoly earns enough to cover its cost of capital, but no other firm can enter the industry offering to supply any or all of the monopolist's products and earn enough to cover its costs.*

Thus, to be deemed sustainable, a set of prices must be profitable for the monopolist and unprofitable for any possible entrant. If a monopolist's prices are sustainable, he need not change them when entry is attempted; he can sit back and await the entrant's financial failure. Hence, a set of sustainable prices may also be described as *stationary limit prices,* that is, prices that can prevent entry without changing in response to an attempted entrant's moves.

However, it is possible that the monopoly firm will not be so lucky as to have available the option of a set of sustainable prices. The preceding discussion of natural monopoly can be related to the availability of a sustainable pricing option as follows:

Proposition III:

> *No sustainable prices are possible for any monopoly that does not meet the cost conditions for natural monopoly, or for any other*

38. It may thus be necessary to estimate the behavior of costs at scales of operation outside the range of currently available experience. For instance, suppose an industry is initially operated as a monopoly; all the available cost data will apply then to only the large outputs of the monopoly firm. There will be no direct statistical evidence about the cost of operation of a small firm in that industry since no small firm may have operated in it recently enough to provide usable information about current costs. In such a case there are indirect ways of providing the required evidence about the costs of smaller firms. Thus, although the requirements of Proposition II, in general, are not impossible to fulfill, they are demanding requirements. The point of Proposition II is that it is insufficient for proof that a monopoly is natural to analyze merely the cost experience of the large firm, even if no other cost information is directly available.

Predatory Pricing

set of firms that does not constitute the cheapest form of organization for the production of the industry's output.[39]

If the monopoly cannot justify its existence on the grounds that it offers costs lower than any combination of smaller firms, it cannot use a set of sustainable prices to protect itself from entry. For public policy, this amounts to the conclusion that if such a monopoly is precluded by law from responding through price changes to the actions of entrants, then the monopoly is doomed in the long run. It will be vulnerable to successful entry if deprived of the weapon of responsive price moves. For if the firm is not a natural monopoly, it follows by definition that a combination of entrants can produce among them the (former) monopolist's output more cheaply than that monopolist can. At any prices that bring the monopolist enough revenues to cover his higher costs, entrants can undercut him and still cover their lower costs.

Unfortunately, the converse of Proposition III is not true. Although sustainable prices will never be available to the "undeserving monopolist," they may also be unavailable to some "deserving" (i.e., natural) monopolists. That is:

Proposition IV:

A firm may have a cost structure that satisfies the requirements for natural monopoly but precludes the possibility of any prices sustainable against entry.[40]

---

39. Formal proof for the monopoly case is provided in Baumol, Bailey, & Willig, *Weak Invisible Hand Theorems on the Sustainability of Prices in a Multiproduct Monopoly*, 67 AM. ECON. REV. 350 (1977). The corresponding theorem for the oligopoly case or for the case where the industry is composed of a larger number of firms is proved in just the same way as that for the monopoly.

40. Faulhaber, *Cross-Subsidization: Pricing in Public Enterprise*, 65 AM. ECON. REV. 966 (1975). This result is easily proved. To prove a theorem of this form, one needs only a single example of the type claimed to exist. The following illustration is very similar to that originally discovered by Faulhaber. Consider three nearby communities, all of which want fixed and equal amounts of electricity. Suppose it will cost $120,000 per month to serve any one of them by itself out of its own generating station, $190,000 to serve any pair of them out of a single plant, and $300,000 for a single plant to serve all three communities simultaneously. This is a natural monopoly, because if the three communities were each served by separate firms, the total cost would be 3 times $120,000 = $360,000, while if any two of them were served by one firm and the third community were served by another, the total cost would be $190,000 + $120,000 = $310,000. Thus, the total cost of any other arrangement would be more than the $300,000 cost of service by a single monopoly firm. Therefore, the costs are subadditive, and the industry is a natural monopoly.

All that remains to be shown is that no prices sustainable against entry are available to this natural monopolist. This argument is also straightforward. With a total cost of $300,000 (including return on capital) for the three communities, suppose the monopolist

The Yale Law Journal   Vol. 89: 1, 1979

While the possibility of a natural monopoly with no sustainable prices available to it is important for analytic purposes, for a very significant class of cases such sustainable prices do always exist. But before proceeding toward this discussion, it is important to examine one other characteristic of sustainable pricing:

Proposition V:

> *If a monopolist (or any other firm) charges for any of its products a price less than the marginal cost of that product, then the firm's prices will not be sustainable against entry.*[41]

The importance of this theorem for policy is that if a monopolist is prohibited by law or regulation from changing prices in response to the threat of entry or to the behavior of entrants, then in seeking stationary limit prices he will consider only prices satisfying the Areeda-Turner criterion. In other words, a policy requiring quasi-permanence of price reductions incidentally will promote behavior that does not violate the Areeda-Turner rule.

On an intuitive level, if a firm were to sell product x at a price below marginal cost, an entrant could, by selling less of product x than the incumbent does, actually earn *more* money than the incumbent earns from this product. For if the marginal cost of the product is, say, $6, while its price is $4, for every unit that the entrant's sale of this product falls short of the incumbent's, his net profit will come out $2 ahead of the incumbent's. Thus, the incumbent must be prepared to change its prices if it is not to lose its market to the entrant; the initial prices cannot be sustainable.

3. *Digression on Ramsey Pricing*

Before explaining the main theorems, it is necessary to digress briefly and explain the nature and meaning of what are known as

---

proposes to be impartial and charge $100,000 to each. In that case an entrant can propose to serve two of the communities, call them A and B, at a price of, say, $97,000 each, and undercut the monopolist's price, while earning $194,000, which more than covers his $190,000 cost. Can the monopolist defend himself by lowering his price to one or both of these communities? Suppose he offered community A a bargain price of $94,000. Then to cover his remaining costs he would have to charge communities B and C together a total of $300,000 − $94,000 = $206,000. Then, the entrant could undercut him by offering B and C prices of $97,000 each, rather than making the offer to A and B. The lower the monopolist's price to any one community, the more he must charge the other two in order to cover his costs and the more vulnerable he becomes to inroads by the entrant. Thus, there is no set of fixed prices that will protect this natural monopoly; we have proved Proposition IV by example.

41. For the proof, see Panzar & Willig, *supra* note 34, at 8-9.

Predatory Pricing

Ramsey prices. Efficiency in the allocation of resources requires the price of each product in the economy to be set equal to its marginal cost. Only then will the marginal cost of a purchase to a consumer —its price—be equal to its true marginal cost to society in terms of the value of the inputs needed to produce the item. Thus, when prices are set equal to marginal costs, consumers' decisions designed to allocate their money as effectively as possible among alternative purchases will automatically allocate the community's resources as efficiently as possible.

The point may be brought out more clearly if we consider a case where prices are not equal to marginal costs. Suppose goods A and B yield equal consumer satisfaction, but A has a marginal cost of $5, while B has a marginal cost of $7 (that is, the production of B requires more valuable inputs). If A is priced, nevertheless, at $10, while B is priced at $9, consumers will buy B in preference to A, thus using more resources than necessary to achieve a given degree of satisfaction. It can be proved, more generally, that any departure of price from marginal cost gives the wrong cost signals to consumers, and thus leads to inefficiency in the sense of yielding less than the maximum total benefit to consumers from the quantities of inputs used.[42]

However, economists also recognize that the ideal of universal marginal cost pricing is chimerical; it cannot be achieved because pricing at marginal cost will not produce revenues equal to total production costs. In particular, where there are diseconomies of scale, marginal cost pricing will yield revenues that exceed total costs. In contrast, where economies of scale exist, setting price equal to marginal cost will not permit producers to break even, as marginal cost will be below average cost.

The question in these circumstances, then, is not whether price should be set equal to marginal cost; in general that will not be possible. Rather, the question is: What is the optimal deviation of prices from marginal costs? What prices will yield the most efficient allocation of resources, subject to the constraint that total revenues under the selected prices be sufficient to cover total costs? The solution, known as Ramsey pricing,[43] is more easily described by considering the simpler case in which cross elasticities of demand are

42. *See* Hotelling, *The General Welfare in Relation to Problems of Taxation and of Railway and Utility Rates*, 6 ECONOMETRICA 242 (1938).

43. The first to solve the problem was Frank Ramsey, a young Cambridge philosopher who produced his result in 1927. *See* Ramsey, *A Contribution to the Theory of Taxation*, 37 ECON. J. 47 (1927).

The Yale Law Journal   Vol. 89: 1, 1979

zero, that is, in which the price of one product does not affect the demand for another. In that case, it turns out that optimal pricing requires the percentage deviation of the price of a product from its marginal cost to be inversely proportionate to its own elasticity of demand. In other words, if the demand for product x is reduced severely by a given rise in price (the demand for product x is highly elastic), then the optimal price of that product will be very close to its marginal cost; the reverse will be true for another product whose demand is quite inelastic.

More explicitly, if Px, MCx, and Ex represent the price, marginal cost, and elasticity of demand, respectively, for product x, then we may define

% Deviation of Px from MCx $= 100 \ (P - MCx)/Px$.

Using this definition, then we have:

Proposition VI:

Optimal Ramsey prices Px and Py for any two products x and y with zero cross elasticities must satisfy

$$\frac{\% \ Deviation \ of \ Px \ from \ MCx}{\% \ Deviation \ of \ Py \ from \ MCy} = \frac{Ey}{Ex}$$

This result can be understood intuitively. If the result of marginal cost pricing is unattainable, the deviations in prices necessary to permit producers to cover their costs should be selected in a way that causes minimal distortion of demands. Thus, if prices have to be raised above marginal costs to sustain producers financially, then these prices should be raised most for products whose demand is least affected by a given price rise, that is, the products with the least elastic demand. That is precisely what the Ramsey rule of optimal pricing requires.

4. *Basic Theorems on Prices Sustainable Against Entry*

We come, finally, to the two basic theorems describing the character of prices that are sustainable against entry. The main theorem is:

Proposition VII:

If a firm is a natural monopoly, satisfying the two sufficient conditions for natural monopoly given in Proposition I, then if it selects as the price for each of its products the Ramsey price for that item, those Ramsey prices will be sustainable against entry.[44]

44. There are some minor additional stipulations that may be regarded as technicalities. This theorem, then, characterizes a broad class of cases in which a natural monopoly

Predatory Pricing

This proposition states, in effect, that the monopoly firm can guarantee itself the fair rate of return and also remain invulnerable to entry by selecting the socially optimal prices satisfying the Ramsey conditions given in Proposition VI. That is, even the monopoly firm whose response to entry is constrained by a quasi-permanent pricing rule can protect itself against entry by instituting the Ramsey optimal prices. Thus, by serving the interests of society, the monopoly firm also serves its own, just as Adam Smith maintained to be true in the absence of monopoly.[45] Thus Proposition VII can be described as an invisible hand theorem for monopoly.[46]

However, Proposition VII is a *weak* invisible hand theorem because, usually, the Ramsey optimal prices will not be the only prices that offer the monopolist the reward of protection against entry. That is, there will generally be other prices that yield the fair rate of return, are sustainable against entry, and yet violate the Ramsey requirements of Proposition VI. These non-Ramsey prices will fail to achieve the maximum consumer benefit from the resources used by the economy, but will offer the monopolist the reward of protection from entry. Although we cannot be sure that the monopolist will pick the socially beneficial Ramsey prices rather than these less-efficient alternatives, two factors render Ramsey prices likely. First, in some cases there will be no sustainable prices other than the Ramsey prices; second, it will be difficult in most cases for the monopolist to determine whether or not sustainable non-Ramsey prices are available to him. Thus, we have the following result:

Proposition VIII:

To determine whether a set of prices other than the Ramsey prices is sustainable, it is not sufficient just to examine costs and consumer price responses at current output levels of the firm. One must also investigate what costs and demand responses would be if output levels were considerably smaller.

The similarity between the phrasing of Propositions II and VIII is worth noting. In each case a difficult statistical task is required: making empirical calculations about material outside the range of

does have sustainable prices available to it, i.e., to which the Faulhaber exception of Proposition IV, *see* p. 19 *supra*, does not apply. Proposition I's two sufficient conditions for natural monopoly play the key role in characterizing the cases in which one can be sure sustainable prices exist.

45. A. SMITH, THE WEALTH OF NATIONS 423 (Mod. Lib. Ed. 1937).

46. A similar result apparently can be formulated for a set of oligopoly firms that adopt Ramsey prices for their outputs and that constitute the cost-minimizing market form for the production of the industry's output. However, no rigorous proof of this extension has yet been constructed.

The Yale Law Journal   Vol. 89: 1, 1979

the available statistics derived from recent experience for the firm or the industry. Proposition II, however, deals with what is essentially a once-and-for-all test to determine whether an industry is really a natural monopoly; Proposition VIII requires calculations that must be carried out every time changing costs or market conditions call for a reexamination by the firm of its prices. And the proposition tells us that these difficult calculations are required to obtain a set of sustainable non-Ramsey prices that will yield, after all, profits no higher than those offered by the Ramsey prices.

The proof of the two weak invisible hand theorems, Propositions VII and VIII, is too technical to describe here.[47] Suffice it to say that the proofs are far more rigorous and definitive than the graphic arguments that are employed by Areeda-Turner and Williamson to support the more modest efficiency claims they make for the policies they propose. But while the mathematical proofs are difficult, their basic rationale is not. From society's viewpoint, a policy that does not discourage stationary limit prices is desirable; it permits the established firm to protect itself from entry only by making itself so attractive to consumers in the first place that they will be left with no motivation to switch to entrants. In the simplest example, if the established firm offers products of high quality at low prices before entry takes place, there will be little inducement for entry to occur. Under stationary pricing, established firms must set their prices in advance lest they be left vulnerable to entry later on. Thus, they are forced to offer consumers the price-quality benefits of competition, even though competition has not yet materialized.

This effect is similar to the pressures besetting a multiproduct firm whose products initially are not priced in proportion to their relative incremental costs. When this is so, the established firm invites "cream-skimming" entry—the entry of competing firms into selected portions of the industry that are most profitable because prices are high relative to costs. To eliminate this cream-skimming opportunity and prevent entry, the firm must realign its prices to correspond more closely to relative costs. It is precisely such a realignment of prices to eliminate deviations from relative costs that is necessary to attain economic efficiency.[48]

47. *See* Baumol, Bailey, & Willig, *supra* note 39, at 355-63 (proofs of Propositions VII and VIII). The proofs employ a full, general equilibrium analysis, taking account of the effects of prices throughout the economy, rather than only those in the industry immediately concerned, as is done in the partial equilibrium analysis used by Areeda-Turner and Williamson.

48. This general approach is entirely practical and in fact sometimes has been adopted. A case in point is the pricing policy undertaken by AT&T for its private line

Predatory Pricing

The logic underlying the virtue of stationary limit pricing is that it forces established firms to give consumers the advantages that true competition provides, because the firms must act in anticipation of competition.

B. *Stationary Limit Pricing versus Quasi-Permanence of Price Reductions*

The quasi-permanent pricing proposal is not identical to a policy of stationary limit pricing. The latter altogether precludes a case-by-case response to entry while the former permits it only once. Under quasi-permanence, the established firm is not inhibited from reducing its price whenever entry occurs; it is precluded only from rescinding such a price cut, at least for the stipulated period. Thus, quasi-permanence of price reductions may not be quite as effective in serving the public welfare as is stationary limit pricing, since it does not offer consumers the advantages of competition before entry occurs. However, in practice it often will be difficult to require established firms to prepackage their responses to any and all potential entrants; such a requirement is necessary for stationary limit pricing but not for quasi-permanence of price reductions.[49] Thus, quasi-permanence seems to be about as close an approximation to stationary limit pricing as we can expect to achieve through public policy. Moreover, it can be argued that the relative flexibility of the policy of quasi-permanence offers more assurance that entry will have an effect upon prices should it occur—a beneficial effect that might not be realized under stationary limit pricing if the established firm is unable to predict entrants' behavior accurately.

It is, of course, difficult to judge the comparative validity of such impressionistic arguments whose relative force may, in any event, vary from case to case. It is sufficient for our purposes to reempha-

services as entry by competitors began. AT&T management, in a series of consultations with Alfred E. Kahn and this author, adopted, instead of a case-by-case response, a stationary pricing policy aligning prices to relative costs so as to reduce substantially the opportunities for cream-skimming. The new pricing program was named the Hi-Lo tariff, referring to the adjustment of relative rates to the lower costs of transmission over high-density routes and the higher costs over low-density routes.

49. The Laker example can be used to bring out the difference more explicitly. In this case, stationary limit pricing would require, presumably, that price reductions by Laker's competitors not be initially confined only to the route where Laker is now offering services. Rather, if Laker's extension to other routes is contemplated as a possibility for the future, these firms would extend the reductions to all other routes ultimately vulnerable to entry by Laker or its imitators. Stationary limit pricing implies that if the established firm chooses not to extend its price reduction simultaneously to all of these routes, it cannot later institute it route-by-route wherever and whenever entry becomes an imminent threat.

size the claim of allocative efficiency that can be made for the broad class of pricing policies that encompasses both stationary limit pricing and quasi-permanence of price reductions. Most important, quasi-permanent pricing creates a strong incentive for full and fair competition both by entrants and by established firms, providing neither artificial protection for the former nor room for hit-and-run tactics by the latter.

Conclusion

An attempt to provide a universally acceptable definition for a vague term such as "predatory pricing" probably can contribute little.[50] However, the term does relate to a problem that is real and significant—the design of means to permit full and fair competitive measures by the established firm, without foreclosure of entry. The problem clearly involves intertemporal behavior patterns that cannot be addressed adequately by the comparison of prices and costs at any single moment. A policy of quasi-permanence of price reductions is advocated because it promises to promote effective competition, to minimize interference with the decisions of both the established firm and the entrant, and to make contributions to general public welfare through low prices and economic efficiency.

---

50. Willig, Ordover, and I have attempted, however, to formulate a working definition that runs along the following lines: Suppose a new entrant establishes himself in an industry. His entry normally will increase the elasticity of the incumbent's demand curve and will call for some reduction in his price. Then any reduction in price beyond that called for by the increase in demand elasticity must be deemed predatory in that it can only benefit the incumbent through a reduction in the probability of the entrant's survival. In other words, any reduction in price, or any other decision, should be judged non-predatory if and only if it is profitable for the incumbent on the assumption either that the entrant is there to stay indefinitely or that the probability that the entrant will withdraw is fixed.

It will be noted that none of the three criteria that have recently been proposed—the Areeda-Turner criterion, the Williamson standard, or the quasi-permanence principle recommended in this article—corresponds with any degree of exactness to the preceding definition of predation. However, that is because this definition is not easily put to use in the complex world of reality where, for example, changes in demand elasticities are often hard to evaluate. The objective of a good rule should not be slavish pursuit of an unattainable ideal. Rather, it should constitute what I have elsewhere described as an optimally imperfect criterion—one that trades off social costs and difficulty of enforcement against the benefits it promises. *See* Baumol & Quandt, *Rules of Thumb and Optimally Imperfect Decisions*, 54 Am. Econ. Rev. 23 (1964).

[11]

William J. Baumol - TECHNOLOGICAL CHANGE AND THE NEW URBAN EQUILIBRIUM

This paper discusses a hypothesis about the economics of the city which is not entirely unfamiliar. It is the view that technical change has deprived the city of many of its former advantages as a location for production and that, consequently, the equilibrium size of the city is now much smaller than it was a half century ago. I will suggest that the transition to the new equilibrium is inherently a slow, lengthy process, and that many of the ills that now beset cities are manifestations of this transition process. The prognosis that follows from this hypothesis offers considerable hope for the long run, but is rather less encouraging for the short run. I will also suggest some implications for public policy.

THE CITY'S HISTORICAL ADVANTAGES IN PRODUCTION

From the late Middle Ages to the beginning of the twentieth century, cities possessed at least three attributes that gave them an absolute advantage in manufacturing. First, they were ideal transportation terminals, earlier offering port facilities for ships[1] and, later central railroad depots. Second, cities were the best location for

I am grateful to the Sloan Foundation whose support greatly facilitated the preparation of this paper. I have also benefited significantly from comments by Daniel Baumol.

4   CITY IN STRESS

economic activities in which easy and rapid communication is of great importance. Third, cities were the only places that could sustain indivisible services with large output capacities. Let us briefly consider each of these advantages in turn to see just how recent technological change has eroded them all.

Both water and rail transportation techniques favor the central terminus. With rare exceptions, neither of them offers door-to-door service, and many of the exceptions are cases in which the shipper has placed himself next to the terminus rather than the terminus being brought to the shipper. There are several reasons for this pattern. First, ships and trains are frequently most economical when their capacity is very large.[2] It therefore does not pay to bring the entire vehicle to the door of a shipper of modest size even when that is physically possible. Second, extension of the route of a railroad requires costly construction and this is at least equally true of the construction of artificial waterways. Where, in addition, loading and unloading require expensive plant and equipment, the advantages of bringing freight to a few central points become clear. So long as there was no efficient means of transportation by which freight could be transferred economically for distribution over a wide geographic area it meant that economic activity which required extensive use of the transportation network secured a substantial advantage from a location close to a terminal. When enough economic activity lay close to a terminal and, for lack of cheap and rapid transportation, the labor force also resided nearby, that place automatically became a city.

Activities which require quick and easy communication also used to need proximity. Banks, stock exchanges and other financial institutions, government agencies and other service organizations whose work is substantially handicapped by long delays in the communication process found it essential to locate cheek by jowl, and they too found their proximity requirements satisfied only within the confines of a city.

Finally, the city's economy benefitted from being the only viable location for many indivisible service institutions. Only in cities could one find shops large enough to offer a very great selection to customers. The non-city resident could meet day to day requirements from local distributors, but customers who desired more than staples had to go to the city for specialized and unusual items, for a large selection from which to choose or for items which offered unusual quality or style. Cultural activities congregated in cities for the same reason. Small towns cannot support a house which provides grand opera or symphony orchestras.

Urban Equilibrium   5

Without any pretense at being exhaustive, one can ascribe to these three elements much of the attraction of the city as a locus of economic activity. Their presence stimulated the growth of our cities in the 19th and early twentieth centuries, with population following the growing economic opportunities. No doubt there were lags in the adjustment process but there seems no reason to believe that the sizes of the populations in the nation's cities were much out of proportion to the available employment.

TECHNOLOGICAL CHANGES AND THE CITY'S LOST ADVANTAGES

At least four developments over the course of the last century have substantially eroded these advantages of the city as a location for productive activity. The first of these was the invention of the telephone and its widespread adoption. This reduced the need for proximity as a means to speed and facilitate communication. I will suggest later that the effect of this innovation upon the city's economy has probably been considerably less drastic than those of the other three changes. The second of our four changes is, of course, the invention of the motor vehicle driven by an internal combustion engine. The automobile has permitted dispersion of the labor force, making it possible for workers to live considerable distances from their work. The truck has played at least as important a role in permitting dispersal of factory sites. No longer was it necessary for a factory to be built close to a central terminal. Indeed, a central location for the factory became a net disadvantage as congestion of urban traffic increased the time and delay involved in getting goods from the terminal to the urban factory even if the distance between the two was relatively small.[3]

This second development brought its full consequences only with the appearance of the third, the construction of the interstate highway system. The network of superhighways permitted rapid road transportation among many localities which before had been all but isolated from one another.

Though they did help to connect the cities to one another, the highway system on balance served to reduce or eliminate what was left of the ancient transportation advantage of the city and also destroyed some portion of the scale economies it offered. The new roads permitted residents of many sparsely settled areas to meet easily at central locations thereby assembling the volume of demand necessary for the viability of enterprises which previously could survive only in a city. Shopping centers began to boast department

6   CITY IN STRESS

stores which soon undermined some of the most venerable shops in central cities. Cultural centers were constructed near convenient superhighway exits, where they were surrounded by rural landscapes and no other activities that one could consider urban in character.

The last of the four significant developments to be mentioned here is the emergence of continuous production processes, probably beginning with the assembly line. The relevant feature of this innovation in productive processes is that it tends to favor single storied factories which occupy more acreage than the old fashioned multi-story plants. This too, has reduced the attractiveness of an urban location for industry, not only because of the higher rents on urban land,[4] but also because in a city it is not easy to assemble continuous parcels of land which together are sufficient for the construction of a large one-story factory.

All of these changes produced the predictable consequences. Industries have closed down urban factories as they were depreciated by age and obsolescence. Their successors were placed in suburban locations, sometimes relatively close to the cities which housed them before, sometimes in distant parts of the country to which they were attracted by lower wages and other economic advantages. In sum, the argument leads us to expect a reduction in the equilibrium volume of economic activity within the city, and the facts seem to fit in with this prognosis.

It should be emphasized that none of this is meant to imply that *all* urban economic activity is destined to depart. Neither the previous nor the prospective equilibrium point is a pure polar case. Even when the city's economic advantages were at their peak a number of economic activities were nevertheless best located in the countryside, agriculture being only the most obvious example. Similarly, the new equilibrium, as I will argue later, will still leave the city as the preferred location for a variety of activities. The change is just a matter of degree. The issue is not whether or not all activity will leave the city, but rather how much will remain there under the new equilibrium and what sorts of activities it will involve. But if the prospective change is limited in scope, its implications for the structure of the city are nevertheless profound.

EFFECTS ON THE URBAN POPULATION

One natural consequence is that the labor force will follow industry out of the city. If the number of jobs available in the city under the

Urban Equilibrium 7

new equilibrium is half what it was under the old we should expect that ultimately the size of the urban population will fall correspondingly. Thus, this analysis leads us to expect that future cities will be very much smaller than they are today, both in volume of economic activity and in sheer size of population.

As we all know, in the postwar period there has in fact been a considerable exodus from the cities, at least by the middle income groups. Much of this migration has probably occurred for reasons other than the cities' lost economic advantages.[5] Until recently, however, the net effect on the overall size of the urban population has been rather modest. The wealthier migrants were replaced by an initial influx of poor from elsewhere in the country. This, too, is partly ascribable to causes other than the process discussed in this paper. But I will argue next that such a temporary inward migration is in fact to be expected during the transition between our two equilibria. Indeed, I will suggest that many of the urban problems of our time can be ascribed to the character of the transition.

LAGS IN THE EQUILIBRIUM PROCESS

Economic adjustments vary enormously in speed. Some can occur in weeks or even days. Money flows, for example, can be redirected with great rapidity, because money is not nailed to any geographic point. The greater the share of the objects destined for relocation which are immobile, the slower will be the adjustment process. Partly this reflects the higher cost of greater rapidity in a process of change. Construction of new facilities requires time and beyond some point hastening of the process is always expensive. But there is a second reason which is important for our analysis. Physical plant is a sunk cost which, when the facility is not to be replaced, essentially becomes a free good. So long as it still can produce output the net value of which is positive, it will continue to be used, even if the net value of the output has been reduced by some change such as the technological developments with which we are concerned. The optimal replacement date will still normally lie in the future when the old plant has deteriorated sufficiently. The move will take the form of construction of the replacement plant at the location which is optimal in the new equilibrium. The optimal replacement date will be that at which the present value of the excess in marginal net output at the new location over that in the old location is equal to the marginal capital cost incurred by earlier plant construction at the new site. Here the margins, of course, refer to a small change in the date of replacement rather than to a small change in output level.

8   CITY IN STRESS

The reason which makes it pay to continue to use industrial plant long after an urban location for a productive process has ceased to be optimal also dictates continued use of the city's excess housing stock. It becomes a free good, a heritage from the past, which can generate a flow of housing services at lower social cost than newly constructed residences despite the latter's superior location.

There is then a parallel reason which dictates both for firms and residents substantial lags in the process of readjustment toward the new equilibrium. In both cases we can expect the transition process to be substantial. But there is also a significant difference between the two adjustment processes. The most striking difference between the standard models of the firm and the consumer is that the latter's maximization process is taken to be circumscribed by budget constraints while the former is not. Business firms have readier access to the capital market, which supplies the resources needed for any outlay that promises to be profitable. Consumers simply do not have equally flexible sources of funds. The presence of the budget constraint which limits the options available to a consumer suggests strongly that consumers, and particularly poor consumers, will have to delay their relocation longer than a firm. That is, their budget constraints will tend to induce them to delay their exodus from the city if earlier departure is costly.[6]

STYLIZED HISTORY OF THE ADJUSTMENT PROCESS

The preceding remarks about the comparative timing of the departure of firms and residents from the city is rather abstract. A description that is a bit more concrete can add flesh to the model. Let us therefore try to summarize what seems to be a "natural" sequence of events in the adjustment of the city to a new equilibrium involving a reduced level of economic activity and a reduced population. This stylized description will, of course, not accord completely with the observed history because the latter is affected by what, for our purposes, may be considered fortuitous developments such as differences in generosity of welfare payments at different locations and other variations in pertinent public policy.

The sequence of events which our discussion should lead us to expect may run somewhat as follows. First, innovation erodes the advantages of the city as a location for production. As a result, with some lag, firms begin gradually to withdraw from it, with earlier departures in those industries which are most heavily affected by the technological changes and whose plant depreciates most rapidly.

Urban Equilibrium   9

One would expect this to single out industries for which truck transportation is particularly well suited, for which transportation cost constitutes a large proportion of value added, and whose plant is not highly durable.

As economic activity begins to withdraw, residences of those able to afford the move can also be expected to change, also with some lag.[7] The departure of these more affluent residents leaves behind it a stock of vacant housing which, essentially, becomes a free economic good, its market value and, consequently, the market value of its rents reflecting this redundancy.[8]

This low cost housing immediately becomes a magnet for the poor who find the city providing them with cheaper places to live. In other words, the transition process disturbs the previous equilibrium in the housing market for the poor and makes the city more attractive on that score than it was previously. True, there is a scarcity of jobs to go along with the low price of housing, but since the exodus of industry is not yet completed, the seriousness of the unemployment problem has not yet reached its peak. Moreover, those who happen already to be unemployed outside the city have nothing to lose on that score by moving into an urban residence. Thus, the stock of housing abandoned by the middle class becomes, in effect, a collection of warehouses in which society stores its impecunious members.

This housing stock is scheduled to deteriorate "naturally," as part of the process of transition to the new urban equilibrium. Since from the long-run point of view it is redundant, it does not pay any private owners to invest heavily in repair and maintenance, let alone, improvement.

But the transition process involves more than this. As the job market for the poor immigrants grows increasingly tight it produces an explosive situation in which the prospect of unemployment for the indefinite future becomes a stimulus to frustration and rage. I shall not indulge myself in an attempt at amateur social psychology, but surely there are grounds for association of high crime rates, violence and destruction of property with this frustration.

Two consequences follow. First, the induced violence hastens the deterioration of the housing stock. The burning of the slums by their residents is, from this viewpoint, no historical accident, but part of the sequence of events in the adjustment toward the new urban equilibrium.

The second consequence is that the induced violence serves to make the city even less attractive than it would have become otherwise to both firms and more affluent residents. The numbers who

10   CITY IN STRESS

are induced to leave exceed the quantities required for adjustment to the new equilibrium. But that is only a temporary phenomenon.

As the housing stock of the poor continues to deteriorate and even to disappear, as jobs fail to materialize and tend to become scarcer, net migration of even the poor can be expected. Those who came into the city will be induced to leave and they will be accompanied by still others who once had a place in the city's economy. This must be so, if the new equilibrium involves a smaller number of unskilled and semi-skilled jobs than the old and therefore calls for a smaller number of impecunious inhabitants. Their equilibrium number will not drop to zero—probably it will be far from that. But it will be significantly smaller than it was before.

This analysis suggests that long-run equilibrium also will require the return of some firms and some of the more affluent workers who have left the city. For as the size of the population of the poor adjusts to the new volume of job opportunities, unemployment will fall correspondingly and with it, the frustrations that lead to the urban violence of recent decades. And as the housing stock declines to its new equilibrium level the deterioration of buildings and neighborhoods will be reduced or eliminated.[9] These changes can be expected to increase the attractiveness of the cities and to bring back marginal emigrants who were induced to leave by the deterioration of social conditions rather than by lack of economic opportunities.[10]

The long-run prognosis, then, is relatively encouraging. After a painful transition process cities will emerge significantly smaller but economically viable and even prosperous, with a more even balance of the different income groups in its resident population. The social ills that have escalated in recent years can be expected to abate. Economic activity will consist far more heavily than before of service and administrative activities and manufacturing will play a considerably smaller role.

This sanguine forecast, unfortunately, does not imply that the new equilibrium is just around the corner. Our cities still have a long way to go in the painful adjustment process, and much of the public urban policy can be expected to protract this period rather than facilitate the transition. I will return to these issues. But first one must examine the grounds for optimism about the viability of a smaller urban economy under the new technological circumstances.

Urban Equilibrium **11**

RESIDUAL ECONOMIC ADVANTAGES OF THE CITY

The main thing to be recognized in seeking to determine what economic advantages the city still offers is that technical change has eroded but not destroyed most of the advantages the city offered before. Specifically, today and for the indefinite future it still offers benefits in ease of communication and in a market sufficiently large to permit the provision of services which cannot survive without it.

While the telephone has reduced some of the benefits of proximity, many types of activity still require frequent face to face communication. This is, for example, true of members of the top management of large corporations who often meet with each other, with lawyers, with representatives of government agencies, etc. When all the parties have their home bases in the same city this advantage is obvious. But even if the people involved have widely separated home bases, the proximity to airports which the city offers is an overwhelming advantage. When travelling to New York to meet with someone from Washington, I often arrive later than the person from Washington even though I have only the 50-mile journey from Princeton. Firms have quickly learned the potency of this advantage. I know of one major corporation which announced some years ago, with considerable fanfare, that it was moving its headquarters from a major city into the countryside some 50 miles away. Today its legal headquarters indeed remains the shiny new edifice outside the city. But it has not given up the urban building which once served as its headquarters, and it is there that the president, the chairman of the board and a preponderance of its vice presidents go everyday.

The city also remains the location par excellence for variety retailing. Paradoxically, it is no longer the giant department stores but the small specialty shops congregate in central cities. Wide selections of unusual electronic components, rare tropical woods, unusual food products can be obtained quickly only in urban centers. But other activities which depend upon ready availability of a wide choice of unusual items also benefit by being nearby.

The dispersal of cultural activities which was mentioned earlier has made the arts and entertainment more accessible to suburban and rural areas but it has not robbed the city of its role as focal point for cultural institutions. Theaters, museums and opera houses continue to be found preponderantly in the major cities, and there is little reason to expect any radical change in this pattern in the foreseeable future.

12 CITY IN STRESS

The variety in retailing including the wide range of services such as restaurants along with the supply of cultural activities in turn serves to reattract some middle and upper income groups, which can become the focus of the rehabilitation of the smaller city of the future. These individuals bring not only themselves and improvements in their neighborhoods. They attract renewed and expanded service activities which are supported by their business. More than that, firms which are on the lookout for this sort of personnel are apt to be drawn to the city whose amenities and cultural activities can make it easier to hire engineers, scientists, technicians, lawyers and management personnel.

The list of attractions of the city in the new equilibrium, like all the attribute lists in this paper, is necessarily incomplete. But that is unimportant for our purposes. For our argument only requires some evidence that while technological change has imposed an economic handicap upon the cities, it has not driven them from the economic race. There is every reason, then, to expect the future city to be a very viable economic entity[11] albeit one which is very much smaller than it once had been.

POLICY IMPLICATIONS

The relatively sanguine view of the city's future is not meant to imply that the concern of policymakers over urban problems is unjustified. While a transition problem is by definition a short-run phenomenon, short-runs have a way of growing distressingly long, and this seems particularly likely to hold for the transition of the cities to their new equilibrium. Thus, policy measures which ameliorate these temporary problems are entirely appropriate, indeed, they are undoubtedly urgent. At stake is the welfare of generations of city dwellers, particularly in the neighborhoods which can be expected to abandon their present form in the next few decades.

But what the analysis suggests is that attempts to rehabilitate and improve these areas to any substantial extent will be disappointing at best. Such measures may serve as palliatives which bring temporary relief. But the reconstruction of housing in a devastated area which, even when rebuilt, cannot be expected to attract jobs for its residents must ultimately prove to be a cruel gift, even if it yields transitory political benefits, and perhaps initially, some benefits for its inhabitants.

But such programs are to be questioned not only because they are wasteful and their benefits destined to be short lived but, more important, because they actually serve to stretch out the unhappy period of transition and impede the readjustment toward the new and more desirable equilibrium. A rebuilt South Bronx can only lure the jobless into remaining longer where they have no economic prospects. One can be fairly confident that the reconstructed homes will be transformed into slums soon enough, and that the torch will be back at the task of destroying them soon enough.

Rather, the analysis suggests that rational policy should emphasize several measures of a different sort: a) improvements in that housing stock which still survives, which offer low costs *at the expense of durability*. For in areas with no long-term economic future there is little justification for investments which are designed to last; b) provision of inducements for emigration from the city, perhaps including subsidies to help cover costs of moving and housing outside the city[12] ; c) special training programs for jobs located in areas of relative labor shortage; d) design of reconstruction plans for devastated areas whose purpose is *not* to restore those areas to anything like their former density, but which instead hasten and cushion the transition to their next stage.

Once more, this list is intended to be illustrative and suggestive, not exhaustive. The basic point is that at least some historical forces cannot be resisted for long. Attempts to undo their effects are not only bound to be fruitless but may well make things worse. This does not mean that we are powerless to influence the course of events. Understanding of the underlying forces offers us knowledge of the constraints which circumscribe our policy options. It is within the limits imposed by these constraints that we are free to act in a way that contributes to social welfare. The preceding policy discussion is meant as a first step suggesting how this can perhaps be done.

CONCLUDING COMMENT

There is probably little in this paper that has not been said before. Certainly, its empirical observations such as the effects of transportation changes upon the urban economy, the devastation of ghetto areas and, more recently, the return of some more affluent residents and "gentrification" of the centers of cities are commonplace observations.

If anything is new here it is the implicit treatment of the subject as an informal exercise in comparative statics—the replacement of one equilibrium by another and, simultaneously, in terms of the time path of the transition process. Viewed in this way, the analysis becomes less of an exercise in casual forecasting than it may at first

14   CITY IN STRESS

appear. Rather, it is an attempt to pull together various well known strands of theoretical analysis and empirical observation. The purpose is to distinguish the degree to which we are faced by what may be described somewhat pompously as "historical inevitabilities" and the degree to which there remains room for maneuver and for choice of effective policies.

If the argument is correct it can account for a number of developments which otherwise may seem almost fortuitous and rather puzzling, such as the burning of the slums and their resistance to policy countermeasures, in sharp contrast to the preliminary signs of success of efforts to reattract less impecunious residents to the city. The analysis also suggests that a number of policy proposals emerging from the highest quarters and attracting considerable popular support are seriously misguided and threaten to exacerbate the problem they are intended to control.

APPENDIX: BUDGET CONSTRAINT AND SPEED OF TRANSITION

In the text it was suggested that tightening of the budget constraint reasonably can be expected to lead to postponement of migration decisions because postponement reduces the cost of the move. However, it was asserted in a footnote that this cannot be proved on the normal premises of comparative statics. This appendix shows briefly why the result cannot be proved from those premises, and indicates some assumptions that can be used to support this inference.

For this purpose let

y represent a vector of dated quantities of goods and services consumed (which may itself be a continuous function of time)

t = the date of emigration from the city

r = the discount rate

$U(y,t)$ = the utility (profit) function giving the present value of expected future benefits

$C(t,r)$ = the cost of moving at date t

By the Hicksian rule, since we shall be holding all prices constant, it is completely legitimate to treat y as a single variable. Then the

Urban Equilibrium 15

standard model of the individual decisionmaker's choice process requires him to

maximize   U(y,t)
subject to the budget constraint

py + C(t,r) = b.

The decision-maker is taken to select those values of y and t which maximize U and the objective is to determine the effect of a change in budget, b, upon optimal timing, t, of the move, i.e., to determine the sign of $\partial t / \partial b$.

Once the problem is posed in this way two things immediately become clear: first, that $\partial t / \partial b$ is a garden-variety income effect the mathematical properties of which are unaffected by the happenstance that the pertinent decision variable is a (utility affecting) choice of moving date rather than a quantity of consumption; second, it becomes obvious that for the usual reasons, the sign of $\partial t / \partial b$ is indeterminate using maximization premises alone because the numerator for the derivative is a non principal minor whose sign, therefore, is not fixed by the second-order conditions. However, a rather crude alternative argument is possible.

By going through the tedious exercise of solving the maximization problem it is readily shown that

$$(1)\quad dt = \begin{vmatrix} O & U_{ty} & -C_t \\ O & U_{yy} & -p \\ -db & -p & O \end{vmatrix} / D,$$

where subscripts denote partial differentiation, and where D, the determinant of system of total differential equations, is positive, by the second order conditions. The numerator of (1) is

$$(1)\ -db \begin{vmatrix} U_{ty} & -C_t \\ U_{yy} & -p \end{vmatrix} = db\,(pU_{ty} - C_t U_{yy}).$$

Here U_{yy} is negative if we can assume that there is declining marginal utility of consumption;

C_t,   the marginal cost of postponement of moving, can also be assumed to be negative and

16   CITY IN STRESS

U_{ty},   the effect of postponed migration upon marginal utility
           of y, can be assumed negative on the argument that, in
           this model, the city is a less desirable place in which to
           live and consume, i.e., that both the total and marginal
           utility of a given amount of consumption are higher in
           the new location.

Hence, each term in brackets on the RHS of (1) is negative, yielding
the expected result, $\partial t / \partial b < 0$.

NOTES

1. Technological change in the late 18th century already profoundly affected
   the character of acceptable port facilities. It is not widely recognized today
   that a ship's crew had no way of determining its latitude until John Harrison invented the first accurate ship's clock in the middle of the 18th
   century and, following him, Arnold and Earnshaw produced the first
   relatively inexpensive ship's chronometers toward the end of the century.
   Before that, wherever possible, ships avoided ports with dangerous areas
   nearby since miscalculations about location were all too easy. There are
   records of ships not making for ports with treacherous areas nearby and
   travelling many additional days to safer habors, even though members of
   of the crew were dying of scurvy daily.

2. Of course, there are exceptions. Thus, canal boats are, typically, relatively
   small.

3. In the long-run equilibrium such handicaps are equalized at the margin.
   But, as we will see, the bulk of our concern will relate to the long period
   of transition toward a new equilibrium which, like all equilibria, probably will never quite be attained.

4. As industry is driven from the city relative land costs are, of course, de-
   pressed and this serves as a partial offset to the comparative static effect
   of the change in productive techniques. Where an equilibrium is stable, a
   shift in one of the relationships generally can be expected to induce a
   cushioning in price. However, except perhaps where the relevant relationships are "pathological," a shift in such an economic relationship cannot
   be expected to cause a price change sufficient to leave equilibrium quantities totally unaffected.

5. Elsewhere I have offered a dynamic model which describes this exodus as
   a cumulative process. To set it off one merely needs a change, such as the
   construction of superhighways, which induces some of the city's more
   affluent residents to move to the suburbs even if they then commute to
   work in the city. It therefore induces deterioration and aggravates other
   problems associated with a lower overall economic status. Simultaneously,
   it tends to raise the per capita tax burden of the remaining residents. Thus
   the first wave of emigration reduces the attractiveness of the city to those

who stay behind and sets off a second wave of outward movement. By the same process, that in turn induces a third and then a fourth wave, each step in this sequence setting the stage for its successor. If the analysis is correct, the cumulative character of this process helps to account for the transitoriness of the effects of many of the urban programs that have been undertaken in recent decades.

6. I deliberately avoid an unqualified statement because, as is shown in the Appendix, a comparative statics analysis of this issue does not give us a categorical answer about the relation between optimal date of relocation and tightness of the budget constraint (where we can interpret the absence of any constraint as the extreme case of a loosened constraint). The reason for the ambiguity is that we are dealing with an income rather than a substitution effect and, as we know, the usual assumptions of comparative statics are insufficient to determine the sign of the income effect.

7. Here is an example of a possible divergence between our stylized history and the actual facts. As already noted, innovation in transportation also independently encouraged suburbanization of residences and may have inaugurated a cumulative process of departure from the city by residents with middle and upper income levels. Thus, in fact, this exodus need not have lagged behind that of industry. Indeed, it may have stimulated the moves of some firms which were induced to follow their key personnel into the suburbs.

8. Apparently, there has been an increase in the ratio of number of households to size of population which has somewhat offset the effect of emigration from the city upon the demand for its housing stock.

9. Here again the conclusion is qualified because other influences are likely to intervene. For example, rent control laws can continue to discourage maintenance expenditures.

10. Other influences, which were more accidental, have also played a role in this. Rising fuel prices and the trend toward several jobs per family have, for example, increased the cost of commuting from the suburbs.

11. I do not mean to imply that all of our cities can be expected to survive. I should not be surprised if a number of middle sized metropolises were to become ghost towns in, say, the next half century.

12. The new housing should presumably be more dispersed than the old to avoid the creation of new centers of unemployment.

[12]

On the Stochastic Unemployment Distribution Model and the Long-Run Phillips Curve

William J. Baumol*

Professor Tobin (1972, p. 9) has characterized the Phillips curve as 'an empirical finding in search of a theory'. But he then proceeds to summarize most admirably the model first suggested by Lipsey (1960) and since expanded upon by Archibald (1970) and others. This model certainly seems an appropriate and convincing theoretical analysis of the Phillips relationship. It indicates why the sort of behaviour described by the Phillips curve might be observed, and suggests some of the influences that might lead it to shift. We believe that it also provides a convenient instrument to examine the contention advanced by Friedman (1968), and since expanded upon by Phelps (1970), that the Phillips curve is essentially a short-run phenomenon and that there may well be no such thing as a long-run Phillips curve — indeed, that *in the absence of money illusion* there may only be a single level of unemployment that is compatible in the long run with a rate of inflation that is neither accelerating or decelerating.

   The purpose of this paper is to show that the class of models following Lipsey's which we may refer to as models of *stochastic unemployment distribution,* serve as a plausible and effective counterexample to the contention that it is logically impossible to have a long-run Phillips curve, other than the trivial vertical curve located at the 'equilibrium' level of unemployment. Of course, only the facts can determine whether the model describes reality to an acceptable degree of approximation. However, any counterexample is sufficient to disprove a contention that such a theory is impossible, and if the model is also plausible, and consistent with

*Princeton and New York Universities. For their very helpful comments the author is extremely grateful to Elizabeth Bailey, Alan Blinder, Stephen Goldfeld, Dwight Jaffee, Janusz Ordover, and Edmund Phelps. In this case, perhaps more than usual, I must be careful to point out that none of them can be held responsible for the remaining error and shortcomings of the paper.

4

the views that have been advanced by a number of observers, then so much the better.

Specifically, I hope to investigate the behaviour of the model in a state of long-run equilibrium (which is, of course, the central issue) to show that its behaviour need produce no 'contradictions'. That is (a) it is compatible with rates of price increase which are not accelerating, (b) those rates of price increase will be higher the lower the (permanent) rate of unemployment, (c) in the absence of productivity changes the wage rate will grow at the equilibrium rate of growth of price level so that no money illusion need be involved, and (d) this occurs whatever the (permanent) rate of unemployment (that is there is no single rate of unemployment consistent with these requirements).

Of course, the contention that one can produce a theory of the long-run Phillips curve does not imply that such a curve will never shift. Just as long-run demand curves for particular products will shift when the values of certain variables are changed, the existence of a long-run Phillips curve will be perfectly compatible with the observations which seem to suggest that in recent years in the United States the curve has not been stationary.

The discussion begins by summarizing the structure of the model, postponing for the moment the difficult questions raised by the monetarist analysis. Then it turns to the role of money illusion and, rather superficially, to the nature of the measures capable of producing long-run changes in the level of employment.

1 The Stochastic Employment Distribution Model: Overview

Let us begin with a summary of the model of the Phillips curve that has grown out of Lipsey's discussion. Assume a world in which labour is not perfectly mobile, at least partly because each economic activity requires particular skills that cannot be acquired overnight. Hence, if unemployment were to decline from a high to a moderate level, it is to be expected, despite the excess supply of labour in the economy overall, that at least temporarily a few activities would exhibit an excess demand, each for the specialized portion of its own labour force. If, instead, the drop in unemployment had been larger still, more industries would initially have found themselves in this position. If the world were otherwise static, this would be a transitory phenomenon. Eventually, so long as employment were not 'full', those involuntarily unemployed would migrate to the industries in which they were needed, having in the meantime acquired whatever skills were necessary for the purpose.

However, where demand patterns are subject to stochastic influences, and where production conditions, too, are not immune from random shocks, it is to be expected that the members of the set of activities in which labour is in short supply will vary constantly and in a manner that is far from perfectly predictable. As soon as one such excess demand is eliminated, another is likely to replace it. No sooner has the work force flown towards industry x, which previously was short of labour, than a shift in tastes produces a new excess demand in industry y and a new excess supply in z. Moreover, at any one time the number of activities beset by such excess demands for labour, as well as the magnitudes of those excess demands, may be expected 'on the average' to vary inversely with the overall rate of unemployment in the economy as a whole.

As is usually assumed in the Walrasian model of price adjustment, we may expect that wages and hence prices will rise more rapidly the greater is the number of industries beset by an excess demand and the greater are the magnitudes of those excess demands. The nature of wage bargaining seems likely to sharpen this relationship. For the workers employed in an industry the spectre of the ready availability of substitute manpower may plausibly be expected to dampen the negotiating ardour of the workers' representatives, and this is simultaneously likely to increase employers' resistance. Lighten that shadow, and wage demands and the negotiators' ability to extract them can surely be expected to increase accordingly The other side of the coin is that industries whose more specialized labour is in short supply may well offer less resistance to wage demands because, as a result of shortages in their areas, they are less subject to immediate competitive pressures and hence can more easily pass along wage increases in the form of higher product prices.

A critical premise implicit in the preceding discussion is that, for reasons to be considered presently, wages are more flexible upwards than downwards. That is, given two otherwise identical industries, if one has a p per cent. excess demand for labour while the other has an equal excess supply of labour, the wages in the former are assumed to rise more rapidly than they will fall in the latter.[1]

This is important because otherwise we must expect the price level to fall so long as there is *any* involuntary unemployment in the economy, for then, by definition, excess supplies must add up to more than the total of excess demand in the economy as a whole. However, with the postulated asymmetry in the price consequences of the two types of supply—demand imbalance, the process will tend to produce an increasing price level, even when involuntary unemployment is positive in the economy overall. Moreover, as involuntary unemployment falls we have seen that the number of lines of economic activity in which there is an excess demand for labour can be expected to grow, along with the average value of that excess demand, and so the net rate of increase in the overall price level will tend to increase correspondingly.

In sum, the stochastic employment distribution model indicates why the rate of price rise can be expected to vary inversely with the level of unemployment. We will argue that such a model can, in principle, associate a stable rate of inflation with any given level of unemployment. Obviously, there will be irregularities in the time path of prices yielded by such a process, since it is so dependent on random elements. But it can be a stationary stochastic process in which a given level of aggregate excess demand for labour is associated with a fixed expected value for the number of activities experiencing excess demand and for the overall magnitude of that excess demand. It is plausible, then, that the expected value of the rate of price increase will also remain constant.

6

2 Towards a Formal Model

To exhibit the workings of the model more explicitly, it is helpful to express matters in terms of a Walrasian price adjustment mechanism in which the rate of change of the price of any good is expressed as a function of the excess demand for that item. Here we are, of course, concerned with the excess demand for labour in each industry, particularly that for more specialized labour. Letting

x_{it} = excess demand for labour by industry i in period t as a percentage of the labour force in i

w_{it} = hourly wage in industry i in period t expressed in nominal terms

x^* = *target* percentage excess total demand for labour aimed at by government policy (explained below)

w_t = average money wage in the economy

p_t = overall price level

r_{it} = a random variable

g = the operator of discrete *expected*[2] growth rates which yields

$$gw_{it} = E \frac{w_{it+1} - w_{it}}{w_{it}}$$

= the expected percentage rate of growth of money wages in industry i in period t, and, similarly,

g_{pt} = the percentage expected rate of growth in the price level

In our comparative dynamic approach we take the government to select the value of the parameter x^*, that is to select its overall excess demand target[3] for labour and then stick to that target value 'forever'. Only in this way can we compare the long-run equilibria (if they exist) corresponding to the alternative values of x^*.

Beginning with what may or may not be a state of equilibrium growth in prices and wages, we may write our Walrasian *market* adjustment equation as

$$gw_{it} = f(x_{it-1}, gp_{t-1}) \tag{1.1}$$

which asserts that the rate of growth of money wages in industry i depends on the level of excess demand for labour in i and the rate of increase in the price level.[4] We must still supplement this equation to make explicit its several peculiarities that distinguish it from the usual Walrasian relationship.

First, we must make explicit the assumed asymmetry in its reactions to excess demands and supplies, that is the upward flexibility and downward inflexibility of wages. This can, for example, be expressed as

$$f(x_{it}, gp) = \begin{cases} f_1(x_{it}, gp) & \text{if } x_{it} > 0, \quad \text{where } \dfrac{\partial f_1}{\partial x_{it}} > 0 \text{ (wages rise more quickly the larger the excess demand)} \\ f_2(x_{it}, gp) & \text{if } x_{it} \leqslant 0, \quad \text{where } |f_1(x, gp)| > |f_2(-x, gp)| \end{cases}$$

$$\tag{1.2}$$

Second, we must describe explicitly the determination of x_{it} in the short run as a product of overall employment policy and of the process of adjustment which works to eliminate excess demands or supplies of labour inherited from the past. For this purpose we utilize the form

$$x_{it} = (1 - \phi_i) x^* + r_{it} + \phi_i x_{it-1} \tag{1.3}$$

where

$$\text{the expected value of } r_{it}, E(r_{it}), = 0, \text{ and } 0 \leqslant \phi_i \leqslant 1 \tag{1.4}$$

The first term in equation (1.3) asserts that excess demand for labour in industry i depends upon x^*, the target level of excess demand for labour overall (which may be negative on balance if, for example, there is a sufficient budget surplus).[5] The second term indicates that, in addition, the excess demand is affected by the value of the random variable r_{it}, whose value is positive or negative, and which distributes the overall excess demand for (supply of) labour among the various industries in accord with shifts in tastes and changes in technology that make up a stationary random process. The last term in equation (1.3), the ϕ_i term, is like an exponential smoothing process which represents the gradual elimination of any past excess demand for (supply of) labour in industry i through mobility, re-training,[6] etc.

Finally, since we have ruled out changes in productivity, we may take the *overall* price level to adjust itself with some lag by growing on the average for the economy at a rate that reflects the recent rate of growth of money wages, that is

$$gp_t = \psi(gw_t, gw_{t-1}) \text{ where, in terms of expected values, } gp_e = gw_e \tag{1.5a}$$

Two suggestive examples of such relationships are

$$gp_t = gw_{t-1} \tag{1.5b}$$

and

$$gp_t = gw_t + b(gw_t - gw_{t-1}) \tag{1.5c}$$

For our purposes we need only assume the latter part of (1.5a), that is the relationship that holds in a state of price growth equilibrium, if such an equilibrium exists.[7]

Together, (1.1) to (1.5) constitute our long-run Phillips model, relating the exogenously determined parameter value x^* to the rate of wage inflation gw_t. A rise in x^* must necessarily increase the *average* values of the x_{it}, by (1.3) and (1.4), and this, in turn, will increase the rate of increase of wages, by (1.1) and (1.2), just as the statistical Phillips curves describe. However, the relationship is stochastic so that the corresponding empirical observations cannot be expected to constitute a smooth and simple curve.[8]

3 Illustration: Generation of a Stable Phillips Curve

Next, I undertake to show explicitly the derivation of a Phillips curve from a model such as that described in the preceding section, and to demonstrate the possibility

8

that it will constitute a stable equilibrium (that is a long-run Phillips curve) with different growth rates of prices corresponding to different rates of excess demand for labour and unemployment. For this purpose, I use a rather simpler variant of the model, taking the wage response functions (1.1) and (1.3) to have the respective forms[9]

$$gw_{it} = agp_{t-1} + k_j x_{it-1} \qquad (0 < a < 1) \qquad \text{where } k_j = \begin{cases} k_1 \text{ if } x_{it-1} > 0 \\ k_2 \text{ if } x_{it-1} \leqslant 0 \end{cases}$$
$$(k_1 > k_2 > 0) \quad (1.6a)$$

$$x_{it} = x^* + r_{it} \tag{1.7}$$

Let us assume for simplicity that the economy is composed of two industries, identical in size and in average wage rates, however those may be measured, and that the random variable r_{it} always takes one of two values: $r_{it} = +r$ or $r_{it} = -r$, with

$$r_{1t} + r_{2t} = 0 \qquad \text{in each period } t \tag{1.8a}$$

Let us consider the range of values of x^* for which $x^* + r > 0, x^* - r < 0$. Then, substituting equation (1.7) into (1.6a) we have, for the economy as a whole (since the two industries are identical in size and start off with equal money wages),

$$gw_t = 0.5gw_{1t} + 0.5gw_{2t} = agp_{t-1} + 0.5k_1(x^* + r) + 0.5k_2(x^* - r) \tag{1.6b}$$

Using equation (1.5b) as our illustrative price adjustment equation,

$$gp_{t+1} = agp_{t-1} + 0.5k_1(x^* + r) + 0.5k_2(x^* - r) \tag{1.9a}$$

This is a first-order linear difference equation whose solution is

$$gp_t = \frac{a^{t/2}gp_0 + 0.5(k_1 - k_2)r}{1 - a} + \left[\frac{0.5(k_1 + k_2)}{1 - a} \right] x^*$$
$$= a^{t/2}gp_0 + gp_e(x^*, r) \tag{1.10a}$$

where the first term on the right-hand side represents the transitory component of the rate of growth of price and the remaining terms represent $gp_e(x^*, r)$, the equilibrium rate of growth of prices. By our premise $a < 1$, equation (1.10a) is stable and does possess an equilibrium value which can be written simply as

$$gp_e = \alpha(r) + \beta x^* \qquad (\alpha, \beta \text{ constant},[10] \ \beta > 0) \tag{1.10b}$$

That is, these equilibrium growth rates of prices are a rising function of expected excess demand for labour.

A numerical illustration will bring out the workings of the model a bit more clearly, also illustrating the relationship of x^* to the actual equilibrium rate of unemployment in the economy.

Let us assume the illustrative values $r = 11$, that is r_{it} equals either $+11$ or -11, $k_1 = 0.4, k_2 = 0.2$, and $a = 0.8$. Let x^*, the governmental target for excess demand for labour, range over integer values from -3 to $+3$, that is from the labour demand generated by a budget surplus to one corresponding to a substantial deficit.

We will use i' to indicate the industry that happens to have an excess demand for labour in a particular period and i'' to designate the industry in which there is an excess supply in that period (where each of our industries will move in a random pattern between these categories in accord with the values of r_{1t} and r_{2t}).

Consider first the lower end of our policy range, the case $x^* = -3$. Then we have in each period, by equation (1.7).

$$x_{i't-1} = -3 + 11 = \quad 8 \text{ per cent excess demand for labour}$$

$$x_{i''t-1} = -3 - 11 = -14 \text{ per cent excess supply of labour}$$

so that (since there can be no negative unemployment in industry i') the overall unemployment rate $= 14/2 = 7$ per cent. With both industries of the same size[11] we can then take the overall rate of growth of wages in the economy to be the (unweighted) average of the growth rates in the two sectors, that is, equation (1.9a) becomes

$$gw_t = 0.5gw_{i't} + 0.5gw_{i''t} = 0.8gp_{t-1} + 0.2(8) - 0.1(14) \tag{1.9b}$$

or, by equation (1.5a)

$$gp_t = gw_t = 0.8gp_{t-1} + 0.2 \tag{1.8b}$$

It follows from the solution (1.10a) to the difference equation (1.8b) that the equilibrium rate of inflation corresponding to $x^* = -3$ must be $gp_e = 0.2/(1 - 0.8) = 1$.

Exactly the same procedure can be used to determine the equilibrium values of our variables for the other values of x^* in the relevant range. Table 1.1 summarizes the results for the cases corresponding to all integer values of the government policy variable x^* in the interval from $x^* = -3$ through $x^* = +3$. In particular, it shows the different values of gp_e associated with the different values of x^*, which vary up to a $gp_e = 10$ per cent. rate of growth of price level when $x^* = +3$.

Table 1.1. Inflation rates, unemployment levels, and other variable values corresponding to different values of government contributions to excess demand for labour (x^*)

x^* (%)	$x_{i't}$ (%)	$x_{i''t}$ (%)	gw_t	gp_e (% p.a.)	Unemployment rate (%)
-3	8	-14	$0.8p_{t-1} + 0.2$	1	7
-2	9	-13	$0.8p_{t-1} + 0.5$	2.5	6.5
-1	10	-12	$0.8p_{t-1} + 0.8$	4	6
0	11	-11	$0.8p_{t-1} + 1.1$	5.5	5.5
1	12	-10	$0.8p_{t-1} + 1.4$	7	5
2	13	-9	$0.8p_{t-1} + 1.7$	8.5	4.5
3	14	-8	$0.8p_{t-1} + 2.0$	10	4

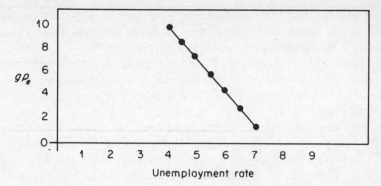

Figure 1.1   Long-run Phillips curve derived from hypothetical data

We see from the last two rows of the table that the premises of our illustrative example yield a long-run Phillips curve relating different inflation rates to different levels of unemployment. As shown in Figure 1.1, this curve is linear, but that is just a consequence of the piecewise linearity of the relationships (1.6a) and (1.7) on which we based our illustrative calculation.

4 On the Role of Money Illusion

We have produced from our theoretical model an explicit example of what appears to be a stable relationship with a unique long-run equilibrium solution, behaving just as we expect a Phillips curve to behave. What, then, are the difficulties that have been raised about the long-run character of the relationship between the level of unemployment and the rate of increase of prices? They reside in good part in two issues which we have left aside up to this point — the role of money illusion in our analysis and the means that are utilized by the policy maker to determine the level of demand for labour, which will be considered presently.

We turn in this section to the first of these issues. It has been suggested that a model such as that which has just been described cannot work without reliance, explicit or implicit, on the assumption that individuals base their decisions at least partly on nominal rather than real values of the pertinent economic variables. To give concreteness to the discussion it is convenient to deal with it in terms of the model of the preceding section.

Equations (1.6a) and (1.7) suggest that our model deals with a Phillips curve relationship of the form

$$gw_t = agp_{t-1} + F(x^*, r) \qquad (0 < a < 1) \tag{1.11}$$

where F is a function whose form will presently be specified.

Since we are trying to deal with a *long-run* Phillips curve, equation (1.11), like all of our other relationships, must be taken to refer exclusively to a situation of stochastic equilibrium. That is to say, apart from random deviations resulting from the stochastic elements built into the model, all of the growth rates in question are equilibrium growth rates. Thus, the time subscripts such as t and $t - 1$ in equation (1.11) and in our other relationships must be taken to relate only to random departures from the corresponding equilibrium relationships.[12]

The premise $a < 1$ in (1.11) is, of course, required for the stability of the solution. But it is this assumption that appears to entail some sort of money illusion, for it seems to imply that growth in wages only *partially* reflects the rate of increase in the price level.[13]

Before discussing the rationale of this premise we may first note that it is not only required for *stability* of the solution. Rather, without it we end up with only one employment level that is consistent with equilibrium in the rate of growth of prices, contrary to the notion of a long-run Phillips curve. To see this, note that, by (1.5a), equation (1.11) implies the following expected value relationship in equilibrium:

$$gp_e(x^*, r) = agp_e(x^*, r) + F(x^*, r) \tag{1.12}$$

or, if $a = 1$,

$$F(x^*, r) = 0$$

Consequently, unless the expected value of F has multiple roots there will be only one expected value of x^* and hence *only one* level of expected unemployment (Friedman's equilibrium unemployment), which is compatible with a fixed equilibrium growth rate in price level. Thus, our analysis requires a value $a < 1$ to yield a long-run Phillips curve, as well as for the stability of that solution.

But further consideration of our postulate $a < 1$ shows clearly that it does *not* imply the presence of money illusion, for if we mean by this that in equilibrium and in the absence of productivity increases workers make certain that their incomes follow the rate of increase in the general price level, despite the assumption $a < 1$, our model will guarantee precisely that — random year-to-year fluctuations apart. To see this, note that from (1.12) we have an interpretation of $F(x^*, r)$ in terms of the equilibrium rate of growth of prices as

$$F(x^*, r) = (1 - a)gp_e(x^*, r) \tag{1.13}$$

Substituting this back into equation (1.11), that basic relationship becomes

$$gw_t = agp_{t-1} + (1 - a)gp_e(x^*, r) \tag{1.14}$$

This confirms that with $a < 1$ the growth rate of money wages does indeed not keep up with the *current* inflation rate during periods of random deviation from full equilibrium. But it *does* follow inflation rates more broadly interpreted, since it is a weighted average of the current inflation rate *and the equilibrium inflation rate*. In other words, equation (1.14) and hence (1.11) embody a 'permanent inflation rate' hypothesis which implies that wage bargains do not follow slavishly every *transitory* change in the rate of inflation, but that they also take into account longer-term price behaviour. In particular, it means that in the long-term equilibrium with which our discussion is exclusively concerned, the apparent role of the premise $a < 1$ as a bearer of money illusion disappears completely. Thus in equilibrium, by

12

definition, $gp_{t-1} = gp_e(x^*, r)$ so that equation (1.14) becomes simply

$$gw_t = agp_e(x^*, r) + (1 - a)gp_e(x^*, r) \equiv gp_e(x^*, r) \qquad (1.15)$$

Indeed, $a < 1$ is perfectly compatible with preservation of expected real wages (that is random effects apart) in *each* industry in the economy taken by itself. Going back to our illustrative linear model of the preceding section we have, as the expected value of wage growth,

$$gw_{it} = agp_{t-1} + \frac{k_1(x^* + r)}{2} + \frac{k_2(x^* - r)}{2} = agp_{t-1} + (1 - a)gp_e(x^*, r) \quad (1.16)$$

by (1.10a) so that, in *any* of the equilibria described in Table 1.1, condition (1.15), the condition for absence of money illusion, is satisfied completely.

Note, moreover, the reason why in our analysis we manage to have $gw_e = gp_e(x^*, r)$ and yet are not forced via equation (1.12) into the conclusion that $F(x^*, r) = 0$, with the implication that there is only one equilibrium expected employment level. Equation (1.13) must represent equilibrium price behaviour. Then so far as $F(x^*, r)$ is concerned, equation (1.12) reduces to the tautology $F(x^*\ r) = F(x^*, r)$ rather than $F(x^*, r) = 0$. This empty requirement is obviously satisfied identically by *any* value of x^* whether or not it is a root of $F(x^*, r)$, even though, as Table 1.1 confirms, equation (1.12) can perfectly well produce for each value of x^* a determinate expected price growth rate $gp_e(x^*)$.

A little more discussion may help to clarify the behavioural implications assumption $a < 1$ in the context of our construct. The model is meant to apply to a situation of long-run *stochastic* equilibrium in which the average (expected) rate of growth in price level is constant. Specifically, it takes the expected value $Egp_t = gp_e$. However, in particular years it is likely to grow somewhat more or less rapidly than this. Thus, the public must realize that the current rate of inflation contains a 'permanent' positive component, gp_e, and a transitory component, $gp_t - gp_e$, which may be positive or negative. In that case, it can hardly be considered to constitute money illusion if they take both components into explicit account. If, year after year, the growth rate of prices has averaged 4 per cent., sometimes going to 5 or 6 per cent. and sometimes dropping to 2 or 3 per cent., a rate of wage increase that does not follow perfectly the year-by-year fluctuations but which averages out at 4 per cent. (plus any increase in productivity, which we have so far assumed away for the sake of simplicity) surely does not represent a preoccupation with nominal rather than real remuneration. This is essentially all that the assumption $a < 1$ in relationship (1.14) really amounts to. Moreover, $1 - a$, the weight accorded to gp_e rather than gp_{t-1}, can be as small as we desire so long as it does not actually fall to zero, that is the model works even if the role of the permanent inflation rate in the wage determination process is as negligible as we care to suppose, so long as it does not disappear altogether.[14]

Nor is any money illusion entailed in our model in the wage floor, if there is a floor, or in the greater stickiness of wages in the downward direction. This merely serves as a cushion which limits but does not prevent reductions in real wages in sectors of the economy that are temporarily doing poorly. Note that in our model, because of the stochastic distribution of prosperity among the various sectors of the economy in the long run, every worker learns not only that prices are rising at $gp_e(x^*, r)$ per cent. per year but also that he can never tell when hard times will (temporarily) hit his industry, since that is determined by random influences. It may be perfectly rational for a worker in a prosperious line of business to prefer an arrangement which offers him some degree of insurance protection against transitory losses in purchasing power if and when it becomes his turn to see a bout of depression hit his industry.[15]

In sum, in our model we need merely treat relationship (1.11) as a description of the market reaction process compounded of the interaction of the labour supply and employer demand relationships. Each of them may also be considered to want to be certain that wage growth follows both current and prospective price movements appropriately, and that is assured by equation (1.14). In particular, for any given value of x^*, it guarantees that there is no erosion of real wages in long-run equilibrium, as gp_{t-1} becomes $gp_e(x^*, r)$ and equation (1.14) reduces to (1.15). Finally, the downward inflexibility of wages protects the worker against the losses in real income that would otherwise accompany the random bouts of adversity that are likely to hit his industry.

Clearly, I have not demonstrated that matters are certain to work out as I have described, or even that they are likely to do so. That is a matter that can only be settled by the empirical evidence. Rather, what I have shown is that there is a *consistent* model and, incidentally, one whose basic components seem to be considered plausible in much of the literature, which by equations (1.14) and (1.15) involves no money illusion, and yet by equation (1.10a) yields a stable rate of growth of prices that varies monotonically with the overall level of excess demand. That is precisely what the Phillips analysis implies.[16]

5 The Transitory Demand Effects of Monetary Measures

The second objection that has been raised against the existence of a long-run Phillips curve is the contention that there are no policy measures capable of sustaining, over the long run, an effective demand for labour beyond that which would result from the market mechanism left completely to itself.

There seems to be no disagreement about the policy maker's ability to increase the effective demand for labour in the short run. Thus, Friedman (1972) has argued that in the short run a government agency wanting to stimulate employment has at its disposal no instrument nearly as powerful as an increase in the money supply.[17] Paraphrasing Tobin, he states that it constitutes an 'alchemy of much deeper significance'[18] than that provided by the usual instruments of fiscal policy — specifically, than a cut in taxes without an offsetting reduction in governmental expenditure. Though he very explicitly concedes that the fiscal measures will have *some* effect, he believes those effects will be 'temporary' and 'minor'.

14

He offers a number of reasons for this view, at least two of which are important for our discussion:

(a) A reduction in taxes automatically brings with it significant offsets which will nullify much of its effect.[19] Specifically, if government does not reduce its outlays and does not increase the money supply, its decreased collection of taxes must be offset by increased borrowing which must result in a decline in consumption expenditure by the lenders or a reduction in their loans to others along with a concomittant rise in interest rates, all of which can offset to a substantial degree the stimulating effects of the tax cut.

(b) If the cut in taxes lasts for only one budgetary period and is not repeated, the stimulating effects will peter out, asymptotically approaching zero in the course of the multiplier process.[20]

In Friedman's words, in such a case 'in the most rigid Keynesian system, the *IS* curve moves to the right and then back again'. In contrast, suppose there were a once-and-for-all increase in the money supply. Then 'the *LM* curve moves to the right as well, *and stays there* after the *IS* curve returns to its initial position. If prices remain constant, real and nominal income stay at a higher level indefinitely.'

So much for the monetarist view of the short run. But it is not here that the difficulties for the long-run Phillips curve are said to arise. Rather, the problem, as Friedman and his followers see it, is that powerful though it may be in short periods, the alchemy of monetary policy tends to evaporate with the passage of time. In this they follow a venerable analysis going back to Cantillon and Hume.

Thus, Cantillon (1755), writing somewhere near 1730, describes clearly the process by which an increase in the money supply stimulates economic activity:

> I consider in general that an increase of actual money causes in a State a corresponding increase of consumption which gradually brings about increased prices.
>
> If the increase of actual money comes from Mines of gold or silver in the State the Owner of these Mines, the Adventurers, the Smelters, Refiners, and all the other workers will increase their expenses in proportion to their gains. They will consume in their households more Meat, Wine, or Beer than before, will accustom themselves to wear better clothes, finer linen, to have better furnished Houses and other choicer commodities . . . . The altercations of the Market, or the demand for Meat, Wine, Wool, etc., being more intense than usual, will not fail to raise their prices. These high prices will determine the Farmers to employ more land to produce them in another year: these same Farmers will profit by this rise of prices and will increase the expenditure of their Families like the others.[21]

However, these earlier authors noted at once that the salutary effects of rising prices upon overall activity levels are likely to be transitory. The increased supply of money stimulates a rise in prices which gradually cuts down the purchasing power of the increased money supply. The nominal supply of money remains at its

15

expanded level but the real quantitity of money falls back to its initial level and in the process loses its stimulating effects. In Hume's (n.d.) words:

> . . . though the high price of commodities be a necessary consequence of the increase of gold and silver yet it follows not immediately upon that increase; but some time is required before the money circulates through the whole state, and makes its effect be felt on all ranks of people. At first, no alteration is perceived; by degrees the price rises, first of one commodity, then of another; till the whole at last reaches a just proportion with the new quantity of specie which is in the kingdom. In my opinion, it is only in this interval or intermediate situation, between the acquisition of money and rise of prices, that the increasing quantity of gold and silver is favourable to industry.[22]

Moreover, as people recognize that prices can be expected to continue their rise, relative prices and incomes will tend to regain their initial relationship. With the economy approaching universal and uniform escalation, rising nominal values of goods will be deprived of any real consequences. They will no longer contribute to real profitability of investment or productive activity and so any earlier gains in employment will evaporate.[23]

In sum, it is the monetarist position that while monetary policy is the only powerful measure in the Keynesian armory, its effects also soon wear out, and cannot continue indefinitely to sustain the gain in employment that it contributed initially. That is, it cannot do so unless, perhaps, by continued and increasing injections that stay one step ahead of inflation and of expectations of inflation each time, the public learns to foresee the rate of growth of prices and to undertake the adjustments that offset its stimulating consequences.

Thus, if such a programme can sustain a level of employment above its 'equilibrium level', it can do so, according to this analysis, only at the price of an accelerating money supply and an accelerating inflation. If the equilibrium level of employment is n, then a policy that maintains a higher level of employment is inconsistent with *any* steady rate of inflation in the long run. Except for relatively brief intervals of time there can be no menu of steady inflation rate – employment combinations among which policy makers can select. From this, too, it is concluded that there can be no stable Phillips curve in the long run.

6 On the Possibility of Durable Fiscal Stimulants

Let us consider, however, whether fiscal instruments can fare better than monetary means in more extended time intervals. It should be noted that the arsenal of fiscal implements goes beyond the mere tax cuts which we have so far considered. It also includes increases in government outlays and, particularly, direct employment by the public sector, which may or may not be accompanied by corresponding tax increases.

First, suppose that the government undertakes to run a deficit not just once, but

16

repeatedly, for the indefinite future and *that it finances it by borrowing rather than by increases in the money supply.* Friedman (1968, pp. 915–917) does not seem to deny at least in principle that this is capable of producing a permanent shift in the *IS* curve. It does not matter for our purposes whether the shift is 'minor'. Surely, even a minor shift can be extended to making the deficit larger. With the money supply constant all that will be changing is the structure of the economy's assets, which at any future date will consist to a greater extent of government debt than it would have otherwise. However, it does not follow that debt must now become with the passage of time an increasing *proportion* of income or of total assets, since that will obviously depend on the relative rates of expansion of debt, productivity, and consumption. In any event it is not obvious why such a shift in the time path of relative asset quantities should lead to accelerating inflation at *any* level of employment above some particular 'natural' rate.

Second, fiscal policy can stimulate demand for labour by increasing government expenditure and taxes equally. For this to be true the balanced budget multiplier need not be equal to unity, as has sometimes been alleged. So long as it is positive it can do the trick, for this means that every increase in government outlay does contribute jobs. Note that while such a course does move us closer to a nationalized economy it involves no cumulative effects on asset holdings. It need produce neither a growing rate of increase of money supply nor of debt.

In a world in which such a programme has been adopted to expand demand for employment permanently beyond Friedman's natural rate, it seems possible to envision in accord with the models of Sections 2 and 3 a state of steady growth of prices which everyone recognizes and accepts, in which workers expect every now and again to suffer a loss in real wages cushioned by the downward stickiness of money wages that is institutionalized by custom. Since monetary policy plays no active role in stimulating job opportunities, there seems to be no reason to expect it to introduce the cumulative inflation that would accompany an attempt to stimulate employment in the long run through the use of this instrument.

7 The Role of the Money Supply: Shifts in the Long-Run Phillips Curve

There is still at least one element missing in our discussion: the long-run behaviour of the money supply and its relation to the stability of the Phillips curve. It should be clear that the steady state envisioned in the last few sections, with employment at some level above Friedman's natural rate and prices rising at a steady rate of $gp_e(x^*, r)$ per cent. per annum, may not be compatible with a constant nominal money supply, for then the real supply of money would be falling, in the simplest sort of model, also at a steady $gp_e(x^*, r)$ per cent. per annum. Thus, this equilibrium would seem to require a corresponding expansion in the nominal stock of cash — one sufficient to keep the real supply constant. 'Inflation neutrality' of the money supply, meaning passive adaptation of the money supply to the rate of growth of prices, is, therefore, an implicit premise of our analysis.

Suppose that the inflation neutrality condition is violated — what then? The answer for the more interesting cases is provided by the Friedman–Phelps analysis.

Suppose that the government decides to use a two-pronged approach to its long-run employment goal, one relying partly on increases in the money supply at a rate more rapid than that required for inflation neutrality. This in turn will lead prices to grow more rapidly than $gp_e(x^*, r)$ per cent. The 'excessive growth' in the money supply will cause an upward shift in the Phillips curve with a higher rate of inflation corresponding to every given employment target. The greater the reliance on monetary policy for the purpose, the larger will be the upward shift in the curve. The slope of the curve may also be affected. Moreover, it may be, for the reason suggested by Friedman and Phelps, that, ultimately, given percentage doses of monetary injection will begin to lose their stimulating effect, so that one may end up with a series of momentary Phillips curves that converge to the long-run curve achievable with an inflation-neutral monetary policy; the alternative is accelerating inflation.

Thus, we see that the Phillips curve is subject to shifting. In terms of our formal model of Section 2, a programme of 'non-neutral' expansion of the money supply, intended to increase employment, may simply shift the f relationship (1.1) and (1.2) upwards, either temporarily or permanently, not necessarily affecting its slope in any predictable direction.

Similarly, increased union militancy may well raise the value of f, that is the wage-raising pressures corresponding to any given level of excess demand for labour. In addition, it can cause an upward shift in the point of discontinuity in the function, the value of x_{it} at which the function f_1 is replaced by f_2. For example, if f_2 is a floor below which nominal wages do not fall, that floor may come into play when excess demand for labour is $x^* + \Delta$ rather than x^* per cent.

It seems clear that these institutional changes are both capable of producing the sorts of shifts in the Phillips curve that appear to have been observed recently, shifts involving increases in the rate of inflation corresponding to any given level of employment.

8 Concluding Comment

The purpose of this paper has been to offer a theoretical basis for a long-run Phillips relationship. Building on the work of Lipsey and others and some standard microdynamic relationships between excess demands and price adjustments, we were able to derive a Phillips relationship which, unlike that in the Friedman model, does not ultimately undermine itself. While outside forces can modify it, as they can any economic relationship, it contains no automatic self-destruct mechanism. The random apportionment of excess demands among lines of economic activities, reflecting intertemporal changes in consumer preferences and production conditions, assures us that the industry in which labour demand is perfectly adjusted to labour supply is the rare exception. There will generally be activities in which labour is in short supply even though, overall, there is a persistent and substantial level of unemployment. In this way, for each such level of employment a stationary *expected* rate of wage (and price) increase will emerge, and that expected value will increase with the level of employment just as the Phillips

18

relationship describes. Moreover, at each level of employment in the economy, in each industry the expected rate of growth of wages will keep up with that of prices, so in the model all decisions are designed in the long run to preserve real and not money wages, and money illusion need play no role in the analysis.

Notes

1. Note the relationship of this portion of our discussion to the Schultze (1959) analysis.
2. Of course, where the rate of growth in question is that for some period in the past (as when we write gp_{t-1}), the operator gives us the rate of growth that actually occurred rather than some expected value.
3. While unemployment will presumably vary directly with the excess supply of labour, the two percentage figures will not be the same. Even a negative excess supply of labour, that is an excess demand, is likely to be associated with pockets of unemployment and, hence, a positive unemployment rate.
4. We could also take account of the rate of growth of labour productivity, but for our purposes that is an unnecessary complication.
5. The relationship between x^* and the unemployment rate in this model is somewhat indirect and is affected by its random variables. The process by which the unemployment rate is determined can be described somewhat loosely as follows. The government, through its fiscal and monetary actions, determines the value of x^*. The random process described in equation (1.3) then transmits the resulting demands to the individual industries and an excess supply in others. The sum of the excess supplies in those latter industries alone, divided by the size of the labour force in the entire economy, yields the overall unemployment rate. An illustrative calculation is shown in the next section.
6. Note that if we do not take ϕ_i to be a constant we can assume that the speed of adjustment can be increased by the magnitude of relative wage changes in industry i, that is we can make it a function of gw_{it}/gw_t.
7. Equation (1.5a) in effect tells us that sellers adjust the prices of their products to match wage increases that in turn were based partly on earlier price rises in accord with equation (1.1). Equation (1.5a) implies that *for a given* value of x^* average real wages will remain constant, at least in equilibrium. However, if x^* changes so will the ratio of w to p and equation (1.5a) will then hold for the new ratio.
8. Equation (1.2) can, clearly, be rewritten to assume that there is a fixed floor under money wages below which they will not fall, no matter what the level of unemployment. Such a floor might represent institutionalized custom or a set of minimum wage laws whose terms are impervious to outside influences such as long-term inflation rates. Such an assumption, however, is neither plausible nor necessary for the analysis. On this matter there is a rather mysterious remark by Tobin (1972, p. 11) who argues that stable Phillips trade-offs in the long run can be preserved only 'if there is a floor on wage changes in excess supply markets independent of the amount of excess supply and of the past history of wages and prices'. The logic of the assertion is just not clear.
9. The premise $a < 1$ has been taken in the literature to constitute money illusion. The reasons for this interpretation are discussed below (Section 1.4), where it is shown that in the context of the present model they are simply not valid.
10. In general, α and β will *both* be random, but the simple assumptions of our illustrative model make only α a function of r, with r in this case a constant.
11. We ignore the temporary differences in unemployment rates in the two industries as a negligible disturbance.

19

12. For similar reasons any two points on the Phillips curve in Figure 1.1 must be interpreted as alternative 'permanent' equilibria corresponding to the choice between two alternative values of x^*. That is, we cannot legitimately use our model to determine what will happen if first one such value of x^* is selected and then the authorities subsequently choose to adopt some other value. Comparison of different points on the curve then represents a piece of comparative statics (or comparative dynamics), rather than an exercise in sequence analysis.

13. The argument of the following paragraph is based on Harry Johnson's distillation of a discussion by Tobin. See Johnson (1971, p. 160). The reader will recognize that the concept of money illusion used here is not quite the usual concept which refers to the behaviour of w_t relative to p_t, and not that of gw_t relative to gp_t. However, the recent discussion seems to have been posed in terms of the latter concept; see Johnson (1971, pp. 167–168). See, however, the discussion of Friedman (1968) below.

14. It should be noted, however, that a *ceteris paribus* decrease in $1 - a$, the weight assigned to the permanent inflation rate, will automatically increase the slope of the long-run Phillips curve. By equation (1.12), $gP_e = F(x^*, r)/(1 - a)$ so that $\partial gP_e/\partial x^* = (\partial F/\partial x^*)/(1 - a)$. Indeed, as the value of a approaches unity the Phillips curve approaches a vertical line. In this respect the Friedman position clearly has considerable force when the weight assigned to the permanent component is small, for it means that, for all practical purposes, the range over which one can expect to vary the employment rate (as determined by x^*) then becomes extremely narrow.

15. On this compare Tobin (1972, pp. 5 and 11). See also Dreze (1973, p. 2, footnote) where wage rigidities are also interpreted as a form of income insurance.

16. That is, no instrument within the set of fiscal and monetary measures. He is careful to suggest that institutional changes such as modification of the minimum wage laws can affect the employment level both in the short run and the long. See Friedman (1968, p. 9).

17. The following characterization of the model of this paper – as a case of a self-fulfilling prophecy – was suggested by Alan Blinder. In a steady-state equilibrium. it posits the following three relations, where a dot over a variable indicates $(1/x)(dx/dt)$;

$$\dot{p} = \dot{w} \tag{a}$$

$$\dot{w} = a\dot{p} + (1 - a)\dot{p}_e \tag{b}$$

$$\dot{p}_e = \frac{F(x)}{1 - a} \tag{c}$$

Given $\dot{p}_e$, which is to say (by (c)) given a fixed aggregate demand policy by the government, (b) is a long-run Phillips curve. The three equations are also consistent.

The question is: how do we rationalize a rule for long-run expectations formation that looks like (c)? One possibility is that people *believe* there is a long-run Phillips curve of the naive kind:

$$\dot{w} = a\dot{p} + F(x) \tag{d}$$

Since they also know that (a) holds in the long run, they can use (a) and (d) to translate their perceptions of government policy into perceptions about the long-run inflation rate. These would appear to be 'rational expectations', that is

20

they use the full model as people perceive it. It is also rational in the sense that they will not be proven wrong. That is, *thinking* that (d) really exists leads them to adopt rule (c). And, in view of (c), (b) and (d) are *observationally equivalent*.

18. See Friedman (1972, especially pp. 914–918). The quotation is taken from p. 916.
19. On this and the materials in the following sections see the extremely illuminating piece by Blinder and Solow (1973).
20. See Friedman (1972, p. 916). Note that Friedman tells us that no part of his argument relies on the assumption that the *LM* curve is (virtually) vertical, a premise frequently attributed to him but one that he now rejects outright (p. 913).
21. See Cantillon (1755, pp. 163–165).
22. See Hume (n.d., p. 170). See also Cantillon (1755, pp. 165–167).
23. Thus, if employment is to be stimulated indefinitely *by a steady expansion in the money supply alone*, money illusion on the part of workers is indeed required – workers must be willing to let their wages fall behind prices indefinitely. It is this role of money that was injected into the discussion by Friedman (1968, pp. 8–10).
24. The discussion of this section is entirely informal. The work of the explicit incorporation of its ideas into our models still remains to be carried out.

Bibliography

Archibald, G. C. (1970). 'The structure of excess demand for labour'. In E. S. Phelps (Ed.), *Microeconomic Foundations of Employment and Inflation Theory*, Norton, New York.

Blinder, A. S., and R. M. Solow (1973). 'Does fiscal policy matter?', *Journal of Public Finance*, 2(4), November.

Cantillon, Richard (1755). *Essai sur la Nature du Commerce en Général*, Higgs ed. (1959), Macmillan, London.

Dreze, J. H. (1973). *Existence of an Exchange Equilibrium under Price Rigidities*, Discussion Paper No. 7326, Center for Operations Research and Econometrics, University of Louvin, Louvin.

Friedman, M. (1968). 'The role of monetary policy', *American Economic Review*, 58(1), March.

Friedman, M. (1972). 'Comments on the critics', *Journal of Political Economy*, 80(5), September/October.

Hume, David (n.d.). *Essays, Literary, Moral and Political*, Ward Lock, London.

Johnson, H. G. (1971). *Macroeconomics and Monetary Theory*, Gray-Mills, London.

Lipsey, R. G. (1960). 'The relation between unemployment and the rate of change of money wage rates in the United Kingdom, 1862–1957: a further analysis', *Economica*, n.s., 27(105), February.

Phelps, E. S. (Ed.), (1970). *Microeconomic Foundations of Employment and Inflation Theory*, Norton, New York.

Schultze, C. L. (1959). 'Recent inflation in the United States'. In *Employment, Growth, and Price Levels*, Study Paper No. 1, U.S. Congress Joint Economic Committee, U.S. Government Printing Office, Washington, D. C.

Tobin, J. (1972). 'Inflation and unemployment', *American Economic Review*, 62(1), March.

16

Planning and Dual Values
of Linearized Nonlinear Problems:
A Gothic Tale

WILLIAM J. BAUMOL

Everyone is aware that the world is rarely *perfectly* linear. Yet planning
analysis continues to rely heavily on linear models. Linear programming is one
of the most attractive tools available for formal planning calculations. Continued reliance upon linear techniques *cannot* be ascribed to unavailability of
good calculation algorithms for nonlinear programmes. On the contrary,
powerful calculation techniques that work in the nonlinear case have been
available virtually from the inception of mathematical programming. Rather,
the propensity toward linearization is to be explained in terms of the difficulty
of empirical estimation of nonlinear functions, at least in regions not very close
to the range of current experience. In a linear world this constitutes no
problem. One can determine precisely the shape of an entire hyperplane from
its height and partial derivatives at a single point. But where a surface may
bend and curve in a manner which the investigator knows he does not know, it
is at best dangerous to draw inferences about distant portions of a surface from
empirical information about its behavior in a relatively small neighborhood.
Apart from that, linear estimation techniques introduce other difficulties:
heavier data requirements, more complex identification criteria, and so on. All
in all, therefore, even with the best of intentions, the planner generally is unable
to determine the shapes of the relevant nonlinear functions. In these
circumstances, recourse to linear programming techniques becomes a great
temptation.

The analyst may comfort himself by the belief, or at least the surmise, that
the nonlinearities involved are realtively minor, though he rarely offers either
evidence for this belief, or even a discussion of the degree of nonlinearity that is
small enough to be neglected with impunity. This is all the more serious since
as was shown elsewhere (Baumol and Bushnell, 1967), even mild nonlinearities
in the underlying problem can and characteristically will introduce very serious
errors into a linear-programming calculation intended to approximate the solution to the problem. The optimal solution to the linear problem is likely to yield
values of the structural variables which differ by orders of magnitude from
their true optima and are very different qualitatively as well. The LP 'solutions'

can easily be worse than answers that are randomly selected. Moreover, reductions in the 'curvature' of the nonlinear functions in question may produce no noteworthy improvements in the results. If correct, these conclusions should be more than a little frightening to casual users of linear programming.

It has been objected that the primal programming calculation is concerned more with the value of the objective function than with the structural variables; that is, it may not matter if the output levels selected are very far from those that are optimal, provided the resulting yields are close to their maximum; and if the objective function is very nearly a hyperplane, it is argued, the approximation can consequently produce little sacrifice in overall yields. Though the argument seems questionable to me, I will not pursue it here. Rather, it is mentioned only because it contrasts so sharply with the case of a calculation whose main purpose is to evaluate the (dual) shadow prices, and for which the behavior of the objective function is only a secondary consideration.

In economic planning the values of the dual variables can be extremely important. Because they indicate the marginal yields of the different resources which constrain the development process, they can play a key role in determination of expenditure (investment) priorities. But it is, of course, crucial, if they are to be used for this purpose that the calculated values bear some reasonable resemblance to the true magnitudes they are intended to approximate.

I will show here that, unfortunately, a linear 'approximation' to a nonlinear programme can yield dual values which bear not the slightest resemblance to the true values of the shadow prices. Not only are the quantities likely to be seriously erroneous, but *the calculation is likely to make free goods of inputs that are in scarce supply* (that is, which have a positive marginal yield) and, perhaps more surprising, *they seem even more likely to impute scarcity value to inputs that are available in excess*. This last result is surprising because we have been taught to expect LP solution vectors to contain large numbers of zeros, a characteristic frequently not shared by a (well-behaved)[1] nonlinear programme. Yet, we will see that the dual values for such a nonlinear programme can easily be made up of nothing but zeros – the null-vector solution.

The Case of the Interior Maximum to the Primal Programme

As we know, the optimal point for a primal nonlinear programme may well lie in the interior of the feasible region. In particular, the solution of a programme with a nonlinear objective function and linear constraints need not lie at one of the corners of the feasible region. Thus, in Figure 16.1, point m inside feasible region Oabcd is the true optimum, if the true objective function is represented by the hill-shaped surface. On the other hand, the solution to an approximating linear programme, if it is unique, always lies at a corner, say, point c on the diagram, where the plane tangent to the graph of the objective function at T represents the approximating linear objective function.

Consider a particular dual variable v, say, that associated with the constraint represented by line segment bc. Let this constraint be

$$k_1 y_1 + k_2 y_2 \leq k. \tag{16.1}$$

Now, assuming the derivative exists,[2] the shadow price property of v is a consequence of the theorem that (whether the problem is linear or nonlinear) the

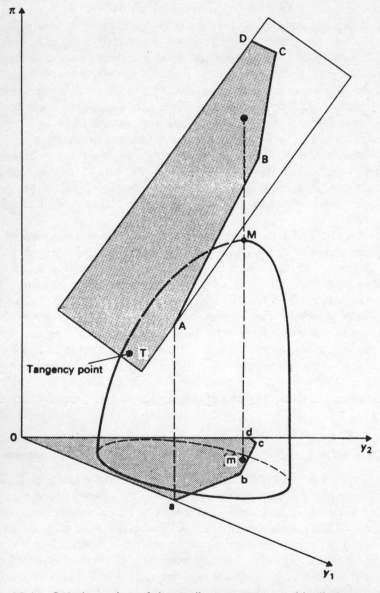

Figure 16.1   *Solution points of the nonlinear program and its linear approximation.*

optimal value $v°$ of the dual variable v, properly defined, must satisfy

$$v° = \partial\pi°/\partial k \tag{16.2}$$

where $\pi°$ is the optimal value of the primal objective function. What 16.2 tells us is that we can determine the value of $v°$ from our diagram by undertaking

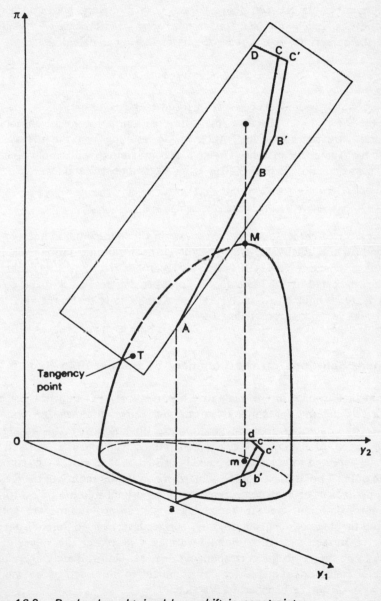

Figure 16.2   *Dual value obtained by a shift in constraint.*

(see Figure 16.2) a small outward shift, from bc to b′c′, in the corresponding constraint segment − a shift that leaves its slope unchanged. We then observe how much the value of $\pi°$ increases as a consequence (it can, clearly, never decrease, since the loosening of the constraint, at worst, will still permit the previous solution). The limit of $\Delta\pi°/\Delta k$ as Δk approaches zero will give us the desired value of $v°$.

In the case shown in Figure 16.2 in the linear calculation $\Delta\pi°$ is given by the difference in heights between points C′ and C on the plane above corners c′ and c of the expanded and the initial feasible regions. In that case we must have (letting the subscript l refer to the results of the linear calculation):

$$\partial\pi_l°/\partial k = v_l° > 0 \qquad (16.3)$$

and we certainly would expect such a result to be common.

On the other hand, because the true solution point m is an interior maximum, the expansion of the feasible region resulting from the increase in k will not *really* improve matters. The nonlinear maximum will remain precisely where it was so that (letting the subscript t connote true values):

$$\partial\pi_t°/\partial k = v_t° = 0. \qquad (16.4)$$

Thus, as asserted earlier, here we have a case in which the input in question is a free good (its true duel value is zero) and yet the linear calculation is likely to assign it a nonzero value. It must be reemphasized that the qualitative difference indicated by 16.3 and 16.4 is not a peculiar result ascribable to any special features built into our illustration. Rather, it is to be regarded as a normal and very likely possibility.

Nonlinear Solutions on the Boundary of the Feasible Region

The immediate source of the qualitative linearization error that has just been described is the interior solution to our illustrative nonlinear programme. However, the solutions to such programmes do not always fall inside the feasible region. One may well ask whether the linear and the true solution cannot be expected to correspond roughly in such a case. For, by hypothesis, the true optimal point must now lie somewhere on the boundary of the feasible region, perhaps at or near a corner point. If the primal solution points for the linear approximation and the underlying nonlinear programme are not far apart and the slope of the linear objective surface is not very different from that of the true surface near those points, we may well expect the values of the $\partial\pi_l°/\partial k$ to be similar to the corresponding $\partial\pi_t°/\partial k$. Unfortunately, there are a number of conditions required for this argument to hold, and as we will see, they may well not be satisfied in practice.

The first source of difficulty is the only one which is quite obvious. Linear approximations are not constructed at the optimal point or, usually, even any-where near it. If one knew the approximate location of the optimal point to begin with, so that one would be able to select an *initial* point known in advance to be nearby, there would be no need for any approximating calcula-tion. A linear approximation is normally constructed on the basis of initial points (such as tangency point T in the figures) for which the required informa-tion happens to be available. Consequently, though the linear surface and the true objective surface may be similar in shape near those initial points, the two may well differ widely near the optimal solution which can be far away. The slopes of the profit function at these points and, hence, the dual values may then also differ substantially.

This difficulty, as already admitted, is an obvious matter and it may be con-sidered a matter of imperfect knowledge which hampers application rather than a fundamental analytical problem. This is, however, certainly not true of the next problem which we will examine. This second problem remains even if the LP and the true solution points are close and the slopes of the two surfaces are very similar. Even then the two partial derivatives of the objective function with respect to k, and hence the two dual values, can well differ substantially.

This second problem arises, because even where the nonlinear optimum lies on the boundary of the feasible region, it may well not fall at a corner point of that boundary. Thus, optimal point m in Figure 16.3 lies in the interior of line segment cb. In our diagram a consequence is that linear profit π_l is bound effectively by two constraint lines, dc and cb, while the true profit π_t is bound by only one. (In a problem with n structural variables, that is, n dimensions, π_l will be bounded by n constraints, while π_t may still be bounded by only one.)

Here, it may be tempting (but incorrect) to surmise that for those derivatives that are nonzero[3]:

$$\partial\pi_l^0/\partial k \leq \partial\pi_t^0/\partial k. \qquad (16.5)$$

This may seem to follow, because additional constraints can only reduce (or leave unchanged) the value of the objective function. However, since we know nothing about the relative *changes* that result in π_l^0 and π_t^0, we can infer no relationship such as 16.5 between their derivatives. Letting π' and π'' refer to the optimal value of the objective function before and after the loosening of the constraint by an increase in k, and assuming for purposes of illustration that the linear values are very close to the true values *near the linear optima*, it is clear that we must have

$$\pi_l' \leq \pi_t' \; \pi_l'' \leq \pi_t''$$

that is, the true optimum must always equal or exceed the corresponding linear optimum. But that tells us nothing about the *differences*, that is,

$$\pi_l'' - \pi_l' \gtrless \pi_t'' - \pi_t'$$

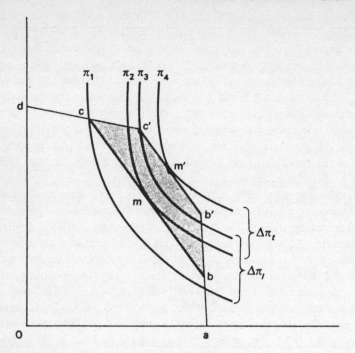

Figure 16.3   *A boundary solution not at a corner.*

since the direction of this inequality clearly depends on the *change* in the loss from linearization before and after the constraint is loosened, namely, on the relative size of $\pi'_t - \pi'_l$ and $\pi''_t - \bar{\pi}''_l$. The problem is illustrated in Figure 16.3, where the loosening of the constraint represented by cb shifts that line segment outward to c'b', changing the linear optimum from c to c' and the true optimum from m to m'. On the assumption we have adopted for the moment, that near c and c' the linear and true values of π are close to one another, the resulting change in the value of the linear profit function will be $\Delta\pi_l = \pi_3 - \pi_1$ and that in the true profit will be $\Delta\pi_t = \pi_4 - \pi_2$. Clearly, the relative magnitudes of $\Delta\pi_t$ and $\Delta\pi_l$ can vary in virtually any way. For example, if we take $\Delta\pi$ to be proportional to the distance between the pertinent curves, the case shown in the figure will yield a relationship the opposite of that of 16.5. Thus, the true dual value can be either larger, or smaller, than its linear proxy, and there seems to be no way to place *a priori* bounds on the difference between them.

There is another, perhaps more fundamental, reason for which we cannot rely on as loose a relationship as 16.5 to characterize the comparative behavior of the linear and the nonlinear dual. For linear approximations to nonlinear programmes are beset by a third and perhaps even more fundamental difficulty. This stems from the fact that there is, in general, not the slightest reason to expect the two solution points to lie anywhere near one another. For, as will be shown now, the linear solution point depends entirely on the choice of initial point from which the linear approximation is constructed, and has no connection with the location of the true optimum. *By an appropriate choice of initial point, virtually any corner of the feasible region can perhaps be made to serve as the linear optimum.* This, as we will see now, can cause critical problems *even where the nonlinear solution lies at a corner of the feasible region* (though it certainly does not help matters if the true optimum lies at a point that is not a corner).

The nature of the problem is brought out by Figure 16.4. In that diagram the curves labeled π_1, π_2 and π_3 are true iso-profit loci. The true optimum is m, the point of tangency between π_3 and the boundary of the feasible region. The solution point of the linear approximation will lie at one of the corners a, b, c, or d. If it happens to fall at c, or even at b, one may hope that things will not work out too badly.

But the corner point that is selected by the linear calculation is by no means certain to be either b, or c. Rather, it is highly sensitive to the choice of initial point. That is, suppose the linearization is in fact carried out by selecting some initial point and fitting a tangent hyperplane to the true nonlinear surface at that point. Then the linear iso-profit curves will be a set of parallel straight lines tangent to the true iso-profit curve at that initial point. For example, suppose the initial point is r. Then c'b', the tangent to the true iso-profit curve at r, will be one of the linear iso-profit curves. In this case r has been selected so that c'b' happens to be parallel to segment cb of the boundary of the feasible region, and all other points on the curve rsm have been selected similarly. This means

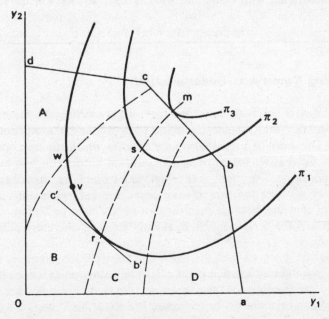

Figure 16.4   *Errors attributable to linearization.*

that for any such initial position all points on cb will be optimal solutions to the linear programme. Similarly, if the initial point is w, the iso-profit curves will be parallel to ba and so any point on that segment will be a linear solution. For the same reason, any point such as v on the arc wr of π_1 will yield point b as its linear solution.

More generally, constructing the other two broken curves as we constructed rsm, we see that they divide the feasible region into four subregions. The one labeled A consists of all points $y^a = (y_1^a, y_2^a)$ such that if y^a is used as the initial point for the linear approximation, the resulting linear programme will select the corner a as its optimum. A similar relationship holds for subregions B, C and D.

We conclude that, if we have no initial information about the location of the true optimum m, we may well happen to utilize an initial point in region D or A, which yields a linear solution very far[4] from *m*. Thus, suppose now that the nonlinear optimum falls at one corner point, and that the linear optimum falls at another. Then the presence of the other constraint lines at these points will generally lead to very different values for $\partial \pi_1^o / \partial k$ and $\partial \pi_1^o / \partial k$. For example, suppose the true optimum lies at c, while the linear optimum is a (see Figure 16.3). Here, the difference is clear, for we have this time:

$$\partial \pi_1^o / \partial k > 0, \quad \partial \pi_1^o / \partial k = 0$$

since the shift in the constraint line cb to c'b' makes no change in the feasible region in the neighborhood of the linear optimum a. Similarly, if *w* is the capacity associated with constraint line segment ab, we will have:

$$\partial \pi_1^o / \partial w = 0, \quad \partial \pi_1^o / \partial w > 0.$$

Concluding Comment: Generalization

Our qualitative conclusions may seem from the preceding discussion to depend on the possibility that the linear solution point will lie far away from the true optimum. This may be suggested by the cases in which the true optimum fell well inside the feasible region or at some distant corner. In fact, however, at least the qualitative distortions in the dual values which we have observed arise *inevitably* even where the two solution points are very close, just so long as they do not coincide, because then the two points must be bound by different constraints and the corresponding dual variables must therefore differ accordingly.

In terms of Figure 16.3 let the linear solution fall, for example, at point c. Then, suppose the true solution point y_t is at *any* other point in the diagram, no matter how far from *or how near* to point c. In that case it is necessarily true that either constraint line dc, or constraint line cb (or both) must not be binding at y_t, so the dual values must differ quantitatively and qualitatively from the

284 *THE THEORY AND EXPERIENCE OF ECONOMIC DEVELOPMENT*

true magnitudes of the corresponding marginal yields. An investment programme based on linear dual values may, therefore, not serve the community very well.

Chapter 16: Notes

I am very grateful to the Sloan Foundation, whose support greatly facilitated the completion of this paper. This note grew out of discussions at the Friday seminar at the Stockholm School of Economics.

1 By a well-behaved programme, I mean here one that involves diminishing returns, diminishing marginal rates of substitution, and so on, so that conventional methods of solution apply.
2 If the derivative does not exist the value of v will, of course, lie between the values of the corresponding right- and left-hand derivatives, but that changes nothing of importance in our discussion. For the derivation of the theorem, see Balinsky and Baumol (1968).
3 Later we will return to the serious problems associated with the zero-valued derivatives.
4 As a practical matter such a choice may be *forced* upon us by the information that happens to be available. Usually, we do not have the luxury of taking as the initial point any point in the feasible region that happens to appeal to us. Rather, the data are generated by current practice which, so far as we can tell in advance, may be distant from any optimum.

Chapter 16: References

Balinsky, M. L. and Baumol, W. J. 'The dual in nonlinear programming and its economic interpretation', *Review of Economic Studies*, vol. XXXV, no. 3 (1968), pp. 237–56.
Baumol, W. J. and Bushnell, R. C. 'Error produced by linearization in mathematical programming', *Econometrica*, vol. 35, nos 3–4 (1967), pp. 447–71.

Part IV
On the History of Economic Ideas

To me, the central theme of this section is the difficulty of communication. Few authors have been talked about more than Marx and Adam Smith (though they have obviously been talked about more often than read). Yet more than a century of discussion has served only to ossify the myths and misrepresentations that characterize many of the writings on their works. No matter how clearly and strongly a proposition was stated by Marx or Smith, no matter how often it was reiterated by them, no matter how vehemently Marx railed against the mischaracterizations of his views during his lifetime, the misrepresentations have persisted and the authors' true opinions have been recognized only by a small number of exceptionally careful scholars.

Obviously, we authors are left in a discouraging position. Readers who think we are likely to have said A seem virtually certain to claim that A is indeed our position no matter how often we protest that A is in direct conflict with our views[1] and that we hold a very different position, B.

In the case of Adam Smith the main popular mischaracterization discussed here is the view that he was an apologist for capitalism and capitalists alike. It is demonstrated here that, on the contrary, merchants and manufacturers were Smith's favourite whipping boys whom he repeatedly cited as untrustworthy plotters against the social interest. It is shown that this was no mere manifestation of dispepsia or prejudice. Rather, it is an integral element in the invisible hand doctrine and its long history, to which Smith provided the culmination.[2]

The paper on Smith also illustrates the care we must exercise in looking at earlier writings through twentieth century spectacles. Though it is well known to specialists, few others recognize that the invisible hand doctrine had a basically religious element and that 'the invisible hand', rather than being mere metaphor, was a standard eighteenth century circumlocution connoting God.

The two papers devoted to Marx deal with myths that are even more pervasive and substantial. It is shown, contrary to popular belief, that Marx did *not* consider the capitalistic wage arrangement to be immoral or that it constituted a valid ground for the struggle against the capitalist system. Nor did he believe that wages have a tendency to be driven to a fixed physical minimum, the so-called subsistence level. Moreover, he believed that wages are determined by a process of supply and demand, a process that in his view could be affected materially by trade union activity. Marx explicitly accepted Smith's and Ricardo's explanation of price determination which he correctly interpreted as a cost of production model, and *not as a labour theory* analysis.

All of those things and more, which fly directly in the face of the common wisdom on the substance of Marxian analysis, Marx said not only once, but again and again. He did not only say them calmly and dispassionately but sometimes with considerable passion supplemented by vituperation aimed at those who had mischaracterized his positions—all to little avail.

The essay which I want to discuss most extensively here is the paper on Say's Law because there is now much to be added to the substance of the paper, thanks to the insights and information contributed by Professor William Thweatt of Vanderbilt University.

Most of the Say's Law article is devoted to the substance of the early writings on the subject, showing that the bulk of that discussion had objectives rather different or, perhaps more accurately, supplementary to the notions we now associate with the idea. While the authors did assert that general overproduction was impossible, they were mostly concerned to show that 'productive consumption', that is, investment, contributes more effectively to national wealth and prosperity than 'unproductive consumption' such as the use of luxury goods and military outlays of governments.

It is also worth remarking that since the appearance of Keynes' *General Theory* one tends to think of the advocates of Say's Law as a reactionary group who sought to provide a prop to ring wing causes. But viewed in terms of the period in which they wrote, this is complete misunderstanding. The group, if anything, was a centre of opposition to the landed interests and the impediments they offered to the recently-launched industrial revolution and to the capitalist mechanism which promoted it. The repeated references of these authors to the waste constituted by luxury expenditures and to the folly and economic cost of military endeavours should confirm that the characterization of these authors as representatives of the right is misleading at best.

My Say's Law paper deals also with the correct attribution of the proposition, discussing whether Say or James Mill should properly be credited as the author. I concluded, and still believe that Adam Smith, if anyone, should be judged to have understood and described the law before either of those authors who previously had been considered the leading candidates for the honour. But in discussing the relative contributions of Say and Mill I had overlooked some crucial pieces of evidence.[3]

Professor Thweatt judges, probably correctly, that as a result I did not give Mill sufficient credit for the extent to which he had mastered the contents of the Law well before Say did in his second edition (1814). Thus he concludes, no doubt justly,

> . . . that Baumol is mistaken in insisting that it was not until the second edition of the Traite that the full structure of [the doctrine] is spelled out . . . . Our own assessment parallels that of Chipman when he concluded that for 'the sharp and excessively doctrinaire version of the principle, priority must certainly go to Mill—doubtless a dubious distinction'. (Chipman, 1969,[4] p. 709N)[5]

I will not deal here with Professor Thweatt's contention that the law is fully explained and enunciated in Mill's *Commerce Defended* (1808), a matter of interpretation on which I am not fully convinced. Whatever may be judged on this point it is clear that I had overlooked three writings by James Mill, two of them earlier than *Commerce Defended*, in which he had dealt with the same subject. These were:

'Lord Lauderdale on Public Wealth', *Literary Journal*, vol. 4, 1804, pp. 1–18.

'Traité d'économie politique (etc.)', *Literary Journal*, vol. 5, 1805, pp. 412–25.

'Mill's commerce defended', *Eclectic Review*, vol. 4, 1808, pp. 554–9.

Let me begin by quoting Professor Thweatt's letter to me (August 23, 1977):

> . . . I imagine you will . . . be interested in learning that James Mill not only mentioned Say's first edition on page 76n of *Commerce Defended*, but that he had reviewed Say's first edition in the *Literary Journal*, vol. V, no. 4 (April 1805), and in that review he quotes extensively from the second volume of Say's *Traité*, but in the end concluding: 'In the execu-

tion of this work very little is to be found which can be considered original. Not only are all the general principles copied from Smith, but . . . the author has copied too slavishly.

You might also be interested to know that Mill reviewed his own *Commerce Defended*, in the *Eclectic Review* for June 1808. I enclose an excerpt which I give out to my students here at Vanderbilt in my course on the history of economic thought from this review.

> James Mill's review of James Mill's *Commerce Defended* (London: 1808) in the *Eclectic Review*, vol. IV, no. 1, art. XIV, pp. 554–9, (June, 1808):
> 'This pamphlet is, in our opinion, a very satisfactory answer to Mr. Spence, and the other advocates of the *Economist* System. It is much more. Its value consists not merely in refuting some dangerous errors, of momentary interest, but also in developing and displaying general principles in political science, which apply to all periods and places, and which are unhappily too little understood . . .
> 'This chapter on Consumption furnishes a clear exposition of Dr. Smith's views on the nature and causes of a nation's progress or declension in prosperity; and it amply confutes, though indirectly, the ridiculous, yet very popular notion, that to consume or destroy articles of manufacture is 'good for trade'. As an excellent specimen of Mr. Mill's acuteness and power of abstraction, we shall quote his remarks on the apprehensions of the Economists, lest capital should increase too fast, and the production of commodities should increase beyond '*the market* for disposing of them' (pp. 554–6).

Here Mill goes on to reproduce the same passage from his *Commerce Defended*, pp. 81–2 which I quote at the end of Section 3 of my article below.

Professor Thweatt, incidentally, notes elsewhere that it is not absolutely certain that Mill is the author of this review of Mill, but indicates that strong internal evidence supports this attribution of his, with which other scholars seem to agree.

In his published comments on my article (1980) Professor Thweatt goes on to provide convincing evidence of Mill's priority:

> . . . in his July 1804 review of 'Lord Lauderdale on Public Wealth' (Mill, 1804), he clearly presented the Law's 'logical underpinnings' which Baumol maintained neither Mill, nor Say, had stated prior to 1814. Concerning the motivation for spending income on commodities rather than holding part of it in the form of cash balances, Mill explored the case of a merchant resolving not to spend all his income, and he asked: 'Why does he not?'
>
>> by employing what he can spare from consmption in augmenting the capital he has in his business, he can increase his revenue next year. Or if he cannot employ it to advantage himself, he may lend it to some other person who can . . . . If he cannot employ what he saves with any advantage, he will not save it. No one thinks of accumulating dead stock . . . no man saves any part of his income which he has not a prospect of employing with advantage. [Mill 1804, 13]

Notice the similarity of the above statement on the matter of motivation of demand which Baumol quoted from Adam Smith. We are expressly told why the excess supply (income) over consumption leads to a demand for investment goods ('reproductive' consumption) rather than cash balances—'No one thinks of accumulating dead stock'. And, in typical Millian fashion, Mill omitted any qualification such as 'the lacunae' which Baumol spotted in Smith's statement which stipulated that savings always are spent only when 'there is tolerable security' in the country.

Mill then quickly demonstrated that the purchasing power generated by production resulted in a demand for commodities '*virtually without* delay' (Baumol, 157). He did this by quoting *the identical passage* from Smith as later did Baumol, thus assuring Lord Lauderdale that savings always were immediately employed as capital, and, in Smith's words 'nearly in the same time too' (Smith, 1976, I, 338, as quoted by Baumol, 158, and Mill 1804, 14–15).

If what Smith wrote in 1776 constituted the rationale of the Law of Markets in the sense that extra income would not result in increased cash balances, but instead represented additional demand for commodities, and 'virtually without delay', then Mill's attack on Lauderdale in 1804, a decade before Say's second edition appeared, must also constitute that rationale. And why not? Mill relied very heavily on what Adam Smith had previously written—paraphrasing him in regard to the 'motivation' of demand and quoting him verbatim as to the 'timing' of that expenditure.

Notes

1. These words are obviously not written disinterestedly, my own work having undergone such misunderstandings. For example, in discussions of the cost disease of the urban services I have repeatedly stressed that the quantities of those services demanded may rise, or decline with the passage of time, depending on income and price elasticities of demand. Yet people have insisted, even to my face, that I believe the rising real costs of the services in question condemns them to eventual extinction. Even more surprising, the Baumol/Bradford article on Ramsey pricing, which is largely devoted to the extensive history of the theorem in the economic literature, has been misread to state that Baumol and Bradford claimed the theorem as their own, while other readers *did* actually attribute the result to them!
2. On this see the excellent little book by Albert Hirschman *The Passions and the Interests* (Princeton: Princeton University Press, 1977).
3. An outright error also crept in somewhere in the writing process. Professor Thweatt has pointed out that though my title refers to 'Say's Eight Laws', in fact I actually describe only seven variations on the theme.
4. The reference is to Chipman, John, 'A Survey of the Theory of International Trade: Part 2: The Neo-classical Theory', *Econometrica*, vol. 53, 1965, pp. 685–760.
5. Thweatt, W. D., 'Baumol and James Mill on 'Say's' Law of Markets', *Economica*, vol. 47, Nov. 1980, pp. 467–9.

[14]

SMITH VS. MARX ON BUSINESS MORALITY AND THE SOCIAL INTEREST

by William J. Baumol*

I believe that among those who know the *Wealth of Nations* mostly by repute there is widespread misinterpretation of its central message about the roles of capitalists and capitalism. The book is neither a tract that opposes all forms of government intervention in the workings of the free market,[1] nor does it dedicate itself to the praise of virtuous intentions and high moral standards of the capitalists. On the contrary, Smith's basic position is that in the operation of the economy there is nothing so untrustworthy as the businessman's good intentions. The economy in the *Wealth of Nations* is populated by a group of individuals intent on pursuit of their own interests, with little concern over the resulting damage to the welfare of others, and businessmen are second to none in their disregard of the public interest.

The basic virtue of the market mechanism, when it is operated without monopolistic restrictions or *inappropriate* governmental interference, is that it not only places a rein upon such selfish behavior, but that it achieves even more, turning pursuit of self interest into an instrument for the promotion of the general welfare. In this mechanism *disregard for the interests of others plays a crucial role*; without it, that is, if the conscience of businessmen were to replace their pursuit of personal gain, the interests of society might not be served nearly as well.

In contrast, Marx's view is that the capitalist as an individual is neither inherently good nor evil, but the inevitable product of historical circumstances which, on the one hand, make him the progenitor of progress over medieval stagnation and, on the other, the destined but transitory exploiter of the working class. Thus it is paradoxical, but entirely consistent with their central purposes, that the book widely considered to be the charter document of the free enterprise system repeatedly attacks the ethics of the merchants and manufacturers, while the volumes that have become the manifesto of the opponents of capitalism do not concern themselves with the capitalist's personal morality.

In sum, it will be my objective to show that while to Marx the capitalist is the product of the historical process, that is, the creation of the capitalist stage of history, to Smith the capitalist system is a mechanism designed, apparently by divine providence, to curb man's inherent selfishness and, indeed, to put it to work for the general good. These are among the central messages of *Capital* and of the *Wealth of Nations*, and so the two authors' contrasting views on the personal morality of capitalists are not incidental quirks of the writers but a direct reflection of their basic views.

1. Smith on Business Ethics

Though most of them are quite familiar, a selection of some more notable quotations giving Smith's views on the ethics of businessmen bear repetition because readers who have not seen them recently may be struck by their force and consistency.

Proceeding more or less in their order of appearance in the book, we start with one in which Smith accuses businessmen of heaping upon labor the blame for high prices, and studiously ignoring their own contribution to the problem:

> Our merchants and master-manufacturers complain much of the bad effects of high wages in raising the price, and thereby lessening the sale of their goods both at home and abroad. They say nothing concerning the bad effects of high profits. They are silent with regard to the pernicious effects of their own gains. They complain only of those of other people. (p. 98)

However, it is not only labor that suffers from the weakness of the capitalists' scruples, and Smith tells us that the public, as a body, is also a likely victim:

> People of the same trade seldom meet together, even for merriment and diversion, but the conversation ends in a conspiracy against the public, or in some contrivance to raise prices. (p. 128)

According to Smith, businessmen as a group try to exercise economic power over their countrymen by restraining trade and monopolizing the domestic markets:

* Princeton and New York Universities.

... merchants and manufacturers, who being collected into towns, and accustomed to that exclusive corporation spirit which prevails in them, naturally endeavour to obtain against all their countrymen, the same exclusive privilege which they generally possess against the inhabitants of their respective towns. They accordingly seem to have been the original inventors of those restraints upon the importation of foreign goods, which secure to them the monopoly of the home-market. (p. 429)

Not only do the capitalists restrain trade, but they seek to deceive the public into believing that high domestic prices somehow serve the general interest:

In every country it always is and must be the interest of the great body of the people to buy whatever they want of those who sell it cheapest. The proposition is so very manifest, that it seems ridiculous to take any pains to prove it; nor could it ever have been called in question, had not the interested sophistry of merchants and manufacturers confounded the common sense of mankind. Their interest is, in this respect, directly opposite to that of the great body of the people. (p. 461)

Indeed, the influence of capitalists upon foreign trade favors impoverishment of other countries, and undermines international tranquility:

... nations have been taught that their interest consisted in beggaring all their neighbours. Each nation has been made to look with an invidious eye upon the prosperity of all the nations with which it trades, and to consider their gain as its own loss. Commerce, which ought naturally to be, among nations, as among individuals, a bond of union and friendship, has become the most fertile source of discord and animosity. The capricious ambition of kings and ministers has not, during the present and the preceding century, been more fatal to the repose of Europe, than the impertinent jealousy of merchants and manufacturers. The violence and injustice of the rulers of mankind is an ancient evil, for which, I am afraid, the nature of human affairs can scarce admit of a remedy. But the mean rapacity, the monopolizing spirit of merchants and manufacturers, who neither are, nor

ought to be, the rulers of mankind, though it cannot perhaps be corrected, may very easily be prevented from disturbing the tranquility of any body but themselves. (p. 460)

It is not surprising, then, that Smith has little use for a government of businessmen:

The government of an exclusive company of merchants is, perhaps, the worst of all governments for any country whatever. (p. 537)

In sum, there should be no doubt about Smith's strong distrust of the ethics of businessmen and their dedication to their social responsibilities.

2. The Invisible Hand and Business Virtue

We have no reason to attribute Smith's vehemence to personal animosity. On the contrary, John Rae in his biography tells us that Smith befriended the Glasgow merchants and manufacturers and apparently learned a great deal from them about current business practices. (Rae pp. 90–95) There is no hint that he had any unpleasant dealings with businessmen even in his role as collector of customs, a post Smith held in Edinburgh for the last twelve years of his life, and one which he seems to have taken very serously.[2]

A much more straightforward explanation is provided in *The Wealth of Nations*. One of the central themes of the book, which is emphasized from its very beginning, is that it is a serious mistake to entrust the economic welfare of society to the good intentions of *any* man. What better way to emphasize this point than to remind us repeatedly of the moral frailty of the group most likely to acquire power over the economy. In a celebrated passage at the beginning of Chapter 2, Smith admonishes us not to rely on anyone's good intentions for the benefits we hope to obtain from the economy:

... man has almost constant occasion for the help of his brethren, and it is in vain for him to expect it from their benevolence only. He will be more likely to prevail if he can interest their self-love in his favour, and shew them that it is for their own advantage to do for him what he requires of them. Whoever offers to another a bargain of any kind, proposes to do this. Give me that which I want, and you shall have this which you want, is the meaning of every such offer; and it is in this manner that we obtain from one another the far greater part of those good offices which we stand in need of. It is not from the benevolence of the butcher, the brewer, or the baker, that we expect our dinner, but from their regard to their own interest. We address ourselves, not to their humanity but to their self-love, and never talk to them of our own necessities but of their advantages. (p. 14)

The passage already suggests the view that reaches its most dramatic expression in the invisible hand passage—the doctrine that self-interest, properly channeled, is a much more reliable protector of the public interest than is any arrangement dependent upon the personal morality of the decision maker. This is the central message of the paragraph on the invisible hand. There, in some of his most telling phrases, Smith tells us how wary we must be of the businessman's committment to his "social responsibilities:"

As every individual endeavours as much as he can ... to employ his capital ... that its produce may be of the greatest value; every individual necessarily labours to render the annual revenue of the society as great as he can. He generally, indeed, neither intents to promote the public interest, nor knows how much he is promoting it .., by directing that industry in such a manner as its produce may be of the greatest value, he intends only his own gain, and he is in this, as in many other cases, led by an invisible hand to promote an end which was no part of his intention. Nor is it always the worse for the society that it was no part of it. By pursuing his own interest he frequently promotes that of the society more effectually than when he really intends to promote it. *I have never known much good done by those who affected to trade for the public good. It is an affectation, indeed, not very common among merchants, and very few words need be employed in dissuading them from it.* (p. 423, my italics)

The point in all this is *not* just that individual virtue, both that of businessmen *and of others*,[3] is untrustworthy, but that there is available a better means, the market mechanism, in which society *can* put its trust. The market mechanism does not merely curb human frailty and prevent its unfortunate effects. Rather it turns matters about

completely, putting that frailty to work in the service of the general welfare. He goes so far as to assert that it succeeds in making the individual do "as much as he can" to promote the general interest.

Moreover, it is no accident that the businessman seeks to subvert this beneficient process. The market mechanism, and its competitive instrument, is a harsh taskmaker—it can impose painful pressures upon the business firm.[4] That is precisely why management can be expected to use every means it can to subvert the process, to conspire against the public, to seek to replace competition by monopoly [which removes from them the pressures for efficiency of operation—(p. 447)].

3. The Invisible Hand as Instrument of Providence[5]

We are inclined nowadays to treat the invisible hand as mere metaphore; but there is some reason to believe that in Smith's mind it was much more than that. Though he occasionally found himself at odds with representatives of the religious establishment (particularly over his friendship with Hume, the skeptic, who took great pleasure in baiting the church), Smith was a theist who believed deeply in the role of God. (Rae, pp. 129, 429–30). *In The Theory of Moral Sentiments*, the Deity is involved frequently and plays an important part in the discussion. In particular, there is one passage (not otherwise germaine to our discussion) in which the invisible hand makes its appearance, and there seems little question that at that point it is the hand of God:

"[The rich] are led *by an invisible hand* to make nearly the same distribution of the necessaries of life, which would have been made, had the earth been divided into equal portions among all its inhabitants, and thus without intending it, advance the interest of the society, and offer a means to the multiplication of the species. *When Providence divided the earth among a few lordly masters, it neither forgot nor abandoned those who seemed to have been left out in the partition.*" (p. 163, my italics)[6]

Now, in a relatively early paper, Viner points out that Adam Smith of *The Theory of Moral Sentiments* does not always hold the same views as the author of *The Wealth of Nations*.[7] However, that does not preclude the possibility that the invisible hand of the two volumes was the same.[8] In his earlier discussion Viner maintained that

"... the emphasis in *The Theory of Moral Sentiments*, upon a benevolent deity as the author and guide of nature is almost, though not quite, completely absent in *The Wealth of Nations*" [1927 p. 221]. However, by 1966 he seems to have changed his mind on this score:

"Modern professors of economics and of ethics operate in disciplines which have been secularized to the point where the religious elements and implications which once were an integral part of them have been painstakingly eliminated ... [H]owever, I am obliged to insist that Adam Smith's system of thought, including his economics, is not intelligible if one disregards the role he assigns in it to the theological elements, to the 'invisible hand'." [11, pp. 81–2]

The point in all this is that it suggests an interpretation of the free enterprise system as an instrument of the Diety designed to curb the frailty of humanity. It is, as it were, a second-best solution, which not merely can undo the mischief that might be produced by the avarice that has afflicted humanity since the fall of man. Rather, it turns that avarice against itself, transforming it into a prime instrument of public virtue. It is a device adopted by a very practical Providence to deal with the unfortunate but very real weakness of human character.

However, whether or not God plays the role in the analysis that I have surmised, the general point seems valid enough. To Smith of *The Wealth of Nations* man in general, and the businessman in particular, is morally weak and untrustworthy. Some rules of the game must therefore be instituted to protect society from the individual. The free enterprise system, whatever the instrument of its design, is a superb mechanism for the purpose. That is the essence of the relationship between the businessman and the free enterprise system as envisaged by Smith.

4. The Marxian Inversion

It is noteworthy that in the Marxian analysis the relative moral positions of the businessman and business enterprise are nearly reversed. Taken as a person, the entrepreneur is not particularly evil (or particularly virtuous). Not that Marx approves of business behavior. One example will suffice to dispell any doubts on that score:

"... the prodigality of the capitalist never possesses the bona-fide character of the open-handed feudal lord's prodigality, but, on the contrary, has always lurking behind it the most sordid avarice and the most anxious calculation ... [The early capitalists] enriched themselves chiefly by robbing the parents, whose children were bound as apprentices to them: the parents paid a high premium, while the apprentices were starved." (*Capital*, Vol. I, p. 651)

Yet to Marx, an historical materialist, the capitalist did evil deeds not because he was born or raised to be a moral cripple but because the material circumstances left him no choice:

And so far only is the necessity for his own transitory existence implied in the transitory necessity for the capitalist mode of production ... Fanatically bent on making value expand itself, he ruthlessly forces the human race to produce for production's sake; he thus forces the development of the productive powers of society, and creates those material conditions, which alone can form the real basis of a higher form of society, a society in which the full and free development of every individual forms the ruling principle. Only as personified capital is the capitalist respectable. As such, he shares with the miser the passion for wealth as wealth. *But that which in the miser is a mere idiosyncrasy, is, in the capitalist, the effect of the social mechanism, of which he is but one of the wheels.* (Volume I, p. 649, my italics).

That is to say, historical forces give the capitalists no choice, be they as morally pure and discerning as Friedrich Engels, the Manufacturer of Barmen and Manchester. Had the accident of inheritance reversed the roles of a particular proletarian and a particular capitalist, the former would readily have fallen into the role of exploiter and the latter would have assumed that of victim.

The doctrine of historical materialism is often misunderstood as naive economic interpretation — as the view that every human action is to be considered the product of careful calculation of self interest. Perhaps this may be true of some recent writings by *non* Marxist economists on the economics of crime, race discrimination and marriage, but it certainly is *not* true of Marx. In his historical materialism economic influences usually exert final control, but often in a subtle manner and at second remove. Human personality does play an important role in history, but the scope for its action is provided by historical circumstances, and the personality itself is heavily influenced by historical conditions.[9]

Moreover, in different historical circumstances, the social implications of the capitalist's role will vary correspondingly. Thus, Marx emphasized consistently that the capitalist was not always the embodiment of reaction. From *The Communist Manifesto* (1847) to *The Critique of the Gotha Program* (1875) Marx reiterated that "the bourgeoisie is . . . a revolutionary class—as the bearer of large-scale industry—relatively to the feudal lords and the lower middle class, who desire to maintain all social positions that are the creation of obsolete modes of production." (*Critique of the Gotha Program*, Comment 4).

Thus, in Marx, the capitalist, with all his crimes, is not the product of a warped morality, but of a set of circumstances that give him no choice. In Smith he is an inherently immoral man whom the capitalist system is designed to restrain. In Marx he is neither inherently moral nor immoral. It is the stage of history that brings capital (rather than the the capitalist) into the world "dripping from head to foot, from every pore, with blood and dirt" (Vol. I, p. 834)

Conclusions

In summary, the difference in the treatment of the capitalist by the two writers reflects both the difference in their view of history and the difference in the purpose of their major works. To Smith even "the early and rude state of society" in which labor is the only scarce resource is a sort of primitive free enterprise system, albeit one without capitalists or landlords. For it is the market mechanism that presumably drives relative prices of deer and beaver into equality with the relative amounts of labor required to hunt them. Thus, Smith's economic history is a progression from a simple to a complex market system, but it is a history in which the institution is permanent, and its workings can be permanently beneficient if they are not subjected to unwise interference which unchains the selfishness of humanity and permits it to do harm to the community rather than working for the public benefit.

To Marx on the other hand, the capitalist system is a transitory phenomenon, and like every other stage in history it makes its people what they are.

The capitalist is not without his virtues—he is a Schumpeterian entrepreneur[10] to be admired for his dynamism of creativity, but he is also a ruthless exploiter. But neither his virtues nor his vices are to be attributed to him alone, for they are ultimately to be ascribed to the stage of society that has created his role. His activities can be redirected to serve the general welfare more effectively, and he himself can be made into a better man, but this can be done only by another historical stage, the communist society that was Marx's goal.[11]

Notes

1. Besides Smith's long discussion, in Book V, of the appropriate general functions of government as the provision of national defense, the administration of justice and the supply of public services, he recognizes explicitly the role of externalities and the justification they provide for governmental intervention. In a passage proposing restrictions on banking practices of which economists were recently reminded by Lord Robbins, Smith wrote: ". . . those exertions of the natural liberty of a few individuals, which might endanger the security of the whole society, are, and ought to be, restrained by the laws of all governments: of the most free, as well as of the most despotical. The obligation of building party walls, in order to prevent the communication of fire, is a violation of natural liberty, exactly of the same kind with the regulations of the banking trade which are here proposed" (p. 308).

2. Indeed, the only person with whom Smith clearly seems to have been involved in a personal clash was Samuel Johnson. Their dislike was apparently mutual and instantanous, though matters seem eventually to have healed. See Rae pp. 35, 154–58, 366.

3. Thus recall Smith's delightful discussion of the dangers of paying university teachers stipends, that do not vary with the number of students they are able to attract, as in 18th century Oxford where " . . . the greater part of the public professors have, for these many years, given up altogether even the pretense of teaching." (p. 718). Note also Smith's quotation of Hume's plea for an exception in the case of churchmen who will be led, if they are paid by results to seek to attract parishioners by appealing to ". . . superstition, folly, and delusion. Each ghostly practitioner, in order to render himself more precious and sacred in the eyes of his retainers . . . [will pay] no regard . . . to truth, morals, or decency in the doctrines inculcated." (p. 743) Thus the market mechanism *can* sometimes backfire.

4. "Their [merchants'] competition might perhaps ruin some of themselves; but to take care of this is the business of the parties concerned, and it may safely be trusted to their discretion. It can never hurt either the consumer, or the producer; on the contrary, it must tend to make the retailers both sell cheaper and buy dearer . . ." (p. 342–43).

5. This section obviously relies heavily on Viner [10]. However, its conclusions are not quite the same as Viner's, as will be noted presently.

6. Quoted in Viner [1927] p. 219.

7. For example, the rejection in the latter volume of benevolence as a reliable source of public welfare is in direct conflict with the basic theme of the former.

8. Perhaps it is suggestive that in the famous passage in *The Wealth of Nations* Smith says that the individual "is . . . led *by* an invisible hand" not "led *as though* by an invisible hand." (my italics)

9. See E. G.; G. Plekhanov, "*The Role of the Individual in History*," Plekhanov discusses at length various noteworthy historical cases to show that even the most accidental events assume their importance from current historical (economic) conditions, and that the long-run influence of such accidental events is usually minimal. Thus, for example he points out "In 1789, Davout, Désaix, Marmont and MacDonald were subalterns; Bernadotte was a sergeant-major; Hoche, Marceau, Lefebre, Pichegru, Ney, Massena, Murat and Soult were non-commissioned officers; Augereau was a fencing master; Lannes was a dyer; Gouvion Saint-Cyr was an actor; Jourdan was a peddler, Bessièrs was a barber; Brune was a compositor; Joubert and Junot were law students; Kleber was an architect; Martier did not see any military service until the Revolution.

Had the old order continued to exist until our day it would never have occurred to any of us that in France, at the end of the last [the 18th] century, certain actors, compositors, barbers, dyers, lawyers, peddlers and fencing masters had been potential military geniuses." (p. 170)

Marx himself never discussed historical materialism at any length or very systematically. That is why so few quotations from Marx have been offered in this section.

10. The Schumpertian process is described in *Capital* very explicitly. Thus note the following passage: ". . . the surplus-profit, which some individual capital may ordinarily realize in its particular sphere of production . . . [is] due, aside from accidental deviations, to a reduction of the cost-price . . . [which arises from] better methods of labor, new inventions, improved machinery, chemical secrets in manufacture, etc., in short, new and improved means of production and methods . . . a circumstance which is neutral-

ized as soon as the exceptional method of production becomes general or is superseded by a still more developed one. . ." (Vol. III, pp. 754–5)

11. See *Critique of the Gotha Program*, comment 3.
cf. also *Grundrisse* p. 610 ff for Marx's view on the role and burdensomeness of labor under varying historical circumstances.

References

1. Marx, Karl, *Capital* Chicago: Charles H. Kerr and Co. Vol. I (1906); Vols. II and III (1909).

2. ———, *A Contribution to the Critique of Political Economy* N. I. Stone, Trans., Chicago: Charles H. Kerr and Co., 1904.

3. ———, *Critique of the Gotha Program*, Moscow: Progress Publishing, 1937.

4. *Grundrisse*, (Martin Nicolaus, Trans., ed.) Harmondsworth: Penguin Books, 1973.

5. ——— and Friedrich Engels, *The Manifesto of the Communist Party*

6. Plekhanov, G. V., *The Role of the Individual in History*, in Plekhanov, G. V., *Fundamental Problems of Marxism*, New York: International Publishers, 1969.

7. Rae, John, *Life of Adam Smith* London, Macmillan, 1895.

8. Smith, Adam, *Theory of Moral Sentiments*, Ward Lock & Co: London, n.d.

9. ———, *Wealth of Nations*, Cannan Edition, New York: The Modern Library, 1937.

10. Viner, Jacob, "Adam Smith and Laissez Faire", *Journal of Political Economy*, 35, April 1927 pp. 198–232, reprinted in Jacob Viner, *The Long View and The Short*, Glencoe, Illinois: Free Press, 1958 pp. 213–45.

11. ———, *The Role of Providence in the Social Order*, Philadelphia, American Philosophical Society, 1972.

[15]

On Marx, the Transformation Problem and Opacity

Editor's Note: *Few articles in the history of the* JEL *have stirred the controversy that Paul A. Samuelson's "Understanding the Marxian Notion of Exploitation: A Summary of the So-called Transformation Problem between Marxian Values and Competitive Prices,"* J. Econ. Lit., *June 1971, 9 (2), pp. 399–431, did. We have already had one "terminal" discussion of the reaction—Bronfenbrenner, M. "Samuelson, Marx, and Their Latest Critics," and "Samuelson's 'Reply on Marxian Matters',"* J. Econ. Lit., *March 1973, 11 (1), pp. 59–63. Professor Baumol has found a history of thought approach to the topic which deserves the attention of all economists who have an interest in Marx, Marxism, or the evolution of classical economic thought. We print his essay here. Professor Samuelson sought to comment on Baumol's work, and we give his views, as well. In the course of Samuelson's reply, he "took on" Professor Morishima, who quite naturally wanted to add a few words of further explanation. We have finally allowed Professors Baumol and Samuelson to share in what we hope are the "last words."* M.P.

The Transformation of Values: What Marx "Really" Meant (An Interpretation)

By WILLIAM J. BAUMOL

Princeton and New York Universities

I would like to thank the students in my seminar on doctrinal history at Princeton University whose discussions contributed greatly to the ideas in this paper. I am also grateful to Elizabeth Bailey, Fritz Machlup, Michio Morishima and Paul Samuelson for their very helpful comments on earlier drafts of this paper. I am particularly indebted to Professor Samuelson for an extensive, illuminating and delightful correspondence on the subject.

THIS PAPER will suggest that the meaning of the relationship between values and prices described in *Capital* has been widely misunderstood. Commentators as eminent as Mrs. Robinson and Professor Samuelson have sought in the transformation discussion issues which Karl Marx never meant it to contain. Writers on "the transformation problem" since L. Bortkiewicz have focussed on an issue that is largely peripheral; and others like E. Böhm-Bawerk have asserted that there is a contradiction between the analyses of Volumes I and III which is certainly not to be found there unless 1ne reads into them an interpretation different from that which Marx repeatedly emphasized.

Interpretation of the intentions of the writings of the dead is always a questionable undertaking, particularly since defunct authors cannot defend themselves. Yet there are some cases in which a careful rereading of the pertinent writings indicates that the author *did* speak for himself and spoke very clearly—the trouble in such cases seems to be that something about the original presentation prevents most readers, even some very careful ones, from seeing what the writer intended.[1]

A notable case in point is D. Ricardo's discussion of the labor theory of value. It is hard to understand how a careful reader of any edition of the *Principles* can overlook Ricardo's recognition of the role of the quantity and the durability of capital in the determination of price. The labor theory is explicitly proposed as a remarkably good approximation to the determination of competitive price. But, ultimately, Ricardo holds to a cost of production theory of pricing, not to a pure labor theory. Yet until Stigler's fine article on the subject (1958),[2] in which this is documented beyond any shadow of a doubt, virtually any text was prepared to ascribe to Ricardo the purest of labor theories, and even J. H. Hollander and E. Cannan (see G. J. Stigler for references) suggested that Ricardo retreated grudgingly under fire to the cost of production model of the third edition. Only a few commentators, notably A. Marshall, J. Viner, and P. Sraffa, saw Ricardo's analysis for what it so plainly was from the first edition on.[3]

I emphasize this case for two reasons; first, because I will try to show that the correct interpreta-

tion of Marx' intentions is equally evident, and second, because I will suggest that the false analogy between Ricardo's and Marx' value theories may help to explain our misunderstanding of the latter.

Marx' Interpretation of the Transformation Problem: Summary

In Ricardo, the labor theory of value *was* meant as a good approximation to a full explanation of the determination of prices. However Marx probably never intended to produce such an approximation and it certainly was not his intention when he wrote about the transformation problem; yet that objective, or something close to it, is often attributed to Marx.

I will provide evidence that Marx did not intend his transformation analysis to show how prices can be *deduced* from values. Marx was well aware that market prices do not have to be deduced from values (nor, for that matter, values from prices). Rather, the two sets of magnitudes which are derived more or less[4] independently were recognized by Marx to differ in a substantial and a systematic manner.[5] A subsidiary purpose of the transformation calculation was to determine the nature of these deviations. But this objective and, indeed, any explanation of pricing as an end in itself, was of very little consequence to Marx, for the primary transformation was not from values into prices but, as Marx and Engels repeatedly emphasize, from *surplus* values into the non-labor income categories that are recognized by "vulgar economists," *i.e.,* profits, interest, and rent.

Thus we must surely reexamine the implications of Samuelson's conclusion:

> The truth has now been laid bare. Stripped of logical complication and confusion, anybody's method of solving the famous transformation problem is seen to involve returning from the unnecessary detour taken in Volume I's analysis of values. . . . [S]uch a "transformation" is precisely like that in which an eraser is used to rub out an earlier entry, after which we make a new start to end up with the properly calculated entry [13, 1971, p. 421].

---

[1] I must emphasize that it is not the purpose of this paper to attack or defend the substance of Marx' transformation discussion or to argue the significance of the insights it offers. This issue can be discussed profitably only after clarification of the content of his analysis—which is the only objective of this article.

[2] Obviously, I disagree emphatically with Samuelson's judgment that "It is a sad reflection on the decadence of literary economics that so much printer's ink has been wasted on the sterile and ambiguous question of whether Ricardo had or didn't have a labor theory of value, or a 93 percent labor theory, or . . ." [13, 1971, p. 405]. If an author speaks for himself as clearly as Ricardo did, it is surely more appropriate to discuss what he did say than what some commentator has somehow inferred he ought to have said.

[3] For references on these matters, see Stigler [15, 1958]. Note that Marx himself understood Ricardo correctly on this issue. Thus in a letter to Engels dated July 6, 1863, Marx wrote "You know that according to *Adam Smith the 'natural' or 'necessary price'* is composed of wages, profit (interest), rent. . . . This nonsense was taken over by Ricardo, although he excludes rent, as merely accidental. . . ." (Marx' italics.) All translations, unless otherwise noted, are taken from [8, 1956]. The preceding quotation appears on p. 174.

I have chosen to follow the published translations of the correspondence, which seem to be reasonably accurate. In a few cases some of the English phrases that Marx scattered through his letters have been edited by the translator.

[4] Not entirely, since labor time (Marxian value) is a technological datum which enters the determination of cost and, hence, competitive price.

[5] R. L. Meek [9, 1956] and M. Morishima [10, 1973, Chapter 7] in my view may be the only current authors who have described the transformation problem correctly.

Colloquium: On Marx, the Transformation Problem   53

I will argue that this conclusion represents no real conflict with Marx' intentions, as Samuelson seems to suggest. Marx knew perfectly well that price determination can be explained in terms of the competitive process by itself, just as the classical economists had done, so that if the objective were an analysis of pricing, Volume I would indeed represent an "unnecessary detour." But Marx' interests were not focused on price theory, and as I will show, he was well aware that competitive prices can be deduced without prior recourse to Marxian values.

My contention is that Marx' interest in the transformation analysis as a sequel to his value theory was not a matter of pricing. Rather it sought to describe how *non* wage incomes are *produced* and then how this aggregate is *redistributed,* the first of these being the substantive issue to Marx and the one he discusses in Volume I, while the latter is the surface manifestation known to all bourgeois economists and which Marx only deigns to consider in Volume III.

The substance of Marx' analysis can be summarized in a simple parable, in which the economy is described as an aggregation of industries each of which contributes to a storehouse containing total surplus value. The contribution of each industry is its total output minus the consumption of its labor force. If we use labor units to measure these quantities, each industry's contribution is proportionate to the quantity of labor it uses, for reasons to be noted in a later footnote. This, then, is how society's surplus value is *produced.*

The *distribution* of society's surplus value from the central storehouse now takes place via the competitive process which assigns to each industry for profit, interest payment, and rent an amount strictly proportionate to its capital investment. This is the heart of the transformation process—the conversion of surplus value into profit, interest, and rent. It takes from each according to its work force, and returns to each according to its total investment.

The object of the discussion of the conversion of surplus value into "average profit" is then straightforward. Given the contribution of some one industry to the social surplus (as described by the value analysis) and the largely independent determination of that same industry's withdrawals in the form of profits, interest payments, and rent, the question is how those two compare. Put another way, the question is, under what circumstances will a given industry withdraw more than it has contributed, and when will the reverse be true?

This is a question which cannot, I believe, be answered with the aid of an eraser. Marx proposed part of the answer, but his argument for even that portion was incomplete. Morishima, (especially pp. 80–84) in his excellent book, is, as far as I know, the first to have supplied a careful answer [10, 1973].

The Value Theory Reconsidered

In Volume I, Marx does occasionally speak of values as if they were meant to approximate prices. For example, he asserts "It is true, commodities may be sold at prices deviating from their values, but those deviations are to be considered as infractions of the laws of the exchange of commodities . . . ."[6] He goes on to describe these deviations as "temporary" ascribing them to "Market disturbances." However, his comments must be interpreted in context: at this point Marx is merely arguing that profits or surplus values cannot be *ascribed* to a process of inflation of prices above values since in such a universal inflation no one can gain. His language at such points generally seems to be explainable primarily in terms of his expository objectives. Certainly by the time we come to Volume III, values and prices are clearly dissociated, with "cost prices" based on equality of rates of return on investment in different industries.

There seem to be three plausible ways to account for the distinction between the role of value in the two volumes. The first is that Marx originally intended his values as equilibrium relative prices and only retreated from this position when he began to realize it was untenable, doing his best to explain away his retreat as a planned regrouping of his forces.[7] This view has been implied by a number of writers.[8] The second and more common interpretation is that Marx intended the value theory as a simplified approximation to the correct analysis

---

[6] Volume I. [6, 1906], Chapter V, pp. 176–77—all references to *Capital* are to the Charles Kerr edition.

[7] R. Hilferding (p. 155) seems to ascribe this view to Böhm-Bawerk but I have not been able to find any such assertion by the latter. Böhm-Bawerk does assert that there is an irreconcilable contradiction between the value theory of Volume I and the price theory of Volume III (p. 29 and Chapter III in general). However, he does not attempt to account for its origin [2, Böhm-Bawerk, 1949].

[8] For an illustrative reference see Sweezy [16, 1942, p. 111].

of prices (somewhat in the manner of Ricardo) and that the transformation calculation of Volume III is his way of producing the appropriate correction.[9] The third explanation, which I suspect is the correct one, is that the value theory was never intended as a theory of price, which, as a superficial manifestation of the bourgeois economy, Marx considered worth very little attention, but was instead designed to explain something to him far more fundamental: the process of production, *i.e.,* the extraction of surplus values in the various sectors of the economy.

Turning to the first of the hypotheses, we cannot hope to prove that Marx never changed his mind on the relation of his values to prices. But we do know that at least half a decade before the completion of the preface to Volume I his views of the transformation problem were quite fully formed. A letter from Marx to Engels, written five years before the publication of Volume I, provides a clear statement of the transformation problem and Marx' proposed solution.[10] Moreover, Engels tells us that

---

[9] See M. Bronfenbrenner [3, 1973] where Marx' "approximation" is explicitly likened to Ricardo's. P. M. Sweezy also argues in a way that tempts the reader to impute this position to him:

> It is perfectly legitimate to postulate a capitalist system in which organic compositions of capital are everywhere equal and hence the law of value does hold. . . . Whether or not this procedure is valid . . . must be tested by dropping the assumption. . . . [I]n Volume III [Marx] abandons this assumption and attempts to show that, from the point of view of the problems which he was attempting to solve, the modifications which result are of a relatively minor character. (*Ibid,* p. 70.)

However, in a very helpful letter to me, Sweezy rejects this interpretation of his views:

> I never had any inclination to accept what you call the "second and more common interpretation . . . that Marx intended the value theory as a simplified approximation to the correct analysis of prices." On certain assumptions, most importantly equal organic compositions of capital, value theory was *also* a valid price theory; but of course Marx never for a moment entertained the notion that the equal organic compositions assumption was realistic, from which it follows that for him the notion of values "approximating" prices was nonsense.

[10] For example, Marx writes in this letter:

> . . . with *equal* exploitation of the worker in *different* trades, different capitals of the *same size* will yield very *different* amounts of surplus value in different spheres of production and therefore *very*

"Volume III . . . was written for the greater part in 1864 and 1865" (Preface to Volume II, p. 9), that is, two years before the appearance of Volume I.[11] In fact, in that same place Engels states Marx had reached his solution "even in his manuscript for His 'Critique of Political Economy' " on which Marx had worked in the 1850's (p. 28).[12]

But substance rather than tedious arguments about dating is our real purpose here. Later, I will show explicitly that what Marx had revealed in his Volume III analysis of price he considered to be no improvement over his Volume I analysis of value. On the contrary, from his point of view the price analysis of Volume III dealt with the "outward

---

> *different rates of profit,* since profit is nothing but the proportion of the surplus value to the total capital advanced. This will depend on the *organic composition* of the capital, *i.e.,* on how it is divided into constant and variable capital. . . . And capitalists are brothers. Competition (transfer of capital or withdrawal of capital from one trade to another) brings it about that *equal sums* of capital in *different* trades, despite their different organic compositions, yield the *same average* rate of profit. In other words: the *average* profit which a capital of £100, for instance, yields in a certain trade it yields not as the capital employed in this particular way, nor in the proportion, therefore, in which it itself produces surplus value, but as an *aliquot part* of the aggregate capital of the capitalist class. It is a share on which, in proportion to its size, dividends are paid from the total sum of surplus value (or unpaid labour) which the total variable capital (laid out in wages) of the class produces [8, 1956, pp. 158–59, Marx' italics].

[11] On p. 209 of Volume III in a footnote, Engels explicitly dates at least that portion of the transformation discussion as 1865.

A bit of chronology may be helpful in following the dating issue.

Marx' preface to Volume I is dated July 24, 1867. The letter telling Engels he had finally finished reading proof for the volume is dated 2 A.M., August 16, 1867. There are at least four letters in which Marx and Engels discuss the transformation problem. The first is dated August 2, 1862, five years before the publication of Volume I. There is an exchange dated June 26 and June 27, 1867, written while Marx and Engels were reading proof for the volume and one dated April 30, 1868, less than one year after publication of Volume I [8, 1956].

Quotations from all four letters are offered later in this paper. They show clearly that there was no significant change in Marx' position on the subject over the period.

[12] Hilferding and Sweezy are among those who have previously pointed out that Marx had worked through the transformation issue before Volume I was published. See Hilferding [2, 1949, p. 155] and Sweezy [16, 1942, p. 111fn].

Colloquium: On Marx, the Transformation Problem 55

disguise" assumed by the subject of his discussion. Only the analysis of the relation of profit and surplus value permitted "the actual state of things [to be] revealed for the first time" (Vol. III, Chapter IX, p. 199). Thus Marx tells us he had something more in mind than mere revision of the value theory in accord with the workings of competitive equilibrating forces.

One must also reject the assertion that Marx thought prices had to be *deduced* from values via his transformation calculation. Marx knew very well that his "prices of production" were the same as the "natural values" of classical economics. He apparently ascribes to Malthus the basic observation underlying their construction: "The theoretical conception . . . according to which every part of the capital yields uniformly the same profit. . . ." [6, 1909, Vol. III, Chapter IX, p. 200; see also, Chapter I, pp. 48–49]. In his first letter on the transformation problem (1862), Marx is quite explicit on the identity of his prices with the classical prices based on cost of production: "*Price* regulated in this way [*i.e.*, via the transformation process] = the expenses of capital + the average profit . . . is what Smith calls the *natural price, cost price*, etc." (p. 160, Marx' italics). Thus, he does *not* accuse the classical authors of having erred in deducing their price relationships without using Marxian values in the process. Rather, the charge repeatedly reasserted is that they dealt only with "this form of appearance."

Prices and values are, in short, not the same thing. Values are not approximations to prices nor a necessary step in their calculation. Rather, one is a surface manifestation, while the latter is intended to reveal an underlying reality. But what are these values and what is their rationale?

An Interpretation of Marxian Values

T. B. Veblen calls to our attention a mystery which no one since seems to have attempted to clear up. Veblen writes

It is scarcely worth while to question what serves as the beginning of wisdom in the current criticisms of Marx; namely, that he offers no adequate proof of his labor-value theory. It is even safe to go farther, and say that he offers no proof of it. The feint which occupies the opening paragraphs of the *Kapital* and the corresponding passages of *Zur Kritik*, etc., is not to be taken seriously as an attempt to prove his position on this head by the ordinary recourse to

argument. It is rather a self-satisfied superior's playful mystification of those readers (critics) whose limited powers do not enable them to see that his proposition is self-evident [17, 1919, pp. 419–20].

This failure to attempt any rationalization should be evident to anyone who rereads carefully the few pages in Volume I that are ostensibly devoted to an explanation of the workings of his value theory. (See especially Chapter I, section 1, pp. 44–46.)

Now, this lacuna seems strange in light of two facts: Marx' near-talmudic skill in conducting an argument and his avowed intention to write *Capital* in as prolix a style as possible.[13] If Marx had in mind or felt he needed some substitute for the competitive mechanism in the Ricardian analysis of prices, why does he not bring it out? In the discussion of values such a mechanism is never mentioned while, by contrast, it plays a clear and explicit role in the determination of prices in Volume III and in the justification of the premise that the rate of surplus value tends to be equal in all industries.[14]

Presumably, the reason Marx attempts no rationalization of his theory of value is, in Veblen's words, that at least to him it was "self-evident."[15] This

---

[13] Letter to Engels, June 18, 1862. "I am stretching out this volume, since those German dogs estimate the value of books by their cubic contents" [8, 1956, p. 156].

[14] The argument for the equality of rates of surplus values in all industries is straightforward, and applies only to a capitalist economy in which labor is free to move. On Marx' assumption (which is shared by Ricardo as well as J. von Neumann, R. Solow, H. Uzawa and many other contemporary writers) that labor is homogeneous and receives equal wages and if all work is equally unpleasant, the working day in all industries must tend to equality, for otherwise workers would move from industries with long working days to those in which working days are shorter. With working days everywhere equal, total value production per laborer (measured in hours of "socially necessary labor") must also be equal. Subtract from this in every industry the same subsistence wage (also measured in value units), and we are left with the same surplus value per worker everywhere. (See Volume III, p. 206.)

[15] In his *Critique of political economy*, the fragment published eight years before Volume I of *Capital*, Marx stated explicitly that he took his value theory to be a tautology:

Since the exchange value of commodities is, in fact, nothing but a mutual relation of the labours of individuals . . . it is a tautology to say that labour is the *only* source of exchange value and consequently of wealth, in so far as the latter consists of exchange values. Similarly, it is a tautology to say that matter in its natural state has no exchange value, because it does not contain any labour. . . . (pp. 31–2, Marx' italics). In other words, "ex-

value theory was intended to explain the gestation, *i.e.*, the production of total surplus value, describing the contribution of each activity in the economy to that total. The tautology used by Marx in this explanation is that each industry contributes to the total surplus its entire output minus the amount used up in supporting labor. The part of the assertion that is not tautological or self-evident is that the "freedom" (mobility) of labor, which Marx stresses so heavily in Volume I as a prerequisite of the historical stage of capitalist production, guarantees a tendency toward equality of surplus value per laborer in every industry, when value is measured in terms of labor.

Moreover, as is now generally recognized, certainly the determination of the magnitudes of the values is straightforward on the Ricardo-Marx-Leontief assumption of fixed production coefficients. To summarize the standard interpretation of the matter as described, *e.g.*, by Morishima, a set of input-output equations can be used to express the value of each output as the amount of labor used directly in its production plus the amount of labor used up indirectly in the form of capital ("congealed labor"), where that indirect labor component is determined by the unit values of the capital inputs.[16]

These values are entirely determined by technological relationships and, under the simple fixed coefficient assumptions shared by both modern and classical models, are entirely independent of pricing.[17] That is, the input-output formulation of the problem puts to rest Joan Robinson's suggestion [11, 1959, p. 362] that ". . . the *values* which have to be 'transformed into prices' are arrived at in the first instance by transforming prices into values."

Values into Prices or Surplus Values into Profits?

Let us turn now to the textual evidence for the preceding discussion. If the interpretation proposed

here is valid, Marx was concerned primarily with the relationship between profits and surplus value and only incidentally (as a means to get at the former) with that between prices and values. As a first piece of evidence, I reproduce in full Engels' famous challenge in the preface to Volume II, the first public statement of the transformation problem, in which it will be noted that the word "price" does not appear even once:

> According to the Ricardian law of value, two capitals employing the same and equally paid labor, all other conditions being equal, produce the same value and surplus-value, or profit, in the same time. But if they employ unequal quantities of actual labor, they cannot produce equal surplus-values, or, as the Ricardians say, equal profits. Now in reality, the exact opposite takes place. As a matter of fact, equal capitals, regardless of the quantity of actual labor employed by them, produce equal average profits in equal times. Here we have, therefore, a clash with the law of value, which had been noticed by Ricardo himself, but which his school was unable to reconcile. Rodbertus likewise could not but note this contradiction. But instead of solving it, he made it a starting point of his utopia (Zur Erkenntniss, etc.). Marx had solved this contradiction even in his manuscript for his "CRITIQUE OF POLITICAL ECONOMY."
>
> According to the plan of "CAPITAL," this solution will be made public in Volume III. Several months will pass before this can be published. Hence those economists, who claim to have discovered that Rodbertus is the secret source and the superior predecessor of Marx, have now an opportunity to demonstrate what the economics of Rodbertus can accomplish. If they can show in which way an equal average rate of profit can and must come about, not only without a violation of the law of value, but by means of it, I am willing to discuss the matter further with them (Vol. II, pps. 27–8).[18]

Turning to Marx' own words, we notice that he entitled the two books in Volume III that are devoted to the subject "Part I: The Conversion of Surplus-value into Profit and of the Rate of Surplus-

---

change value" is, *by definition*, related to labor content, and consequently not necessarily the same as price [5,1904].

[16] For an explicit discussion of this construction, see Morishima, [10, 1973, Chapter 1]. Of course, this interpretation also appears in various other writings.

[17] Note also that by treating the training of labor as investment in human capital it removes any difficulty of comparing the value contribution of different *qualities* of labor. When the coefficients of production of different types of labor are constant, the Ricardian and Marxian treatment of an hour of skilled labor as several hours of unskilled labor, with their ratio based on relative training costs, runs into no logical difficulty.

[18] In a letter to me Samuelson writes:

> By the way, Engels' 'challenge' is absurd; there was no 1830's crisis of the Ricardian system; there was no contradiction in it, for as you remind people, when Ricardo is not assuming the labor theory of value he is not assuming it and there is no reason why such cases should not disagree with the labor-theory-of-value cases. . . . When you revise your paper you might point this out.

value into the Rate of Profit" and "Part II: Conversion of Profit into Average Profit." Pricing is again not mentioned. It is true that in Chapter IX of Part II he does get around to dealing with prices and says so in the title "Formation of a General Rate of Profit (Average Rate of Profit) and Transformation of the Values of Commodities into Prices of Production." But is should be clear from the ordering which issue has the star billing.

Finally, we may note how Marx described the issue to Engels in his 1868 letter:

> . . . it is proper that you should know the method by which the rate of profit is developed. I will therefore give you the *most general features* of the process. . . . In Book III we come to the transformation of surplus value into its different forms and separate component parts. . . .
>
> *Profit* is for us first of all only *another name* or another category of *surplus value* . . . *surplus value* gets the form of *profit, without any quantitative* difference between the one and the other. This is only the illusory form in which surplus value appears [8, 1956, pp. 245–6; all italics are Marx'].

The Parable: "Capitalist Communism"

I have attempted to explain the transformation process in terms of a parable in which the economy's total surplus value is first aggregated[19] and then redivided by the competitive process. It is easy to show by a quotation from *Capital* that this parable describes Marx' intentions accurately.[20]

. . . the capitalists in the various spheres of production . . . do not secure the surplus-value, and consequently the profit, created in their own sphere by the production of these commodities, but only as much surplus-value, and profit, as falls to the share of every aliquot part of the total social capital out of the total social surplus-value, or social profit produced by the total capital of society in all spheres of production . . . . *The various capitalists, so far as profits are concerned, are so many stockholders in a stock company in which the shares of profit are uniformly divided for every 100 shares of capital,* so that profits differ in the case of the individual capitalists only according to the amount of capital invested by each one of them in the social enterprise, according to his investment in social production as a whole, according to his shares. (Vol. III, Chapter IX, pp. 186–7. My italics.)

The Transformed Profits as a Mere Surface Manifestation

We economists have always had a somewhat warmer spot in our hearts for Volume III, and have tended to treat Volume I as an "unnecessary detour" to the issue that really matters—the explanation of competitive pricing. But that is merely a reflection of our own prejudices as bourgeois (shall I say, "vulgar"?) economists. From the point of view of the objectives of Marx' analysis, what is all that important about an explanation of the determination of competitive prices?[21] To Marx, indeed, it was worth discussing only to reveal its irrelevance

---

[19] To Marx this aggregation was of fundamental importance. He lists it as the first of

> . . . the three fundamentally new elements of the book [*Capital*, Vol. I] . . . that in contrast to *all* former political economy, which *from the very outset* treats the particular fragments of surplus value with their fixed forms of rent, profit, and interest as already given, I first deal with the general form of surplus value, in which all these fragments are still undifferentiated—in solution, as it were (Marx to Engels, January 8, 1868, p. 238).

The other two fundamentally new contributions of Volume I, are, in Marx' view, the difference between the use value and the exchange value of labor, and the evaluation of wages as an "irrational form in which a relation hidden behind them appears." Note these are all matters relating to income distribution, not pricing of commodities in general.

[20] The parable is also described several times in Marx' correspondence. For example in his later 1868 transformation problem letter he wrote:

> What competition between the various masses of capital—differently composed and invested in dif-

ferent spheres of production—is striving to produce is *capitalist communism,* namely that the *mass of capital belonging to each sphere of production* should snatch an aliquot part of the total surplus value proportionate to the part of the total social capital which it forms [8,1956, p. 248, Marx' italics].

Recall from our first quotation from that letter, that the parable also appears in the earliest (1862) transformation letter, which uses the phrase "and all capitalists are brothers" for what has here become "capitalist communism." In the text of Volume III it becomes the metaphor about proportionate dividends on shares in a joint-stock company, a metaphor that had also been used in the 1862 letter.

[21] Note that to Marx, Volume I deals with "The *Process of Capitalist* Production" (Marx' italics), that is, not (primarily) with *price* theory (Marx to S. Meyer, April 30, 1867, p. 224). Similarly, in two letters to Engels, dated August 24, 1867 and January 8, 1868 (the one cited in the preceding footnote) Marx gives his lists of the main contributions of Volume I, none of which relates to the pricing of commodities [8, 1956].

and to tear away the curtain it formed before our eyes, so that the basic truth about the production of surplus value could be revealed. *That* is why the first volume is indeed the important one for Marx and his followers. To argue that he and Engels stuck by Volume I in order to put up a brave show when they had realized the weakness of its analysis is to reveal one's own misunderstanding of Marx' purpose.

Once again it is easy to document this conclusion. I quote a rather long but very significant passage from *Capital:*

> . . . the mass of the surplus-value produced in any particular sphere of production . . . has any importance for the individual capitalist only to the extent that the quantity of surplus-value produced in his line plays a determining role in regulating the average profit. But this is a process which takes place behind his back, which he does not see, nor understand, and which indeed does not interest him at all. The actual difference of magnitude between profit and surplus-value—not merely between the rate of profit and of surplus-value—in the various spheres of production now conceals completely the true nature and origin of profit, not only for the capitalist, who has a special interest in deceiving himself on this score, but also for the laborer. By the *transformation of values into prices of production, the basis of the determination of value is itself removed from direct observation* . . . The fact that the actual state of things is here revealed for the first time; that political economy up to the present time . . . [has clung] to the obvious phenomena of these differences—this confusion of the theoretical economists demonstrates most strikingly the utter incapacity of the capitalist, when blinded by competition, to penetrate through the outward disguise into the internal essence and the inner form of the capitalist process of production. (Volume III, Chapter IX, pp. 198–99, my italics.)

The Significance of the Transformation to Marx

If Marx considered pricing an unimportant phenomenon which only served to obscure the relevant relationships, then why did he devote so much effort and space to the transformation problem? The answer has already been suggested in the preceding section—it must be explained in order to get it out of the way. It is important because it had misled so many people—capitalists, laborers (see the preceding quote), vulgar economists and even economists as considerable as Ricardo.

But—and this is the essential issue—what is this truth that Marx is trying to reveal? In other words, what is the value theory really about? Is it just a bit of revolutionary propaganda, or mere playing with persuasive definitions, or a bit of Hegelian mysticism?[22]

I believe that the answer is none of the above, but to see why, it is suggestive to look ahead in time. Think of the economists at the turn of the century who were seeking evidence of justice in the capitalistic process of distribution with the aid of marginal productivity theory. It is not totally unfair to characterize their argument as proceeding from the position that labor, land,[23] and capital each contributes toward the production of society's output. It is surely only just, therefore, that each of these should share in that output. Since, regrettably, mother nature is not available to collect her share, it is indeed fortunate that the landlord is willing to accept it in her stead.[24]

Such nonsense is precisely what Marx' analysis anticipates and what it is intended to expose. Again, let Marx speak for himself.

> In Capital—Profit, or better Capital—Interest, Land—Rent, Labor—Wages of Labor, in this economic trinity expressing professedly the connection of value and of wealth in general with their sources, we have the complete mystification of the capitalist

---

[22] "Taken on the Hegelian (neo-Hegelian) ground, and seen in the light of the general materialistic conception, the proposition that value = labor-cost is self-evident, not to say tautological. Seen in any other light, it has no particular force." (Veblen, *loc. cit.*)

[23] Marx was at pains to emphasize the contribution of land to the *productive process:*

> The use-values, coat, linen, etc., *i.e.*, the bodies of commodities, are combinations of two elements—matter and labour. If we take away the useful labour expended upon them, a material substratum is always left, which is furnished by Nature without the help of man. . . . As William Petty puts it, labour is its father and the earth its mother. (Vol. I, Chapter I, section 2, p. 50.)

Why Marx denied that "land" contributed *value* to the product should soon become clear.

[24] Marx' objections to Adam Smith on this score presumably arise out of passages such as the following:

> . . . rent may be considered as the produce of those powers of Nature, the use of which the landlord lends to the farmer. . . . It is the work of Nature which remains after deducting or compensating every thing which can be regarded as the work of man [14, 1937, Book II, Chapter V, pp. 344–5].

mode of production. . . . It is an enchanted, perverted, topsy-turvy world, in which Mister Capital and Mistress Land carry on their goblin tricks as social characters and at the same time as mere things . . . it is . . . natural that the actual agents of production felt completely at home in these estranged and irrational forms of Capital—Interest, Land—Rent, Labor—Wages of Labor, for these are the forms of the illusion, in which they move about and in which they find their daily occupation. It is also quite natural that vulgar economy, which is nothing but a didactic, more or less dogmatic, translation of the ordinary conceptions of the agents of production and which arranges them in a certain intelligent order, should see in this trinity, which is devoid of all internal connection, the natural and indubitable basis of its shallow assumption of importance. This formula corresponds at the same time to the interests of the ruling classes, *by proclaiming the natural necessity and eternal justification of their sources of revenue* and raising them to the position of a dogma. (Volume III, Chapter 48, pp. 966–67, my italics.)

This discussion is clearly pertinent to an understanding of the significance of the value theory to Marx. But if it is relevant for the transformation analysis it may well be asked why he let some 700 pages intervene between this passage and the transformation discussion in Volume III. We can never be sure of the answer but it must be remembered that Engels tells us (in the preface to Volume II) that the manuscript from which he produced Volumes II and III was made up of many bits and pieces which he fitted together as best he could. Part VII of Volume III, from which the preceding quotation is taken, is one of the most fragmentary, with sentences reported to have been illegible, (*e.g.*, Ch. 48, p. 948) and pieces of manuscript left uncompleted, (*e.g.*, p. 950). It might only have been natural for Engels to have put it off to the end.[25]

But we are not forced to rely on conjectures on this issue either. Once again, Marx tells us about the matter; for in his later transformation letter to Engels (1868), he juxtaposes the two issues very clearly, completing his discussion of the transformation issue thus:

V. We have now reduced profit to the form in which it appears in practice . . . *Next comes the splitting*

[25] Engels also reported that the transformation discussion "(relation of Mehrwertsrate to Profit rate)" required "a great deal of work" on his part to prepare it for publication (Letter to N. F. Danielson, November 13, 1885.) [8, 1956, p. 464].

up of this profit into entrepreneur's profit and interest. Interest-bearing capital. The credit system.
VI. *Transformation of surplus profit into ground rent.*
VII. At last we have arrived at the *forms of appearance* which serve as the *starting point* in the vulgar conception: ground rent coming from the earth, profit (interest) from capital, wages from labour. But from our point of view the thing is now seen differently. The apparent movement is explained. Moreover, Adam Smith's nonsense, which has become the *main pillar* of all economics hitherto existing, that the price of a commodity consists of those three revenues, *i.e.*, only of variable capital (wages) and surplus value (ground rent, profit (interest)), is overthrown. Then—the whole movement takes place in this form of appearance. Finally since these three (wages, ground rent, profit (interest)) constitute the respective sources of income of the three classes of landowners, capitalists and wage labourers, we have, in conclusion, the *class struggle*, into which the movement and the smash-up of the whole business resolves itself. . . .[26]

The point of the value theory may then be summed up as follows: goods are indeed produced by labor and natural resources together. But the relevant *social* source of production is labor, not an inanimate "land." Thus profits, interest, and rent must also be attributed to labor, and their total is equal (tautologically) to the total value produced by labor minus the amount consumed by labor itself. The competitive process, that appears to show that land is the source of rent and capital the source of profits and interest, is merely a distributive phenomenon and conceals the fact that labor is the only socially relevant source of output. This is the significance of the value theory and the transformation analysis to Marx.

Conclusion: Sources of Misunderstanding

Having come to so unequivocal a conclusion about what Marx hoped to accomplish through his notion of a transformation process one may well ask how the apparent misunderstanding of so many commentators might have arisen. But before turning to this it should be noted again that Meek and Morishima are very clear cut exceptions and that my interpretation is very close to theirs. Thus, Morishima reminds us of Samuelson's remark that

[26] The (anonymous) Russian translator exhibits some delicacy in this rendition. The word he translates as "business" is *"scheisse"* in the original [8, 1956, p. 250].

"the proportionality of market price to labor content applies validly only when surplus value is zero and not worth talking about!" [12, 1957, p. 888].

On this Morishima remarks:

> . . . in the transformation problem Marx did not intend to establish a proportionality between values and prices but, on the contrary, to show that individual exploitation and individual profit are disproportional unless some restrictive conditions are imposed. . . . Thus it is clear that the transformation problem has the aim of showing how 'the aggregate exploitation of labour on the part of the total social capital' is, in a capitalist economy, obscured by the distortion of prices from values; the other aim is to show how living labour can be the sole source of profit" [10, 1973, pp. 85–6.].

Meek begins his discussion with a statement of the issue that is just as clear. However, he does go on to treat the transformation problem as though it were primarily a matter of explaining *price* determination.

Sweezy [16, 1942, esp. pp. 125–130] also comes close to the Meek-Morishima position arguing that prices and profits of individual capitalists are micro issues while Marxian values are intended to deal with the macro issues of distribution in which Marx is interested (pp. 125–6). He notes that the "price calculation . . . mystifies the underlying social relations of capitalist production. Since profit is calculated as a return on total capital, the idea inevitably arises that capital as such is in some way 'productive' " (p. 129).

His book does follow the Bortkiewicz tradition in treating prices as magnitudes to be determined from values. However, Sweezy's letter to me also casts additional light on this matter. He writes:

> To the best of my recollection, I never treated 'the transformation problem primarily as a matter of determining prices from values.' Values are in fact an abstraction from capitalist reality, not an observable phenomenon, and could not possibly 'determine' prices of production (which are also an abstraction albeit on a lower level). The justification for such abstractions, esp. value, is that they reveal the essence of capitalist reality as opposed to the appearance—an argument which orthodox economics of course is totally unable to comprehend.

In any event, it is clear that with these and perhaps a few other exceptions, the interpretation I have offered and sought to document is hardly the view that is held universally. I have already suggested one explanatory hypothesis—that many readers may have been misled by the analogy with Ricardo. Ricardo tells us explicitly when he gets to the role of capital in price determination that the "labor theory" model gives us answers that are still very nearly correct, so that in his view it remains a good model to use in explaining the determination of individual prices. Marx, on the other hand, points out that the deviations between the two models are systematic and significant enough to conceal the underlying relationships from other observers. Moreover, as we have seen, at this point, at least, Marx is not even interested to any significant degree in the theory of price.

Yet Marx himself must bear a good share of the blame for the confusion. Since it seems true that Volume I and Volume III were written with perfectly consistent intentions he should surely not have adopted the word "value" for the magnitude on which he focuses his discussion. He was perfectly aware that "value theory" was used in the economic literature to refer to the theory of price determination (though he felt that Ricardo had also groped, albeit unsuccessfully, for a deeper phenomenon when he discussed values). Consequently, if he deliberately used the term to denote a magnitude that differs from price in a significant and systematic manner he was certainly asking for the sort of misunderstanding to which the work has been subject. Moreover, in the bulk of Volume I Marx does speak as though the "exchange value" which he explains in terms of labor were a normal market price. If he meant otherwise he hardly hinted at it.[27]

[27] There seem to be only three points in Volume I where the reader is given some warning on the matter; on pp. 184–5, footnote, p. 244, footnote, and on pp. 335–6. In the second of these, he writes "We have in fact assumed that prices = values. We shall, however, see, in Volume III, that even in the case of average prices the assumption cannot be made in this very simple manner."

Similarly on p. 335–6 we have the statement

> This law [that the masses of surplus value produced by different capitals vary directly as the variable constituents of these capitals] clearly contradicts all experience based on appearance. Everyone knows that a cotton spinner, who, reckoning the percentage on the whole of his applied capital, employs much constant and little variable capital, does not, on account of this, pocket less profit or surplus-value than a baker, who relatively sets in motion much variable and little constant capital. For the solution of this apparent contradic-

Colloquium: On Marx, the Transformation Problem 61

This too constitutes something of a mystery. Since Marx did have his transformation analysis worked out before Volume I was published, why is there no clear statement of the issue there? But this mystery does have a known solution. The definitive answer is provided in an exchange of letters between Marx and Engels. As they were making the final corrections for Volume I, Engels (gently) rebuked Marx for his failure to deal with the issue in Volume I. In a letter dated June 26, 1867 he wrote

> . . . As for the origin of surplus value, the following: The manufacturer, and with him the vulgar economist, will at once object: If the capitalist pays the worker only the price of 6 hours for his 12 hours of working time, no surplus value can originate from this, for then every hour of labor of the factory worker is only equal to half an hour of labor—equal to what is paid for it—and enters into the value of the product of labor as worth only that much. . . . No matter how terribly shallow this argument is, no matter how much it identifies exchange-value and price, value of labor and wages, no matter how absurd its assumption that one hour of labor enters into value as only half an hour if it is paid for as only half an hour, I marvel that you have not taken this into consideration already, for it will *quite certainly* be held up to you at once and it is better to dispose of it in advance. Perhaps you will return to it in the next [printer's proof] sheet . . . (Engels' italics).

To this Marx replied on the next day . . .

> . . . As for the inevitable objections you mention of the philistine and the vulgar economist . . . [The answer to this problem] presupposes [among other matters] . . . that the *conversion of surplus value into profit, of profit into average profit*, etc., is set forth. This presupposes a previous account of the *process of the circulation of capital*, since the turnover of capital, etc. plays a part here. Hence this matter can be set forth only in the third book. . . .
>
> If I were to *silence* all such objections *in advance*, I should ruin the whole dialectical method of development. On the contrary, this method has the advantage of continually *setting traps* for these fellows

which provoke them to untimely demonstrations of their asininity. (Marx' italics.)[28]

REFERENCES

1. BLAUG, M. *Economic theory in retrospect.* Revised edition. Homewood, Ill.: Richard D. Irwin, 1968.
2. BÖHM-BAWERK, E. VON *Karl Marx and the close of his system and Böhm-Bawerk's criticism of Marx by Rudolf Hilferding with an appendix by L. von Bortkiewicz.* Edited by P. SWEEZY. New York: Augustus M. Kelley, 1949.
3. BRONFENBRENNER, M. "Samuelson, Marx and Their Latest Critics," *J. Econ. Lit.,* March 1973, *11* (1), pp. 58–63.
4. ENGELS, F. *Engels on capital: Synopsis, reviews, letters, and supplementary material.* Translated and edited by L. MINS. New York: International Publishers, Inc., 1937.
5. MARX, K. *A contribution to the critique of political economy.* Translated by N. I. STONE. Chicago: Charles H. Kerr and Co., 1904.
6. ———— *Capital. A critique of political economy.* Chicago: Charles H. Kerr and Co., Volume I (1906); Volumes II and III (1909).
7. ———— AND ENGELS, F. *Correspondence 1846–95; with explanatory notes.* Translated by DONA TORR. New York: International Publishers, [1934, 1936] 1942.
8. ———— AND ———— *Selected corrrespondence.* Moscow: Foreign Languages Publishing House, 1956.
9. MEEK, R. L. "Some Notes on the Transformation Problem," *Econ J.,* March 1956, *66,* pp. 94–107.
10. MORISHIMA, M. *Marx's economics: A dual theory of value and growth.* New York: Cambridge University Press, 1973.
11. ROBINSON, J. "Review of SWEEZY, P., *Karl Marx and the close of his system* . . . ," *Econ. J.,* June 1950, *60,* pp. 358–63. [see ref. 2.]

[28] I came across this exchange of letters quite accidentally (thanks to a fortunate find by my secretary in a 6th Avenue trash can!) after an earlier draft of this paper had been completed. Note how remarkably it confirms Veblen's conjecture about Marx' attitude toward some of his expected readers, as well as several of the hypotheses of this article. The translation here is taken from Mins, in whose little volume (presented to me by my secretary) I first came across the exchange [4, 1937].

tion, many intermediate terms are as yet wanted. . . . It will be seen later how the school of Ricardo has come to grief over this stumbling-block. Vulgar economy which, indeed, "has really learnt nothing" here as everywhere sticks to appearances in opposition to the law which regulates and explains them [6, 1906].

12. SAMUELSON, P. "Wages and Interest: A Modern Dissection of Marxian Economic Models," *Amer. Econ. Rev.*, Dec. 1957, *47*, pp. 884–912; reprinted in SAMUELSON, P., *Collected scientific papers*, edited by J. STIGLITZ. 2 vols. Cambridge, Mass.: M.I.T. Press, 1965, Ch. 29, pp. 341–69.

13. ———— "Understanding the Marxian Notion of Exploitation: A Summary of the So-called Transformation Problem Between Marxian Values and Competitive Prices," *J. Econ. Lit.*, June 1971, *9* (2), pp. 399–431.

14. SMITH, A. *An inquiry into the nature and causes of the wealth of nations.* Edited by EDWIN CANNAN. New York: Modern Library, [1776] 1937.

15. STIGLER, G. J. "Ricardo and the 93% Labor Theory of Value," *Amer. Econ. Rev.*, June 1958, *48* (3), pp. 357–67.

16. SWEEZY, P. M. *The theory of capitalist development.* New York: Oxford University Press, 1942.

17. VEBLEN, T. B. *The place of science in modern civilization, and other essays.* New York: Viking Press, 1919.

[16]

CLASSICAL ECONOMICS: THE SUBSISTENCE WAGE AND DEMAND-SUPPLY ANALYSIS

Marx and the Iron Law of Wages

By WILLIAM J. BAUMOL*

Marx den Laf [argue] sagte: Ce qu' il ya de certain c'est que moi je ne suis pas Marxiste.

Letter from Engels to Bernstein London 2/3, November 1882

I find few things as discouraging as the persistent attribution of positions to a writer whose works contain repeated, categorical, indeed emotional, denunciations of those views. Marx's views on wages are a prime example. Both vulgar Marxists and vulgar opponents of Marx have propounded two associated myths: that he believed wages under capitalism are inevitably driven near some physical subsistence level, and that he considered this to constitute robbery of the workers and a major evil of capitalism. Yet Marx and Engels tell us again and again, sometimes in most intemperate language, that these views are the very opposite of theirs. These observations, incidentally, are hardly new discoveries. Thus, for example, Roman Rosdolsky (1977, p. 287 ff.) disposes of the subsistence wage allegation and Robert Tucker (1969, ch. 3), and Allen Wood (1972) cover Marx's view on the morality of capitalist distribution very effectively.

I. Wages and Subsistence

I will show that to Marx the value of labor power does not normally equal physical subsistence; moreover, wages need not be equal to the value of labor power; with Marx's ascerbic rejection of the Malthusian model this system is denuded of *any* explicit wage equilibrium process; the omission of any fixed equilibrium point was deliberate, because Marx was anxious to show that workers

*Princeton University and New York University.

have the power to raise wages substantially even under capitalism; Marx considered the iron law of wages a monstrosity. These are not things he said once or twice, by indirection and in obscure places. They recur over and over, in *Capital* and in other writings including private notes and correspondence. Moreover, these are views Marx held to the end of his life.

A. *Value of Labor Power and Physical Subsistence*

A key statement in *Capital* does seem to support the subsistence allegation: the value of labor power is "...the labour-time necessary for the production and consequently also the reproduction, of this special article" (*Capital*, I, p. 189). But almost at once Marx points out that

> ...the number and extent of [the worker's] so-called necessary wants, as also the modes of satisfying them, are themselves the product of historical development, and depend therefore to a great extent on the degree of civilization of a country, more particularly on the conditions under which, and consequently on the habits and degree of comfort in which, the class of free labourers has been formed.
> [*Capital*, I, p. 190]

This view was, of course, shared by Marx's predecessors (see, for example, Adam Smith, *Wealth*, p. 744; Ricardo [Sraffa, I, p. 97]). But it seemed particularly crucial to Marx. For example, he severely criticized the physiocrats (whom he generally admired) for maintaining that wages have a *fixed* floor (*Theories of Surplus Value*, I, p. 45). Similarly, in *Wages, Price and Profit*, to whose

304   AEA PAPERS AND PROCEEDINGS   MAY 1983

history I must return, Marx tells us

> Besides [the] mere physical element, the value of labour is in every country determined by a *traditional standard of life*...the satisfaction of certain wants springing from the social conditions in which people are placed and reared up.... This historical or social element, entering into the value of labour, may be expanded, or contracted, or altogether extinguished....
>
> [pp. 50–51, Marx's italics]

Other such quotations are easy to find. There simply can be no doubt about the matter. "The labour-time necessary for the production and...reproduction" of labor power is a flexible magnitude which is not "determined...by nature," that is, it is neither bare subsistence, nor any other preset amount.

B. *Wages and Value of Labor-Power*

Wages are, of course, the price of labor power. To most economists the "value of good x" connotes its price. But, to Marx, value clearly meant something else. His extensive discussion in Volume III of *Capital* of the transformation of values into prices deals with the persistent and systematic deviations between the two, even in equilibrium. Value was *defined* by Marx to equal a good's labor content (he repeatedly tells us it is a tautology) (see, for example, *A Contribution to the Critique...*, 1904, pp. 31–32), while Marx explicitly followed Smith and Ricardo in taking price to equal cost of production, including the normal return on capital (*Capital*, III, p. 233).

Now, since Marxian price differs from value, the wage rate, the price of labor power, like that of wheat, can and does differ from its value. It must be admitted that this distinction does not occur frequently in Marx's writings, but it certainly occurs explicitly. It is found, for example, in *Capital* (III, 1966 ed., p. 235) and in *Marginal Notes on Adolph Wagner*: "[Wagner claims I say] ...in the determination of the *value of labour power*, that its value is really paid, which is *not in fact the case*" (p. 43).

C. *Absence of an Equilibrating Mechanism*

Even though the Ricardians also did not believe that wages approach a fixed physical subsistence level, their model did have a mechanism driving wages toward the subsistence level *currently customary*. This mechanism was, of course, the Malthusian population principle which Marx rejected vehemently, for reasons I will discuss.

It has been suggested that the reserve army of the unemployed was substituted by Marx for the population principle. Marx does say that when wages rise, machinery is substituted for labor, and the resulting excess supply of labor limits these increases. But this only means that the slope of the labor demand curve is negative. There is clearly no way one can deduce from such a demand curve that the equilibrium wage must always (or ever) equal subsistence. We will see that Marx emphatically rejected such a conclusion, and why.

D. *The Power of Workers over Wages*

To understand the main piece of evidence on the degree to which Marx believed wages can be influenced by the workers, some biographical information is pertinent.

In 1865, two years before publication of Volume I of *Capital*, Marx was hard at work on the manuscript. Just then a member of the Council of the International Working Men's Association (John Weston, a follower of "Utopian" socialist Robert Owen) argued before the Council that unions can never raise real wages because wage increases must cause proportionate price increases. Marx pronounced this conclusion "theoretically false and practically dangerous" and undertook two lectures in reply to the Council. Marx wrote to Engels (May 20, 1865) that he did so most reluctantly both because it would give away some of *Capital*'s ideas and would take him away from his writing so that, to save time, his talks would be extemporaneous. It must have been a surprise when the manuscript (written in English) was discovered three decades later among Marx's papers by his daughter, Eleanor. The issue had evidently been most important to Marx.

VOL. 73 NO. 2   CLASSICAL ECONOMICS   305

In these talks, published as *Value, Price and Profit* (or *Wages, Price and Profit*) Marx was quite unambiguous on our subject:

> By comparing the standard wages or values of labour in different countries, and by comparing them in different historical epochs of the same country, you will find that the *value of labour* itself is not a fixed but a variable magnitude, even supposing the values of all other commodities to remain constant...although we can fix the *minimum* of wages, we cannot fix their *maximum*.... It is evident that between the two limits...an immense scale of variations is possible. The fixation of its actual degree is only settled by the continuous struggle between capital and labour, the capitalist constantly tending to reduce wages to their physical minimum, and to extend the working day to its physical maximum, while the working man constantly presses in the opposite direction....
>
> As to the *limits* of the *value of labour*, its actual settlement always depends upon supply and demand, I mean the demand for labour on the part of capital, and the supply of labour by the working men.   [pp. 51–52]

Thus, Marx clearly believed that "an *immense* scale of variations" in wages is possible under capitalism and that it is the responsibility of unions to take full advantage of it. He emphatically did *not* believe that fate condemns workers to subsistence wages which they must accept passively. Note incidentally, that Marx believed unions to have a very valuable role, a piece of information which, one hopes, was some comfort to his daughter who had devoted much of her life to union activity, when she found the manuscript a few months before her suicide (see the superb biography of Eleanor Marx by Yvonne Kapp, 1972, 1976).

E. *The Iron Law of Wages*

A later manuscript, published as a *Critique of the Gotha Programme* (henceforth "*Gotha*") can complete my discussion of Marx on wages and subsistence. Written in 1875 (and not intended for publication) it denounced a platform before a German socialist group meeting in the town of Gotha. The platform was an attempted compromise between Marxian principles and the sentimental notions of romantic socialist Ferdinand Lassalle, Marx's ancient nemesis, then dead eleven years. (*Gotha* is the source of the phrase "from each according to his abilities, to each according to his needs".) Several weeks before Marx wrote *Gotha*, Engels, undoubtedly with Marx's knowledge, had written to one of the German Marxist leaders a letter that was to serve as an outline for much of *Gotha*. Engels wrote:

> ...our people have allowed the Lassallean "iron law of wages" to be foisted upon them...namely, that the worker receives on the average only the *minimum* in wages, and indeed because, according to Malthus' theory of population, there are always too many workers.... Now Marx has proved in detail in *Capital* that the laws regulating wages...are in no sense iron but on the contrary very elastic.... The Malthusian argument in support of the law...has been refuted in detail by Marx in the section on the 'Accumulation of Capital.' Thus by adopting Lassalle's "iron law" we commit ourselves to a false thesis with a false argument. [*Gotha*, Appendix, pp. 40–41]

Marx, in *Gotha*, denounces the Lassallean slogan: "the abolition of the wage system together with the iron law of wages," writing:

> ...Lassalle's attack on wage labour turns almost solely on this so-called law.... But if I take the law with Lassalle's stamp on it and, consequently, in his sense, then I must also take it with his substantiation for it. And what is that?...it is the Malthusian theory of population.... But if this theory is correct, then again I *cannot* abolish the law even if I abolish wage labour a hundred times over, because the law then governs not only the system of wage labour but *every* social system. Basing themselves directly on this, the economists have been proving

306   *AEA PAPERS AND PROCEEDINGS*   *MAY 1983*

for fifty years and more that socialism cannot abolish poverty, *which has its basis in nature*, but can only make it *general*, can only distribute it simultaneously over the whole surface of society!   [*Gotha*, pp. 22–23]

Later I will show that this crucial passage helps to explain the reasons behind Marx's views. For now I use it just to confirm his abhorrence of anything like the "iron law" of wages.

II. The Morality of Surplus Value

Marx repeatedly expresses contempt for the view that wages under capitalism are immoral and constitute grounds for revolution. In *Capital*, where he discusses the value of labor power, he describes as "a very cheap sort of sentimentality" the view that the method by which wages are determined under capitalism is "brutal" (Vol. I, p. 192). Similarly, about three years before he died, in *Marginal Notes on Adolph Wagner*, perhaps his last piece on economics, Marx remarked

[Adolph Wagner] foists on me the idea that "the *surplus-value* produced by the labourers *alone improperly* remains with the capitalist entrepreneurs".... In fact, I say the direct opposite: namely that at a certain point commodity production necessarily becomes 'capitalist' commodity production and that according to the *law of value* governing the latter, the "surplus-value" is necessarily the capitalist's and not the labourer's.   [p. 61]

The same views appeared more than twenty years earlier, in the *Grundrisse*, and again in Engels' introduction to the first German edition of *The Poverty of Philosophy*:

According to the laws of bourgeois economics, the greatest part of the product does *not* belong to the workers who have produced it. If we now say: that is unjust, that ought not to be so, then that has nothing immediately to do with economics. We are merely saying that this economic fact is in contradiction

to our moral sentiment. Marx, therefore, never based his communist demands upon this...he says only that surplus value consists of unpaid labour, which is a simple fact.   [pp. 10–11]

Marx himself returns to the morality of wages in *Capital*:

...The circumstance, that on the one hand the daily sustenance of labour-power costs only half a day's labour, while on the other hand the very same labour-power can work during a whole day...this circumstance is, without doubt, a piece of good luck for the buyer, *but by no means an injury to the seller*.   [Vol. I, p. 216, emphasis added]

III. Accounting for Marx's Positions

In sum, Marx consistently held views on the level, determination, and morality of wages very different from those attributed to him in popular legend. In his words, his positions are "the direct opposite" of those in the folklore. Why did Marx argue so vehemently that wages are not fixed at physical subsistence, and that the manner in which they are set is not immoral? We have rather clear indications of his own explanations.

First, as we have seen, Marx was anxious to encourage the activity of trade unions both "as centres of resistance against the encroachments of capital [upon wages... and] organized forces...for the final emancipation of the working class, that is to say, the ultimate abolition of the wages system" (*Wages, Price and Profit*, p. 55).

Second, the "iron law of wages" and the Malthusian model underlying it ascribe poverty not to any feature of capitalism but to human psychological propensities. As we have seen, Marx tells us in *Gotha* that this concedes everything to the opponents of socialism. For, if valid, it should be equally so in a socialist society which, consequently, could do nothing to eliminate poverty, aside from sharing the wealth or, rather (as Marx notes), sharing the poverty. No wonder Marx rejected the Malthusian model so vehemently, describing it as "a libel on the human race."

VOL. 73 NO. 2 CLASSICAL ECONOMICS 307

Third, Marx believed as a fundamental matter of philosophy that there is no such thing as an absolute standard of morality. A basic component of historical materialism is the view that no phenomena, and, emphatically, no social phenomena can be understood except in their historical context. Any proposition is robbed of its sense if it is taken as an eternal verity or as a truth independent of historical circumstances. Moral values (including value judgments on distribution) are no exception—a behavior pattern which is considered monstrous today may have to be adjudged ethical and appropriate for another society.

> The idea of equality, therefore, both in its bourgeois and in its proletarian form, is itself a historical product, the creation of which required definite historical conditions which in turn themselves presuppose a long previous historical development. It is therefore anything but an eternal truth.
> [Engels in collaboration with Marx, *Anti-Dühring*, p. 121]

This was one of the prime grounds on which Marx and Engels rejected the doctrines of the utopian and the romantic socialists. As Engels wrote:

> To all these Socialism is the expression of absolute truth, reason and justice, and has only to be discovered to conquer all the world by virtue of its own power. And as absolute truth is independent of time, space, and of the historical development of man, it is a mere accident when and where it is discovered. With all this, absolute truth, reason, and justice are different with the founder of each different school... there is no other ending possible in this conflict of absolute truths than... a kind of eclectic, average Socialism... a mish-mash allowing of the most manifold shades of opinion; a mish-mash of such critical statements, economic theories, pictures of future society by the founders of different sects, as excite a minimum of opposition.
> [*Socialism*: *Utopian and Scientific*, end of Section 1]

Given Marx's and Engels' fear of the vulnerability of the socialist movement to seduction by indefensible romantic notions which can undermine both its effectiveness and its purpose, their anxiety to hammer home such philosophical points is entirely understandable.

Finally, Marx was determined to battle the "iron law" and those who considered it a primary indictment of capitalism because it cheapens and trivializes the entire socialist cause.

> It is as if, among slaves who have at last got behind the secret of slavery and broken out in rebellion, a slave still in thrall to obsolete notions were to inscribe on the programme of the rebellion: Slavery must be abolished because the feeding of slaves in the system of slavery cannot exceed a certain low maximum! Does not the mere fact that the representatives of our Party were capable of perpetrating such a monstrous attack on the widespread understanding among the mass of our Party prove by itself with what criminal levity and with what lack of conscience they set to work.... [*Gotha*, p. 24]

REFERENCES

Engels, Frederick, *Anti-Dühring*, London: Lawrence and Wishart, 1878, 1934.

_____, *Socialism*: *Utopian and Scientific*, pamphlet extracted by Engels from *Anti-Dühring*, with a forward by Marx, Paris, 1880; Peking: Foreign Language Press, 1975.

Kapp, Yvonne, *Eleanor Marx*, New York: Pantheon Press, 1972, 1976.

Marx, Karl, *Capital*, Chicago: Charles H. Kerr, Vol. I, 1894, 1909; Moscow: Progress Publishers, 1966.

_____, *Critique of the Gotha Programme*, 1875, Moscow: Progress Publishers, 1937.

_____, *A Contribution to the Critique of Political Economy*, 1859, Chicago: Charles H. Kerr and Co., 1904.

_____, *Grundrisse*, Martin Nicolaus, ed., trans., Harmondsworth: Penguin Books, 1973.

_____, *Marginal Notes on Adolph Wagner's*

'*Lehrbuch der politischen Ökonomie*', (1879–1880), in Marx-Engels, *Werke* (MEW) Vol. 19, pp. 355–383; Trans. by Athar Hussain in *Theoretical Practice*, Issue 5, Spring 1972.

_____, *The Poverty of Philosophy*, London: Martin Lawrence [1846–1847], N.D.

_____, *Theories of Surplus Value*, Moscow: Progress Publishers, 1963.

_____, *Value, Price and Profit*, New York: International Publishers, 1898, 1935.

Ricardo, David, *Principles of Political Economy and Taxation*, P. Sraffa, ed., Vol. I, *The Works and Correspondence of David Ricardo*, Cambridge: Cambridge University Press, 1951.

Rosdolsky, Roman, *The Making of Marx's 'Capital'*, London: Pluto Press, 1977.

Smith, Adam, *The Wealth of Nations*, Cannan ed. Modern Library, New York, 1937.

Tucker, Robert, *The Marxian Revolutionary Idea*, New York: W. W. Norton & Co., 1969.

Wood, Allen, "The Marxian Critique of Justice," in *Philosophy and Public Affairs*, Vol. 2, Spring 1972.

[17]

Economica, **44**, 145–162

Say's (at Least) Eight Laws, or What Say and James Mill May Really Have Meant

By WILLIAM J. BAUMOL

Princeton and New York Universities

I. THE SAY'S LAW DISCUSSION AS A COMPLEX OF IDEAS

Revisionism usually supplies whatever excitement there is to be found in writings on *dogmengeschichte*. Here, achievement often consists in showing that a writer had been badly misinterpreted, or that his contribution is far greater than is generally supposed. This paper can, however, pretend to propose no more than a modest revision of our ideas on the early writings on Say's Law. It will be argued that J. B. Say and his contemporary James Mill, who is also sometimes credited with the notion that "supply creates its own demand", really seem to have had in mind a set of ideas rather more complex than that and, moreover, that the main policy implications they drew from their discussion went well beyond the comforting thought that fears of universal glut are baseless.

Certainly, their discussion was not Panglossian in spirit, for one of their main points was the superiority, from the point of view of growth in economic welfare, of investment outlays over idle consumption (either in the form of luxurious living by wealthy individuals or the military and other unproductive outlays of prodigal governments). Moreover, these authors maintained that only production can create real purchasing power, so that an impecunious community is in no position to provide effective demand in abundance. Restriction in output must necessarily limit effective demand and is certainly not a way to promote it, particularly in the long run.

These are ideas, it will be noted, that the modern literature does not reject, at least not with the universality with which it denies the notion that supply creates its own demand. Indeed, they are thoughts that may still be of some pertinence, particularly for development theory and policy. Moreover, for the time in which these authors were writing, these ideas can certainly not be considered a manifestation of conservatism. Rather, they can be interpreted as a reply to the defenders of the landed aristocracy and their consumption patterns, and as support for the expanding spirit of capitalist enterprise that accompanied the young industrial revolution.

Obviously, there is no limit to the extent to which one can subdivide the notions composing Say's discussion of markets or exchanges (*débouchés*), his related remarks on consumption, or the parallel materials in Mill. I will confine myself to those relationships that have played a substantial role in later discussions, particularly in recent literature, and to those observations that seem clearly to have been uppermost in the minds of the authors as indicated by the degree of emphasis devoted to them.

But before getting to that, it is appropriate first to recapitulate the contents of Say's Law, as it is understood nowadays, and as contrasted with the main proposition espoused by Say himself.

When discussing Say's Law, the literature since Ricardo seems generally to refer to one of two propositions—a strong assertion, which Becker and I have referred to elsewhere as "Say's Identity", and a weaker variant, which we labelled "Say's Equality".

The first of these, the identity, is the assertion that no one ever wants to hold money for any significant amount of time, so that, as a result, every offer (supply) of a quantity of goods automatically constitutes a demand for a bundle of some other items of equal market value. Thus, as in a barter economy, supply must automatically create its own demand and a general over-production of goods and services is logically impossible.

The second, equality, form of the law admits the possibility of (brief) periods of disequilibrium during which the total demand for goods may fall short of the total supply, but maintains that there exist reliable equilibrating forces that must soon bring the two together.

It should be noted that both of these propositions relate to the shorter run—the period relevant for the analysis of economic crises, recessions and unemployment. It is one of my main contentions that many of Say's central propositions are quite distinct either from the equality or the identity and that it is, in fact, not until the second edition of the *Traité* in 1814 that the full structure of either idea is spelled out in the book.

I believe that the related issues that Say *did* stress in his first edition give us some idea of the order of priorities in his mind, and this, as well as the amount of space and emphasis he accorded them, suggests to me that some of the associated propositions may have held even greater significance for him. To help the reader to judge these issues for himself, I have included in this article a translation of the pertinent sections of that book which I believe of interest in themselves, and which are fairly brief and quite easy to follow.

II. ON PRIORITY IN FORMULATION OF SAY'S LAW

This paper may, incidentally shed some light on a more minor matter—the issue of priority in the formulation of Say's Law.

In the history of ideas, few things are more foolhardy than attribution of the parenthood of some proposition to a particular individual. The ascription is little more than a sporting act that will ultimately serve as a challenge to others, virtually certain in due course to come up with a predecessor who anticipated the idea with more or less exactitude.

As is well known, Say's Law is a notion whose lineage is older than its name suggests. Its roots in the writings of the Physiocrats have been investigated with great care by Spengler (1945). There are clear precursor statements in *The Wealth of Nations* (see Sowell, 1972, pp. 15–17, and Spengler, 1945, pp. 182–184). It has also been suggested that James Mill anticipated Say in the formulation of the principle. While the first edition of the *Traité* appeared in 1803, it has been argued that in 1807 Mill the elder, in his *Commerce Defended*, published something much closer to "Say's Law" as it is now generally understood. Spengler (1945) and Sowell (1972) show that this conclusion probably rests on a superficial reading of Say's first edition. Readers may have been misled because much of the pertinent discussion appears much later in the book than the chapter on *débouchés*, the chapter into which most of this material was collected in subsequent editions. Winch (1966, p. 34) disposes of the issue even more effectively. He reminds us, as Sowell did, that Mill was acquainted with the *Traité* when he wrote *Commerce Defended* and in fact cites it there. Moreover, he shows that Mill explicitly credited Say with the idea. I will, however, argue that the issue is a bit more convoluted. While it is true that Mill's version of the discussion did not differ all that much from Say's, I will suggest that neither of them offered an explicit exposition of Say's Law until some time later. Only the second edition of Say's *Traité* in 1814 describes explicitly the logic of Say's Law as we interpret it nowadays.

Let us now turn to the related issues that Say and Mill emphasized in their discussions.

III. PRODUCTION AS THE SOURCE OF DISPOSABLE INCOME

The focal chapter's title, "Des Débouchés", is often translated as "on markets". However, it should be borne in mind that the term "market" is used as in "making a market", to denote the availability of effective demand, not as an institution (such as a marketplace) that facilitates the process of exchange. Perhaps a better translation of *des débouchés* is "on outlets for goods". I begin with the propositions which are the main subject of the extremely brief chapter on *débouchés* in the first edition of the *Traité*. These can be summarized as:

Say's First Proposition. A community's purchasing *power* (effective demand) is limited by and is equal to its output, because production provides *the means* by which outputs can be purchased. Furthermore,

Say's Second Proposition. Expenditure increases when output rises.

Note that the first proposition deals with purchasing *power*, not with actual purchases. It tells us, as Keynes did, that output is the source of effective demand—that output is purchasing power. But it does *not* say that all of that purchasing power will always be used to buy goods. Rather, these assertions state, in effect, that the marginal propensity to consume and invest is greater than zero and that the average propensity is (generally) not greater than unity. That is, they tell us that people who produce more are in a position to consume more and will generally do so. These points, which most of us would still accept, are made most emphatically in the very brief chapter on *débouchés* in the first edition, which I now present in its entirety:

Chapter 22 *On Markets*

Every producer produces a quantity of a particular good that considerably exceeds his own consumption. The farmer harvests more grain than is required to feed him and his household; the hatter makes substantially more hats than he produces for his use; the wholesale grocer handles more sugar than he can consume. Each of them needs many other products to live comfortably. The exchanges they carry out of their own products for those of others, constitute what are called the *markets* for those products.

In this operation money serves approximately the same role as the posters and the handbills in a large city which facilitate the intercourse of persons who may want to do business with one another. During the course of the year each producer handles a very large quantity of money, but aside from small balances of little consequence, at the end of the year there ordinarily remains in his hands no more money than he had at the beginning. What matters is what he purchases with that money, that is, the products of others that he has exchanged against his own, a portion of which he has consumed, and a portion saved according to his needs, his saving habits and the state of this wealth.

I trust this shows that it is not the abundance of money but the abundance of other products in general that facilitates sales. This is one of the most important truths of political economy.

Imagine a very industrious individual having everything he needs to produce things: both ability and capital; if he were the only industrious person in a population which, aside from a few coarse foods, does not know how to make anything; what could he do with his products? He will purchase the quantity of rough food necessary to satisfy his needs. But what can he do with the residue? Nothing. But if the outputs of the country begin to multiply and grow more varied, then all of his produce can find a use, that is to say, it can be exchanged for things which he needs or for additional luxuries he can enjoy, or for the accumulation of the stocks that he considers appropriate.

What I have just said about a single industrious individual can be said equally of one hundred thousand. Their nation will offer them as much of a market as it can pay for additional objects; and it can pay for additional objects in proportion to the quantities it produces. Money performs no more than the role of a conduit in this double exchange. When the exchanges have been completed it will be found that one has paid for products with products.

Consequently, when a nation has too large a quantity of one particular type of product, the means of disposing of them is to create goods of another variety. It is when one can no longer produce any exchangeable object that exportation becomes advantageous. That is the case when it serves as a means to purchase products that cannot be furnished domestically, such as fruits from another climate. But the most profitable sales are those that a nation makes to itself; for they can take place only because of the two values produced: that which is sold and that which is purchased. Exportation should therefore be considered only as a supplement to and less advantageous than domestic consumption. [Say, 1803, Vol. I, Book 1, pp. 152–155]

Exactly the same point is emphasized by James Mill:

No proposition however in political economy seems to be more certain than this which I am going to announce, how paradoxical soever it may at first sight appear; and if it be true, none undoubtedly can be deemed of more importance. The production of commodities creates, and is the one and universal cause which creates a market for the commodities produced. Let us but consider what is meant by a market. Is any thing else understood by it than that something is ready to be exchanged for the commodity which we would dispose of? When goods are carried to market what is wanted is somebody to buy. But to buy, one must have wherewithal to pay. It is obviously therefore the collective means of payment which exist in the whole nation that constitute the entire market of the nation. But wherein consist the collective means of payment of the whole nation? Do they not consist in its annual produce, in the annual revenue of the general mass of its inhabitants? But if a nation's power of purchasing is exactly measured by its annual produce, as it undoubtedly is; the more you increase the annual produce, the more by that very act you extend the national market, the power of purchasing and the actual purchases of the nation. Whatever be the additional quantity of goods therefore which is at any time created in any country, an additional power of purchasing, exactly equivalent, is at the same instant created; so that a nation can never be naturally overstocked either with capital or with commodities; as the very operation of capital makes a vent for its produce. [Mill, 1807, pp. 81–82].

It is to be noted that both Mill and Say apparently misinterpreted the logic of their own propositions. From the valid assertion that a high income level *permits* a high level of demand, they seem to jump to the conclusion that demand will *necessarily* be high when output is high. This is an issue to which we will return later.

IV. INVESTMENT V. CONSUMPTION AS STIMULANTS TO WEALTH

There is a pair of related propositions which may have been even of more importance at least to Say, judging by the space he devoted to them and the vehemence with which he espoused them. Those observations, which deal with the relation between consumption and investment ("unproductive" and "reproductive" expenditures), can be described as:

Say's Third Proposition. A given investment expenditure is a far more effective stimulant to the wealth of an economy than an equal amount of consumption.

This proposition is the main substance of Say's chapter on consumption, whose translation now follows:

Chapter 3. *Is the Wealth of a State Increased by its Consumption?*

Reproductive consumption that ordinarily replaces with greater values those values that it destroys, is not ordinarily referred to as *consumption*, and I myself, when I happen to have used that word without explanation, have meant unproductive consumption, whose only purpose is to satisfy men's needs or to multiply their pleasures. It is only that sort of consumption that is referred to in the title of this chapter.

Many people, seeing that, overall, total production always equals consumption (because it is quite necessary for everything that is consumed to have been produced), imagined that the encouragement of consumption was favourable to production. The *Physiocrats* seized upon this idea and made it one of the fundamental principles of their doctrine. *Consumption is the measure of reproduction* they said;[1] that is, *the more there is consumed the more there is produced.* And since production brings wealth, they concluded that a state enriches itself through its consumption, that saving is in direct conflict with public prosperity, and that the most useful citizen is the one who expends most.[2]

This system is well designed to win the favour of the vulgar and so it has many partisans. The manufacturer and the merchant perceive general prosperity only in the sale of their wares, only in the greatest possible consumption of them. But when one considers this doctrine more attentively one finds that it leads to results quite different.

The consumption of each family can exceed, equal or fall short of its income. The consumption of all families together, that is, that of the nation, can follow the same course. That is, a nation, all things compensated for, can spend more or less than its income or exactly the amount of its income.

In the first of these cases the nation every year causes a dent in its capital; and, as a result, each year decreases its income; first, from the profits that would have corresponded to the capital that was eaten up and, second, from the profits from the industry which this capital would have supported. Far from being the way to stimulate exchanges it is the way to reduce them. Each year production rises to the level of consumption; but it declines along with consumption, to the point where the entire nation with no more capital, no more cultivated land, no more industry, no more population, disappears entirely or pursues a sad and miserable existence. It is the situation into which many parts of Greece and Syria have fallen under Turkish rule.

If a country or the families that compose it consume no more than their income, since that country does not deplete any part of its capital, it will keep its income constant, and will offer every year the same market for the product of its industry.

Let us also note, in passing, that it is difficult for a nation encouraged to spend its entire income not to over-spend it quickly, and consequently to fall more or less rapidly into the same grievous extremes as those that consume a portion of their capital along with their income. Both individuals and a government that raise their regular expenses exactly to the level of their ordinary income take no account of accidents and unforeseen risks that never fail to take something away from income and to add something to expenses.

As for a nation that does not expend its entire income, and annually augments its capital, that is the one and the only one that provides the greatest annual markets for its product. In effect, each year it experiences growth in the profits from its capital and in the power of its industry and, consequently, in its income; that is to say, its means of consumption either direct or through exchange, in one word, its markets.

The public interest is consequently not served by consumption, but it is served and served prodigiously by saving, and though it seems extraordinary to many persons, not being any the less true as a consequence, the labouring class is served by it more than anyone else. These persons think, perhaps, that the values which the wealthy save out of outlays on their personal pleasures in order to add to their capitals are not consumed. They are consumed; they furnish markets for many producers; but they are consumed reproductively and furnish markets for the useful goods that are capable of engendering still others, instead of being evaporated in frivolous consumption.

I will explain this doctrine through an illustration expressed in terms of the most common of activities.

A wealthy individual who has an income of a hundred thousand francs, and who is in the habit of consuming them totally, decides one day to decrease his outlays. He gives up some of his domestic servants, and is better served, he purchases fewer jewels, and is not criticized quite so much; he gives less splendid dinners and makes better friends. In brief, instead of spending a hundred thousand francs per annum he expends no more than eighty thousand. From the first year on, he thereby adds twenty thousand francs to his productive capital. The hundred thousand francs that constitute his income are always spent in their entirety, but no more than eighty thousand of them are spent unproductively; the remaining twenty thousand are spent in a manner that reproduces them with profit. He lends them to a manufacturer of handkerchiefs whose enterprise was languishing for lack of funds. The class comprising the lackeys, jewellers, and merchants of fine foods do indeed experience a decrease in the demand for their services and their products; but the class that provides to handkerchief makers their clothes, their food, and their raw materials see theirs increase precisely by the same proportion. The encouragement given by reproductive consumption is thus the same as that which would have resulted from the satisfaction of the needs and pleasures of a single person. But it does not cease here.

In effect, there has been *in addition* an increase in income for the wealthy capitalist, and an increase in income for the manufacturer and his workers. On the basis of a very moderate evaluation based on experience,

the capitalist may find his income increased by   1,000 francs
the chief manufacturer may find his increased by the
                                                                    same amount   1,000 francs
and the class of workers may find their total salaries
                                                                    augmented by   3,000 francs
                                                                                    ———
                                                                    total 5,000

That year's consumption, consequently, will be 105 thousand francs rather than the 100 thousand to which they would have added up if the person with the large income has spent it all unproductively.[3] And what is even more, the same 20 thousand francs that increased that year's incomes by 5 thousand francs are reaccumulated and can yield the same service in all the years that follow for so long as one considers it appropriate to use them productively.

There are a thousand ways to invest savings. While the happy effects which we have just seen continue, the following year gives the same consumer the opportunity to carry out similar savings. He uses them for the construction of a steam engine, to irrigate a field; the effect on general wealth is the same: the yield of his lands is increased by a thousand francs, more or less, and the activity that is introduced into their cultivation yields an annual income to many workers.

Thus, many persons are in error when they imagine that the poor obtain resources only from the expenditures of the rich. The true resource of the poor man is his labour. To exercise his labour he has no need for the rich man's consumption; he needs only his capital. Similarly, a country or a district could be most fortunate if no rich men were to reside or consume there, so long as they were to invest their capital in it. The farmer would labour there for the manufacturer and the merchant, the merchant for the farmer and the manufacturer, and the latter for the other two. All would be well supplied with all the necessities of life. With frugality they could enrich themselves and they would also have the means to pay to the absentee capitalist the interest and the rents on the capital and the land which, so to speak, he would have lent to them.

I have insisted on carrying out this demonstration because the error it exposes is among those that are the most widespread. It is shared by those who advocate the mercantilist doctrine, and those who advocate the agriculturist doctrine, that is to say, the Physiocrats. They all consider consumption to be useful in relation to production, while it is in fact, useful only for the pleasure that it procures.[4] A consumer offers no advantages by *that which* he consumes, but by *that* which he provides as a replacement; now, he can give that much more in replacement as he undertakes less unrewarding consumption and more reproductive consumption. If an idle rich man who eats up an enormous income, does not ruin his country, at least he contributes nothing to its prosperity. A

---

[1] See Mercier de la Rivière, *Ordre essentiel des Sociétés polit,* Vol. 2, p. 138, and the other writings of the Physiocrats.

[2] A reviewer notes that the physiocratic concept of "consumption" was very different from Say's (or from ours) so that "Say's reading of his own definition into the physiocrat's words created a complete distortion of their doctrines." [W.B.]

[3] One may think there is double counting here, and that the profit of the entrepreneur and his employees merely are substitutes for those that would have been earned by the jeweller and the chef on the assumption of unproductive consumption. But there is really no double counting. The profits of the jeweller, the chef and all the suppliers of unproductive consumption are replaced by the suppliers of productive consumption. These suppliers have sold to the manufacturer or his workers 20 thousand francs in goods, in place of the same quantity of goods that would have been sold to the rich consumer. Besides, there have been 5 thousand francs in income by which the year's consumption can have risen. That is to say, with 20 thousand francs and labour, 25 thousand francs in handkerchiefs have been produced. One should not be astonished that I evaluate the gross product of a manufacturer at 25 per cent of his capital; the net product itself often reaches this proportion.

[4] I knew a young man who threw crystal flasks out of the window as soon as he had emptied them. *This is necessary, he said, to encourage workshops.* In this way, he diminished total social wealth, precisely by the amount the artisan had increased it in producing the flask. He should have given it to a household too poor to be able to procure one. In this way he would have provided its inhabitants one of the pleasures of wealth, and manufacture would have been given an advantage comparable to that which it would have received from an increase in general opulence.

wealthy man who does not expend his entire income does contribute to it; a wealthy man who increases his capital and, moreover, occupies himself usefully, contributes to it still more.

If there is any one habit that merits encouragement, in monarchies and republics alike, in large and small countries alike, it is saving. But does it need encouragement? Is it not enough to avoid honouring dissipation? Is it not enough to respect all savings and all of their uses, that is to say, the growth of all economic activity that is not criminal? For I am not speaking here of the vague and inadequate protection that is sometimes referred to as *respect for property*. It is not enough merely to protect individuals from being stripped by arbitrary acts, by injustice, by fraud and violence; it is also necessary to guarantee them from attack by chicanery, from increases in taxes even if freely consented to, because though a contribution may well be voted freely, it becomes obligatory the moment it is made into a requirement. Then, man's desire to accumulate goods, to prepare his resources for the future, will suffice to balance off his love of present enjoyment, and to provide for the general prosperity that is made up of the prosperity of individuals. [Say, 1803, Vol. II, Book 5, pp. 358–368]

While in this first edition of the *Traité* the issue of superiority of investment over consumption as a stimulus to growth is not referred to directly in the chapter on *débouchés*, it is explicitly incorporated into this chapter in later editions (see, e.g., p. 139 of the English translation of the third edition). To Mill, too, this is a central point: "The greatness of the produce of a country in any year, is altogether dependent upon the greatness of the quantity of the produce of the former year, which is set apart for the business of reproduction. The annual produce is therefore the greater, the less the portion is which is allotted for consumption". (Mill, 1807, p. 71).

Mill quotes approvingly Say's tale of the young man who threw crystal vases out of the window in order to encourage manufactures. He also points out that

... it is the maintenance of great fleets and armies, which is always the most formidable weight in the scale of consumption, and which has the most fatal tendency to turn the balance against reproduction and prosperity. It is by the lamentable contrivance of wars, almost always nourished by puerile prejudiced and blind passions, that the affairs of prosperous nations are first brought to the stationary condition, and from this plunged into the retrograde. [Mill, 1807, p. 74]

(This passage also reminds us of the circumstances in which Mill was writing. He was here involved in a debate on foreign trade, the hegemony of agriculture, war expenditure and under-consumption—issues arising out of Napoleon's attempted blockade of the British Isles.)

V. In the Very Long Run Demand Will Catch Up with Supply

Like all classical economists, Say was very much interested in the longer run. From the first edition on, Say never ceased to emphasize, as an empirical observation:

Say's Fourth Proposition. Over the centuries the community will always find demands for increased outputs, even for increases that are enormous.

In other words, there was in his opinion no basis for fear of secular stagnation. This view he based on the argument that production provides *the purchasing power* with which output can be acquired. Thus, from the first edition on, he recalled to the reader how much the output of his country had risen since the humiliating days of Henry V, and the end of the Hundred Years' War. He points out that the total income accruing to factors of production expands equally with the total output of the community. "Otherwise, by what means could one purchase nowadays in France at least to two or three times the quantity of things that were purchased in the miserable and unfortunate reign of Charles VI?" (Say, 1803, Vol. II, p. 180.) A translation of the full selection from which this quotation is taken is provided later in this paper. Charles VI (1368–1422) was the mentally unstable king of France who was forced by the English to adopt Henry V as his heir, disinheriting his son, later Charles VII (Jeanne d'Arc's Dauphin), and to give Henry his daughter, Catherine, in marriage.) Subsequent developments seem generally to have supported Say on this score. Real *per capita* GNP has no doubt risen at least tenfold since Say wrote, when the Industrial Revolution was only in its beginnings. Demand certainly seems to have risen comparably.

Now, it must be admitted that Say seems never to have devoted much space to a discussion of the very long-run correspondence of demand with supply, and I have not found any place where Mill dealt with it at all. Yet it seems to me to be implicit in their emphasis on production as the source of *growth* in the wealth of a nation. The fact that in his second edition Say moved his remark on Charles VI into the body of the chapter on *débouchés* and that he kept it there in the subsequent editions attests to the value he placed on the observation that demand in the long run is capable of keeping up with the most enormous increases in output.

Note that this proposition, which is clearly of some considerable importance for the analysis of economic development, is virtually irrelevant for stabilization policy. Say's observation that in the long run demand keeps up with rises in production is perfectly consistent with the existence of protracted periods of substantial unemployment. There is nothing in the principle that is inconsistent with a "general glut" whose possibility is denied by Say's identity. Note in this connection, Sowell's (1974, pp. 64ff) contention (against Patinkin and Blaug) that even Malthus' position in the glut controversy did *not* include a secular stagnation argument.

VI. Money No More than a Means to Facilitate Exchange

We come now to the first of the propositions that relate closely to "Say's Law". This is the emphasis that both Say and Mill place on the *un*importance of money as a contributor to effective demand. Say stresses the conclusion that money is no more than a conduit for, or a lubricant of, the exchange process but itself ultimately contributes nothing to effective demand. (Mill deals with the role of money only obliquely. He does say that his propositions are seen most clearly by considering ". . . the circumstances of a country in which all exchange should be in the way of barter, as the idea of money frequently tends to perplex" (p. 82). He also makes much of

Spence's observation, "Let it not be urged that what they might save would not be hoarded (for misers now-a-days are wiser than to keep their money in strong boxes at home) but would be lent on interest", emphasizing that these loans will finance effective demand in the form of reproductive consumption (p. 75).) We have already seen that two of the seven paragraphs that constitute the first edition chapter on *débouchés* are devoted to a description of the unimportance of money. Say makes this point by likening the role of money to that of advertising and stressing that producers generally add negligibly to their stock of money over the course of a year. Thus we may describe:

Say's Sixth Proposition. Production of goods rather than the supply of money is the primary determinant of demand. Money facilitates commerce but does not determine the amounts of goods that are exchanged.

This assertion gets closer to implying Say's identity than anything we have discussed up to this point. If in fact he had said that no one wants money for its own sake and that any cash accumulations will always and immediately be respent, Say's identity would indeed have been implied. However, to Say of the first edition, the irrelevance of money would seem to arise in quite another way—it is unimportant not because only goods are demanded, but because it is a poor means for the stimulation of demand. We are back at the Keynesian point that effective demand is a rising function of *real* output, and that money merely facilitates the working of that relationship. If that is what Say had in mind (and on this we can only guess from his inconclusive wording), then even his monetary discussion is still only distantly related to "Say's Law".

VII. General v. Particular Gluts

So far as I have been able to judge, Say in his first edition and Mill in *Commerce Defended* make only one point that is really related directly to either the equality or identity form of Say's Law. This is an assertion which we may characterize as:

Say's Seventh Proposition. Any glut in the market for a good must involve relative underproduction of some other commodity, or commodities, and the mobility of capital out of the area with excess supply and into industries whose products are insufficient to meet demand will tend rapidly to eliminate the overproduction.

Certainly this argument suggests strongly that both authors believed in some form of Say's Law. However, this argument would appear to be a conclusion one draws from the Law rather than a bit of logic that argues its validity. It is a corollary rather than an underpinning of the Law.

Mill makes the point with characteristic force:

> It may be necessary, however, to remark, that a nation may easily have more than enough of any one commodity, though she can never have more than enough commodities in general. The quantity of any one commodity may easily be carried beyond its due proportion; but by that very circumstance is implied that some other commodity is not provided in sufficient proportion. What indeed is meant by a commodity's exceeding the market? Is it not that there is a portion

of it for which there is nothing that can be had in exchange. But of those other things then the proportion is too small. A part of the means of production which has been applied to the preparation of this superabundant commodity, should have been applied to the preparation of those other commodities till the balance between them had been established. Whenever this balance is properly preserved, there can be no superfluity of commodities, none for which a market will not be ready. This balance too the natural order of things has so powerful a tendency to produce, that it will always be very exactly preserved where the injudicious tampering of government does not prevent, or those disorders in the intercourse of the world, produced by the wars into which the inoffending part of mankind are plunged, by the folly much more frequently than by the wisdom of their rulers. [Mill, 1807, pp. 84–85]

Note that in this passage Mill not only emphasizes the possibility of a partial glut but also asserts explicitly the impossibility of an excess "of commodities in general". In other words, Mill does assert his adherence to Say's Law. Yet it seems to me that nowhere here or in Say's first edition does either author try to spell out the logical foundation for any variant of Say's Law. To make this point I shall now present a last passage from the *Traité*. This one is perhaps particularly significant because both Spengler (1945) and Sowell (1972) cite it as the passage containing the heart of Say's first discussion of the subject.

Chapter 5. *In What Proportions the Value of Products is Distributed Among the Three Factors of Production*

The magnitude of the demand for factors of production in general does not depend on *the magnitude of consumption* as all too many persons have imagined. Consumption is not at all a cause, it is an effect. In order to consume it is necessary to purchase; now, one can make purchases only with what one has produced. Is the quantity of outputs demanded consequently determined by the quantity of products created? Without any doubt. Everyone can, at his pleasure, consume what he has produced; or else he can buy another product with his own. The demand for products in general is therefore always equal to the sum of the products available.[1] A nation that produced annually no more than a value of two billion, would be able neither to purchase nor to consume three billion during the same period of time without drawing the billion deficit from its capitals every year. We see that the best way to provide markets for outputs is to produce more, not to destroy them. If this conclusion is obvious, as I believe it to be, what are we to think of the systems that encourage consumption in order to stimulate production?

It is not true that total output cannot exceed total consumption. Can one not accumulate a portion of the products created each year? Cannot everyone accumulate either some of his own products or some of those he acquires by exchange? Is not a market provided by this accumulation just as effectively as if that same value had been consumed?[2] Total output is consequently not limited by the magnitude of consumption. Limitation of consumption does not close off markets; rather the fostering of production will open new ones. A nation that enriches itself enjoys an advantage comparable to that acquired by one that extends its foreign commerce. It experiences the opening of new markets and the appearance of new customers. It extends its commerce, and does not wage wars to achieve this.

If production is not bounded by the magnitude of consumption,[3] if one can produce more than is consumed, what then are the bounds to production? They consist of the availability of the factors of production.

But, it may be said, *if there are goods that cannot be sold, there are necessarily more productive factors employed than there are opportunities for the consumption of their outputs*. Not at all. No glut ever occurs except when too large a quantity

156   ECONOMICA   [MAY

of factors of production is devoted to one type of production and not enough to another. In effect, what is the cause for the inability to carry out a sale? It is the difficulty of obtaining some other good (either an output or money) in exchange for the one that is offered. Means of production are consequently lacking for the former to the extent that they are superabundant for the latter. A region deep in the interior of a land finds no sale for its wheat, but if some factory is established there and part of the capital and the labour that formerly was devoted to the land is redirected to another type of production, the products of the one and the other can be exchanged without difficulty, even though these outputs have expanded rather than diminished. Inability to sell, therefore, arises not from overabundance but from the misallocation of the factors of production.

In the notes that Garnier has included in his excellent translation of Smith he states that in old nations like those of Europe, in which capital has been accumulated over several centuries, overabundance of the annual product would *obstruct trade, if it were not absorbed by proportionate amounts of consumption.* I realize that trade can be obstructed by the overabundance of particular products. It is an evil that can never be anything but temporary, for participation in the production of goods whose outputs exceed the need for them and whose value is debased will rapidly cease and it will instead be devoted to the production of the goods that are sought after. But I cannot conceive that the products of the labour of an entire nation can ever be overabundant since one good provides the means to purchase the other. The sum of its outputs composes the total wealth of a nation, and wealth is no more of an embarrassment to nations than it is to individuals.

This point having been thoroughly cleared up, it provides us an answer to the question with which we are concerned and which I repeat: *upon what elements does the demand for factors of production in general depend?* It depends on the volume of production, and since the volume of production depends on the quantity of factors of production, the demand for factors of production expands proportionately to the quantity of means of production themselves. That is to say, as a result, a nation always has the means to purchase everything it produces. Otherwise, by what means could one purchase nowadays in France at least to two or three times the quantity of things that were purchased in the miserable and unfortunate reign of Charles vi? [Say, 1803, Vol. II, Book 4, pp. 175–180]

This passage clearly summarizes all of the seven propositions we have listed so far. In particular it states emphatically that "... trade can be obstructed by the overabundance of particular products ... goods whose outputs exceed the need for them. ... But ... the products of the labour of an entire nation can never be overabundant because one good provides the means to purchase the other".

VIII. Incompleteness of the Statement of the Law

What then, if anything, is lacking in this passage to qualify it as an explicit statement of Say's Law? The Law is surely enunciated in the latter

---

[1] A product consumed by its maker is a product that has been supplied and demanded by the same person. It constitutes part of the total supply of goods and of the total demand for them.

[2] Moreover, we will see later that the portion saved out of income and added to capitals is just as surely consumed every year, but in another manner; that is to say, in a reproductive manner.

[3] Here our subject is only unproductive consumption, not the use of capital for its reproduction with profit.

part of Mill's assertion "That a nation may easily have more than enough of any one commodity, *though she can never have more than enough of commodities in general*" (Mill, 1807, p. 84, my italics); and the same is obviously true of Say when he tells us that "The products of the labor of an entire nation can never be overabundant".

Thus the proclamation of Say's Law is found in both writings. As I have already suggested, all that is missing is its rationale. Thus, note that Say completes the preceding quotation by telling us that he "... cannot conceive that the products of the labor of an entire nation can ever be overabundant since one good provides the *means* to purchase the other" (my italics). In other words, the community can *afford to* purchase the goods *if it wishes to do so*. We are back at what we have labelled Say's first proposition, which asserts that production creates the *power* to purchase itself.

But this sidesteps the basic issue in the entire subsequent controversy over Say's Law. The issue is not whether the purchasing power needed to buy a nation's output is available, but whether it will in fact be used.

Mill treats the issue virtually as a tautology and, hence, as one whose logic requires no discussion: "What indeed is meant by a commodity's exceeding the market? Is it not that there is a portion of it for which there is nothing that can be had in exchange? But of those other things then the proportion is too small". (Mill, 1807, p. 85). In other words, every excess supply is, by definition, an excess demand for something else. But what is that something else? Must it necessarily be a commodity?

IX. Say's Second Edition: The Missing Ingredient Supplied

There are, it seems to me, two missing ingredients to the Say's Law discussion on the preceding paragraphs. For they fail to discuss the nature of the demand generated by the holders of the community's purchasing power, and they do not deal with the timing of that demand.

Other discussions both afterwards *and before* treated both these matters very explicitly. They asserted that people will always use their purchasing power to seek either consumers' or producers' goods in exchange; that is, they will demand goods rather than cash balances, because to do otherwise would be irrational. Moreover, it was (sometimes but not always) stated that this demand must accompany the acquisition of purchasive power through production *virtually without* delay. These statements clearly add up to Say's identity, with supply automatically and immediately creating an equivalent demand, or to a strong form of the equality, with fast acting and powerful equilibrating forces that either usually or always channel demands into commodities.

It is curious that Adam Smith had already discussed both these matters nearly thirty years before Say. (On the other side of the matter, Tucker (1960, pp. 92–99) points out that Ricardo was induced to emphasize his Say's Law discussion by his opposition to Smith's view that accumulation tends to *reduce* the rate of profit through a growing abundance of capital-seeking employment.) Concerned to support the idea that saving does not reduce the demand, he deals with the issues we have just raised in two

158   ECONOMICA   [MAY

well-known passages. The first examines the motivation of demand:

> In all countries where there is tolerable security, every man of common understanding will endeavour to employ whatever stock he can command, in procuring either present enjoyment or future profit.... A man must be perfectly crazy who, where there is tolerable security, does not employ all the stock which he commands, whether it be his own or borrowed of other people, in some one or other of those ... ways. [Smith, 1776, p. 268]

In the second passage he considers the timing of these expenditures:

> That portion of his revenue which a rich man annually spends, is in most cases consumed by idle guests, and menial servants, who leave nothing behind them in return for their consumption. That portion which he annually saves, as for the sake of profit it is *immediately* employed as a capital, is consumed in the same manner, *and nearly in the same time too*, but by a different set of people. [Smith, 1776, p. 321, my italics]

In other words, as has been pointed out before, Smith all but enunciated Say's Law and certainly spelled out its logic more completely than either Say or Mill in their first writings on the subject. The only lacunae in Smith's discussion are his stipulation that a state of "tolerable security" must prevail for (*ex ante*) investment always to equal saving (would he have considered a period of bad business prospects or great uncertainty to involve intolerable security?) and his failure to state explicitly the conclusion that total supply must, consequently, always be equal to the demand.

Say only gets around to these matters in his second edition where he tells us in his revised and expanded chapter on *débouchés* that:

> ... It is worthwhile to remark, that a product is no sooner *created* than it *from that instant* offers a market for other products to the full extent of its own value. For every product is created only to be consumed, whether productively or unproductively, and indeed to be consumed as quickly as possibly, since every value whose realization is delayed causes a loss to the individual who is currently its possessor of the interest earning corresponding to that delay.... A product is therefore, so far as everyone can arrange, destined to the most rapid consumption. From the moment it exists, it consequently seeks another product with which it can be exchanged. Gold and silver are no exception since no sooner has the merchant made a sale than he seeks to employ the product of his sale. [Say, 1814, pp. 147–148, his italics. A somewhat modified version of this passage is found in later editions. See, e.g., the 1821 English translation of the fourth edition, pp. 134–135. The translation here follows that one so far as possible.]

From the second edition on Say also deals far more directly with the role of money and its irrelevance as a determinant of demand. For example, in the English translation of the fourth edition of the *Traité* we are told

> Should a tradesman say, "I do not want other products for my woollens, I want money", ... You say, you only want money; I say, you want other commodities, and not money. For what, in point of fact, do you want the money? Is it not for the purchase of raw materials or stock for your trade, or victuals for your support? ... Thus, to say that sales are dull, owing to the scarcity of money is to mistake the means for the cause....
> There is always money enough to conduct the circulation and mutual interchange of other values, when those values really exist. Should the increase of traffic require more money to facilitate it, the want is easily supplied.... In such cases, merchants know well enough how to find substitutes for the product

serving as the medium of exchange or money:[1] and money itself soon pours in, for this reason, that all produce naturally gravitates to that place where it is most in demand.... [Say, 1821, pp. 133–134]

What is noteworthy in this comment is Say's implicit adherance in this passage to an equality rather than an identity form of the law. He admits that an excess demand for money can arise, but he tells us that it will only be temporary. If it is only local, supplies of money will soon flow in from elsewhere. And, in any event, the excess supply will be eliminated not by anything like the cash balance effect which trims demands down to the available (nominal) supply of cash, but by an increase in the supply of cash or substitutes for cash.

Thus the eighth (and for our purposes the last) of Say's eight propositions is Say's Law itself. Apparently this takes the form of a type of Say's equality, i.e., supply and demand are always equated by a rapid and powerful equilibration mechanism. However, we should be careful not to attribute to him thoughts on what he would have considered fine distinctions, such as that between the equality and the identity forms of the law. For very likely the subject was never explicitly considered by him.

Of course, one can go on indefinitely, listing observations that Say considered pertinent to his subject. My choice is consequently and unavoidably rather arbitrary. Note that I have not listed the rather curious tautological version of Say's Law that Say enunciated in his correspondence with Malthus. In a letter dated Paris, July 1827, Say wrote:...

> Our discussion on *débouchés* begins to be no more than a dispute on words. You wish me to accord the name products to goods that can satisfy a certain number of wants and which possess a certain value, even though that value is insufficient to repay the totality of their production costs. But the logic of my doctrine on production establishes clearly that there is no complete production unless all the inputs necessary for that piece of work are repayed by the value of the product ... everything that is truly produced that cannot be sold is an outlay made thoughtlessly and without producing anything; and my doctrine on *débouchés* remains intact. [*Cours Complet d'Économie Politique Pratique*, Brussels 1844, p. 649. See also Malthus's comment on p. 647.]

X. CONCLUDING COMMENT

Several conclusions emerge from this discussion of Say's and Mill's discussion of Say's Law. First, on the relatively unimportant issue of priority matters are hazy, and the answer must depend on our definition of the Law itself. Obviously, it is at least hinted at from the first edition of the *Traité* onward. My own conclusion is that Spengler (1945), Winch (1966) and Sowell (1972) are right in awarding priority to Say. But they are right for the wrong reason. To me, the first statement of the Law as we understand it today appears complete with its logical underpinnings *neither* in the first edition of the *Traité* nor in *Commerce Defended* but in the second edition of Say's work. On that interpretation, Say's Law can be said to have achieved its first full codification in 1814, even though, as is always the case in the

---

[1] By bills at sight, or after date, bank-notes, running-credits, write-offs, & c. at London and Amsterdam.

160   ECONOMICA   [MAY

history of ideas, any one who seeks to pinpoint its first origins must do so at his peril.

However, the major conclusion that emerges from our re-examination of Say's and Mill's texts is that the Say's Law discussion was, first and foremost, an examination of the influences that promote long-term economic growth, and not primarily a matter of short-term problems of unemployment and overproduction. The major emphasis of Say's and Mill's arguments was that investment (productive consumption), rather than consumption of luxuries, pyramid building or military expenditure (unproductive consumption), are the effective means to promote growth.

There is also a second observation, going beyond our textual examination, which also seems worth making. We tend to think today of the Malthusian side of the argument as Keynesian in spirit and consequently "progressive", while the Say–Mill–Ricardian position is interpreted to be the opposite. But viewed in terms of the circumstances of the early nineteenth century, when the debate was underway, this is the reverse of the truth. Malthus was the open defender of the role of the landed proprietors as against the rising capitalist class. (Marx characterizes those writings which "... regard *consumption* as a necessary spur to production" as "apologetics ... partly for the rich idlers and the 'unproductive labourers' whose *services* they consume, partly for 'strong governments' whose expenditure is heavy, for the increase of State debts, for holders of sinecures, etc". (1963, p. 281). It was on their behalf that he defended protective tariffs and it was their consumption of luxury goods and their employment of personal retainers that he was defending when he argued that they were necessary for the prevention of over-production. On the other hand, Say, Mill and Ricardo sought, against this position, to encourage the new industrial activity and, with it, the expansion of the output of the economy (See Blaug, 1958, pp. 94–97). It is always dangerous to interpret the political colour of earlier works in terms of the state of affairs of the reader's own era.

ACKNOWLEDGEMENTS

I am grateful to Elizabeth Bailey, Fritz Machlup and Donald Winch for their comments and suggestions, and to George de Menil and Arthur Laurie for their corrections of my translations.

REFERENCES

BLAUG, MARK (1958) *Ricardian Economics: A Historical Study*. New Haven: Yale University Press.

MARX, KARL (1963 edition). *Theories of Surplus Value*. Moscow: Progress Publishers, I.

MILL, JAMES (1807).*Commerce Defended*. London: C. and B. Baldwin.

SAY, J. B. (first ed. 1803). *Traité d'économie politique ou simple exposition de la manière dont se forment, se distribuent et se consomment les richesses* Paris: Deterville.

—— (2nd ed., 1914). *Traité d'économie politique ou simple exposition de la manière dont se forment, se distribuent et se consomment les richesses* Paris: A. A. Renouard.

—— (1821) *A Treatise on Political Economy; or the Production, Distribution and Consumption of Wealth*, Boston: Wells and Lilly.

—— (1844). *Cours complet d'économie politique pratique* Brussels: Société Typographique Belge.

SMITH, ADAM (1776). *An Inquiry into the Nature and Causes of the Wealth of Nations.* London: Methuen & Co. (Cannan ed. 1925).

SOWELL, THOMAS (1972). *Say's Law: An Historical Analysis.* Princeton: University Press.

—— (1974). *Classical Economics Reconsidered.* Princeton: University Press.

SPENGLER, J. J. (1945). The Physiocrats and Say's Law of Markets. *Journal of Political Economy,* 53, 193–211, 317–347. Reprinted in Spengler and Allen (1960).

—— and ALLEN, W. R. (1960). *Essays in Economic Thought: Aristotle to Marshall.* Chicago; Rand McNally.

TUCKER, G. S. L. (1960). *Progress and Profits in British Economic Thought, 1650–1850.* Cambridge: University Press.

WINCH, DONALD (1966). *James Mill: Selected Economic Writings.* Chicago: University Press.

Acknowledgements

The author is grateful to the following for permission to reproduce the material in this book.

Chapter 1: 'Scale Economies, Average Cost and the Profitability of Marginal Cost Pricing'. Reprinted by permission of the publisher from *Public and Urban Economics: Essays in Honor of William S. Vickrey* edited by Ronald E. Grieson. (Lexington, Mass.: Lexington Books, D. C. Heath and Company. Copyright 1976, D. C. Heath and Company.)

Chapter 2: *American Economic Review.*

Chapter 3: *American Economic Review.*

Chapter 4: 'Quasi Optimality: The Price We Must Pay for a Price System', Journal of Political Economy, Vol. 87, No. 3 (1979), pp. 578–599, © 1979 by The University of Chicago. Reprinted by permission of The University of Chicago.

Chapter 5: *Kyklos.*

Chapter 6: *Intermountain Economic Review.*

Chapter 7: *Bell Journal of Economics and Management Science.*

Chapter 8: *American Economic Review.*

Chapter 9: *Eastern Economic Journal.*

Chapter 10: Reprinted by permission of the Yale Law Journal Company and Fred B. Rothman & Company from *The Yale Law Journal.*

Chapter 11: From *Cities Under Stress, The Fiscal Crisis of Urban America* (Burchell and Listokin, eds), Center for Urban Policy Research, Rutgers University.

Chapter 12: From *Stability and Inflation, Essays in Honor of Professor A. W. H. Phillips* (Bergstrom et al., eds), John Wiley and Sons.

Chapter 13: From *The Theory and Experience of Economic Development, Essays in Honour of Sir W. Arthur Lewis* (Gersovitz et al., eds), George Allen and Unwin.

Chapter 14: *The American Economist.*

Chapter 15: *Journal of Economic Literature.*

Chapter 16: *American Economic Review.*

Chapter 17: *Economica,* London School of Economics and Political Science.

Index